Welcome to
Arkham Asylum

Welcome to Arkham Asylum

Essays on Psychiatry and the Gotham City Institution

Edited by
SHARON PACKER, M.D., *and*
DANIEL R. FREDRICK

Foreword by Jason W. Ellis

McFarland & Company, Inc., Publishers
Jefferson, North Carolina

ALSO BY SHARON PACKER, M.D.

Neuroscience in Science Fiction Films (McFarland, 2015)

*Cinema's Sinister Psychiatrists:
From Caligari to Hannibal* (McFarland, 2012)

ISBN (print) 978-1-4766-7098-0
ISBN (ebook) 978-1-4766-3742-6

LIBRARY OF CONGRESS AND BRITISH LIBRARY
CATALOGUING DATA ARE AVAILABLE

Library of Congress Control Number 2019041211

© 2020 Sharon Packer and Daniel R. Fredrick. All rights reserved

*No part of this book may be reproduced or transmitted in any form
or by any means, electronic or mechanical, including photocopying
or recording, or by any information storage and retrieval system,
without permission in writing from the publisher.*

Front cover image: © 2020 Shutterstock

Printed in the United States of America

*McFarland & Company, Inc., Publishers
Box 611, Jefferson, North Carolina 28640
www.mcfarlandpub.com*

In memory of Christine Quigley, a prolific McFarland author, retired Georgetown University Press editor, and blogger at Quigley's Cabinet, whose long, brave battle with MS ended in 2018

Acknowledgments

My thanks to McFarland editor Layla Milholen for her patience, encouragement, and insights. Belated thanks to the late Christine Quigley, who introduced me to McFarland and who set an unmatchable example of perseverance and productivity in the face of illness. My thanks to participants at American Psychiatric Association workshops for many years of feedback and encouragement and to my fellow members of the New York Academy of Medicine History of Medicine Steering Committee. My thanks to Professor Jason W. Ellis for organizing City Tech Symposiums on Science Fiction and spearheading interdisciplinary scholarship in this field. Thanks to Danny Fingeroth for organizing Comic-Con symposia and other comics-related venues and to Graphic Medicine for hosting presentations of comics and medicine-related presentations. My thanks to Mount Sinai Beth Israel's Department of Psychiatry, Brooklyn VA Department of Psychiatry, Montefiore Hospital of Albert Einstein College of Medicine, Brookdale Hospital and Metropolitan Hospital for hosting Grand Rounds on "Post-Traumatic Strength Disorder & Superhero Stories" and "Sinister Psychiatrists in Cinema" and opening opportunities for the invaluable comments by the medical center staff. My thanks to Professor Sean Moreland and Professor Christian Perring, to editors Natalie Timoshin and Laurie Martin of *Psychiatric Times*, and Robert Rubin, M.D., and George Fink, M.D., for publishing my chapters and articles on this topic and adding their invaluable insights. Thanks to artist Jason Soles for his Cthulhu sculpture, to Jim Carlson for his much-appreciated technology support and especially to George Higham and Wood Stock Photos for their photographs of *Batman* toys.—Sharon Packer, M.D.

Table of Contents

Acknowledgments — vi

Foreword by Jason W. Ellis — 1

Preface by Sharon Packer, M.D. — 3

Introduction: Why Arkham, Why Now?
SHARON PACKER, M.D. — 7

Section I: Clinical Psychiatric Controversies

The Differential Diagnosis of Elizabeth Arkham
ELYSE D. WEINER, M.D. — 25

ECT in Arkham Asylum: Pacification, Assassination and Electrocution
TIMOTHY W. KNEELAND — 35

Hallucinations and Psychedelics in Arkham
MATTHEW BROWN, D.O., *and* FERNANDO ESPÍ FORCÉN, M.D. — 43

Section II: Forensic Psychiatric Controversies

I'm [Virtual] Batman: Violence and Video Games
RYAN C.W. HALL, M.D., *and* SUSAN HATTERS FRIEDMAN, M.D. — 55

Deadly and Dysfunctional Family Dynamics: When Fiction Mirrors Fact
SUSAN HATTERS FRIEDMAN, M.D., *and* RYAN C.W. HALL, M.D. — 65

Murderous Minds, Arkham Villains and Real (Not Reel) Life
Movie Massacres
SHARON PACKER, M.D. — 76

Section III: Medical-Ethical Controversies

Anti-Psychiatry and the Arkham Asylum
FERNANDO ESPÍ FORCÉN, M.D. — 91

Harley Quinn and the Joker: Pitfalls of Doctor-Patient Romances
SHARON PACKER, M.D.   101

Unethical Experiments in Arkham and Elsewhere
SHARON PACKER, M.D.   110

Section IV: Big Screen Parallels

Arkham's Sinister Psychiatrists and the Continuum with Caligari
SHARON PACKER, M.D.   123

Haunted by Madness: Horror and the Supernatural in Arkham Asylum
MICHAEL MARKUS   134

Breaking Out: The Escaped Mental Patient in the Batman Universe
JEFFREY BULLINS   145

The Suicide Squad: From Bad to Good and Back Again
JAQ GREENSPON and RASA GREENSPON   155

Section V: Small Screen Parallels

Animated Arkham: Television and Children's Perceptions of Psychiatric Treatment
KRISTI ROWAN HUMPHREYS   165

The Fine Line Between Sanity and Madness in *Star Trek*'s "Whom Gods Destroy" and *Arkham Asylum: A Serious Place on Serious Earth*
DARREN HARRIS-FAIN and ERIC J. STERLING   173

Section VI: Video Screen Parallels

If Walls Could Scream: Embedded Narratives and Mazes of Madness in the Virtual Space of Arkham Asylum
SHAWN EDREI   183

Excavating Arkham: The Mental Asylum as Horrible Homecoming
BRENDA S. GARDENOUR WALTER   191

Section VII: Literary and Artistic Influences

Bizarro Arkham, Bizarro World: The Looking Glass Looks Back
AARON BARLOW   203

The Neo-Expressionist Agony of Arkham Asylum
ROSA JH BERLAND   211

Surrealism's Influence on Arkham and Psychiatry's Influence on Surrealism
SHARON PACKER, M.D.   222

Poe's Place in Arkham Asylum: Precursors and Parallels
   CALEB PUCKETT   233

H.P. Lovecraft, Literary Heritage and *Batman: Arkham Asylum*
   ERIC SANDBERG   243

Section VIII: Mythic and Religious Parallels

Evil Clowns and Acrobats: The Joker and Harley Quinn
   ADAM W. DARLAGE   255

Matricide and Myth
   DANIEL R. FREDRICK   264

Appendix: Unethical Experiments in Modern Genetics Research   273
About the Contributors   275
Filmography   277
Bibliography   281
Index   291

Foreword
by Jason W. Ellis

Welcome to Arkham Asylum: Essays on Psychiatry and the Gotham City Institution is a new, interdisciplinary essay collection that explores the cultural significance of Arkham Asylum, the fictional, secure mental health facility designated to hold Batman's nemeses who are judged to be criminally insane. The editors have assembled a multidisciplinary team of medical professionals and researchers, literary and media scholars, historians, and art curators to share their Arkham Asylum–focused research and foster dialogue between and among disciplines of study. While these writers apply their own discipline's critical lenses to explore the influence of Arkham Asylum on our culture, each also establishes connections across disciplines. Furthermore, the collection forms an interdisciplinary scaffolding for future research on this unnerving location in DC Comic's Batman mythology and its significance to our culture and the medical profession as a touchstone of mental health issues.

Arkham Asylum is an important cultural image for study because it collapses the history of psychiatry, popular understandings of psychological treatment, and anxieties surrounding mental health within its various forms through its historical development across media, including comic books, animated television series, films, and video games. In its various appearances, it is a nexus of science (psychology, biology, and chemistry), technology (psychopharmacology and mental health treatment devices), and engineering (architecture, incarceration management) that creates the narratological space where stories play out with a focus on humanistic concerns, such as rationality, identity, autonomy, and ethics.

Considering the asylum in general, its meaning has changed historically from a place of refuge protected by the threat of sacrilege to one of incarceration—first for the purposes of isolation of those considered mad from society and later for the purposes of treatment and possible reintroduction of the mentally ill to society. This institutionalization of the asylum feeds into popular ideas about its role as a place of despair and promise, which is also influenced by social, ethical, political, and medical debates on the treatment of mental illness. Further, the meaning of the asylum and its popular conceptions filter into generalized anxieties about mental health that reveal the fictional Arkham Asylum's walls to be quite permeable—patients escape with alarming regularity, the asylum threatens the mentally well with madness, and the asylum, with its deep foundations in Gotham City, creates an uneasiness about the madness contained within, which could erupt and envelop the entire citizenry with insanity. It evokes questions about the nature of madness, the treatment of mental health, and the public's understanding of and response to mental health issues.

The essays contained in this collection investigate Arkham Asylum from these and

Mamoulian's definitive 1931 version of Stevenson's *The Strange Story of Dr. Jekyll and Mr. Hyde* (1886) shows a barely visible Dr. Jekyll (Fredric March) seated in his laboratory, where he concocts a potion to unleash libidinous instincts that turn him into the destructive Mr. Hyde. This iconic mad scientist laboratory scene is not so different from Dr. Strange's bigger and better-equipped laboratory and surgical amphitheater in TV's *Gotham* (2015–2019).

other perspectives with the goal of creating dialogue about the role of this place within the overlapping domains of culture, science, ethics, and policy. Due to the long shadow cast by Arkham Asylum both within the Batman mythos and in popular culture combined with contemporary debates about mental health treatment and ameliorating mental health stigmas, I am confident that this collection is an early and important contribution to a developing and needed discourse.

Preface
by Sharon Packer, M.D.

This book began in earnest over a decade ago, in 2007, although I did not expect this exact essay collection to emerge so many years later or evolve in the direction it did. Let me explain how that happened.

The book you hold in your hands (or see on your screen) has been through many permutations and incarnations. It started as a monograph on Medical Controversies in Superhero Stories—and I can assure you that there are many—but the chapters related to Arkham Asylum multiplied out of proportion and screamed for their own edition. Since Arkham Asylum for the Criminally Insane is a psychiatric hospital, and since I am a physician who specializes in psychiatry, a collection that focuses on psychiatric controversies in the Arkham Asylum mythos was a logical outgrowth. A criminal justice approach to Arkham Asylum for the Criminally Insane by qualified scholars would also be in order, since this fictional institution is as much a penal institution as a medical facility, but this is not that book.

The seeds for this book about Arkham were sown when I presented a workshop on "Sinister Psychiatrists in Cinema" at the Institute of Psychiatric Services, hosted by the American Psychiatric Association and held in Chicago. That workshop led to five more annual psychiatric services workshops on the same subject (each one updated). My monograph *Cinema's Sinister Psychiatrists* (2012), also published by McFarland, collated those lengthy lectures and elaborated on them in book form.

The first conference took place at the Palmer House near Chicago's Magnificent Mile. Delighted by the opportunity to return to my home city, I prepared the presentation diligently, perhaps even obsessively, except for one part: the end film clip (on a CD, since film clips embedded in PowerPoint were not yet possible). I decided to play it by ear and gauge the audience's reactions before locking in my closing comments. I brought several choices for that last leg of the workshop. One clip came from *Batman Begins* (Nolan, 2005), set in Arkham Asylum for the Criminally Insane, with Cillian Murphy playing Dr. Jonathan Crane, sometimes known as Scarecrow. A consummate example of a sinister psychiatrist, Dr. Crane clandestinely exposes his patients to aerosolized hallucinogens to convince them they are psychotic.

As relevant as it was to the topic, I didn't dare add the *Batman* clip from the get-go, for I was still embarrassed to admit my preference for superhero action-adventure films over more sophisticated fare. Psychiatrists of my generation were expected to extol films like Bergman's *Persona* or, better yet, Shakespearean dramas like *King Lear,* seen on screen

4 Preface

if not on stage. When I began my residency training, Shakespeare was quoted regularly at morning rounds, in emulation of Freud, who often compared his own dreams to dramas penned by the British bard.

Fearing that superhero films would be rejected by this educated audience—even though the superhero subgenre had gained more and more traction among the public after 9/11—I packed two more choices, the first being *The Jacket* (Maybury, 2005), starring Adrien Brody as a peripatetic and pathetic veteran with PTSD (post-traumatic stress disorder), TBI (traumatic brain injury) and accompanying amnesia. The other option was David Cronenberg's equally bleak and uncharacteristically serious film *Spider* (2002) about a schizophrenic man (played by the characteristically sensitive Ralph Fiennes). The film is set in a dilapidated adult home in London's shabby East End, where Fiennes' character struggles to distinguish his own persecutory auditory hallucinations from the accusations hurled by the hateful woman who runs the half-way house.

I asked the crowd to choose among the three. To my surprise (and relief), the reaction was overwhelming: everyone in the packed auditorium wanted the superhero film. *Batman Begins* was true to the topic, although casting a youthful Cillian Murphy as head of the sprawling forensic psychiatric hospital—instead of a withered Leo G. Carroll–type as seen in the *Spellbound* sanitorium—added insult to injury. But so it was: lowbrow (but high grossing) entertainment was elevated to star status and earned an unofficial stamp of approval at an official psychiatric conference. How times had changed!

To be fair, other factors may have influenced the audience's choice of a pop culture /action-adventure/superhero film that day. That was an unusual day. The night before, the stock market crashed. Scenes on the television screen were scarier and more sinister than the worst Hammer horror clips screened at the workshop. Real estate val-

In *Batman Begins* (2005), Batman (Christian Bale) assaults psychiatrist Dr. Crane (Cillian Murphy) after Crane sprays patients with hallucinogenic gas to make them psychotic enough to transfer to Arkham Asylum for the Criminally Insane. Dr. Crane's misuse of hallucinogens contrasts with recreational hallucinogen use and with recent psychiatric studies of hallucinogens in the treatment of suicidal depression and end-of-life anxiety.

ues plummeted. In a few short hours, 401ks shriveled up. Years of savings vaporized as stock prices shrank to the size of Ant-Man. The markets—the stock market, the real estate market, and the job market—would continue to decline for a few more years. The yet-unnamed Great Recession had begun.

It's well known that desperate times invite desperate solutions and that superhero fantasy films (along with new religions) gain steam when real life opportunities contract and hopes for saviors from the sky expand.[1] The superhero comic book genre started in 1938 when the economy was still reeling from the Great Depression and when almost 20 percent of Americans were out of work.[2] To make matters even more uncertain, a Second World War was percolating across the Atlantic. The U.S. had not yet joined the Allies and would not do so until the bombing of Pearl Harbor in 1941, but Hitler had already invaded parts of Europe.

In Nazi Germany, Draconian anti–Semitic Nuremberg Race Laws had expanded, limiting the rights of Jewish doctors, lawyers, civil servants, students, academicians, accountants, actors and more. Siegel and Shuster, the two Jewish authors of *Superman,* the first official superhero, had no way of knowing that 1938 would also mark the start of the Shoah (Holocaust), with the *Kristallnacht* (Night of Broken Glass) pogrom on November 9–10, 1938. Siegel and Shuster had been shopping their work around for years before finding a publisher, and before their inaugural *Action Comic* book hit the stands, dated June 1938,[3] with Superman on the cover.

Superhero film popularity skyrocketed after 9/11 claimed nearly 3,000 innocent civilian lives and pummeled America's confidence in its ability to foresee and forestall terrorist attacks on its own soil. So, perhaps the conference attendees would have voted for *Batman* regardless, or perhaps that dire day demanded escape from more serious films.

Whatever the reasons for the crowd's choice of the Arkham Asylum scene, or a peek at the Batman universe, the Arkham mythos was perfectly suited to discussions about ethical dilemmas faced by the field of psychiatry, either in the present or the past or perhaps even in the future. Contemporary clinical controversies about neuropsychiatry, psychiatric diagnosis and prognosis, and psychiatric genetics are often embedded in over-the-top formats that distract from the seriousness of the situations. Administrative issues, such as the criminalization of and/or incarceration of persons with psychosis, their segregation from the general prison population, and the value of institutions versus "community care" (or even old-fashioned "funny farms") are implicit in story arcs that revolve around a so-called "asylum for the criminally insane."

The project expanded beyond its original scope. It drew from my earlier work on *Cinema's Sinister Psychiatrists* (2012) but added essays written by scholars from a wide range of fields, as well as by practicing psychiatrists and forensic psychiatrists.

As this project neared completion, Latin scholar and rhetoric professor Daniel R. Fredrick joined the project as coeditor. Fredrick previously published on matricide and myth in an essay entitled "Medea, Madness, and Mothers" in my earlier collection on *Mental Illness in Popular Culture* (ABC-Clio, 2017).[4] Bringing his background on myth, music, and rhetoric into the mix, Fredrick expands on his earlier publication and compares Greek and Latin lore to Arkham Asylum's "origin story" about Amadeus Arkham's murder (or mercy killing?) of his demented, bedbound and bug-eating mother.

The meme of matricide is but one of many allusions to mental illness in the Arkham mythos. Perhaps the weight accorded this meme functions as a Rorschach test for each individual reader, player or spectator. Or perhaps we can read this as a Rorschach test of the creators. Or perhaps this meme and every other meme in the mythos simply represents art for art's sake and reflects the blended efforts of the many editors, artists, writers, pencillers, inkers, game designers, producers, directors and actors who contributed to the Arkham mythos along the way and who responded to the reactions of fans. Then again, Rorschach tests are not held in high esteem by contemporary psychiatry or psychology, though they often make for excellent art.

What I can say for sure is that there are many, many layers of meaning in *Arkham*. As always, readers are invited to add their own interpretations along the way. Sadly, this single volume cannot cover all the important issues concerning the Arkham mythos and the crossovers with psychiatry. The essays ahead represent a small sampling of an ever-expanding subject.

NOTES

1. Similarly, religion in general, with sometimes extreme or unusual religious groups, surge under the same circumstances. See Sharon Packer, "Stress, Religion & Superheroes," in M. Fink, ed., *Stress: Concepts, Cognition, Emotions & Behavior* (Cambridge, MA: Academic Press, 2016), 465–475; Sharon Packer, "Stress & Religion" (updated and revised), in M. Fink, ed., *Encyclopedia of Stress*, Second Edition (Cambridge, MA: Academic Press, 2007); Sharon Packer, "Stress & Religion," in M. Fink, ed., *Encyclopedia of Stress* (Cambridge, MA: Academic Press, Vol. III, 1998), 348–355; Sharon Packer, "Stress and Religion After 9/11," in M. Fink, ed., *Encyclopedia of Stress*, Second Edition (Cambridge, MA: Academic Press, 2007).

2. Burton Folsom, Jr., and Anita Folsom, "Did FDR End the Depression?" *Wall Street Journal*, April 12, 2010. Accessed online September 24, 2018.

3. The date on comic book covers is not the date of publication, whereas the date on daily newspapers marks the date of publication.

4. Daniel R. Fredrick, "Medea, Mothers and Madness: Classical Culture in Popular Culture," in Sharon Packer, ed. *Mental Illness in Popular Culture* (Santa Barbara, CA: ABC-Clio, 2017), 183–192.

Introduction:
Why Arkham, Why Now?

SHARON PACKER, M.D.

Arkham Asylum has a formidable presence in contemporary fiction, if only because it exists in the Batman universe and the Batman universe also enjoys a prominent presence, now and for the past 70 years. There are more reasons why Arkham is important, and there are extra reasons why the crossover between Arkham and psychiatry is especially significant.

In addition to its association with the perennially popular Batman universe, Arkham has many media manifestations, far more than the traditional cinema, comics, cartoons, costumes and children's toys and trinkets. The popularity of newer venues, such as video games and graphic novels, has been increasing steadily. The Arkham games and graphic novels are riding those waves and it is those media that moved Arkham Asylum from an obscure corner of the Batman universe to center stage. Moreover, the Arkham mythos includes many allusions to psychiatry, as should be expected of a series that revolves around a psychiatric asylum for the criminally insane. Psychiatry itself consistently provokes debates and elicits strong opinions, now more than ever, as more and more Americans seek mental health care or take psychotropic medications.[1]

Arkham Asylum the institution has immutable connections to Batman and to Batman's fictional universe. The game-changing video game is titled *Batman: Arkham Asylum* (2009). The graphic novel that cemented Arkham's position in the popular imagination is similarly named *Batman Arkham Asylum: A Serious House on Serious Earth* (1989). Batman himself is a prime player in the plotline; the asylum uprising was a ploy to lure Batman into the Arkham building. Once inside, Batman himself hovers between sanity and psychosis and thereby reifies the philosophical and clinical themes that reverberate throughout the series.

The dreamlike illustrations in the graphic novel deliberately depart from other Batman depictions of that dark decade, and self-consciously tap into an oneroid reality (or unreality), yet Morrison and McKean's *Batman Arkham Asylum: A Serious House on Serious Earth* remains part of the Batman canon, and an important part at that. At the same time, it sets a precedent.

Some say that the chronological correspondence between Tim Burton's blockbuster *Batman* (1989) film and the 1989 publication of Morrison and McKean's *Batman Arkham Asylum* propelled the popularity of the graphic novel. The timing was propitious on many levels, for graphic novels were attracting wider audiences and garnering critical acclaim. This timely association increased the public's awareness of the Arkham mythos, extending this facet of Batmania far beyond the usual fanboys and fangirls who follow comics and flood comic-cons.

All links to Batman are significant in their own right since Batman the superhero remains so popular and is one of only three superheroes who have survived since the superhero genre started just before the 1930s ended.[2] Historically, Batman has been the preferred superhero because he functions as a detective as well as a superhero. This dual function enabled him to withstand the anti-superhero sentiment that arose in the aftermath of the Comics Code of 1954, which is ironic, because Batman in particular (as his alter ego Bruce Wayne and alleged consort of Robin the Boy Wonder) was singled out for perceived improprieties.

Over the decades, the fictional Batman survived attacks by fictional villains who drive the plot and enrich the story line. Batman the comic book character also survived the 1950s, when real life attacks threatened to cripple the comics industry. In the same decade when anti–Communist crusader Senator Joe McCarthy's HUAC (House Un–American Activities Committee) upended Hollywood and condemned many screenwriters as well as actors and directors for pro–Communist proclivities, anti-comics activist and psychiatrist Fredrick Wertham, M.D., (and others) harpooned comics. Batman comics stood accused of promoting a pedophilic and homoerotic relationship between Bruce Wayne and Robin the Boy Wonder. Yet Batman persisted and adapted to the changing times many times over. In the interim, Wertham's testimony, plus Senator Kefauver's televised hearings on juvenile delinquency, prompted the self-imposed Comics Code. Comic books tamed their violent currents and tempered their socially offensive sexual innuendoes (real or imagined)—until social changes of later decades welcomed back some of the very trends that offended the staid 1950s-era mindset.

Over time, Arkham Asylum (and Arkham Island and Arkham Hospital) became increasingly important to the Batman universe, even though the forensic psychiatric institution is a relative newcomer to the series. It first appeared in October 1974, in issue #258, where it was identified as "Arkham Hospital." Created by Dennis O'Neil and Irv Novick, Arkham merited only an anemic mention in a single-story arc. Clearly, the concept eventually exploded far beyond the page and a half allotted in the original pulp pages of the 1974 comic book.

In that historic issue, Arkham Hospital looks more like a prison than a hospital, with bars blocking the windows. Its future as a forensic institution is cemented. An etched cornerstone sign reads: Arkham Hospital. One character mentions Arkham by name. A panel explains Arkham's significance: "Four hours later, at a New England institution *called* a *hospital*—a polite name for an *asylum* which houses the *criminally insane*..." [bold print that appears in comics is italicized here].

Arkham Hospital houses the Joker and Two-Face, among others, until Two-Face escapes. Two-Face decides to leave the Joker behind after he tosses his trademark coin. A retired army general, imprisoned for transporting uranium intended for sabotage, breaks Two-Face out. A few pulp pages later, the disgraced general commits suicide in an act of remorse. It is the story and the characters, rather than the asylum per se, that lures readers, writers, and artists.

Even that modest 1974 debut was long delayed, given that *Detective Comics* introduced *Batman* in 1939. The little hospital on the hill is unimpressive, save for its historic significance. The refurbished, repurposed and rededicated Elizabeth Arkham Asylum for the Criminally Insane, which appears much later, stands in stark contrast to the opulent Wayne Manor, where Bruce Wayne was born and reared and where Bruce cum Batman "holds court," lives with his butler Alfred, and parks his trademark Batmobile in a concealed underground getaway.

Arkham Asylum has since become an icon of popular culture. *Batman: Arkham Asylum* has outsold all other video games to date.[3] The original *Arkham Asylum* spawned several more Arkham-based video games and morphed into its own franchise. Arkham Asylum the edifice enjoys greater prominence in animated versions and in Fox network's television series *Gotham* (2015–2019), which ran five full seasons through 2019. On TV's *Gotham*, the asylum sparks real estate feuds, social class wars and financial conflicts (much like TV's *Arrow* series, a spin-off of *Green Arrow* comics, which is yet another creation by Dennis O'Neil).

At first glance, Arkham Asylum's appearance in *Gotham* appears to be little more than an architectural backdrop for the "real action" that pushes this police procedural. However, the institution takes on a life of its own as the series progresses. Arkham Asylum weaves its way into the lives of the antagonists and protagonists and serves as the stage for many dramatic escapades. A super-sized (but not yet superpowered) police captain enters Arkham as a patient after the blood-born Tetch virus enters his system and turns him psychotic.[4] The beefy former Marine named Nathaniel Barnes gains enormous strength yet loses all reason and self control after exposure to a very fictional virus spread by the blood of Alice Tetch, sister of the man who became the Mad Hatter. The eccentric Edward Nygma (E. Nygma) (soon to be reborn as The Riddler) is also committed to the asylum, as is the beak-nosed, wobbly footed crime lord Penguin. Penguin loves his mother unequivocally but later professes love for the unsuspecting and rejecting Nygma. Other colorful characters, including Jerome, are already incarcerated. Detective Jim Gordon's enduring love interest, Dr. Leslie Thompkins, practices general medicine at Arkham when she is not functioning as a physician in even more eccentric environments.

Besides being a colorful form of speculative fiction, Arkham Asylum in its many manifestations informs and reflects the public's attitudes toward mental illness, persons who manifest such illnesses and the professionals who treat (or mistreat) the persons with the illnesses. Conveniently, and in accordance with tried-and-true cinema and literary tropes, doctors often become patients in the very same asylums where they worked. The inmates repeatedly take over the asylum. Inmates occasionally impersonate the psychiatrists and sometimes seduce the psychiatrists. Other aspects of the Arkham mythos are remarkably relevant to today's society—even though its backstory is nearing its 50th anniversary and even though the graphic novel *Batman Arkham Asylum: A Serious House on Serious Earth* celebrates its 30th birthday in 2019. The graphic novel already spawned two annotated anniversary editions and inspired some not-very-competitive competitors.[5]

A Detour Away from Dementia and into the Author's Annotations

At this point, I must make a confession. My original research on Arkham Asylum revolved around filmic representations of sinister psychiatrists who treat inmate-patients in this institution for the "criminally insane." This data appeared in another McFarland book, *Cinema's Sinister Psychiatrists* (2012). Focusing on the best-selling *Arkham Asylum* graphic novel or the record-breaking video game came later and opened more vistas—and more surprises and errata.

As this collection was nearing completion, I stumbled upon a curious factoid in the annotations to the 25th Anniversary Edition, published in 2014. The author of *Arkham Asylum: A Serious House on Serious Earth* elaborates on his original ideas about Dr. Amadeus Arkham and on Len Wein's contribution to the concept in *Who's Who*.[6] There, Grant Morrison writes that Amadeus' descent into psychosis was a reaction to the devastating 1929 stock market crash. According to the backstory, Amadeus was admitted to Arkham as a patient after he murdered his stockbroker. Since the Arkham mansion opened as an asylum in 1921, this timeline fits the storyline perfectly. Morrison then speculated that Dr. Arkham's mental decline was a response to the horrific deaths of his wife and daughter at the newly renovated and renamed asylum.

Oddly enough, the author does not directly connect Amadeus' deteriorating mental state to an inheritable neurodegenerative disease that afflicted his mother Elizabeth and his nephew, Jeremiah, another blood relative—although, in an eerie, elongated panel, Dr. Amadeus Arkham exclaims that "madness is born in my blood. It is my birthright, my destiny."[7]

That sentence reified my initial reaction. Perhaps the text functions as a Rorschach test for the reader. As a physician who has researched various history of medicine topics, *Arkham* immediately reminded me of 1980s-era breakthroughs in Huntington's Disease (HD), a dreaded autosomal dominant neurodegenerative disease. HD came to public attention largely because it affected folk singer legends Arlo and Woody Guthrie. The older Guthrie appears as a tragic bedbound character in *Alice's Restaurant* (1969). HD is inherited in the same pattern as the Arkhams' familial condition, so it seemed a likely inspiration, even if the Arkhams never show the defining HD motor movements along with their dementias. More about HD later.

As a practicing psychiatrist, inheritable mental conditions are always on my mind, and neurodegenerative disorders (such as Alzheimer's and other dementias) are among the "diseases of the day." Huntington's is uncommon, so it rarely comes up in conversations, but fears about developing dementia loom large in almost anyone past middle age. Concerns about inheritable memory problems (or any memory problem) are prominent among patients, especially since medicine has not yet concocted an adequate cure for most dementias (contrary to vigorous pharmaceutical advertising of products with very limited proven benefits). Lifestyle changes begun twenty years earlier appear to protect against some forms of dementia but probably cannot reverse the course of decline once it has begun, although exercise improves prognosis.[8] Research in this field is expanding exponentially as I write, but advances in understanding the epidemiology (distribution of disease) and the cellular pathology and anatomical changes that distinguish one type of dementia from another far exceed gains made in treatment options.

In the 1980s, in the same decade that birthed Morrison and McKean's graphic novel, different concerns emerged after scientists uncovered the genes behind the still incurable Huntington's disease. HD was previously known as Huntington's chorea, named for the British doctor who described the hereditary affliction in 1872. In a rural region of Venezuela where many residents suffer from the inheritable neurodegenerative disease, it was called "mal de San Vito" [sickness of Saint Vitus[9]]. Dr. Americo Negrette, a local doctor practicing in those isolated and ostracized communities, diagnosed the disease in many of his intermarried patients, published his observations in book form in 1963 and presented his findings at a world conference in 1972 and thereby increased the visibility of his discovery far beyond South America.[10]

Dr. Negrette's data led a clinical psychologist turned geneticist, Dr. Wexler, to start fieldwork in the impoverished lakeside Venezuelan villages identified by Negrette. The year was 1981. Dr. Wexler was already all-too-familiar with Huntington's, for her mother developed the inheritable disease in 1968 and later died from it. With help from her psychologist father and her historian sister, Dr. Wexler established a foundation to study HD. By 1983, collaborating scientists identified a genetic marker for HD. Their discoveries made worldwide news.

Once a test for HD became available, medical journals agonized about the ethics of testing for a deadly disease with no known cure. Arguments pro and con went both ways, but the early arguments proved unnecessary when most persons at risk declined testing. It is difficult to believe that reasonably well-read persons (such as Morrison) were not aware of this discovery, and perhaps incorporated such ideas unconsciously. But this hypothesis cannot yet be proven.

What *does* this prove, apart from the fact that one should "never assume" (and the childlike yet true reasons why)? Was Roland Barthes right when he wrote about the "death of the author" in an era when everyone can add personal interpretations to the text? Barthes' contention is probably more correct than ever, in our information era, when anyone with an internet connection can access data—or publish data, proven or not—with the flick of a fingertip.

My medical mind pushed me to diagnose the Arkham clan as suffering from an inheritable neurodegenerative disorder and to pigeonhole them into existing paradigms, paradigms that are medically correct and that also represent pressing contemporary concerns. The rise of those concerns among the public and among health professionals—along with several other issues mentioned below—propelled the publication of this book at this time. The popularity of the Arkham mythos is a secondary concern, but surely not an irrelevant concern.

Let's look at some of the most prominent of those psychiatric and medical concerns alluded to by *Arkham* (however inadvertently) before summarizing the essays that follow.

Contemporary Concerns: Aging and Alzheimer's, Dementia and Diagnosis

The inheritability of dementia is an ever-present issue. Cognitive decline is often reflexively but incorrectly attributed to Alzheimer's disease even though 15 percent of dementias arise from conditions other than Alzheimer's and only a tiny percentage of persons who develop Alzheimer's disease inherit a gene that causes "early-onset Alzheimer's" before age 55. Extra APOE genes increase the likelihood of later-onset Alzheimer's, but so do many lifestyle factors.

In the 1980s, when the HD genetic marker was identified, testing caused controversy. Home genetic testing is currently an expanding industry, despite its contested accuracy. Many loopholes limit the utility of the few isolated tests that are currently approved by the FDA. Tests related to Alzheimer's and Parkinson's diseases are available to the public without prescription but do not identify all the relevant markers, making their predictive value dubious.

As noted in Clare Ansberry's 2018 *Wall Street Journal* article, "The Call to Care for Aging Parents Comes Sooner Now,"[11] sometimes such concerns extend beyond those who are directly afflicted. All too often, these issues impact younger relatives who care for them. Writing for a noted financial publication, Ansberry emphasizes the financial pitfalls that may befall members of the millennial generation. Caring for aging and/or memory-impaired parents can detour career courses of younger workers who leave jobs to relocate or leave the work force prematurely to attend to family members who lose abilities for self-care. Women may be affected even more than men, since female relatives tend to assume more care-taking responsibilities. Thus, the nameless and mysterious neurodegenerative disease inherited by the Arkhams represents more than fictional fears portrayed on the pages of graphic novels or screens of video games.

Contemporary Concerns: Euthanasia vs. Physician-Assisted Suicide vs. Right-to-Die

Let's go one step further and step into speculation about other contemporary medical-ethical controversies. Given that the death of Elizabeth Arkham may have been closer to euthanasia than murder and given the possibility that her psychiatrist son Amadeus acted on explicit wishes expressed when Elizabeth was mentally competent, this central story arc reflects much more than a continuum with the classical myths about matricide in Orestes and Alcmaeon.

The sparse text of the graphic novel offers multiple opportunities to "fill-in-the-blanks" or add free associations, surrealist style, so it is not so far-fetched to fathom such a communication occurring between Amadeus the son and Elizabeth the mother in the past. This possibility is eerily prophetic, given that physician-assisted suicide (PAS) of persons with incurable illnesses (including mental illness) was legalized in a few U.S. states despite public and professional outcry and hand-wringing debates that went both ways. This practice has been permitted in some European countries for several years, provided that enough medical documentation is available, although one country to date has legalized euthanasia on request. Some countries are so well known for their liberal suicide policies that the expression "going to Switzerland" has become a euphemism for (one-way) "suicide tourism." In other cases, and in other places, persons assisting such suicides are prosecuted, physicians included.

The "right-to-die" remains a source of contention in the U.S. The role of hospice care, and the forgoing of "heroic measures" at life's end, is discussed in detail by psychiatrist and palliative care specialist Lewis Mitchell Cohen, M.D., in his book *No Good Deed: A Story of Medicine, Murder Accusations, and the Debate Over How We Die.*[12] Cohen explains how a nursing assistant misinterpreted the motives of palliative care nurses who removed an oxygen cannula, possibly because the nursing assistant was not made aware of the medical details underlying the two RNs' decision-making. Cohen shows how this inadvertent omission (and the aggrieved assistant's personal belief system) spurred legal charges against well-meaning and otherwise well-respected nurses.[13] While it is doubtful that the fictional Amadeus Arkham was as well-meaning as the registered nurses at Dr.

Cohen's hospital, this book offers an excellent and engaging clinical overview of this polarizing topic.

Contemporary Concerns: Institutionalization vs. Trans-Institutionalization, Violence and Illness

The concept of Arkham Asylum for the Criminally Insane comes at a time when "trans-institutionalization" (moving from one institution to another, in this case from state hospitals or hospital inpatient wards to penal institutions or prisons) gets more press than ever, although it is not a new issue. Mental health professionals (and some of the public) have been chagrined—even outraged—by the trend toward criminalization of mental patients and their wholesale incarceration in jails and prisons in lieu of treatment facilities or chronic care hospitals (many of which were shuttered). Colativa and colleagues' essay, "Orange Is the New Color of Mental Illness," compares this phenomenon to the popular television show, *Orange Is the New Black*, where a clearly psychotic woman called "Crazy Eyes" is incarcerated with the general prison population.[14]

There is yet another side to the story, as told by the press and as paralleled in Arkham. Judging by laws enacted in recent years, it seems that public sentiment has shifted in response to the upswing in mass shootings in America (which began in earnest with Columbine High School in 1999 but expanded to grade schools, concert halls, shopping malls, movie theaters, churches and synagogues, and video game tournaments, not to mention workplaces and post offices). Many wonder if untreated, undertreated, undiagnosed or misdiagnosed mental illness (as well as easy gun access) influenced these tragedies. Many citizens (as well as lawmakers) are unappeased by data that shows the difficulty in predicting such violence, much less preventing it. Laws limiting gun purchases by persons who were hospitalized for mental illness or who were admitted involuntarily have been enacted by many states—but mandates are not always followed as carefully as expected, as is true of any law. Different states have different statutes and these statutes are constantly changing in response to recent tragedies.

My own state—New York—mandates that psychiatrists and other mental health professionals report patients whose delusions or other signs of illness pose a threat to others, even though psychiatrists' abilities to predict violence are poor and even though mental illness in isolation does not necessarily correlate with violent outbursts. (Mental illness compounded by substance use follows different patterns.) Previously, the Tarasoff law required treaters to warn potential that protect themselves, provided that their patient voiced credible death threats against a specific person—but not all states follow the Tarasoff law. Some states have even more stringent requirements than New York state. Laws requiring health care providers to function as both treating professionals and policing agents typically elicit objections, on the part of individuals as well as on the part of professional societies, as this puts treaters in a double bind and demands that they figuratively "serve two masters." Some hypothesize that such laws potentially deter high risk persons from seeking needed psychiatric consultation and thereby act contrary to the very purposes for which they were intended.

New laws related to this topic are minted by the day, sometimes in haste, and often in response to horrific school shootings. Publications such as *Wall Street Journal* print opinion pieces on "A Parkland Father's Quest for Accountability," where writer Tunku

14 Introduction

Varadarajan introduces a soon-to-be published book by Andrew Pollack, a bereaved father-turned-activist and author.[15] The "Government News" section of *Psychiatric News*, a publication of the American Psychiatric Association, highlights Linda M. Richmond's article on "State Laws Provide New Tools for Removing Guns from Individuals at Risk."[16] Richmond elaborates on gun violence restraining orders, also known as "extreme risk protective orders" or "ERPO." No matter how comprehensive the reporting, we can be sure that the data will become outdated soon because this field is in constant flux.

A dizzying array of research on this topic exists. Many studies conflict with one another, and each is as confusing as the next. Virtually all such studies prove the power of statistics, and of statistics' abilities to deceive and distort data, since focusing on one parameter instead of another or circumscribing the subject of study to carefully demarcated groups leads to dramatically different conclusions—but at the same time produces "publishable statistics."

Forensic psychiatrist and former APA president Paul Appelbaum, M.D., publishes always intriguing and sometimes contrarian data on related topics. Scholarly articles by Jonathan Metzl, M.D.,[17] and others synthesize these studies for public health professionals.[18] Dinah Miller and Annette Hanson approach this ever-vexing issue from a different angle in their well-received 2016 Johns Hopkins publication *Committed: The Battle Over Involuntary Psychiatric Care*. Robert Whitaker's books and his blog, www.madinamerica.com, offer alternative arguments. The list of erudite and occasionally inflammatory opinions goes on and on.

But what about the public? Where do they weigh in and where do they "hold court" (metaphorically, that is)? And how can they escape the contradictory and confusing cavalcade of "facts" on this topic, some of which are presented by obviously partisan organizations with explicit agendas or economic incentives? The Arkham franchise, for one, offers opportunities to contemplate these heady questions, under the guise of entertainment or diversion. Hours of video games provide a distraction from the realities of the day—or open floodgates for more sophisticated queries.[19]

Transvestism, Transsexualism and Shamanism

Another concern relates to transvestism, transsexualism and shamanism—and the portrayal of cross-dressers as killers in Arkham and elsewhere. Transgender legal and medical rights make headlines regularly. A December 2018 issue of the *New England Journal of Medicine*, a weekly beacon of medical information for physicians of all specialties, features articles and editorials about the increasing prevalence of "non-binary" sexual identities and the pressing need to learn more about the nuances of gender transitions and sexual minorities.[20] *NEJM*'s emphasis on medical care counterbalances the attention accorded legal disputes and cultural conundrums highlighted by less specialized resources. Admittedly, both the tone and the intent of these articles is much more serious than *A Serious House on Serious Earth*, but Morrison mentions the ritual transvestism of shamans in his annotations, and the author's emphasis makes this tangent important to our exegesis of Arkham.

Ordinarily, shamanic rituals primarily concern anthropologists, or perhaps cultural psychiatrists, and do not enter everyday discourse, although New Age subcultures have aped some shamanic rituals. Then there are those persons who learned of these rites when they read the small print of the annotated *Arkham*. Yet the cross-dressing proclivities of Dr. Amadeus Arkham and of Dr. Cavendish, the Arkham psychiatrist who orchestrated the inmate uprising that lured Batman into the locked and guarded institution, are prominent in the graphic novel. Should there be any doubt about the significance of this subject to the author, the graphic novel includes portraits and quotes from Anthony Perkins, who played the cross-dressing matricidal Norman in Hitchcock's *Psycho* (1960).

Above and beyond these arcane references in this book, and increased visibility in general medical journals (as opposed to subspecialty journals), transgender issues are very much in the public eye as celebrities such as Caitlyn [Bruce] Jenner or Chaz [Chastity] Bono have changed genders and as military courts deliberated about Chelsea Manning's proposed sex-reassignment/gender-affirming surgery when he still self-identified as male during the trial. The court of public opinion addressed public subsidies for such pricey procedures. Questions about insurance coverage for surgeries and hormones are ever-present in America. Those financially motivated and philosophically driven debates are relevant in real life, even if they not as colorful as stories of cross-dressing Siberian shamans who consume concentrated quantities of hallucinogenic amanita mushrooms by drinking their own urine.

In the heyday of the counterculture, when hallucinogens were promoted for recreational use, those exotic amanita rituals received much attention. The transvestism/transsexualism accompanying those rituals were lesser concerns in that era. Times changed. Because Grant Morrison, the author of the graphic novel *A Serious House on Serious Earth*, mentions them, American Indian *berdache* or transvestite rituals are also relevant, although practitioners of such traditions have been renamed "two-spirited" to avoid any negative associations of *berdache*. Yet *A Serious House*'s portrayal of cross-dressers as murderers and its glorification of Anthony Perkins/Norman Bates only adds to their pejorative connotations and is anything but neutral. It is only a matter of time before activists condemn such portrayals and reignite the ire expressed when De Palma's *Dressed to Kill* (1980) starred a cross-dressing killer psychiatrist at an especially importune time, a year before the AIDS epidemic emerged in America.

Carl Jung, Occultism and Grant Morrison's Authorial Interest in Jung

Essays on *A Serious House*'s occult symbolism (and the author's acknowledged interest in occultism, Tarot and Carl Jung) and the crossovers with the writings of Jung deserve exploration, if only because Morrison endorses Jung, mentions a visit to "Professor Jung" in the graphic novel and adds a pencil portrait of Jung. Jung's books outsell all other psychology books, attesting to his popularity with the public in spite of his lukewarm reception by fellow psychiatrists who practice outside of C.G. Jung foundations. Jung's appeal to visual artists in particular is well-established, as is his contribution to "New Age" ideology, even though the founder of "analytical psychology" and the author of visually spectacular *Man and His Symbols* (and much more) fell from the grace of the psychoanalytic establishment early on and has long been marginalized in medical circles. Jung is rarely taught in psychiatry curricula or medical schools, apart from specially devoted institutes. Jung himself remains a consistently curious and controversial character, partly because of his notorious associations with anti–Semitism, Nazism, and the Third Reich but also because of his over-the-top interest in occultism and in communicating with poltergeists that inhabited his home. Jung's recognition of his own poltergeists has parallels with the bat spirits that reportedly occupied the Arkham home. Such essays are not included here due to space constraints.

Review of the Sections of This Book and the Essays

Since so many psychiatric controversies weave their way in and out of the Arkham mythos, we cannot expect the 24 essays in this collection to cover each concern that *Arkham Asylum* uncovers. Equally important, comics mythology is ever-evolving and new adaptations of source material surface far too frequently to cover all sources in print form. Luckily, several impressive websites and blogs regularly update this material and keep readers current. With those caveats, it is our hope that the topics included (as well as the omissions) will stimulate readers to build upon this foundation and pursue their own projects.[21] The essays here hail from a wide range of researchers: humanities professors, practicing psychiatrists and forensic psychiatrists as well as entertainers and artists (some of whom are also academicians).

The book you hold in your hands (or see on your screen) is divided into eight sections. The first section, "Clinical Psychiatric Controversies," opens with "The Differential Diagnosis of Elizabeth Arkham," by Elyse D. Weiner, M.D., a consultation-liaison psychiatrist who treats patients in general hospital settings and differentiates chronic and progressive neurodegenerative diseases from acute-onset and time-limited (and often deadly) delirium, which can include visions, delusions, and disorientation. History professor Timothy W. Kneeland's essay "ECT in Arkham Asylum: Pacification, Assassination and Electrocution" explains the clinical benefits and potential side effects of ECT, and its political, legal and gender-related implications. He highlights Harley Quinn's enthusiasm for ECT and Amadeus Arkham's murderous misuse of ECT. Psychiatrists Matthew Brown, D.O., and Fernando Espí Forcén, M.D., review the convoluted history of medicinal hallucinogens, their promises and their pitfalls, their uses and abuses in "Hallucinations and Psychadelics in Arkham." They contrast contemporary clinical research to the diabolical drugs used by Arkham's doctors.

The second section, "Forensic Psychiatric Controversies," opens with an essay by forensic psychiatrists Ryan C.W. Hall, M.D., and Susan Hatters Friedman, M.D., "I'm [Virtual] Batman: Violence and Video Games." Using Batman and Arkham as touchstones, they address current (often contradictory) data about violence and video games, which recollect remarkably similar debates about comic book violence and censorship from the mid–1950s. These authors also coauthored the essay, "Deadly and Dysfunctional Family Dynamics: When Fiction Mirrors Fact." Grounded in Friedman's first-hand clinical experience with women in prison, and fortified by academic research on matricide and parricide, Friedman and Hall compare the matricide "McGuffin" in the graphic novel to real-life statistics on family murder. They also elaborate on Amadeus' amnesia of the event and elucidate the clinical and forensic nuances of "dissociation" after committing such an act. After that, I write about the shooting at a movie theater in Aurora, Colorado, perpetrated by a psychiatrically compromised graduate student during a screening of *The Dark Knight Rises.* A fanatical Batman fan, the neuroscience student identified himself as "The Joker" although his flame-colored hair and his neuroscience pursuits also resembled the Mad Hatter, the red-headed neuroscientist incarcerated at Arkham. This essay, "Murderous Minds, Arkham Villains and Real (Not Reel) Life Movie Massacres," expands on my earlier entry in *Evil in American Popular Culture* (2014)[22] and explores the consistently controversial but rarely successful "insanity defense" that failed to exculpate the Batman movie murderer.

The third section, "Medical-Ethical Controversies," opens with an essay by a practicing psychiatrist who also holds a doctorate in the history of psychiatry. In "Anti-Psychiatry and the Arkham Asylum," Fernando Espí Forcén, M.D., compares attitudes implicit in *Arkham Asylum* to unabashedly anti-psychiatry academic writings published since 1960. Forcén updates us on the residual "anti-psychiatry" grass roots movement among "consumers." The next essay, written by me, is "Harley Quinn and the Joker: Pitfalls of Doctor-Patient Romances." This essay compares the Harley-Joker romance to fantasies fossilized by daytime TV hospital soap operas and Dr. Jekyll's dalliance with a saloon singer. Added to that are realistic concerns voiced by early 20th century psychoanalytic circles, and contemporary medico-legal sanctions against such professional boundary-breaking and compromised clinical care. The next essay, "Unethical Experiments in Arkham and Elsewhere," is also written by me, and connects the long literary history of mad scientists and evil experimenters to Arkham psychiatrists Jonathan Crane (Scare-

Updated technology notwithstanding, Arkham Asylum's sinister psychiatrists follow in the footsteps of 19th century literary predecessors. Fredric March appears in many guises in this lobby card for Mamoulian's *Dr. Jekyll and Mr. Hyde* (1931). In the upper right, wearing a top hat, he is Dr. Jekyll, with his transformed simian "shadow self," Mr. Hyde, just below, surrounded by a silhouette shadow. Rose Hobart, his "proper" fiancée embraces him in the upper left, while a head shot of saloon singer Ivy Pearson (Miriam Hopkins) is at bottom left. Dr. Jekyll's pre–Hyde humanitarian streak sets him apart from diabolical Arkham doctors.

18 Introduction

crow) and Dr. Hugo Strange (to be distinguished from the Marvel superhero and disabled neurosurgeon Stephen Vincent Strange). This essay also addresses real-life horror stories of human experimentation perpetrated by the Nazis, the U.S. Public Health Service and others.

The next section, "Big Screen Parallels," backtracks to the early days of silent cinema and German Expressionism, to compare the likes of Dr. Caligari and Dr. Mabuse to Arkham Asylum's ever-expanding cadre of diabolical doctors. My essay, "Arkham's Sinister Psychiatrists and the Continuum with Caligari," draws on research from my earlier *Cinema's Sinister Psychiatrists* (2012). Next comes an essay by historian and horror film expert Michael Markus, "Haunted by Madness: Horror and the Supernatural in Arkham Asylum." Markus links Arkham Asylum, with its ghostly inhabitants, to other haunted houses in the horror genre. His historical overview of supernatural motifs in "madhouse movies" reminds us that psychosis was conflated with possession until the 19th century, if not later in some circles, making this meme especially appealing and almost plausible.

The lobby card for *Island of Lost Souls* (1932), a film based on H.G. Wells' 1896 novel, shows Katherine Burke as part-human, partly-clad Panther Woman (left), while the portly star Charles Laughton, who plays Dr. Moreau, stands between her and Richard Arlen (right), cast as the shipwrecked sailor who stumbles onto this strange site. Dr. Moreau (Laughton) experiments on animals like Panther Woman Lota (Burke) in his House of Pain and trains them to act human. Dr. Hugo Strange inverts Dr. Moreau's legacy by creating monstrous humans in Indian Hill.

"Breaking Out: The Escaped Mental Patient in the Batman Universe," written by Jeffrey Bullins, a professor of communications and a sound designer for horror films, dissects the meme of the escaped mental patient, and murderous ones at that, to show when and why mental patients supplanted mad scientists as movies' most popular villains. He tells us why the mentally ill, murderous Arkham Asylum inmates continue this legacy from late 1950s, which began in earnest with *Psycho* (1960) and corresponded in time with the "closing of the asylums" in the mid–1950s. He suggests that Arkham's increased visibility in comics from the late 1970s onward may also reflect attempts to mirror the success of Carpenter's horror classic, *Halloween* (1978), with its asylum, a murderous (but morally just) psychiatrist, and an "incurable" Michael Myers, who escapes the confines of the asylum, only to kill again. Jaq Greenspon tackles yet another aspect of *Arkham* and Harley Quinn in his essay "The Suicide Squad: From Bad to Good and Back Again." A Ph.D. candidate in comics studies, and a professional writer with hands-on Hollywood experience, Greenspon traces *Suicide Squad* (2016) to its less-celebrated cinematic precursors—even though trailers and posters advertise Harley Quinn's prominence in the feature film. He shows how Amanda Waller morphed and mutated over time, evolving into a femme fatale–like character who resembles the seductive Harley Quinn far more than her unappealing comic book appearance. This essay explains why *Suicide Squad*'s action cannot logistically occur in Arkham Asylum itself and moves to a full-scale prison.

The section "Small Screen Parallels" follows, beginning with "Animated Arkham: Television and Children's Perceptions of Psychiatric Treatment" by Kristi Rowan Humphreys. Humphreys examines daytime TV cartoon representations of mental illness, mental hospitals and sinister psychiatrists in *Batman* (where Arkham Asylum held a prominent place). She speculates about their impact on youthful audiences' attitudes toward psychiatry and how those ideas percolate later in life. In "The Fine Line Between Sanity and Madness in *Star Trek*'s 'Whom Gods Destroy' and *Arkham Asylum: A Serious Place on Serious Earth*," English professors Darren Harris-Fain and Eric J. Sterling compare and contrast the Arkham plotline to a single episode of the influential *Star Trek* TV series (1966–1969), where psychotic and violent criminals assume control of an insane asylum, and blur the distinction between sanity and madness. Their research convinces readers that *Star Trek* also influenced Morrison's plotline.

We then move to "Video Screen Parallels," beginning with an essay by narratologist and video game scholar Shawn Edrei. "If Walls Could Scream: Embedded Narratives and Mazes of Madness in the Virtual Space of Arkham Asylum" explains how video games such as *Batman: Arkham Asylum* configure the physicality of the asylum in the virtual space and simulate the perceptual and cognitive experiences of psychosis in ways that are unattainable via other media. "Excavating Arkham: The Mental Asylum as Horrible Homecoming," by historian of medicine and pharmacy college professor Barbara S. Gardenour, Walter offers cross-cultural and historical perspectives on the representation of "brick and mortar" mental hospitals in virtual space. She compares the Arkham franchise (inspired by Scottish-born Morrison and McKean's graphic novel) to Japanese video games such as *Silent Hill* (1999) and *The Evil Within* (2014) and to the American game, *Outlast* (2014), an even more disturbing mental hospital game which was banned in several countries on account of its graphic depiction of castration and other grisly scenes. Walter traces theories about hospital architecture's impact on treatment.

The section "Literary and Artistic Influences" begins with "Bizarro Arkham, Bizarro World: The Looking Glass Looks Back," by literature professor and science fiction specialist Aaron Barlow. Barlow reminds readers of Arkham's literary roots in Lewis Carroll's *Alice and the Looking Glass*, where a person's very presence in a psychiatric asylum ipso facto proves that they are mad (which is polar opposite of conclusions by anti-psychiatry academicians such as Goffman and many more). Barlow alludes to Ray Bradbury's "Usher II," Perkin's "The Yellow Wallpaper," *Cuckoo's Nest*, and Poe's enduring short story about Tarr and Fether [sic], as he explains how Arkham Asylum's topsy-turvy world parallels the better-known Bizarro world of DC's Superman comics, where all values and cultural preconceptions are inverted into mirror images. The next essay, "The Neo-Expressionist Agony of Arkham Asylum," is written by MOMA (Museum of Modern Art) curator and German expressionist expert Rosa JH Berland. Berland ties masterpieces of the German expressionist art movement to psychiatric after-effects of World War I trauma. She unmasks parallels in Arkham Asylum's origin story and recollects Bob Kane's appropriation of German expressionist aesthetics for his early Batman comics creations.

My essay, "Surrealism's Influence on Arkham and Psychiatry's Influence on Surrealism," mines material from my earlier book *Dreams in Myth, Medicine & Movies* (2002), updating it with annotations in the graphic novel anniversary editions, where Morrison elaborates on his intent to evoke the dream state advocated by surrealists. Surrealism itself was inspired by Freud's *Interpretation of Dreams* (1899), as reinterpreted by André Breton, who was a medical student prior to enlisting in World War I. In response to wartime experiences that left him and many others a "changed man," he put his formal medical studies behind but salvaged experiences from working with brain-injured soldiers during the war. Breton abandoned aspirations to practice psychiatry or neurology and subsequently became a surrealist impresario.

"Poe's Place in Arkham Asylum: Precursors and Parallels" addresses Edgar Allan Poe's influence on Arkham and on authors and filmmakers who influenced Arkham directly. Caleb Puckett, a published poet as well as a scholar, brings his broad knowledge of Poe's pre–Civil War short stories about familial "degeneration," psychotic psychiatrists, and arcane neuropsychiatric illnesses. To highlight how Poe's memes are reborn in Arkham, Puckett shows similarities between William Wilson, Roderick Usher and Doctor Tarr and Professor Fether of Poe lore and the Arkham clan members. In keeping with Morrison's admiration for Jung's tenets, he identifies Jungian constructs, such as the shadow self and the anima, in Arkham-specific characters and in Batman himself. An essay by literature professor Eric Sandberg connects Arkham to influential horror writer and horror critic H.P. Lovecraft. In "H.P. Lovecraft, Literary Heritage and *Batman: Arkham Asylum*," Sandberg traces Arkham Asylum's lineage to a fictional town in a Lovecraft short story and also identifies Lovecraftian characteristics of Arkham story arcs. He relates Lovecraft's repeated literary renditions of psychosis to Lovecraft's personal and familial experiences with mental illness and institutions, since both parents died separately in the same mental asylum and Lovecraft himself had multiple mental breakdowns.

The concluding section, "Mythic and Religious Parallels," mines early medieval as well as classical Greek theater. Its essay, "Evil Clowns and Acrobats: The Joker and Harley Quinn," is written by Adam W. Darlage, who holds a Ph.D. in the history of Christianity. After reviewing the long history—as well as recent history—of evil clowns, jesters, and tricksters, Darlage connects Harley Quinn to the Harlequin character (Arlecchino) of 16th-century Italian street theater, Commedia dell'Arte. He traces the Joker's smile to Paul Leni's silent film, *The Man Who Laughs*, starring Conrad Veidt and based on a tragic

19th-century story by Victor Hugo. Daniel R. Fredrick also draws on history in his essay, "Matricide and Myth." A classicist by training who previously performed death metal music, and who teaches university-level rhetoric, Fredrick situates Elizabeth Arkham on a continuum with Eriphyle and Clytemnestra. After reviewing these myths about matricide, and the circumstances that catalyzed their sons' actions, he poses a most provocative question: are these mothers guilty of provoking their sons to commit matricide? And if so, how and why? He exonerates Elizabeth Arkham of any wrong-doing, but inevitably leads us full circle to Friedman and Hall's clinical research on matricide, making readers wonder if Elizabeth's enmeshed relationship with Amadeus contributed to this act. The essays conclude with this provocative question and hopefully provokes readers to add their own answers or ask more questions.

The volume ends with an appendix, "Unethical Experiments in Modern Genetics Research," and includes a filmography and bibliography of works cited throughout the book.

Notes

1. The American Psychiatric Association lists the following statistics on their website, https://www.psychiatry.org/newsroom/reporting-on-mental-health-conditions:
    In any given year,
One in five adults in the United States has a diagnosable mental disorder.
One in 24 adults has a serious mental illness.
One in 12 has a substance use disorder.
Suicide is the 10th leading cause of death for all ages. It is more common than homicide.

2. Sharon Packer, *Superheroes and Superegos: Analyzing the Minds Behind the Masks* (Westport, CT: Praeger, 2010).

3. The 2018 *Spiderman* video game may unseat *Arkham*, if sales remain steady.

4. The Tetch virus and its alleged ability to induce both psychosis and extra strength nearly merited a chapter in this book, since certain infectious diseases do indeed invade the brain and cause neuropsychiatric symptoms, if not death. However, the fact that the virus supposedly originated in a girl with an inheritable blood disease (rather than an infectious disease) makes this otherwise interesting story arc too implausible to pursue in this essay collection.

5. Michelle Madsen, Sam Kieth, and Dave Stewart's *Arkham Asylum Madness*, published by DC Comics in 2010, plays off the artwork and formatting of Morrison and McKean's 1989 graphic novel, without the intensity or the popularity of the Morrison and McKean collaboration.

6. Len Wein died September 10, 2017, after a long and illustrious comics career.

7. Some might consider the possibility of more "generic" and more common inheritable psychiatric disorders, such as bipolar disorder or schizophrenia, but Elizabeth's dementia and the mid-life onset of psychotic symptoms make these diagnoses less likely, as detailed in Dr. Weiner's essay on "The Differential Diagnosis of Elizabeth Arkham." Those disorders are also not inherited so predictably—and are not controversial or incurable enough to push the plot.

8. Knowing about these protective lifestyle changes—such as exercise and diet in midlife and extra education in early life—does not reverse age-related memory problems and gaining this little bit of knowledge after the fact may even make matters worse because guilt results from *not* having taken these measures. Still, recent studies suggest that late life exercise helps a bit.

9. "St. Vitus' Dance" often refers to the choreiform movements or "Sydenham's Chorea" (SC) which can follow infection with certain strains of streptococcus infection (also known to cause rheumatic fever), although there does not appear to be any other relationship between those disorders other than the colloquial names and the jerky involuntary movements themselves.

10. Although Dr. Negrette identified the endemic disease in the 1950s, his book entitled *Corea De Huntington: Estudio De Una Sola Familia a Traves De Varias Genereaciones* was published in 1963. the world learned about HD in this isolated, intermarried and otherwise ostracized community when Negrette's work was presented at the 1972 Centennial Symposium. Another extended family in Columbia, South America suffers from early-onset Alzheimer's Disease (AD) and is the subject of much research on the genetics of this variant of AD. This inheritable disorder is distinct from HD although there could be cause for confusion between these two inheritable but unrelated dementias that afflict extended families in South America.

11. Clare Ansbery, *Wall Street Journal* (Updated August 6, 2018). Accessed online August 13, 2018.

12. Lewis Mitchell Cohen, *No Good Deed: A Story of Medicine, Murder Accusations, and the Debate Over How We Die* (New York: HarperCollins, 2010).

13. Medical literature on palliative care as well as medical ethics include lengthier discussions of this polarizing topic than general psychiatry journals. Interested readers may wish to consult such specialty journals for more detailed data.

14. Mary L. Colativa et al., "Orange Is the New Color for Mental Illness," in Sharon Packer, ed., *Mental Illness in Popular Culture* (Santa Barbara, CA: ABC-CLIO, 2017), 99–108.

15. *Wall Street Journal,* January 11, 2019, online.

16. Linda M. Richmond, "State Laws Provide New Tools for Removing Guns from Individuals at Risk," *Psychiatric News,* published online December 31, 2018.

17. Jonathan M. Metzl and Kenneth T. MacLeish, "Mental Illness, Mass Shootings, and the Politics of American Firearms." *American Journal of Public Health* (Published Online: December 12, 2014).

18. The American Psychiatric Association lists the following on their website, https://www.psychiatry.org/newsroom/reporting-on-mental-health-conditions:

> People with mental illnesses are no more likely to be violent than those without a mental health disorder. in fact, those with mental illness are 10 times more likely to be the victims of violent crime. [Persons with certain psychiatric conditions who use non-prescription recreational drugs pose higher risks than the general population and higher risks than persons with serious psychiatric illness who do not use such drugs.]

19. Television's longest-running drama, *Law & Order: SVU* has addressed related questions about insanity and criminal culpability over the past 20 years. the success of this TV series attests to the public's intrigue with such questions, especially when controversies are spiced up with salacious stories about sex crimes handled by the "special Victims' Unit."

20. K.L. Ard and A.S. Keuroghlian, "Training in Sexual and Gender Minorities—Expanding Education to Reach All Clinicians," *New England Journal of Medicine* (December 20, 2018) 379:25. Accessed online December 24, 2018; "Persons of Non-Binary Gender—Awareness, Visibility, and Health Disparities," *New England Journal of Medicine* (December 20, 2018) 279: 25. Accessed online December 24, 2018.

21. Criminal justice approaches to this topic do not appear in this collection, as important as they are, since impressive publications from that field already exist.

22. Sharon Packer and Jody Pennington, ed. *Evil in American Popular Culture: What Hannibal Lecter, Stephen King, and Vampires Reveal About America*, Santa Barbara, CA: ABC-CLIO, 2014.

Section I
Clinical Psychiatric Controversies

The Differential Diagnosis of Elizabeth Arkham

Elyse D. Weiner, M.D.

The Elizabeth Arkham Asylum for the Criminally Insane is a later addition to the Batman series, first appearing in Batman #258 in October of 1974.[1] Earlier on, Arkham Asylum was called "Arkham Hospital." This fictional forensic psychiatric hospital housed many famous patients over the years but its namesake, Elizabeth Arkham, is the subject of this essay. We will create a neuropsychiatric differential diagnosis to explain her symptoms, as is done for any patient evaluated in a hospital. In short, this essay strives to teach readers to "think like a shrink."

To start, we must gather everything we know about Elizabeth Arkham. In medical terms, this is called "taking a history." Since she is deceased, and, of course, a fictional character, we use "collateral sources." Collateral sources in medicine can be anything written or known about a patient, including interviewing people who may have had contact with the person. After we reconstruct everything we know about Elizabeth Arkham, we will review various possibilities that might explain what ailed her. This will generate a "differential diagnosis."

To start, who was Elizabeth Arkham? Elizabeth Arkham was the mother of its chief psychiatrist, Dr. Amadeus Arkham. She was reported to have had a long history of mental illness, which, in later years, could be described as a dementia with visual hallucinations.[2] Mrs. Arkham reportedly would see a bat and, in fear, yell for her son. After witnessing his mother's misery for years, Dr. Arkham eventually killed her, presumably to "take her out of her misery." He goes on to repress the memory of her murder for many more years and comes to believe his mother's death to be a suicide, until he treats a patient, Martin "Mad Dog" Hawkins, who awakens buried memories in Amadeus.

Martin "Mad Dog" Hawkins had escaped from prison around the time the Arkham family estate was being remodeled into the future Elizabeth Arkham Asylum forensic hospital. Unfortunately for Dr. Arkham and his family, this turned out to be a terrible coincidence. The Mad Dog broke into the poorly secured home which was under renovation and murdered Dr. Arkham's wife and only daughter. In true comic book fashion, there seemed to be no problem with the psychiatrist treating the man who murdered his family, even though this is a terrible conflict of interest. One day while administering Martin Mad Dog Hawkins a prescribed electroshock therapy session, Amadeus gave too much electrical power which killed Mad Dog. Dr. Arkham was not arrested at the time of the death or even sued for malpractice. The error is deemed accidental and the only other consequences seem to be to the good doctor himself. Sometime after Mad Dog Hawkins's "shocking" death, Dr. Arkham spirals into mental illness and is hospitalized in the Arkham asylum. There are reports that he became extremely paranoid.

Even though our information is sketchy, we find prominent features that help us formulate a rudimentary differential diagnosis for this fictional character. One important characteristic is chronicity. We know that Mrs. Arkham suffered from mental illness for a long time. The second is visual hallucinations. Visual hallucinations are a rarity in primary psychiatric illnesses such a schizophrenia. They usually point to an underlying medical cause as a driver of the psychosis. The fact that it was a bat—which is important to Batman fans— is what doctors call a "red herring" which distracts us from the pertinent medical data because it seems so interesting on the surface. While hallucinatory bats are fun for comic book readers, the actual content of a visual hallucination rarely makes much of a difference in identifying the disease state responsible for the hallucination.[3] What is most important is that those visual hallucinations are either present or absent.

The third major piece of medical information found in the history is that Dr. Arkham also eventually developed psychotic symptoms (as did other second-degree relatives). It is always notable when a history reveals that a first degree relative has a major psychiatric illness. Since Dr. Amadeus Arkham was an only child without siblings and since he himself had no children who survived into adulthood—his daughter having been murdered before reaching the age when she might manifest such later life psychosis—we cannot say for certain that first-degree relatives did not show similar symptoms. Nor can we say that this psychosis affected only males but spared females, which typically occurs in x-linked recessive conditions that are transmitted from mother to son, but which appear in female progeny who inherit two such genes, one from the mother and one from the father. Without belaboring the point further, this fact alone opens questions about inheritable familial diseases and especially about "autosomal dominant" inheritance patterns.

We cannot say for certain that Dr. Arkham did or did not have visual hallucinosis, but we can be relatively confident in saying that Dr. Arkham's most prominent neuropsychiatric symptom is paranoia, which adds more options to the differential diagnoses at hand.

Finally, we must consider Mrs. Arkham's "downhill course" which is cited by multiple sources. This trajectory is a hallmark of dementia (rather than time-limited delirium). She eventually confined herself to her bedchamber. Let us not, however, put her in the Alzheimer's type of dementia category too quickly. Many factors can cause a decline in personal care. Other issues may have caused or contributed to her illness such as long-term toxin exposure, an infectious disease, uncontrolled seizures, or untreated mental illness, all of which can take their toll. In summary, for Elizabeth Arkham, we need to keep an open mind. We start with exploring causes of dementia along with other medical causes of personal decline, accompanied by visual hallucinations, since this is the most we know about her clinical signs before she was felled by her son in an act of comic book physician-assisted homicide. Since we have no idea if Mrs. Arkham would even have consented or wished to die, despite her persistent visions of bats, we unfortunately cannot dignify with the doctor's act with the wording, "physician-assisted suicide."

First, consider that Mrs. Arkham simply has pure visual hallucinations because of low eyesight. This is called Charles Bonnet syndrome. Dr. Bonnet lived in the 1700s and described visual hallucinations in people who had visual but no other psychiatric problems. These visual hallucinations can be very complex and distressing but otherwise harmless. We can think of them as "phantom limb" pain for the eyes. When people are so visually impaired, they do not see normally anymore, their brain still retains images of things they may have seen in the past. There is no mention of blindness or other visual symptoms in the comic book series so while this would be considered, we can quickly rule it out as a cause.

We can then talk about her general metabolic state. Is she visually hallucinating because of low oxygen saturation or hypoxemia? Patients with poor oxygenation can have visual hallucinations. Does she have trouble with her lungs or heart or maybe she has anemia? Is she losing blood, perhaps from a cancer that has gone undiagnosed? Does she have heart or lung disease that has not been worked up? A complete blood count is a starting test to see if blood loss is involved. If there is an anemia, then a doctor might suspect a malignancy given other aspects of her presentation. Doctors then must see what other workup is needed but this is getting beyond our scope of Mrs. Arkham and her hallucinations of bats. We then have basic blood chemistries and thyroid tests that we check on all patients who present with hallucinations. Could her sodium be off the charts? Could her blood chemistries show evidence of dehydration? Could she be in thyroid storm? These would be answered in hours with routine blood tests.

We then move to rule out toxin exposure. Could Mrs. Arkham have been exposed to a toxin and if so, what? Certainly, an untreated toxin exposure would have a downhill course. Could someone have poisoned Mrs. Arkham or continued to give her a medication, seemingly innocuous, that in large amounts have led to visual hallucinations? The first most common cause of visual hallucinations is alcohol exposure, either intoxication or withdrawal. As much as we do not like to think of alcohol as a "toxin," in large doses it does indeed function as a toxin. Too much, and then subsequently too little, of a good thing is never a good thing. People can experience visual hallucinations from drinking large amounts of alcohol. When people habitually drink, they become tolerant to a specific amount of alcohol. One day the patient either decides to quit or is no longer able to obtain the quantity of alcohol they had been drinking. The reasons run the gamut from, running out of money to entering an institution where no one knows that they were drinking. Within 48 hours of abruptly stopping alcohol consumption, they begin to experience an alcohol withdrawal delirium or what was called in the old days, delirium tremens (DT's). One of the hallmarks of this phenomenon is visual hallucinations. It is a medical emergency. If not treated, delirium tremens can lead to permanent medical problems, seizures, coma or death. It is not treated, however, by killing your mother.

There are so many medications and illicit drugs that can cause visual hallucinations. The most notable ones are LSD, mescaline, MDMA and PCP, but even cocaine and amphetamines in high doses can cause visual hallucinations, as can over-the-counter (OTC) stomach medications such as cimetidine and ranitidine, prescription medications for the heart or blood pressure. Other OTC medications associated with visual hallucinations include phenylpropanolamine and ephedrine. Steroids even, which are used for a whole host of conditions, are well known to cause psychosis and visual hallucinations. People have hallucinated on Viagra, which is especially known to cause people to see blue. Could someone have been feeding any of these to Mrs. Arkham on the sly? If we think about a woman who is going downhill for no discernible reason and being visited by an imaginary bat, a sneaky poisoner could explain a lot.

To what other toxins could Mrs. Arkham have been exposed? Heavy metals can be ruled out by blood tests. Lead, for example, can be filtered out of patient's blood with the proper medications. Could Ms. Arkham have Wilson's disease, or hepatolenticular degeneration, which is an inborn error of metabolism that causes high levels of copper in the body? Left untreated, this would explain both her and her son's psychiatric illnesses and downhill courses. Coincidentally, the upper extremity tremor associated with Wilson's disease is called a "wing-beating tremor." A simple blood test for copper and a slit-lamp eye exam to look for the signature Kayser-Fleischer rings in the cornea can diagnose Wilson's disease, as can a liver biopsy after the fact. They could have taken medication to rid themselves of the excess copper, had it been available at the time of diagnosis. Coincidentally (or perhaps not so coincidentally), Dr. Wilson first described the illness (and the pathology) that bear his name in 1912, around the same time that Mrs. Arkham became ill enough to enter the hospital. It is unclear if Dr. Arkham knew of Dr. Wilson's recent breakthrough, which is on every board exam in psychiatry today.

Two treatable neurologic disorders, not initially thought of as associated with visual hallucinations, are migraine and narcolepsy. These disorders imply that Mrs. Arkham is probably psychiatrically intact. She may have become isolated because she had difficulty functioning due to the chronicity of the medical disease. Severe migraines can be incapacitating. One can imagine Mrs. Arkham with intractable, untreated migraines that require her to sit in a dark room. Usually the visual symptoms are in the form of shapes such as lines, halos, circles and prisms. Rarely, the visual hallucinations are figures, such as Elizabeth Arkham's recurrent bat.

The other treatable disease with relatively normal psychiatric functioning is narcolepsy. Narcolepsy is associated with sudden onset REM periods that intrude into the day. People with narcolepsy fall asleep suddenly and have muscle paralysis and other symptoms such as hypnogogic hallucinations. Hypnogogic hallucinations occur when going to sleep. These types of hallucinations are primarily visual and are especially frightening—as are bats!

Seizure disorders are abnormalities of the electrical functioning of the brain with many and varied physiological symptoms that follow. The classic is the grand mal or tonic-clonic seizure where the abnormal electric impulses involve so much of the brain that the patient loses consciousness and manifests generalized motor muscle contractions. It is not well known that there are many other kinds of seizures whereby a patient remains fully conscious—or perhaps in a dreamlike (oneroid) state. These are called partial seizures because enough of the brain is still awake and aware of the outside. With partial seizures, the patient can experience visual hallucinations, especially if the seizure-causing lesion is in the temporal or occipital lobes. Could a seizure disorder account for Mrs. Arkham's hallucinations? Sometimes seizure disorders just occur and other times there is an underlying abnormality in the electrical disturbance. Some such abnormalities could include brain tumors (both benign and malignant), bleeding in her brain or bleeding around the coverings. General tests that tell us about the health of her brain such as a CT scan or MRI can show these types of problems. Untreated seizures and certainly an underlying medical condition causing those seizures can account for the visual hallucinations plus a downhill course. Even a brain tumor or stroke could cause Elizabeth Arkham's symptoms without the development of seizures. In either case, a patient such as Mrs. Arkham in a modern-day hospital would certainly have had her brain imaged to rule out any demonstrable cause of her visual hallucinations and downhill course.

There are infectious diseases, many of which can infect the brain and cause both mental illness, possibly visual hallucinations and a downhill course. First, we can start with blood-borne illnesses such as hepatitis B or C, which eventually cause liver failure, confusion and psychiatric signs. Depending on when Mrs. Arkham acquired this type of infectious disease, she might have passed it on to her son. As her liver failed, she would have had progressively worsening psychiatric symptoms. Her son would experience the same problems. Another blood borne illness with mother-to-child transmission is HIV/AIDS, which, when left untreated, can result in dementia and neuropsychiatric symptoms in the later stages, before death intervenes.

A third infectious disease would be neurosyphilis. While uncommon in the 21st century because it is responsive to readily available antibiotics, syphilis has historical importance and was prevalent in the early 20th century, when Elizabeth showed symptoms and well before Fleming's 1947 discovery of penicillin. Syphilis was brought to Europe by Christopher Columbus and his crew who acquired the disease through sexual relations with the Native Americans. The first outbreak was then recorded in Naples, Italy in 1494–5. Among the many historical figures who were either alleged to have had syphilis or to have died from it are Hitler, Franz Schubert, Leo Tolstoy, Vladimir Lenin, Vincent Van Gogh, Charles Baudelaire, Guy de Maupassant and even Shakespeare. The evidence for some is more compelling than others.

One of the most interesting current theories of syphilis is that Abraham Lincoln (as well as his assassin John Wilkes Booth) may have had neurosyphilis. Mr. Lincoln had frequented prostitutes before marriage. Mrs. Lincoln, well known to have had psychiatric problems for the rest of her life, showed erratic behavior, a downhill course, and eventually went blind. Blindness is a well-known manifestation of tertiary syphilis that affects the central nervous system. Blindness does not fit a purely psychiatric picture and suggests the presence of another medical cause. Since the organism that causes syphilis, Treponema pallidum, can be transmitted during pregnancy, to cause so-called "congenital tabes," some theorize that tabes may have affected President Lincoln's children, who died young. However, all-cause infant mortality secondary to infectious disease was already high in the days before vaccination and antibiotics.

Before the advent of modern antibiotics, such as penicillin, this killer disease would cause severe psychiatric disturbance. Unfortunately for these patients, the (partial) treatment was mercury or arsenic. So, if what ails you did not kill you, the treatment most certainly did. Mercury poisoning causes multiple psychiatric symptoms as does arsenic. Lincoln was often seen taking blue pills that were supposedly prescribed for constipation. The active ingredient of these pills, however, was mercury. A syphilis test is part of the routine psychiatric blood screening tests today. This disease does fit into the potential differential diagnosis for the Arkhams, with its long indolent course, eventual intense psychiatric symptoms with hallucinations, impulsivity, rage and mother-to-son vertical transmission. However, late-stage syphilis affects several other organ systems as well, causing life-threatening aortic disease and other cardiovascular manifestations, as well as paralysis (general paresis of the insane) and we have no data suggesting that impairment of the Arkhams' medical health or shortened lifespans (except by murder/euthanasia).

What about prion diseases or transmissible spongiform encephalopathies which fall under the rubric of Creutzfeldt–Jakob disease? We can recall Britain's mad cow disease craze of the 1990s, when people feared that they had consumed infected beef. Mad cow disease or bovine spongiform encephalopathy is one of these prion diseases. In the 1980s and 1990s, animals (mostly in Europe) were fed nervous system parts mixed into meal and a bovine spongiform encephalopathy epidemic resulted. Although the practice was banned by the 1990s, a total of 229 variant Creutzfeldt–Jakob disease cases were identified between 1996 and 2014. This prion disease can also affect humans consuming sick cattle. Because most cases were in the United Kingdom, the European Union banned British beef from 1996 to 1999.

These are very unique diseases because the particles causing these conditions do not have any DNA or RNA. They are just folded proteins that enter brain matter and start replicating to the point of destroying the functioning brain. They are called "spongiform" because they leave sponge-like holes in the brain. Often these diseases take years to manifest themselves after initial exposure because the prions need time to cause damage to the brain. Prion diseases are universally fatal. They are easily and insidiously transmissible and are feared by treating physicians as well as forensic pathologists who perform post-mortem exams.

There are much less common familial types of prion disease, if we want to revisit mother-to-son transmission. Should Mrs. Arkham have had a prion disease, visual hallucinations would have only been the beginning of a precipitous decline.

Finally, and perhaps most importantly, we must discuss heritable neurodegenerative diseases, which can cause hallucinations or delusions and other psychiatric symptoms as the brain deteriorates. Alzheimer's disease, fronto-temporal dementia (FTD) and Lewy body dementias are examples that are most often sporadic but, in a minority of cases, also have genetic components. For instance, 34 percent of persons with FTDbv (behavioral variant) carry a specific gene linked to this condition. Huntington's Disease (HD) is an excellent example because of its Mendelian genetics, and its transmission as an autosomal dominant disorder that can affect all genders equally (as opposed to "sex-linked" disorders that are transmitted on the X-chromosome and mostly affect males), so I will discuss HD to illustrate how we can construct a theory that incorporates all our Arkham characters into our hypothesis. Yet even HD has become more complicated than previously realized, since the number of "repeats" of the culpable chromosome impact the age of onset of motor (movement), psychiatric and cognitive symptoms.

We know that Elizabeth Arkham's son developed serious psychiatric symptoms in mid-life, after which he also showed a downhill (rather than cyclic) course, but we should discuss all known biological relatives as well. That brings us to Elizabeth's great-nephew (and Amadeus' nephew), Jeremiah Arkham. Jeremiah took over the asylum after his uncle became too psychiatrically impaired to continue his directorial role. Yet both Amadeus and Jeremiah were cognitively intact enough to complete their medical education and their psychiatric specialty training, suggesting that their symptoms did not emerge until the third or fourth decade of life.

How did Jeremiah know that he would become a psychiatrist? When he was a teenager, he went to a nearby store that was being robbed by an Arkham patient. The patient had killed the owner and was about to kill Jeremiah. Jeremiah managed to talk the patient out of killing him and the patient committed suicide instead. Inspired by these events, Jeremiah planned to become a forensic psychiatrist like his uncle. He did another renovation of the Arkham Asylum.

Unfortunately, Jeremiah eventually became a paranoid leader of the inmates, grooming them for a criminal empire. He implants chips into villainous patients. The chips could explode if patients do not cooperate. In some comics, he operates as the Black

Mask. Finally, like his uncle, he, too, became a patient at Arkham Asylum. These three successive generations of precipitous decline with multiple psychiatric symptoms point to a heritable disease such as Huntington's Chorea, more recently known as Huntington's Disease (HD)—except for the fact that the Arkhams do not display abnormal motor movements that characterize HD.

HD results from the dominant inheritance of a single gene defect on chromosome 4. This means that if a parent has the gene, a child has a 50 percent risk of inheriting that gene from that parent. Inheriting the gene for Huntington's disease means that an affected person will probably develop the symptoms between ages 30 and 50, although symptoms may start sooner, depending upon the number of chromosomal "repeats." HD symptoms are progressive (rather than intermittent). The psychiatric and neurological symptoms progress to a need for total care. HD is invariably fatal, commonly due to complications such as pneumonia.

The idea that the Arkham family carried a genetically dominant disease such as Huntington's brings up many ethical issues related to genetic testing. For instance, if the Arkhams knew Elizabeth Arkham had Huntington's disease, would Amadeus have had earlier testing, had it been available at the time? Patients are divided on getting genetically tested for a dreaded disease such as Huntington's. Some patients choose to know the results to circumvent the burden of not knowing, while others feel that they will become hyper-alert for symptoms if they confirm that they inherited the gene. Had Amadeus known that he might develop neurological impairment, he might not have been allowed to treat patients. That might have aborted his plans to euthanize his mother and electrocute a patient. Alternatively, restricting activities because of future potential—in the absence of clinical symptoms—is equally unethical.

Genetic testing for Alzheimer's disease is even more confusing in that certain genes such as the APOE-e4 gene are more strongly associated with early Alzheimer's disease but do not guarantee that the afflicted person will develop the disease. It is not currently recommended to have the test on a routine clinical basis. There is a form of autosomal dominant Alzheimer's disease which has the same genetics as Huntington's Disease, but this accounts for only 1 percent of all the Alzheimer's disease cases in the U.S. It brings up the same ethical issues we are discussing with Huntington's disease with regards to prenatal and genetic testing in adults.

What about his nephew Jeremiah? Had Elizabeth Arkham been tested for Huntington's disease and proved positive, then the niece or nephew who was the biological parent of Jeremiah might have chosen prenatal testing (or more advanced embryo selection, had that been available and affordable). In doing so, they could have decided not to conceive a child affected by this genetic disease. Currently, there are three types of pre-natal genetic testing. PGD, or pre-genetic diagnostic testing, can be used in conjunction with in-vitro fertilization, so that a cell of an embryo is tested before implantation in the uterus, to ensure that the developing fetus will not be affected by the disease. In an already developing embryo, chorionic villus sampling performed at 10–11 weeks or amniocentesis at 14–18 weeks will provide genetic material for testing. The parents then confront an ethical/religious decision regarding the continuation of the pregnancy of an affected child or the termination of that pregnancy before the end of the second trimester (when pregnancy terminations are still legal in most states).

We have reviewed the reasoning patterns and "differential diagnosis" used by psychiatrists before concluding that behavioral symptoms are purely psychiatric and based on the mind alone. After we rule out all the medical, toxic and neurologic causes of Mrs. Arkham's illness—or treat any treatable diseases identified during this laborious process, we can start to think about our psychiatric differential diagnosis. Could Mrs. Arkham have been simply psychotic and visually hallucinating? Could she have schizophrenia, a chronic psychotic disorder? Could the natural course of untreated schizophrenia account for her downhill course? While visual hallucinations alone are rare as the cardinal symptom of schizophrenia (without accompanying auditory hallucinations), it is possible and as we well know, in Gotham City, anything is possible. These symptoms of schizophrenia are described by the American Psychiatric Association's *Diagnostic and Statistical Manual of Mental Disorders 5 (DSM-5)*[4]:

Diagnostic Criteria
  295.90 (F20.9)

  1. Two (or more) of the following, each present for a significant portion of time during a 1-month period (or less if successfully treated). At least one of these must be (1), (2), or (3):
    1. Delusions.
    2. Hallucinations.
    3. Disorganized speech (e.g., frequent derailment or incoherence).
    4. Grossly disorganized or catatonic behavior.
    5. Negative symptoms (i.e., diminished emotional expression or avolition).
  2. For a significant portion of the time since the onset of the disturbance, level of functioning in one or more major areas, such as work, interpersonal relations, or self-care, is markedly below the level achieved prior to the onset (or when the onset is in childhood or adolescence, there is failure to achieve expected level of interpersonal, academic, or occupational functioning).
  3. Continuous signs of the disturbance persist for at least 6 months. This 6-month period must include at least 1 month of symptoms (or less if successfully treated) that meet Criterion A (i.e., active-phase symptoms) and may include periods of prodromal or residual symptoms. During these prodromal or residual periods, the signs of the disturbance may be manifested by only negative symptoms or by two or more symptoms listed in Criterion A present in an attenuated form (e.g., odd beliefs, unusual perceptual experiences).
  4. Schizoaffective disorder and depressive or bipolar disorder with psychotic features have been ruled out because either (1) no major depressive or manic episodes have occurred concurrently with the active-phase symptoms, or (2) if mood episodes have occurred during active-phase symptoms, they have been present for a minority of the total duration of the active and residual periods of the illness.

Opposite: A 1962 advertisement for the anti-psychotic medication Thorazine (phenothiazine), from SKF Labs. Although this outdated medication is not prescribed in *Batman Arkham Asylum* games, Thorazine revolutionized schizophrenia treatment after arriving in the U.S. in 1954. It catalyzed the closing of long-term hospitals that housed persons with previously incurable psychosis. Thorazine eventually fell out of favor after disabling and disfiguring movement disorders followed long-term use. This scary ad appeared long before the era of calming, bucolic direct-to-consumer ad campaigns; it promises to "quickly put an end to his violent outburst" "when the patient lashes out against 'them'" [their hallucinatory voices].

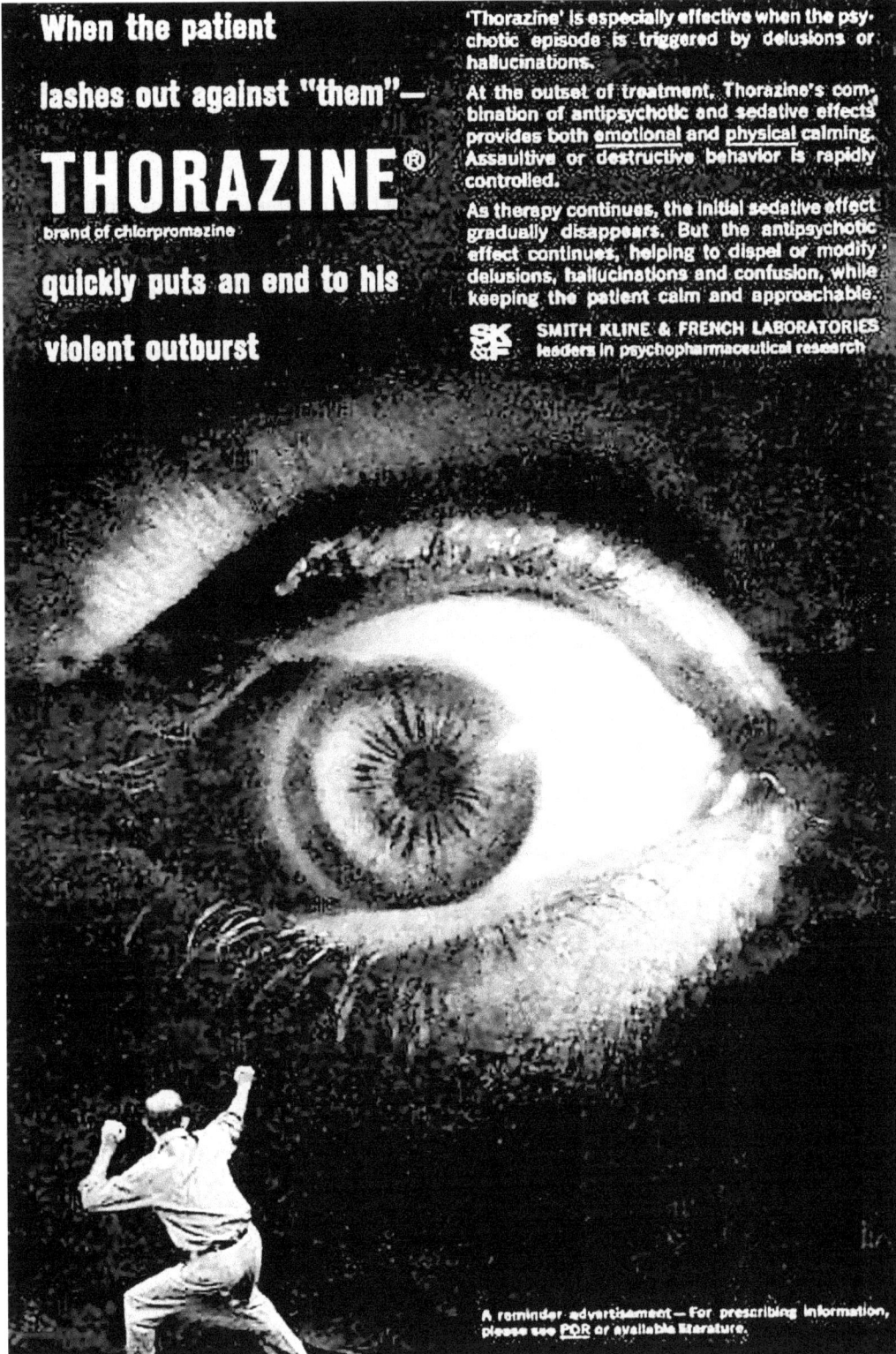

5. The disturbance is not attributable to the physiological effects of a substance (e.g., a drug of abuse, a medication) or another medical condition.

> If there is a history of autism spectrum disorder or a communication disorder of childhood onset, the additional diagnosis of schizophrenia is made only if prominent delusions or hallucinations, in addition to the other required symptoms of schizophrenia, are also present for at least 1 month (or less if successfully treated).[5]

Significantly, we also know that schizophrenia runs in families. We have long known through twin studies that if one twin has schizophrenia, the second twin has a high risk of developing the disease, up to 85 percent.[6] The cardinal symptoms of schizophrenia are delusions, hallucinations, thought disorganization, paranoia, and what we call "negative symptoms." These can include flattening of emotional expression, slowing of cognition, or lack of motivation. Elizabeth Arkham's symptoms do fit this profile. The treatment would include antipsychotic medication. Haloperidol and Thorazine are classic first-generation anti-psychotics, which have largely been replaced by the atypical antipsychotics with improved side effect profiles with respect to movement disorders (tardive dyskinesia) that follow the blockade of dopamine receptor by these medications. Examples are Risperidone, Olanzapine, Quetiapine, Aripiprazole, Lurasidone, to name a few.

The real question is why did Amadeus not try to treat his mother's symptoms? Are we to assume that there were no antipsychotic medications in Gotham City at the time? That is not an unreasonable assumption, considering that Elizabeth was hospitalized in the early 20th century; the phenothiazines (such as Thorazine) were not developed until the mid–20th century. Mrs. Arkham was already dead by the time that ECT was introduced in 1938. Even the more dangerous insulin coma therapy was not discovered until 1927 in Berlin. We must wonder whether Amadeus would have tried to alleviate his mother's distress if effective anti-psychotic medications or other treatment modalities were available when she was most ill. Or would he have chosen to euthanize her anyway, before trying available albeit ineffective treatments? Another question to consider is whether Amadeus himself may have already been subtly deteriorating, unbeknownst to the reader? His mantle passed onto his nephew, who had many reasons to be vulnerable to psychosis as well. The deconstruction of Arkham Asylum and its namesakes is a lesson in medical psychiatry. Elizabeth Arkham and her symptoms have taken us on an unexpected journey from comics to the real world and how doctors think about patients, their diagnoses, their treatments and the ethics implicit in whatever course of action they choose (or dismiss).

Notes

1. Bob Kane and Bill Finger, *Batman #1* (DC Comics, 1940). on the controversy over Jerry Robinson's role in the creation of the Joker, see *The Joker: A Serious Study of the Clown Prince of Crime*, ed. Robert Moses Peaslee and Robert G. Weiner (Jackson, MI.: University Press of Mississippi, 2015), XVI.
2. Victoria Pelak and Grant Liu, "Visual Hallucinations," *Current Treatment Options in Neurology* 6: 75–83. doi:10.1007/s11940-004-0041-4.
3. Sometimes, the size of the visions is relevant, such as Lilliputian hallucinations of "little People" that characterize atropine psychosis.
4. American Psychiatric Association: *Diagnostic and Statistical Manual of Mental Disorders, Fifth Edition (DSM-5)*. Arlington, VA: American Psychiatric Association, 2013.
5. Ibid., 99.
6. Alistair Cardno et al., "Heritability Estimates for Psychotic Disorders: the Maudsley Twin Psychosis Series," *Archives of General Psychiatry* 56: 162–168. doi:10.1001/archpsyc.56.2.162; Cannon Tyrone et al., "The Genetic Epidemiology of Schizophrenia in a Finnish Twin Cohort: a Population-Based Modeling Study," *Archives of General Psychiatry*, 55: 67–74. doi:10.1001/archpsyc.55.1.67

ECT in Arkham Asylum

*Pacification, Assassination
and Electrocution*

TIMOTHY W. KNEELAND

"I love electroshock. It's a shiatsu message for the brain."—Harley Quinn[1]

"The door opens into the Electroconvulsive Therapy room ... there seems to be someone strapped to what we see of the couch ... the figure on the couch jerks violently."[2] Harley Quinn's quote and the description above provide glimpses into the use of electroconvulsive therapy (ECT), or electroshock, in Arkham Asylum, the fictional institution for the criminally insane in the Batman universe.

Sending an electrical current through the brain in order to induce a grand mal seizure may not sound therapeutic, but that is exactly how ECT works to alleviate the symptoms of mental illness.[3] The practice began in the 1930s because clinicians believed that individuals suffering from epilepsy were immune to schizophrenia and other forms of mental illness. To cure or treat mental illness, psychiatrists artificially created seizures by using chemicals such as Metrazol and Insulin. These chemically induced seizures effectively reduced the symptoms of madness but were time consuming, dangerous, and terrified the patients. To create a faster, more effective and controlled seizure, Italian psychiatrist Ugo Cerletti invented electroshock in 1938.[4]

Depending on the amount of electricity needed to induce the grand mal seizure, patients received anywhere from 70 to 100 volts. Before muscle relaxants were developed in the 1940s, the convulsions created by ECT were so violent that patients broke bones and bit off their tongues. Some patients turned bright blue from apnea, involuntarily urinated, defecated, or ejaculated. After ECT, patients had short-term memory loss. In rare cases, a patient suffered long-term persistent memory loss.[5] The practice was and is still controversial. Psychiatrists and neurologists condemned it and warned that memory loss was a symptom of much deeper brain damage and cognitive impairment.[6] Improvements to the procedure became common in the 1970s. Today, patients receive anesthesia and muscle relaxants before the treatment to reduce pain and prevent injuries.[7] Rather than bi-lateral electrodes on both sides of the brain, unilateral placement of one electrode on the right temple is sufficient to convulse the patient. Instead of continuous electrical current, pulse waves of electricity are sent into the brain. Overall, these refinements minimized many of the most damaging side effects. Over a million people were treated with ECT through the 20th century, and Americans are probably unaware that as many as a hundred thousand patients a year undergo ECT for drug resistant mood disorders, suicidal ideation, or as an alternative to psychopharmacology during pregnancy.[8]

Electroshock is a popular trope in literature, movies and television shows about villainous psychiatrists. Both the procedure and the machine appear as metaphors of social control, punishment for deviancy, and as a method of torture and execution. It may also represent the machine-like inhumanity of psychiatric professionals. These metaphors sometimes have quasi-religious overtones. ECT is imagined as a form of crucifixion and punishment for sin.[9] Several of these tropes appear in storylines in the Batman universe, especially stories involving Arkham Asylum.

Arkham Asylum, a.k.a. Elizabeth Arkham Asylum for the Criminally Insane, became an integral part of the Batman universe, or multiverse, of comics, graphic novels, radio dramas, television series, films, and video games in 1973.[10] Depending on the imaginationof the writer, the asylum may appear as a Gothic mansion from the 19th century, a maze, or a prison. In whatever form it takes, Arkham is the backdrop for interactions between Batman and villains such as the Joker, Poison Ivy, the Riddler, Killer Croc, Penguin, Two-Face, and Zsasz. The asylum itself is the antagonist in various graphic novels and video games.[11] The staff workers at Arkham are as likely to be mentally ill as the inmates. Arkham hosts former mental health professionals such as the Scarecrow (a.k.a. Dr. Jonathan Crane), Dr. Hugo Strange, and Harley Quinn (a.k.a. Harleen Quinzel).[12]

Psychiatry is frozen in time at Arkham, set in Batman's version of 1950s noir. Nurses in the facility wear a white uniform and hat, popular in that profession in the 1950s but

Entryway to Arkham Asylum Intensive Treatment, where electroshock therapy is administered. Dr. Amadeus Arkham intentionally murders his murderous patient "Mad Dog" during ECT treatments, to retaliate against Mad Dog's rape, murder and mutilation of the doctor's wife and daughter. This portal recollects Dr. Moreau's "House of Pain," used to experiment on humans.

In James Whales' 1931 adaptation of Shelley's story, Boris Karloff stars as the misunderstood monster. This dark, deep German Expressionist–style cavern reminds us of Bob Kane's appropriation of German Expressionist aesthetics for *Batman* comics and Gotham City. The "science-gone-awry" meme in Mary Shelley's *Frankenstein* (1818) is especially relevant to ECT, for *Frankenstein* comments on recent discoveries in electricity and galvanism and in the use of electricity to reanimate frogs. Amadeus does the opposite when he electrocutes his murderous patient Mad Dog while pretending to provide curative care.

ultimately discarded after the 1970s. The asylum is an admixture of prison and hospital. Patients appear as inmates, involuntarily committed to the asylum and forced into wearing prison garb while living in cells. The head of the institution is likely to be a warden rather than a physician, and the staff includes thuggish orderlies and armed police assigned to the asylum.[13] It is a place where the residents are more likely to be tortured than treated.

The use of ECT is infrequent in the Batman series but when it does appear, it reinforces the idea that psychiatrists and their treatments are malevolent.

Therapy at Arkham includes psychotherapeutic techniques offered usually by female characters such as Ruth Adams and Harleen Quinzel. The use of talk therapy in the institution harkens back to the days of psychoanalysis in the U.S., which dominated psychiatry in the 1950s.[14] The male doctors at Arkham are sadistic figures straight from the pages of anti-psychiatry novels, and they use somatic treatments like ECT to manipulate and control the patients.[15] The use of ECT at Arkham is slightly farfetched because the patients in the asylum are nearly all suffering from a form of unnamed psychosis, but few practitioners today consider ECT an effective treatment in such cases. The ECT practiced at Arkham echoes some of the historical reality of the treatment, but like much in the Batman universe, it is a distorted and violent version of that history.

The ECT given in Arkham Asylum is more electric chair than electrotherapy. In *DCU: Assault on Arkham* (2014), the Riddler explains ECT to the Suicide Squad and correctly notes that electroshock is used to induce a grand mal seizure in patients. However, The Riddler erroneously suggests that patients receive 1,000 volts of electricity, an amount ten times stronger than any recorded dosage. The depiction of ECT in this direct-to-video animated film is congruent with most iterations of ECT in the Batman universe. Patients sit in chairs, physically restrained so they cannot move. ECT at Arkham is unmodified, bi-lateral electroshock, given without the benefit of muscle relaxants or anesthesia. The patients convulse, but they do not flail around due to their restraints. Instead they looked tortured like Jack Nicholson in the film version of *One Flew Over the Cuckoo's Nest*.

The ECT machines at Arkham are located in the Intensive Therapy room or building. In the 2009 videogame, *Batman Arkham Asylum,* Batman must go to that room to rescue Mike the security guard from the hands of Zsasz who has strapped Mike into the electroconvulsive machine. Batman's shocking rescue of Mike from Zsasz saves the guard from an electrical death. Later in the game Batman will have to save Commissioner Gordon from a similar fate at the hands of the Joker.[16] Here the machine represents psychiatric brutality, torture, and death. This resonates in the character Zsasz, named to honor the psychiatrist Thomas Szasz, author of *The Myth of Mental Illness* (1961). Dr. Szasz, a psychiatrist employed at the Upstate Medical School in Syracuse, New York, believed mental illness was a social problem, not a medical issue, and that the involuntary treatment of patients was unethical.[17]

At Arkham Asylum, electroshock is equated with electric death. In the origin story of Arkham Asylum, Grant Morrison's *Arkham Asylum, A Serious House on Serious Earth* (1990), the founder of Arkham, Amadeus Arkham, appears as a kindly figure who wants to help those who are mentally ill, such as Martin "Mad Dog" Hawkins. Amadeus loses his sanity after Mad Dog rapes, tortures and murders his wife and daughter. Deciding that revenge is a dish best served cold, Amadeus provides free therapy to Mad Dog until the one-year anniversary of the death of his loved ones. On that date, April 1, 1922, he straps his client "into the electroshock couch and I burn the filthy bastard."[18] This is one of many ECT anachronisms within the Batman universe because the plot point occurs 14 years prior to the invention of ECT by Cerletti. Arkham puts Mad Dog on a couch to receive the electroshock and this is incorrect. In actuality, ECT patients were always supine but laid on a gurney, table, or cot, but never a couch or chair. Morrison may be using the couch as a reference to psychoanalysis, which was popular in the 1920s. He may also be thinking of the electric couch, a device used in the days of electrotherapeutics. In the 1800s patients diagnosed with maladies such as neurasthenia and hysteria were often given mild forms of electricity along the spine, but rarely if ever to the brain. Electrotherapeutics peaked in 1910s, and by the 1920s electrotherapy was dismissed by medical authorities as quackery.[19]

At least one doctor at Arkham frequently used ECT. Doc Cavendish was introduced by Grant Morrison in *Arkham Asylum: A Serious House on Serious Earth* (1990), where he is described as "our current administrator, a man who just loves to administer current to ECT patients."[20] Cavendish's fetish for ECT is reflective of the first twenty years of ECT use. Between 1940 and 1960, many doctors saw ECT as a cure-all for mental illness. Psychiatrists and general practitioners used ECT in large state mental institutions, private hospitals, at the doctor's office, and even made house calls with their portable ECT machines. One patient remarked of his physician: "The doctor was shock happy—I mean he shocked everybody.... He thought shock was a miracle treatment."[21] Prior to 1960, ECT was deployed to treat nearly every mental illness: mood disorders, autism, schizophrenia, and anxiety disorders. Patients included toddlers, children, pregnant women, senile cases and everyone in between. By today's standards, some of those given ECT would not be considered mentally ill. Before the 1970s heteronormative cultural norms labeled gender fluidity, homosexuality, lesbianism, and cross-dressing as symptomatic behavior of underlying mental ailments as well as criminally deviant behavior.[22] Psychiatrists used ECT on non-heterosexuals to control their sexual orientation and make them "well" by the socially constructed standards of the 1950s. This clearly demonstrates the duo function of ECT as therapy and social control.[23]

Doc Cavendish's employment of ECT at Arkham suggests a desire to control, torture, punish, and execute disruptive patients. This motif reappears in the television series, *Gotham* (2014), which depicts electroshock therapy as a means of control of others. Jack Gruber, a.k.a. the Electrocutioner, and Dr. Strange find that ECT can bend people to their wills. Dr. Strange uses ECT on the Penguin to make him docile and easily controlled.[24] To an extent, this abuse of ECT is a distorted version of reality. There are documented cases of abuse at Stockton State Hospital in the 1950s, in which patients were controlled and punished with electroshock.[25] Similarly, Peter Cranford, a doctor at a large state mental hospital in Georgia, recalled that at his hospital patients thought that the term "punish" and "shock treatment" were synonymous.[26] Author Ken Kesey worked at a state mental hospital in Oregon in the 1950s where he witnessed patient abuse, which became fodder for his novel *One Flew Over the Cuckoo's Nest*. In the novel, protagonist Randle McMurphy is introduced to ECT by a fellow patient, who describes the procedure: "You are strapped to a table shaped ironically like a cross, with a crown of electric sparks in place of thorns. You are touched on each side of the head with wires. Zap! Five cents worth of electricity through the brain and you are jointly administered therapy and punishment for your hostile go-to-hell behavior."[27]

The mention of crucifixion and ECT evokes the quasi-religious overtones to ECT in Arkham Asylum. One of the patients in Arkham is Maxie Zeus who believes he is the "Electric Messiah." In Morrison's *Arkham Asylum (1990)* Batman finds Zeus connected to the ECT machine and perpetually receiving the current which Maxie calls "fire from heaven." The equation of ECT with religious ritual was one metaphor that the writer Sylvia Plath used to recreate her own experience with ECT in "Johnny Panic and the Bible of Dreams"[28]:

> The white cot is ready. With a terrible gentleness, Miss Milleraverage takes the watch from my wrist, the rings from my fingers, and the hairpins from my hair. She begins to undress me. When I am bare, I am anointed on the temples and robed in sheets virginal as the first snow. Then, from four corners of the room and from the door behind me come five false priests in white surgical gowns and masks whose one lifework is to unseat Johnny panic from his own throne. They extend me full-length on my back on the cot; the crown of wire is placed on my head, the wafer of forgetfulness on my tongue.[29]

There are overtones of punishment for sin the scene depicting Maxie Zeus. Zeus, under the Joker's direction, has taken control of the asylum with other members of the Rogues' Gallery. Maxie captures an unnamed guard, strips him and straps him into the electric couch, on which the semi-naked guard is continuously plied with shocks from the ECT machine. At one point, the guard looks up, "fixes us with a deranged slack grin. He's enjoying this," the narrator tells us.[30] Guards in Arkham are often vicious and cruel toward the patients and Maxie is punishing the guard for his sins. Studies of patients who received ECT show that some thought they were receiving the treatment as punishment for their sins.[31] As one patient explained, he was condemned to the asylum for his behavior. "They're going to electrocute me for my sins."[32]

The equation of ECT with death is actually part of the psychiatric literature on ECT. Some patients and practitioners imagined the shocks as a kind of death. One patient described his experience as "a jolt of power jars you into the darkness of temporary death." One patient asked another if he died in the shock treatment room.[33] Another patient told his therapist that every ECT "was (like) going through the crucifixion again."[34] In the 1950s a number of practitioners saw the equation of ECT with death as an explanation for why treatment worked. Cerletti formulated a theory that convulsions bring the person close to death, which arouses a reaction of extreme biologic defense, creating the therapeutic effect.[35] Psychologist Thelma Alper believed "the treatment threatened the patient with death and offers him an opportunity of rebirth cleansed of previous fear anxieties."[36] This fits the thesis proposed by psychoanalyst Otto Fenichel, who analyzed other psychiatrists and found that the "attitude of the doctors toward the treatment was regularly that of killing and bringing back alive again."[37]

At Arkham Asylum ECT is used to kill the persona as much as the person. In *Arkham: Living Hell* (2004) both Dr. Ruth Adams and Dr. Jeremiah Arkham, nephew of Amadeus, seek to cure the inmates by destroying their old personalities.[38] In *Gotham* (2014) Dr. Strange used ECT to obliterate Penguin's memory and change his personality. Strange cured Penguin from his violent tendencies then released him from Arkham.[39] In *Batman: Savage City* it is revealed that Bruce Wayne once volunteered for electroshock, hoping it would erase his sad memories. However, at the last minute, Bruce fled before receiving the treatment.[40] This idea that memory loss and the obliteration of the old personality were therapeutic was recognized by early practitioners of ECT. The co-inventor of ECT, Lucio Bini, went so far as to advocate annihilation therapy. He gave patients thousands of electroshocks until he obliterated their old memories and former personality.[41]

Despite the semi-realistic depiction of ECT in Arkham Asylum, the use of ECT in the Batman universe is merely a Halloween version of psychiatry. Here ECT works on the darkest fears of mental medicine and echoes the employment of electroshock as a literary device meant to show cruel and power-hungry psychiatrists wielding this therapeutic weapon on their tormented patients. It always appears in the unmodified form utilized in the 1950s and assumes the role of social control, punishment, torture and death.

Notes

1. Quoted in *DCU: Batman Assault on Arkham*, Directed Jay Oliva and written by Ethan Spaulding (New York: DC Entertainment, 2014).
2. Grant Morrison and David McKean, *Arkham Asylum: A Serious House on Serious Earth 15th Anniversary Edition* (New York: DC Comics, 2004; 1990), 45.
3. Timothy Kneeland and Carol Warren, *Pushbutton Psychiatry: A History of Electroshock in America* (Westport: Praeger, 2002).
4. Kneeland and Warren, *Pushbutton*, 46; Joel T. Breslow, *Mental Ills and Bodily Cures: Psychiatric Treatment in the First Half of the Twentieth Century* (Berkeley: University of California Press, 1997).
5. This was the case for Marilyn Rice and Linda Andre; see Daniel Smith, "Shock and Disbelief," *The Atlantic Monthly* 287, 2 (February 2001): 79–90.
6. Franklin G. Ebaugh et al., "Fatalities Following Electric Convulsive Therapy," *Archives of Neurology and Psychiatry* 49 (1) (1943): 107–117; H.H. Fleischhacker, "Some Neurological and Neurovegetative Phenomena Occurring During and After Electroshock," *Journal of Nervous and Mental Disease* 102 (4) (1945): 185–190; Alexander Gralnick, "A Fatality Incident to Electroshock: a Review of the Subject and Autopsy Report," *Journal of Nervous and Mental Disease* 102 (5) (1945): 483–495; Peter Breggin, *Electroshock: Its Brain- Disabling Effects* (New York: Springer, 1979).
7. Jonathan Sadowsky, *Electroconvulsive Therapy in America: The Anatomy of a Medical Controversy* (New York: Routledge, 2017), 5.
8. Histories of ECT include *Kneeland and Warren Push Button Psychiatry (2002)*; Edward Shorter and David Healy, *Shock Therapy: A History of Electroconvulsive Treatment in Mental Illness* (New Brunswick: Rutgers University Press, 2007; Jonathan Sadowsky, *Electroconvulsive Therapy* (2017). My work with Carol Warren is a chronological examination of the treatment in the context of the American fascination with electro technology, the use of medical treatment as a form of gendered social control, and the medical, social and legal debates over involuntary treatment. Healy and Shorter see ECT as medically beneficial, and Sadowsky reviews the history of ECT topically and includes issues of efficacy and therapeutic value.
9. Timothy Kneeland, "ECT as Miracle Maker, Crucifier & Resurrector: Christian Imagery and ECT 1940–Present" (Unpublished Paper, Popular Culture Conference, 1999).
10. For more on the origin and mental health backdrop of Batman see Sharon Packer, *Super Heroes and Super Egos: Analyzing the Minds Behind the Mask* (Santa Barbara: Praeger, 2010).
11. The graphic novels in this series include, David Hine and Jeremy Haun, *Batman: Arkham Reborn* (New York: DC Comics, 2010); Dan Slott, Ryan Sook, and Lee Loughridge, *Arkham Asylum Living Hell* (New York: DC Comics, 2003); video games include *Batman Arkham Asylum* (London: Rocksteady, 2009).
12. J. Knight writes, "A Remarkable Number of Arkham Inmates Are Former Psychiatrists" whose pursuit of the madness within has conquered them see "Comic Books and Psychiatry an Innovative Way to Teach Mental Health Issues," *British Medical Journal* 340 (2010): 1388; a similar point is made in Joseph Kane, "Batman and Psychiatry," *British Journal of Psychiatry* 199 (2011): 359; and in *Icons of the American Comic Book: From Captain America to Wonder Woman*, ed. Randy Duncan and Matthew J. Smith (Santa Barbara, ABC-CLIO, 2013), 40.
13. Arkham is prominently featured in the *Batman* animated series, and is the backdrop for episodes of the live action *Gotham*. on the role of the asylum as a hybrid hospital prison see H. Erik Bender, Praveen R. Kamban, and Vasilisk Pozios, "Putting the Caped Crusader on the Couch," *New York Times*, September 20, 2011.
14. Nathan G. Hale, "American Psychoanalysis Since World War II," in *American Psychiatry After World War II, 1944–1994*, ed. Roy W. Menninger and John C. Nemiah (Washington, D.C.: American Psychiatric Press, 2000).
15. Nathan G. Hale, "American Psychoanalysis Since World War II," in *American Psychiatry After World War II, 1944–1994*, ed. Roy W. Menninger and John C. Nemiah (Washington, D.C.: American Psychiatric Press, 2000); Joseph Kane, Batman and Psychiatry: *British Journal of Psychiatry* 199 (2011): 359; anti-psychiatry is a movement by patients, doctors and advocate that condemns psychiatrists or psychiatry for doing more harm than good, See Kneeland and Warren, *Pushbutton Psychiatry* (2002), 60–70.
16. Video games include *Batman Arkham Asylum* (London: Rocksteady, 2009).
17. Thomas Szasz, *The Myth of Mental Illness* (New York: Hoeber-Harper, 1961); Alan Grant, *Batman: The Last Arkham* (New York DC Comics, 1992), 7.
18. Morrison, *Arkham Asylum* (1990).
19. The use of electrotherapeutics to treat mental illness is discussed in Kneeland and Warren, *Push Button Psychiatry*, 28–40.
20. Grant Morrison, *Arkham Asylum: A Serious House on Serious Earth*, 15th anniversary edition (New York: DC Comics, 1989; 2004).
21. Quoted in John Friedberg, *Shock Treatment Is Not Good for Your Brain* (San Francisco: Glide Publications, 1975), 102.
22. Sadowsky, *Electroconvulsive Therapy*, 69–70.

23. See for example my review of the documentary *Hurry Tomorrow* available at Educational Media Reviews Online http://emro.lib.buffalo.edu/emro/emroDetail.asp?Number = 4253; this is a point also made by Sadowsky, *Electroconvulsive Therapy*, 75.

24. *Gotham* "Rogues Gallery" 11, Directed by Oz Scott Written by Bruno Heller (Fox, January 2015); Gotham," This Ball of Mud and Meanness," 68, Directed by John Behring, Written by Bruno Heller (Fox, January 2016); David Sims, Gotham's Arkham Asylum Is Too Bland to Be Scary," *The Atlantic*, January 6, 2015. https://www.theatlantic.com/entertainment/archive/2015/01/gothams-arkham-asylum-is-too-bland-to-be-scary/384244/

25. Sadowsky, *Electroconvulsive Therapy*, 88–90.

26. *Ibid.*; 76; Ken Kesey's experience led him to write the novel *One Flew Over the Cuckoo's Nest* (New York: Signet 1962).

27. Kesey, *One Flew Over the Cuckoo's Nest*, 64–65.

28. *The Age of Madness: The History of Involuntary Mental Hospitalization*, ed. Thomas Szasz (New York: Jason Aronson, 1974), 315.

29. *Ibid.*, 316.

30. Morrison, *Arkham Asylum*, 45.

31. John A.P Millet and Eric P. Mosses, "On Certain Psychological Aspects of Electroshock Therapy," *Psychosomatic Medicine* (July 1944): 341 found that electric shock treatment is desired because it felt to be a fitting punishment.

32. Jack Kerkhoff, *How Thin the Veil: A Newspaper Man's Story of His Own Mental Crackup and Recovery* (New York: Greenberg, 1952), 10.

33. Cyril Kolocotrnis, "The Truth About Electro-Shock Treatments" *Madness Network News Reader* (San Francisco: Glide Publications, May 1973) reprinted in Freidberg 166.

34. Quoted in Friedberg, 108.

35. Lothar Kalinowsky and Paul Hoch, *Somatic Treatments in Psychiatry: Pharmacotherapy: Convulsive, Insulin, Surgical Other Methods* (New York: Grune & Stratton 2nd edition, 1952).

36. Thelma Alper, "An Electric Shock Patient Tells His Story," *Journal of Abnormal and Social Psychology*, 43 (1948): 201–210.

37. Otto Fenichel, *The Psychoanalytic Theory of Neurosis* (New York: Norton, 1945), 138.

38. Dan Slott and Ryan Sook. *Arkham Living Hell* (New York: DC Comics, 2004).

39. *Gotham*," This Ball of Mud and Meanness," 68, Directed by John Behring, Written by Bruno Heller (Fox, January 2016).

40. Scott Snyder, *Batman Zero Year Savage City*, 2, 33 (New York: DC Comics, September 2014).

41. Kneeland and Warren, *Push Button Psychiatry*, 57.

Hallucinations and Psychedelics in Arkham

MATTHEW BROWN, D.O., *and*
FERNANDO ESPÍ FORCÉN, M.D.

Hallucinogens, as well as mind control, have been important to Arkham Asylum and to the CIA. Hallucinogens once held promise for use in general psychiatry but were banned because both patients and renegade researchers misused them. However, today, those who practice mainstream psychiatry as well as those who study academic psychiatry are rediscovering the value of hallucinogens and recognizing that hallucinogens can offer hope to suffering patients. In the *Arkham* universe, in contrast, hallucinogens cause—rather than cure—suffering. This essay explores how settings and intentions ("set") alter the impact of psychedelics and hallucinogens in Arkham. *Arkham*'s hallucinogen scenes offer an ideal opportunity to kindle discussions about psychiatry's use (or misuse) of hallucinogens in the distant past and to trace the trajectory of contemporary controversies surrounding psychedelic substances in treatment settings.

Background

Soon after the discovery of LSD's psychoactive effects, the scientific community was eager to identify potential clinical applications. In the 1950s, the CIA started a research project called MKUltra to study the effects of mind-altering substances and to see how such substances could be used for "mind control" during interrogation of subjects. The CIA study involved up to 80 institutions across the country. The outcomes of the MKUltra study are not known since most project files were destroyed in 1973.[1] However, the methodology itself evoked criticism because the studies violated participants' autonomy and overrode informed consent.

During the same decade, John Lilly, a psychiatrist and psychoanalyst, took psychedelic research to a whole new level. While working at the prestigious National Institute of Mental Health (NIMH), Dr. Lilly constructed the first isolation tank in 1954. An isolation tank, also called a sensory deprivation tank or a floatation tank, is a completely dark, soundproof tank with salt water heated to skin temperature to allow a person to float comfortably. Dr. Lilly deemed this state of sensory deprivation as ideal for experimentation with LSD, since it could theoretically allow subjects to navigate in the inner space of their minds. Lilly narrated these experiences in his book *Center of the Cyclone*.[2]

Several other researchers became interested in LSD's potential to treat psychiatric disorders. This innovative technique became known as psychedelic therapy. For instance, Bill Wilson, the co-founder of Alcoholics Anonymous (AA), conducted several trials with patients struggling with alcoholism and concluded that not only was this drug helpful for alcohol cessation but that it could also help patients enhance their connection to a higher power.[3] Subsequent studies that explored the therapeutic properties of LSD in alcoholism showed encouraging results. LSD was also studied in the treatment of autism and obsessive-compulsive disorder. Some researchers proposed that LSD could have clinical use in psychotherapy.

Traditional psychoanalytic thinking deemed psychosis to be a manifestation of the unconscious mind. Some therapists believed that they could reach the unconscious via LSD. Studies emerged, encouraging clinicians to use LSD with their therapy patients. Later, psychedelic therapy (with higher doses) was distinguished from psycholytic therapy (with lower doses). Some considered LSD as a potential enhancer of trance states in hypnosis.

Due to its massive recreational use and potential behavioral disturbances, LSD was outlawed in the U.S. in 1968. In the previous year, an article in the *Archives of General Psychiatry* discouraged clinicians from using LSD because it could aggravate psychotic symptoms and worsen mental states. Sandoz Laboratories, which manufactured the chemical, had already withdrawn support for LSD research and refused to ship their product to the U.S. Research into LSD stopped and recreational use in the general population gradually declined.[4]

Action figure of Jonathan Crane, unmasked, with his straw-covered Scarecrow hat tossed aside, lying at his feet. By DC Direct, based on an Alex Ross design for "Justice League" toy line. This bespectacled Dr. Crane looks professorial although he lost his college teaching post for firing fear-inducing weapons in class. In *Batman Begins* (2005), a more corpulent Dr. Crane, played by Cillian Murphy, administers hallucinogens to potential patients to convince a crime boss (and the courts) that a mobster requires transfer to Arkham Asylum (photograph by George Higham).

With the resurgence of psychedelic research in the last two decades, better quality studies appeared in the scientific literature. In addition, neuroimaging studies with functional MRIs have shown that the potential therapeutic effect may relate to psychedelics' action in the amygdala, which is an almond-shaped area of grey matter inside the cerebral hemisphere. The amygdala is involved in the experiencing of emotions. One neuroimaging study of healthy individuals without previous psychiatric histories showed that occipital cortex (the visual cortex) activity increased while the subject was under the influence of LSD. This change could explain the visual effects of psychedelic substances. The same study showed decreased activity in the white matter connecting the retrosplenial cortex (RSC) and the parahippocampus—but only in individuals who experienced so-called ego dissolution.[5]

Recently, psychiatrists have been revisiting the usefulness of psychedelics in the treatment of psychiatric symptoms. The first studies were performed on patients who experienced anxiety related to cancer or life-threatening diseases. This population showed benefit from treatment with psychedelics, since psychedelics can enhance transcendence and decrease existential and eschatological anxiety about the end of life. For instance, in 2011, Grob and colleagues administered psilocybin to twelve advanced cancer patients and confirmed reductions in their anxiety scores after this treatment.[6]

In 2016, another study involving 51 cancer patients found dramatic reductions of anxiety and depressive symptoms as well as high remission rates in patients who took higher doses of psilocybin as compared to patients who took lower doses. This study was double-blinded, which means neither the researchers nor the patients knew who received the larger dose. Intriguingly, six months after the treatment, patients who took the higher dose continued to show significant reductions of anxiety and depression symptoms. In other words, a single dose provided six months of symptomatic relief.[7]

Psychedelics are thought to be potentially beneficial in the treatment of tobacco, alcohol and opioid use, obsessive-compulsive disorders, anorexia, bulimia nervosa and cluster headaches. Within the last few years, researchers have been desperately looking for effective treatments for patients with severe depression and currently, some are focusing on ketamine, an anesthetic with psychedelic properties. A NIMH study of patients with severe depression showed symptomatic improvement within 30 minutes after intravenous administration of ketamine. Also, many centers across the country are studying the therapeutic effects of an intranasal form of ketamine.[8]

After the decades-long lag in psychedelic research following its ban in 1968 and Sandoz's decision to stop shipment of laboratory-quality LSD to the U.S., these encouraging results brighten once again the future of psychedelics in psychiatry.

Psychedelics in the Media

The CIA's use of LSD took an entirely different turn, and a dark turn at that, after one prominent scientist committed suicide after being dosed clandestinely with LSD. One of the participants in the CIA-led project MKUltra was American novelist Ken Kesey. Inspired by his experiences with LSD and by his encounters with patients with psychiatric disorders, Kesey wrote *One Flew Over the Cuckoo's Nest*, first published in 1962. The novel had a huge cultural impact and influenced both the so-called antipsychiatry movement and the counterculture of the 60s.

A psychedelic art movement inspired by the emotional, visual and auditory effects of LSD and other psychedelic substances emerged. In 1967, The Beatles released *Sgt. Pepper's Lonely-Hearts Club Band*, an album deeply impacted by the psychedelic aesthetic. Whether the Beatles intended it or not, the *Sgt. Pepper* album came to symbolize the ambitions, the longings, and even the fears of a generation. Sixties rock, along with the civil rights and anti–Vietnam War movements, fueled widespread willingness to experiment with marijuana and LSD, giving young people a new sense of empowerment.[9]

Jimi Hendrix, Jefferson Airplane, Cream, and The Grateful Dead all played pivotal roles in the consolidation of psychedelic music in the United States. The posters that announced such psychedelic concerts became true art pieces. Several of these artists lived in San Francisco, among them were Rick Griffin (leading designer of album covers of the Grateful Dead), Wes Wilson, and Victor Moscoso. Moscoso emigrated from Spain to study art at Yale University and became the first psychedelic artist with an academic background. Pink Floyd worked with the group Hypgnosis for their album covers. Psychedelic art was influenced by the dreamlike representations of surrealism (which was rooted in psychoanalytic theories and reinterpretations by a medical student turned poet named André Breton). Additionally, psychedelic art used brilliant and colorful fractal images to depict the effects of LSD.

Psychedelia was also reflected in cinema. In 1967, the film *The Trip* was released. Written by Jack Nicholson, *The Trip* tells the story of a man who uses psychedelic therapy to resolve conflicts in his troubled marriage. In Hitchcock's *Spellbound* (1945), Salvador Dalí's dream-like paintings of eyes embedded in curtains appear during trance states. *Psych Out* (1968), also written by and starring Jack Nicholson), represents hippies' values, whereby a group of friends live in Haight-Ashbury, drive a Volkswagen van, practice free love, play in a psychedelic band, and consume acid almost daily. In 1969, Dennis Hopper directed and starred in the film *Easy Rider* with co-stars Peter Fonda and Jack Nicholson. *Easy Rider* represents the 1960s social changes and became a cult classic.[10]

In 1973, Alejandro Jodorowsky directed *The Holy Mountain*. Jodorowsky was able to obtain substantial funding for this ambitious project, thanks to the success of his film, *El Topo* (1971) and to John Lennon, Yoko Ono and The Beatles' manager Allen Klein who helped produce it. Charged with iconographic symbolism, each scene in *The Holy Mountain* could be the subject of its own discussion. Multiple Freudian and Jungian concepts are directly or indirectly reflected in the film. Congruent with the counterculture of the time, the director was interested in helping audiences understand the effects of LSD without taking the drug themselves to experience its effects. In another sense then, *The Holy Mountain* can be interpreted as a beautiful depiction of a psychedelic trip.[11]

Psychedelics in the Arkham Asylum

In the world of Gotham City, and more specifically within the confines of Arkham Asylum for the Criminally Insane, psychedelic compounds are rarely if ever viewed in a positive light. In contrast to the more typical experience of feeling love and unity, in Gotham, psychedelic compounds produce feelings of fear and isolation. Participants feel as if they are unwillingly pulled into a black mirror to face their fears, rather than gaining the ability to walk through the mirror on their own accord, and the equally important ability to emerge from the mirror transformed.[12]

The catalyst driving this negative experience is the Scarecrow's atomized "fear toxin," which is sprayed on unwitting subjects. Dr. Jonathan Crane (the Scarecrow's alter ego) perfected the agent while studying the effects of fear and trying to replace study participants' current fears with new fears. In other Batman universe stories, and especially in the made-for-television series *Gotham*, the fear toxin traces back to Jonathan's father, Dr. Gerald Crane, a biology teacher who developed the fear toxin and exposed his son Jonathan to his invention, hoping to spare his son of the intolerable phobias that he himself endured. At the time of exposure and for years afterwards, Jonathan hallucinates scarecrows until he adopts the Scarecrow person and essentially "identifies with the aggressor." He dresses like a scarecrow; he even renames himself "Scarecrow."

Over time, the younger Dr. Crane (Jonathan) became more obsessed with fear reactions and their debilitating effects on his participants and less concerned with curing their phobias.[13] Perhaps the best examples of the Scarecrow's induced hallucinations can be found in the *Arkham Asylum* video game and *Batman: The Animated Series* as well as in the more recent FOX TV series *Gotham* (Season 1. Episode 14). As typically happens in the comics' universe, story arcs and even characters are constantly added; plots grow more convoluted, making it likely that even more allusions to the fear toxin and hallucinogens will appear, guaranteeing that any data in this essay will soon become outdated.

With that caveat in mind, let us return to one of the more interesting examples of the fear toxin in Arkham Asylum, where Joker gases Batman with Scarecrow's fear toxin while the two are in a freight elevator. When his descent ends, Batman begins walking through the catacombs and air shafts in the hospital basement, and then meanders through the morgue, where he is haunted by images of Jim Gordon's death. While in the morgue, he opens two body bags containing the remains of his deceased parents. Scarecrow emerges from the final

Scarecrow statue by Iron Studios, based on design from *Batman: Arkham Knight* (2015), dir. Sefton Hill. Also called Dr. Jonathan Crane, this one-time psychology professor turned forensic psychiatrist became administrator of Arkham Asylum. His syringe-like fingertips inject fear serum into victims. Jonathan's biology teacher father, Dr. Gerald Crane, developed this fear toxin and used it on Jonathan, hoping to spare his son the phobias endured by the elder Crane (photograph by George Higham).

bag to start a side scrolling playable sequence where Batman must defeat the Scarecrow by shining the light of the Bat-Signal on him. Two other playable hallucinations follow a similar pattern.

In the next sequence, Batman finds himself in a hallway where he starts to experience auditory hallucinations about the death of his parents. He is transported back in time when he witnessed their murder. He relives this scene, literally transformed into his childlike self. After emerging from the scene, Scarecrow reappears, and a similar battle recurs. In the third scenario, Batman is not faced with the death of his parents, but of his own death. After a brief "glitch" in the game, we find Batman passed out in the back of the Batmobile with the Joker behind the wheel. Batman awakens, strapped to a gurney surrounded by Harley Quinn, Bane and of course the Joker. The Joker then kills Batman and the player is greeted by a game over screen. However, in the next shot, we find Batman crawling out of his grave, having emerged from a sort of graveyard in the center of Arkham. All around him he sees versions of himself in some form of torture. The player ascends a staircase to find a Batman character feasting on a dead rat. Scarecrow shows his face and the final Scarecrow boss battle occurs.[14]

The themes depicted here are very interesting, for several reasons. There is no reference to Batman gaining new knowledge or overcoming his past, even though such achievements would not be foreign to a psychedelic session. According to Stanislav Grof, one of the pioneers in the study of psychedelic medicine, it is common to encounter "postnatal biography" (or a recollection of all things that have happened to us after we were born) upon entering a "non-ordinary state of consciousness" (when one perceives the world differently from the way we perceive it during our day-to-day lives). In the case of Bruce Wayne, one of the most significant events in his life was witnessing the death of his parents. Once he fully processes these events, there is a strong tendency to uncover more commonly shared traumas, including the trauma of his own birth or even death. This is a way of reliving the various states of birth which Grof has divided into the four Birth Perinatal Matrices (BPM), which begin with the experience of blissfully floating in the warm womb during development (BPM1), followed by the onset of labor, a time in which the amniotic fluid drains from the uterus, pressing the fetus up against the cervix. This tense situation often results in fear and dread not to mention pain as the fetal head is compressed while approaching the birth canal (BPM2). The next stage, which is even worse, involves going through the birth canal, a narrow passage which is often associated with various bodily fluids and the feeling of being crushed or pulled apart (BPM3). The final stage involves the resolution and emergence into the world by exiting the vaginal canal. This stage is often represented by falling, before being caught and lifted, ideally to the mother's breast, to find peace and comfort (BPM4).[15]

In the game, Bruce Wayne is forced to deal with the death of his parents and his own death/rebirth which can conclude when he conquers the manifestation of his fear (Scarecrow) using the power of "Light" (the Bat-Signal) over darkness. This is a more metaphorical rather than literal interpretation. In the end, it is unclear what Bruce Wayne would have learned from the experience, but that seemingly empty result is not unusual, given that the effectiveness of a psychedelic session tends to be limited by the post-processing and integration work that is done in the aftermath of the session.

We can see how this example plays out in modern clinical or laboratory research on this subject. Two primary models of psychedelic therapy are under study. In one case, the subject receives the drug, has an experience, and is sent home without the benefit of therapeutic intervention. This approach has been studied with a drug called Ketamine which has long been used as an anesthesia medication but has been more recently studied for the treatment of acute suicidality and treatment-resistant depression (TRD). Outcomes from such interventions typically show benefits for up to two weeks after treatment.[16] In contrast, studies done with both MDMA and psilocybin (the active ingredient in hallucinogenic mushrooms) tend to pair psychotherapy before, during, and after the drug session and show superior results, with reduction of symptoms of anxiety and depression for nearly three to six months.[17]

Part of the differences in effect and outcome mentioned above can be attributed to "Set Setting," since the effects of a specific drug are not limited to the drug in and of itself. Both the "Set," features which the participant brings to the session (e.g., the participant's intentions, thoughts, other substances in their body, or just their own personal biology), and the "Setting," the place where the subject undergoes the experience (which is not limited to the physical environment, but could include other people, noises, sights, smells and any other things that happen just before, during and after the experience) can color the user's experience.[18] It is no wonder then that we see Batman transcend fear utilizing a mere glimmer of light, at best, in the dark, grim world of Gotham.

In an early episode of *Batman: The Animated Series* entitled "Dreams in Darkness," Batman is once again infected with the Scarecrow's fear toxin. As he heads to Arkham Asylum to confront Scarecrow, he crashes the Batmobile. He is rescued, brought into the hospital, put in a straitjacket, and strapped to a unit. Monitoring the caped crusader, Dr. Bartholomew attempts therapy, but is too judgmental, characterizing Batman's visions and ideas as "delusions," even verbalizing this to the patient rather than trying to understand Batman's experiences. While alone in his room, Batman again re-experiences the death of his parents. After escaping from his room, Batman encounters images of the Joker, Penguin, Poison Ivy and even evil versions of Robin and Alfred.[19] One might assume that such an experience would be more intense when facing it alone or with others telling you that you are crazy. Such a setting provides little hope for a positive experience. This ineffective setting can be compared to today's settings of big concerts and festivals with panoramic light shows and myriads of people yelling and cheering, which also lead to less-than transcendent experiences with psychedelic substances.

At the end of the episode, Batman returns to the Batcave, presumably on the comedown from the high of his trip. His butler Alfred gives him an "antidote" and then tucks him into bed. Before the scene fades, Batman comments that he now feels safe and comfortable at home. Again, this concept of safety and comfort—which is minimal in the Gotham universe—is very important for fully processing one's biological and birth traumas and finding connection with the universal unconscious.

In a psychedelic therapy session, one is typically in a room, reminiscent of a bedroom, lying down with an eye mask and headphones that play soothing music. A therapist stands by the patient's side in case things get too scary or "crunchy." Even if one does experience true terror during the trip, in the end, ideally, they are able to "walk through it" and will no longer feel plagued by that uncomfortable unconscious memory, such as those associated with PTSD. When done properly, not only do subjects show a reduction in symptoms, but many reduce symptoms to the extent that they no longer meet criteria for PTSD. Again, studies about PTSD are underway yet incomplete, but so far, the results are promising, and we may be able to utilize such techniques with MDMA as soon as 2021 in a regulated and legal fashion.[20]

50   Section I: Clinical Psychiatric Controversies

In Stanley Kubrick's *A Clockwork Orange* (1971), the imprisoned sociopathic anti-hero Alex (Malcolm McDowell) undergoes the Ludovico Technique and is forced to watch images of violence while dosed with a nausea-inducing drug. Television's *Gotham* series shows a strikingly similar scene, where Dr. Strange turns the crime lord and multiple murderer Penguin (Oswald Cobblepot) into a mild-mannered and polite person before releasing him from Arkham.

At the beginning of this section we began the discussion of psychedelics with talk of the MKUltra experiments done by the U.S. government in the mid–20th century. While not as detailed as the work done in the real world, Dr. Hugo Strange was indeed known to experiment on many residents of Arkham Asylum over the years. Although many of his experiments involved genetic manipulations, he did use many different drugs including the Scarecrow's fear toxin as well as Bane's Venom. Most of his "experiments" were largely failures and resulted in the increase in the numbers of "lunatics" that live in the Asylum.[21]

Dr. Strange also happened to be the prescriber of the one pseudo-positive outcome of a hallucinogenic agent found in the Batman comic universe. In Gotham Knights 8–9 Bruce Wayne is required to undergo a "routine psychological assessment" as part of a screening for insurance benefits. Unknown to Bruce, Dr. Strange was the treating provider who claimed to have "poisoned" the couch on which Bruce was lying with a hallucinogenic agent. While Bruce does not have any hallucinogenic experience, towards the end of the second book, the narrator makes a comment that he seems "contented" in a way he has not felt in a long time. Unfortunately, this moment of bliss and clarity is short lived, for just after Bruce leaves the building and enters his vehicle, the vehicle explodes.[22] This finale suggests that the most we can expect from the psychedelic experience in the world of Arkham and Gotham in general is a momentary beacon of light, with a transient glimmer of hope, before the darkness and chaos again take over.

Notes

1. United States Senate 95th Congress, *Joint Hearing Before the Subcommittee on Intelligence and the Subcommittee on Health and Scientific Research of the Committee on Human Resources* (Washington D.C.: U.S. Government Printing Office, 1977). Accessed from the New York Times: http://www.nytimes.com/packages/pdf/national/13inmate_ProjectMKULTRA.pdf
2. John Lilly, *Center of the Cyclone: Considering Inner Space* (Oakland: Ronin Publishing, 1972).
3. Francis Hartigan, *Bill W.: A Biography of Alcoholics Anonymous Cofounder Bill Wilson* (New York: St. Martin's Press, 2000).
4. Fernando Espí Forcén, "Sex, Rock and Psychedelia: Psychiatry and the Counterculture of the 1960s," *Journal of Humanistic Psychiatry* (1)(3) 2013: 15–17.
5. Robin L. Carhart-Harris l., "Neural Correlates of the LSD Experience Revealed by Multimodal Neuroimaging," *Proceedings of National Academy of Sciences of the United States of America* 113 (17) 2016: 4853–4858.
6. Charles S. Grob, "Pilot Study of Psilocybin Treatment for Anxiety in Patients with Advanced-Stage Cancer," *Archives of General Psychiatry* 68 (1) 2011: 71–78.
7. Roland R. Griffiths, "Psilocybin Produces Substantial and Sustained Decreases in Depression and Anxiety in Patients with Life-Threatening Cancer: a Randomized Double-Blind Trial," *Journal of Psychopharmacology* 30 (12) 2016: 1181–1197.
8. James W. Murrough, "Antidepressant Efficacy of Ketamine in Treatment-Resistant Major Depression: a Two-Site Randomized Controlled Trial," *American Journal of Psychiatry* 170 (10) 2013: 1134–1142.
9. Mikal Gilmore, "Inside the Making of "Sgt. Pepper,"" *Rolling Stone*, June 1, 2017.
10. Forcen, "Sex, Rock and Psychedelia," 15–17.
11. Fernando Espí Forcén, "The Holy Mountain," *Journal of Humanistic Psychiatry* 4 (3) 2016: 28–29.
12. Judith Reeves-Stevens and Garfield Reeves-Stevens, "Dreams in Darkness," in *Batman the Animated Series,* dir. Dick Sebast, 1992; *Batman Arkham Asylum* (Eidos Interactive: Warner Bros. Interactive, 2009), Xbox360; *Batman: Arkham City* (Rocksteady Studios: Warner Bros. Interactive, 2011), Xbox360.
13. Bob Kane et al., "Riddle of the Human Scarecrow," *World's Finest* 1(3) 1941: 83–96.
14. *Batman: Arkham City* (Rocksteady Studios: Warner Bros. Interactive, 2011), Xbox360.
15. Stanislav Grof, *Realms of the Unconscious: Observations from LSD Research* (New York: Viking Press, 1976).
16. Sanjay Mathew et al., "Ketamine for Treatment-Resistant Unipolar Depression: Current Evidence," *CNS Drugs* March 2012; 26 (3): 189–204.
17. Michael C. Mithoefer et al., "Novel Psychopharmacological Therapies for Psychiatric Disorders: Psilocybin and MDMA," *Lancet Psychiatry* 3(5) 2016:481–8.
18. Matthew Brown and Fernando Espí Forcén, "Psychedelics and Psychiatry: Past, Present, and Future Research" (paper presented at Students for a Sensible Drug Policy Midwest Regional Conference, Chicago, Illinois, October 23, 2016).
19. Forcen, "Sex, Rock and Psychedelia," 15–17.
20. MAPS, "MDMA Assisted Psychotherapy." http://www.maps.org/research/mdma.
21. *Batman: Arkham City* (Rocksteady Studios: Warner Bros. Interactive, 2011), Xbox360.
22. Devin Grayson et al., "Transference," *Batman: Gotham Knights* 8–9, 2000.

Section II

Forensic Psychiatric Controversies

I'm [Virtual] Batman

Violence and Video Games

RYAN C.W. HALL, M.D., *and*
SUSAN HATTERS FRIEDMAN, M.D.

Video games and computer games did not come into mainstream fruition until 1972 with the release of the arcade game *Pong*. By 1979, the first superhero video game, *Superman*, came out on the Atari 2600 home system, in all its 8-bit glory. Although Superman may have started off the superhero video game genre, it is arguably Batman who rules it, in no small part to the *Arkham Asylum* video game franchise (release date, 2009 noted in the Guinness Book of World Records as the most critically acclaimed superhero video game of all time after having sold 2 million copies in its first month of release).[1] The *Arkham Asylum* video game to date is as close as Batman fans have come to seeing the *Arkham Asylum* graphic novel adapted to a cinematic presentation. This video game was groundbreaking in that it had exquisite production value, wonderful voice actors (Kevin Conroy, Mark Hamill, and Arleen Sorkin), inventive game play mechanics, and was based on the comic book source material, not a Hollywood movie tie-in.

It is Batman's longevity in the video game world, in no small part thanks to *Arkham Asylum*, and the pop culture world, which makes him an interesting vehicle to explore the current controversies that surround the medical, scientific, and social impacts of video games, especially violent video games. In addition, the superhero and comic roots of the character make the parallels to Fredric Wertham's criticism of comic books in the 1950s impossible to miss. Once again, Batman (and the many mediums in which he is represented) is raising questions regarding societal influences, protective measures, scientific research, advocacy, and how society will look back on the discussion.

The Issue of Media's Influence on the Individual and Society

One of the common questions raised about media and popular culture is the impact it has on groups and society as a whole. Unfortunately, this discussion is often confused with the impact of a particular medium on one susceptible individual, such as someone with mental illness or antisocial agendas. It is clear from anecdotal case reports that media can influence the individual. Classic examples of this occurring include The Beatles

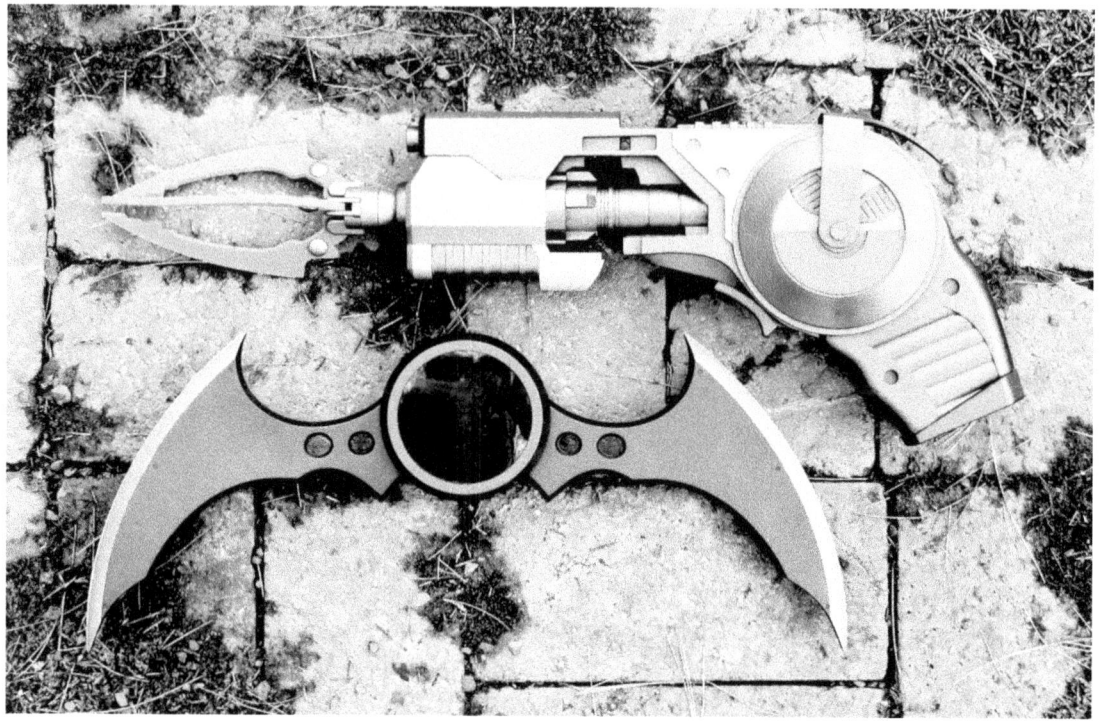

Grapnel gun (above) and batarang (below) prop replicas seen in *Batman Arkham Knight* (2016) video game. Batman avoids deadly force and uses these non-lethal "weapons" against adversaries, along with mental cunning, martial arts skills and equipment that compensates for missing superpowers. His grapnel gun shoots cables that allow him to climb tall buildings, since he cannot fly like Superman. His batarang functions as a multi-purpose, high-tech boomerang. Very early *Batman* comics were not so benign, but Batman's character was soon modified. Newer *Batman* films starring Ben Affleck reclaim the dark side of the Dark Knight (photograph by George Higham).

music influencing Charles Manson; the book *Catcher in the Rye* influencing David Mark Chapman, who assassinated John Lennon; and John Hinckley's obsession with the movie *Taxi Driver*, which influenced his attempt to assassinate President Ronald Reagan. Also, horrific acts have occurred with themes from media being evident even if they are not necessarily the inciting cause. Potential examples include James Holmes (a.k.a. the Aurora, Colorado, theater shooter, Batman fan, and role-playing video gamer) dying his hair orange, allegedly referring to himself as the Joker, and choosing a movie theater that was showing the *Dark Night Rises* for his mass shooting; Anders Behring Breivik, the convicted Norway Shooter, whose primary motivation was political though he was also a video game enthusiast who made comments about using video games as a way to prepare for large scale societal attacks; and Charles McCoy, the Ohio Highway (I-270) shooter, who allegedly played "lone gunman" mass shooter games (a.k.a. first person shooters), and later shot at drivers from highway overpasses.[2]

Currently, there is a trend in the medical community to consider violence using a disease contagion model, which suggests that violence can be treated and prevented the same way as an infectious disease. Although there may be some benefit to studying violence this way, the medical community and the community at large need to realize that multiple factors influence violence (e.g., biology, social, economic, political, health, developmental, life experience, substance use) and—just as not all disease can be prevented—neither can all acts of violence or potential influences be identified.[3] In addition, unlike an infectious disease with a single causative agent (e.g., a bacteria, virus, or parasite)—with violence, literally any of these factors can become an influencing or inciting cause. For example, traditional virtuous works such as the Bible, Koran, and Torah have at times become an influencing factor for an individual or group to commit acts of violence—whether suffering from a mental illness or not. In addition, video games have become such a popular medium that at some point in time most people have had some contact with them (e.g., more than 90 percent of youths have played video games).[4] For example, *Batman: Arkham Knight* (ESRB rating M for Mature due to Blood, Language, Suggestive Themes, Violence), the concluding chapter in the *Arkham Asylum* video game franchise, sold over five million copies within five months.[5] Given the number of copies out there, it is likely that sooner or later someone who has played it will commit a violent act. This is similar to what happened with *The Catcher in the Rye,* where 65 million copies were sold, including copies which were owned by Mark David Chapman, Lee Harvey Oswald, and John Hinckley, Jr.[6] One must not forget the millions who have read *The Catcher in the Rye* and did not assassinate someone famous.

This implies that any form of media with any type of content can have a negative impact on the susceptible individual. This then can sometimes lead to debate about whether the potential benefit of media outweighs the negatives. After all, millions have enjoyed and been positively inspired by The Beatles yet there was only who was negatively influenced. His name was Charles Manson.

This also raises questions on why some individuals are drawn to violent media. On a very simple level this speaks to the classic debate about whether life imitates art or art imitates life. For example, many of the current "story lines" in games like *Call of Duty* and *Arkham Asylum* look very similar to real life concerns and news headlines (e.g., terrorism, North Korea's nuclear programs, mass shootings/crime committed by people with mental illness). Do these games that address real world concerns allow for children, adolescents, and adults to process and cope with fears and concerns or do they magnify them? After all, traditional children's fairy tales contain violence and death as a way to teach moral lessons (e.g., Hansel and Gretel learned not to be gluttonous in the process of killing the witch). For some it may be helpful to learn and develop coping mechanisms based on exposure to fictional violence while for others it may be detrimental.

Legal Issues Regarding Access to Video Games

Historically, in the United States, authorities have limited access to information which was deemed harmful to certain groups while making it available to other groups. An example would be limiting access to erotica/pornography to adults only. The court case of *Ginsberg v. New York* ruled that material that is not obscene for adults may still be considered obscene for minors (variable-obscenity standard) and, therefore, could be regulated so that minors could not purchase it.[7] Many have expressed similar concerns that violent video games may be harmful to children, therefore similar regulation should be imposed. This has led to numerous states trying to pass laws, which mirrored the *Ginsberg* ruling.[8] many of the laws referenced the scientific literature and the harmful effects, which were purported to occur from playing violent video games, as justification for the restriction.

In 2011, the United States Supreme Court case of *Brown v. Entertainment Merchants Assoc.* found the laws regulating the sale of violent video games to children to be unconstitutional. When the Supreme Court issued its majority opinion (7–2) for *Brown*, it found:

> These studies have been rejected by every court to consider them, and with good reason: They do not prove that violent video games *cause* minors to *act* aggressively (which would at least be a beginning). Instead, "[n]early all of the research is based on correlation, not evidence of causation, and most of the studies suffer from significant, admitted flaws in methodology." *Video Software Dealers Assn.* 556 F.3d, at 964. They show at best some correlation between exposure to violent entertainment and miniscule real-world effects, such as children's feeling more aggressive or making louder noises in the few minutes after playing a violent game than after playing a nonviolent game. … the *same* effects have been found when children watch cartoons starring Bugs Bunny or the Road Runner, … or even when they "vie[w] a picture of a gun."[9]

What Is the State of the Literature?

Given the majority opinion of the U.S. Supreme Court in 2011 (e.g., "[literature does] not prove that violent video games *cause* minors to *act* aggressively"), what is the state of the scientific literature regarding video games? Two of the more cited authors in this field are the psychologists Anderson and Bushman. Most of their findings and conclusions are in a similar vein as to what was reported in their 2009 paper entitled *Comfortably numb: desensitizing effects of violent media on helping others*.[10] In that study, 320 college students played either a violent video game (randomized between *Armageddon, Duke Nukem, Mortal Kombat, Future Cop*) or non-violent video game (*Glider Pro, 3D Pinball, Austin Powers, Tetra Madness*) and were then exposed to a staged confrontation. The outcome was that individuals who played violent video games were less likely to help the victim in the staged confrontation (21 percent vs. 25 percent p = 0.38), rated the fight as less serious (5.91 vs. 6.44 out of 10; p<0.04), took longer to help (medium time 73.3 s vs. 16.2s; p<0.02), and were less likely to "hear" the confrontation (94 percent vs. 99 percent; p<0.05). It is important to note that the measure looking to see if there was an active behavioral change (e.g., helping) was not a statistically significant result. Bushman and Anderson commented in the paper that the effects of violent video games were similar to results they had found for violent movies in that both media "make people numb to the pain and suffering of others." In many ways, the results of this study highlight the concerns raised in the majority opinion of the Supreme Court: that these types of studies do not answer the ultimate question whether video games cause minors to act aggressively, because the data obtained was how one responds after exposure to violence with similar effects found with exposure to different media (films). This study also raises the question: just because a statistical finding was found, does it actually have a real-world effect? For example, would the half-point difference on a rating scale for severity of a fight actually lead to people in the real world to be more likely to engage in prosocial or violent behavior themselves?[11] Given that the helping measure of actually getting involved was statically non-significant, it would seem to indicate it would not.

Anderson and Bushman were also authors of a meta-analysis that was published in 2010 prior to the Supreme Court's ruling on *Brown*. In that meta-analysis it was noted that:

> The evidence strongly suggests that exposure to violent video games is a causal risk factor for increased aggressive behavior, aggressive cognition, and aggressive affect and for decreased empathy and prosocial behavior.... Results of various sensitivity analyses revealed these effects to be robust, with little evidence of selection (publication) bias.[12]

These views were at odds with the commentary by psychologists Ferguson and Kilburn's *Much Ado About Nothing: The Misestimation and Overinterpretation of Violent Video Game Effects in Eastern and Western Nations: Comment on Anderson et al.*:

> The issue of violent video game influence on youth violence and aggression remains intensely debated in the scholarly literature.... In a new meta-analysis, Anderson et al. (2010) has several methodological issues that limit the interpretability of their results. Anderson et al. included many studies that do not relate well to serious aggression, an apparently biased sample of unpublished studies, and a "best practices" analysis that appears unreliable and does not consider the impact of unstandardized aggression measures on the inflation of effect size estimates.... Despite a number of methodological flaws that all appear likely to inflate effect size estimates, the final estimate of r = .15 is still indicative of only weak effects.[13]

In addition, there are studies that have found some potential beneficial effects to playing video games. In a 2010 study of middle school students in Iran (n = 444), Allahverdipour et al. found that the average student played video games 6.3 hours per week, with 47 percent playing one or more intensely violent games.[14] Surprisingly, non-gamers were found to have poorer mental health measures (GHQ -28 score 8.96 ± 7.7) than excessive gamers (GHQ -28 score 6.67 ± 6.0). Both non-gamers and excessive gamers overall reported poorer mental health scores compared to those who were low level (5.43 ± 5.6) or moderate game players (4.97 ± 5.0). As with much of the literature on video games and their effects, it is sometimes difficult to distinguish what is a correlation vs. a causative effect. For example, did playing video games result in better reported psychological wellbeing because it allowed for "healthy fantasies enactment" (e.g., "safety valve theory") or a way to express and cope with negative emotion and hostility? Or is playing video games a correlative marker for general health and adjustment? For example, are children who play no video games in today's world either depressed or in a social environment which prevents them from participating in a mainstream activity? At the same time, the parabolic curve could suggest that playing up to a point may be positive, but too much playing begins to negatively affect functioning. On the other hand, this could indicate excessive gamers have pre-existing trouble interacting with peers or self-regulating, which leads to increased game play.

What is interesting is that the "safety value theory" versus the "gateway," acceleration, or learning theories of exposure have been debated in other areas of violence research as well. For example, Fischer and colleagues found similar problems in studying pornography and its effects:

> Little clarity concerning the causal impact of pornography on sexual aggression ... has been achieved in the scientific literature. Laboratory experimentation demonstrates that violent pornography may contribute to antiwoman aggression, but the artificiality and constraints of the experimental setting severely limit generalization of these findings to real-world situations, and observational studies in natural settings consistently find no association or an inverse association of pornography with sexual aggression.[15]

It should be noted that studying violence, much like pornography, in a prospective double-blind reproducible manner is difficult. There are often questions of whether the authors' perspective influenced results (either consciously or unconsciously) and how a propensity for violence can be ethically tested in a laboratory setting. Many of these issues became evident when Tear and Nelson attempted to replicate findings from an earlier study by Greitemeyer and Osswald.[16] In Tear's paper, as well as the original study, participants played violent, pro-social, or neutral video games and then were subjected to a "pencil drop test" (examiner "accidently" drops a container of pencils or pens to see if participants will offer to help as a marker of pro-social behavior). The original study had used older games such as *Lemmings* (pro-social game where the object is preventing cute characters from accidently killing themselves), *Lammers* (anti-social knock off *Lemmings* game where player tries to kill as many lame characters as possible) and *Tetris* (neutral puzzle game). The updated studies used games with more realistic graphics (e.g., *Grand Theft Auto IV*, *Call of Duty: Black OPS*), which has been hypothesized to further increase desensitization to violence given the realism. When the updated games were used, it was found that about the same number of people who played the violent games offered to help pick up pencils (*Grand Theft* 2/16, *Call of Duty* 6/16) as those who played the neutral puzzle game (*Portal 2*, 5/16) and the pro-social game (*World of Zoo*, 3/16). When other factors were analyzed and studied, the factors determined to have the most effect were: how much time passed since playing any game and if there was an expectation of the subject spending additional time with the researcher (expected to spend more time: anti-social games 14/16, non-violent 10/16; not expected: anti-social 6/16, non-violent 4/16). This raised the question if pro-social behavior is more likely to occur when an individual thought they would be spending more time with someone who might judge them for not helping, rather than having anything to do with the video stimulus.

When using the original games of *Lemmings* and *Lammers*, conflicting results were found compared to the original study. In the original study, two-thirds (67 percent) of the *Lemmings* players stayed to help (12/18) with only 28 percent of the *Lammers* staying (5/18). With the reproduction study, two-thirds (68 percent) of the *Lammers* picked up the pencils (11/16) with only 56 percent of the *Lemmings* players helping (9/16). The implications of this replication study do call into question the overall validity and generalizability of many of the studies investigating violent video games. For example, although the same games were used, the Greitemeyer study was done with predominately female (63 percent) German college students, while the Tear study was done with predominately male (56 percent) Australian college students. So, are the differing results due to the researchers, methodology, the makeup of the subjects, or the small sample size used for both studies?

Unfortunately, since the 2011 Supreme Court ruling, the question of whether playing violent video games causes real world aggression has not become clearer. Two large-scale international studies have had conflicting results. A 2013 British study including 11,000 seven- year-olds from the UK Millennium Cohort Study found:

> Playing electronic games was not associated with conduct problems. No associations were found between either type of screen time [TV and Video games] and emotional symptoms, hyperactivity/inattention, peer relationship problems or prosocial behaviour.[17]

This contrasts with a three-year study published in 2014 of 3000 Singapore children (age range, 8–17 years), which found:

> Longitudinal latent growth curve modeling demonstrated that the effects of violent video game play are mediated primarily by aggressive cognitions. This effect is not moderated by sex, prior aggres-

siveness, or parental monitoring and is only slightly moderated by age.... understanding the psychological mechanisms by which [video games] can influence behaviors is important for parents and pediatricians and for designing interventions to enhance or mitigate the effects.[18]

The lead author Gentile explained in an interview that "the effect was statistically small but might be a serious issue for individual parents worried about their kids."[19] The effect was determined based on questionnaires which asked about views on aggression, violence and frequency of violent fantasies. However, the study also noted that there were methodological/administrative errors which impacted the applicability of the results:

> 27 items were rated on a 4-point scale (strongly disagree to strongly agree). Due to an administrative error, this scale was not administered in wave 1.... Another limitation is that [aggressive behavior] was not measured at wave 1. Obtaining 3 or more measurement waves in future studies would make it possible to explore growth rates of aggression.[20]

As noted in the *Brown* decision, many studies prior to the court case suffered from methodological flaws which complicated how to interpret the findings. In addition, the finding from self-reported "theoretically relevant measures" regarding violent thoughts may not be a finding just related to video games, but rather a common occurrence. For example, Kenrick and Sheets found 73 percent of male undergraduates and 66 percent of female undergraduates self-reported having at least one homicidal fantasy in their lifetime.[21] This study from the early 1990s was likely before many of the participants had been impacted by more complex realistic violent video games, although they had likely been exposed to movies, TV, Beatles music, and, potentially, even Grant Morrison's *Arkham Asylum* graphic novel.

Although the issue of violent video games is not likely to be resolved any time soon, DeCamp and Ferguson sum up the current state of the literature as:

> Despite decades of study, no scholarly consensus has emerged regarding whether violent video games contribute to youth violence.... Models examining video game play and violence-related outcomes without any controls tended to return small, but statistically significant relationships between violent games and violence-related outcomes. However, once other predictors were included in the models and once propensity scores were used to control for an underlying propensity for choosing or being allowed to play violent video games, these relationships vanished, became inverse, or were reduced to trivial effect sizes.[22]

What Is Old Is New Again

As noted above, the current debate about the effects of video games mirrors the 1950s debate about the effects of comic books on juvenile delinquency. Although another essay addresses that issue in greater depth, certain similarities are important to acknowledge here. In both instances, mental health professionals took on advocacy roles claiming that media needed to be limited to protect children. In the 1950s, Dr. Wertham famously said at the United States Senate Subcommittee on Juvenile Delinquency:

> I may say here on this subject, there is practically no controversy. Anybody who has studied [comic books] and seen them knows that some of them have bad effects ... as long as the crime comic books industry exists in its present forms, there are no secure homes. You cannot resist infantile paralysis in your own home alone. Must you not take into account the neighbor's children?[23]

Dr. Wertham's advocacy was very effective, with some countries (including Canada) even banning certain comic books and the American comic book industry voluntarily developing the Comics Code Authority (CCA) to self-regulate content.[24] Although effective, Wertham's advocacy may have had the unintended consequences of perpetuating stigma regarding mental illness in comic books. For example, Grant Morrison notes he intentionally made reference to Dr. Wertham's work in the graphic novel, *Arkham Asylum*, in his Special Edition notes ("the Joker does Fredric Wertham" in the section tauntingly implying Batman and Robin have a homosexual relationship).[25] Although there may be many positive messages to take away from Batman comic books and video games (e.g., problem solving, being aware of one's environment, improved hand-eye coordination, realizing sometimes it is best to avoid confrontation), how psychiatry and mental illness are represented is usually not one of them (e.g., in the video game story line, a corrupt psychiatrist is manipulated by the Joker, allowing him to take over Arkham Asylum).

In addition, it is hard to assess if the Comics Code brought into existence by Wertham's work prevented comics from potentially doing good, such as discussing important societal topics like drug use. This societal concern was not covered until Stan Lee addressed the topic in *Amazing Spider-Man* issues 96–98.[26] These issues of *Spider-Man* were literally published without the CCA seal of approval.

Much of Wertham's research was presented in his book *Seduction of the Innocent*, where he outlined how comic books influenced children on certain themes, such as violence (e.g., The Superman Complex: sadistic joy in seeing other people punished over and over again while you yourself remain immune) and sexuality (e.g., speculation on Batman and Robin having a homosexual relationship).[27] In his zeal to be an advocate, Dr. Wertham may have misrepresented some of his findings—although psychiatrists contend that Wertham obscured patient identities in case reports to protect patient confidentiality and to comply with medical ethical standards.

As noted in a *New York Times* article:

> While the findings of Wertham (who died in 1981) have long been questioned by the comics industry and its advocates, a recent study of the materials he used to write "Seduction of the Innocent" suggests that Wertham misrepresented his research and falsified his results.[28]

Hopefully, current researchers will not allow their desire to be an advocate, either pro or con, impact the quality of their research. Although not implying wrong-doing, video game studies being withdrawn due to problems with the data were recently a *Fox News* story:

> The now-retracted study argued that training with a violent video game can actually make people better at shooting with a real gun.... But the study has now been retracted because two other researchers, who were not involved in the study, pointed out "irregularities in some variables of the data set."[29]

Will researchers in the future look back on the Batman *Arkham Asylum* games with fondness compared to the state of the video game industry of their time? Although this may sound unlikely, as noted at a 2010 American Psychological Association meeting, some current research psychologists are touting the virtue of the very comic book heroes that Wertham criticized, while at the same time expressing concern with the current incarnation of superheroes. Dr. Lamb, a distinguished professor of mental health at University of Massachusetts–Boston was noted to say:

Today's superhero is too much like an action hero who participates in non-stop violence; he's aggressive, sarcastic and rarely speaks to the virtue of doing good for humanity.... The comic book heroes of the past did fight criminals, but these were heroes boys could look up to and learn from because, outside of their costumes, they were real people with real problems and many vulnerabilities.[30]

If the Superman complex of yesterday can no longer be seen as a negative influence on kids, there may be hope for the superhero videogames of today.

Acknowledgment: Special thanks to Terri Day, JD, and Marcia Chapman for reviewing this manuscript.

NOTES

1. Darry Huskey, "A Complete History of Batman Video Games," http://www.ign.com/articles/2014/10/08/a-complete-history-of-batman-video-games (April 2, 2017); IMDB: *Batman: Arkham Asylum* (2009), http://www.imdb.com/title/tt1282022/ (May 31, 2017).
2. Derrik Lang, "Colo. Massacre Casts Ugly Scar on Batman Mythology," *Associated Press*, July 26, 2012, https://www.usnews.com/news/entertainment/articles/2012/07/26/colo-massacre-casts-ugly-scar-on-batman-mythology (April 2, 2017); Helen Pidd, "Anders Breivik 'trained' for Shooting Attacks by Playing Call of Duty," *The Guardian*, April 19, 2012, https://www.theguardian.com/world/2012/apr/19/anders-breivik-call-of-duty (April 2, 2017); Bob Fitrakas, "The Columbus sniper, video games and the new Manchurian Candidates," *The Free Press*, August 29, 2004, http://freepress.org/article/columbus-sniper-video-games-and-new-manchurian-candidates (April 2, 2017).
3. Larry Siever, "Neurobiology of Aggression and Violence," *American Journal of Psychiatry* 165 (2008): 429–442; Christopher Patrick, "Psychophysiological Correlates of Aggression and Violence: an Integrative Review," *Philosophical Transactions of the Royal Society B: Biological Sciences* 363 (2008): 2543–2555.
4. Douglas A. Gentile et al., "Mediators and Moderators of Long-term Effects of Violent Video Games on Aggressive Behavior: Practice, Thinking, and Action," *Journal of American Medical Association Pediatrics* 168 (2014):450–457.
5. Dianne Dedra, "5,000,000: Number of 'Batman: Arkham Knight' Copies Sold Since Launch," *Tech Times*, October 15, 2015, http://www.techtimes.com/articles/95196/20151015/5–000-000-number-of-batman-arkham-knight-copies-sold-since-launch.htm (April 2, 2017).
6. [Atomicpoet], "Is Catcher in the Rye an Assassination Trigger?" *Wordpress*, January 31, 2012, http://atomicpoet.wordpress.com/2012/01/31/is-catcher-in-the-rye-an-assassination-trigger/ (April 2, 2017).
7. *Ginsberg V. New York*, 390 U.S. 629, 88 S. Ct. 1274, 20 L. Ed. 2d 195–1968.
8. Terri Day and Ryan C.W. Hall, "Déjà Vu: from Comic Books to Video Games: Legislative Reliance on 'Soft Science' to Protect Against Uncertain Societal Harm Linked to Violence V. the First Amendment." *Oregon Law Review* 89 (2010): 415–452.
9. *Brown V. Entertainment Merchants Ass'n*, 131 S. Ct. 2729, 564 U.S. 786, 180 L. Ed. 2d 708—Supreme Court, 2011.
10. Brad J. Bushman and Craig A. Anderson, "Comfortably Numb: Desensitizing Effects of Violent Media on Helping Others," *Psychological Science* 20 (2009): 273–277.
11. Ryan C.W. Hall, Terri Day, and Richard Hall, "A Plea for Caution: Violent Video Games, the Supreme Court, and the Role of Science," *Mayo Clinical Proceedings* 86 (2011):315–321.
12. Craig A. Anderson et al., "Violent Video Game Effects on Aggression, Empathy, and Prosocial Behavior in Eastern and Western Countries: a Meta-analytic Review," *Psychological Bulletin* 136 (2010):151–173.
13. Christopher J. Ferguson and John Kilburn, "Much Ado About Nothing: the Misestimation and Overinterpretation of Violent Video Game Effects in Eastern and Western Nations: Comment on Anderson Et Al. (2010)," *Psychological Bulletin* 136 (2010):174–178.
14. Hamid Allahverdipour et al., "Correlates of Video Games Playing Among Adolescents in an Islamic Country," *BioMed Central PublicHealth* 10 (2010):286. doi: 10.1186/1471–2458-10-286.
15. William A. Fisher et al., "Pornography, Sex Crime, and Paraphilia," *Current Psychiatry Reports* 362 (2013): doi:10.1007/s11920–013-0362-7.
16. Morgan J. Tear and Mark Nielsen, "Failure to Demonstrate That Playing Violent Video Games Diminishes Prosocial Behavior," *Plos One* 8 (2013): doi: 10.1371/journal.pone.0068382; Tobias Greitemeyer and Silvia Osswald, "Effects of Prosocial Video Games on Prosocial Behavior," *Journal of Personality and Social Psychology* 98 (2010): 211–221.
17. Alison Parks et al., "Do Television and Electronic Games Predict Children's Psychosocial Adjustment? Longitudinal Research Using the UK Millennium Cohort Study," *Archives of Disease in Children* 98 (2013): 341–348.
18. Gentile, "aggressive Behavior," 450.
19. Kathryn Doyle, "Violent Video Games May Be Tied to Aggressive Thoughts" *Reuters Health News*,

March 24, 2014, http://www.reuters.com/article/us-violent-videogames-idUSBREA2N1MC20140324 (April 9, 2017).

20. Gentile, "aggressive Behavior," 451.

21. Douglas Kenrick and Virgil Sheets, "Homicidal Fantasies," *Evolution and Human Behavior* 14 (1993): 231–246.

22. Whitney DeCamp and Christopher Ferguson, "The Impact of Degree of Exposure to Violent Video Games, Family Background, and Other Factors on Youth Violence," *Journal of Youth and Adolescence* 46 (2017): 388–400.

23. Senate Subcommittee Hearings into Juvenile Delinquency, with the special focus on Comic Books, April 21, 1954, testimony by Dr. Fredric Wertham, http://www.thecomicbooks.com/wertham.html (April 9, 2017).

24. Day, "Déjà Vu," 415–452.

25. Grant Morrison and David McKean, *Batman Arkham Asylum 25th Anniversary Paperback—Deluxe Edition* (New York: DC Comics, 2014).

26. Joe Sergi, "Tales from the Code: Spidey Fights Drugs and the Comics Code Authority," July 18, 2012, http://cbldf.org/2012/07/tales-from-the-code-spidey-fights-drugs-and-the-comics-code-authority/(April 9, 2017).

27. Day, "Déjà Vu," 415–452.

28. Dave Itzkoff, "Scholar Finds Flaws in Work by Archenemy of Comics," *New York Times* February 19, 2013, http://www.nytimes.com/2013/02/20/books/flaws-found-in-fredric-werthams-comic-book-studies.html (February 29, 2017). Psychiatrists have found flaws in some critiques by the first scholar, who holds a Ph.D. in Library Science and who views Wertham's obscuring of identifying information in his patient case presentations as misrepresentation, and hence scientific dishonesty, whereas psychiatrists note that medical ethics expressly prohibit disclosure of identifying patient information, even in academic case reports, so it is customary to obscure demographic specifics to protect patient confidentiality. See Hannah Means-Shannon, "On the Scene: Sparks Fly at 'Surely, You're Joking, Dr. Wertham' Event," www.comicsbeat.com. Accessed December 21, 2018.

29. *Fox News*, "Controversial Video Game Gun Study Gets Retracted," http://www.foxnews.com/tech/2017/01/25/controversial-video-game-gun-study-gets-retracted.html (April 9, 2017).

30. American Psychological Association, "Today's Superheroes Send Wrong Image to Boys, Say Researchers: Masculine Stereotype Not Healthy for Relationships," http://www.apa.org/news/press/releases/2010/08/macho-stereotype-unhealthy.aspx (April 9, 2017).

Deadly and Dysfunctional Family Dynamics
When Fiction Mirrors Fact

SUSAN HATTERS FRIEDMAN, M.D., *and*
RYAN C.W. HALL, M.D.

Introduction

The Batman canon spans over 75 years with seminal pieces of work exploring or reinterpreting classic aspects of the characters' dynamics. This can be seen from the works of visionaries, such as Alan Moore in *The Killing Joke,* which explores one of many potential origins for the Joker, and Frank Miller's *Year One,* which updates Batman's origins, relationship with James Gordon, and flushes out Bruce Wayne's first year as the caped crusader. However, as any comic aficionado understands and appreciates, there are certain fixed points in comic lore which, if changed, would fundamentally damage the character and irreversibly change continuity, no matter how many "flashpoints" occur. This has become a running joke in the comic world canonized by the following sentiment: that Uncle Ben (*Marvel Universe*) and Thomas and Martha Wayne are the only deaths that are irreversible. (Even Jason Todd came back as the Red Hood after "A Death in the Family"). Without Thomas and Martha Wayne's deaths outside of a theater, young Bruce Wayne would not have experienced the fear and guilt that led him to become the Batman. This has led to many comic book writers using proxy characters which mirror Bruce Wayne's experience to explore the psychological make up of Batman/Bruce Wayne in a "compare and contrast" fashion to try to answer the question if Batman is truly sane or not.

Many of these stories take an ancillary character in comic book history and imagine how they would have turned out if they were placed in a similar position to young Bruce Wayne in Crime Alley. Even though they may be placed in a similar position (loss of family), the surrogates' unique circumstances (different back-story, no Alfred Pennyworth character as a support, different lessons learned from the tragedy) allow the readers to see how different motivations and ethical decisions could have changed what the Batman became. In most instances, this leads to the surrogate characters developing pathology which highlights that no matter how obsessive Bruce Wayne/Batman is in his vigilante search for justice, his mental health and ethical code is the best that could be hoped for. For example, in Geoff Johns' 2011 *Flashpoint* story, which led into the re-launch of the

Dr. Linda Friitawa, also known as Fright, as a custom action figure. An albino, the white-haired Dr. Friitawa is a geneticist who lost her medical license because of her unethical experiments. Unable to find legitimate medical positions, she assists in Scarecrow's fear gas studies and works for the Black Mask (Dr. Jeremiah Arkham), joining his stable of sinister scientists. She also collaborates with Dr. Hugo Strange and the two resurrect The Reaper as they distract Batman (photograph by George Higham).

DC universe with the *New 52*, Thomas and Martha Wayne serve as the stand-ins by witnessing the death of their beloved son, Bruce. Thomas becomes a more dysfunctional, sadistic, gun-toting, borderline alcoholic version of the Batman who funds his activities through his casino empire, while Martha Wayne was driven to total insanity and becomes that continuity version of the Joker.

One of the more interesting and earlier Batman stands-ins is Grant Morrison's Amadeus Arkham in the 1989 *Arkham Asylum: A Serious House on Serious Earth*.[1] Unlike the Waynes, who had an "idyllic life" of power and wealth prior to experiencing trauma, Amadeus had to cope with his mother's mental illness from an early age (approximately the age when Bruce Wayne lost his parents), especially after his father's death (from a never-specified cause). Instead of being consumed with vengeance the way Bruce Wayne was, Amadeus' single purpose became taking care of his mother and the mentally ill. This was typified in the graphic novel by the line "In the years following my father's death I think it's true to say that the house became my whole world." Amadeus eventually become a philanthropist (e.g., founding the Elisabeth Arkham hospital), physician, and family man just as Thomas Wayne had done. Although Amadeus deals with a similar tragic loss of his family at the hands of Mad Dog Hawkins, as both Bruce Wayne and

Thomas Wayne in *Flashpoint* did, and does eventually develop an obsession for justice/vengeance (ultimately killing Hawkins in an ECT "accident" after the initial goal of treatment fails), he is different from both Wayne men in that he had experienced mental health challenges before the trauma of the loss of his family. There was the obvious experience of dealing with his mother, but there were also his own personal challenges—that he just was not initially cognizant of. Over the course of *Arkham Asylum*, it is revealed that Amadeus Arkham had previously killed his deranged mother in his early adulthood—either in a dissociative state or as a conscious act of which he later repressed the memory.

Amadeus saw his mother's death and his subsequent actions as altruistic, as noted in his journal entry:

> I returned to the family home on a cool spring morning in 1920, shortly after mother's funeral. She opened her own throat with a razor. In the end perhaps, it was for the best. I have to believe that…. Alone in a gloom that smells of dust and childhood, I dedicate myself to the prevention of such suffering as my poor mother knew. And I begin to make plans. For the first time in twelve years I spend the night in my old room. I do not sleep well, my dreams are haunted by beating wings.[2]

Later journal entries appear to support the notion that Amadeus Arkham rationalized his actions to a point that he had even convinced himself for a period of time that he had not killed her. Again, as noted in his journal:

> Oh my poor mother…. Don't be afraid mother. I love you [raising and then slashing with the razor blade]. I understand now what my memory tried to keep from me. Madness is born in my blood. It is my birth right. My inheritance. My destiny.[3]

So, Amadeus Arkham is the stand-in for how Batman would have developed if he was already flawed or potentially mentally ill, even with good intentions, before he developed his obsession for vengeance and justice. Grant Morrison (in the anniversary edition of his graphic novel) notes that he intentionally included general psychological concepts, symbolism, and theories from Jung and others in his story to explore the Batman universe and the character itself. Further review specifically about matricide adds another layer to the psychological profile of Amadeus Arkham and the comparison to the Batman, Thomas Wayne, and even Martha Wayne that could have been from *Flashpoint*.

Common Features of Matricide

Matricide, murder of the mother, has historically been viewed as "[a] schizophrenic crime."[4] However, while people with schizophrenia are over-represented among those who kill their mothers, more people without schizophrenia kill their mother and, of course, the majority of people with schizophrenia do not kill their mother. In addition, it can be difficult to classify what is a true case of matricide vs. a larger scope crime that happens to also include the killing of the mother. For example, mass shooters like the Texas Bell Tower shooter Charles Whitman and the Sandy Hook School shooter Adam Lanza killed their mothers immediately before engaging in larger acts of homicide. There are also times when acts of matricide may be better conceptualized as unsuccessful murder-suicides, in which the mother was killed first, but for whatever reason the suicide was not completed (e.g., could not bring self to commit suicide, or attempted suicide but did not die).

Overall, studies find unusual long-term dysfunctional mother-child relationships prior to the murder, where the mother is perceived as either intrusive/controlling and/or the child is overly dependent. The mother is often described as controlling or smothering, usually in the context of an absent or ineffectual father. Underlying the smothering relationship is often hostility and a mutual dependence. However, it should be noted that in many of the high profile legal cases where forensic psychiatrists are directly involved (e.g., determination of competency to stand trial, insanity at the time of the act, or mitigating factors) the perpetrator is suffering from some psychotic event (e.g., schizophrenia, bipolar disorder, or substance-induced psychosis) and the mother may have been more traditional and nurturing, legitimately looking out for the (adult) child's best interest. This sometimes explains why the mother/caregiver was around psychotic individuals—who most other people avoided or were concerned could be dangerous. It needs to be noted that these cases are often different from cases where more traditional motivations for murder exist, such as money/wealth/inheritance, anger (non-psychotic), crimes of the heart (if kill mother, can be with romantic love) or crimes of opportunity (if mother is gone then I can get on with my own life) occur.

On average, in the United States, 100 mothers are killed by their son or daughter annually.[5] Interestingly, more offspring kill their fathers, with a rate of about 150 fathers killed per year. American data reveals that one-third of matricide offenders were under age 25, with one in seven matricide offenders under 18 when they killed their mother.[6] The vast majority of matricide offenders are male, with five out of six matricides being committed by sons.[7]

A national study in Scotland which considered three decades of matricide offenders—persons who were charged with murder or culpable homicide—found many more sons than daughters (23 vs. 3).[8] They found that one-quarter of the matricide offenders had schizophrenia, one-fifth had a personality disorder, 16 percent alcohol dependence, and several suffered mood disorders. However, it is important to note that one-quarter had no mental health diagnosis, which again implies that matricide (like any murder or crime) can occur for rational motivations (e.g., money or anger).

Among a sample of 58 psychiatrically hospitalized men at England's Broadmoor Hospital who had killed their mothers, schizophrenia was most common diagnosis (74 percent), followed by depression and personality disorders.[9] The majority (83 percent) of psychiatric patients were not taking medications at the time of the matricide despite their mental illness history. There was often a "close confining mother/son relationship … characterized by a dominant mother and an immature, dependent son, who had frequently lost his father some years before the homicide."[10] More than half of the sons had no significant romantic/sexual relationship history themselves.

In another study, Green found that offenders fit into specific motivational categories for matricide. He defined the categories as "paranoid and persecutory reasons," "altruistic," and other. The "persecutory/paranoid" group had delusional beliefs about their mother (such as that she was the devil). As well, Green found sexual elements in half of the matricides in the schizophrenia group.[11]

Green's "altruistic" group had selfless reasons for the killing—similar to what is seen in altruistic infanticide cases in which the mother, acting out of love rather than anger, believes she is doing what is best for her child.[12] In altruistic infanticide cases, the mother may be psychotic (e.g., believing she is protecting the child from some fate worse than death) or depressed (and planning to take her own life, not wanting to leave her infant in the world that she is departing.) In altruistic matricides, the murder is seen as an act of love and mercy because the mother has been suffering from a physical or psychiatric illness (e.g., dementia) or that they (the adult child) themselves were dying and wouldn't leave their mother to care for herself. Just because the perpetrator's motives are altruistic, it does not mean that they are not also suffering from a mental illness. As seen in altruistic infanticide, perpetrators of altruistic matricide often suffer from depression or psychosis which may affect their judgment, limit their ability to problem solve, or prevent them from appreciating the larger significance of their action at the time. Motives in the "other" category included "accidental," jealousy, rage, and impulsivity.[13] Often, when precipitants were identifiable, they were trivial—for example arguments over food. Yet, excessive violence (over-kill) was common.

In a study of 15 men admitted to the NYU-Bellevue Hospital Forensic Psychiatry Service, who were charged with killing their mothers, diagnoses included eight with schizophrenia, four with substance-induced psychosis, and three with impulse disorders.[14] Most commonly, mothers were home alone with their sons when they were killed and none of the sons were living independently—supporting the notion of an abnormal mother-child relationship (e.g., co-dependent) or one where the mother was still engaging in a caretaking role for an adult child with difficulties (e.g., "failure to launch," or too ill to launch). Among the schizophrenia group, several reported being assaulted by their mothers, with the actual matricide potentially occurring as a response to an assault, while for some others, the act of matricide was a response to persecutory delusions about their mothers. Again, the fathers were often absent or weak. Campion and colleagues noted "a serious chronic derangement in the relationships of most matricidal men with their mothers."[15] None of these men reported amnesia and almost all used excessive levels of violence to kill (over-kill). They often had a prior history of violence and/or a suicide attempt. Psychometric testing indicated that they felt weak, dependent, and unable to accept an adult role that was separate from their mothers.

Campion and colleagues noted "in this group of schizophrenic men who killed their mothers the act of matricide may[be] understood as a reaction to a fantasy of physical or psychological annihilation, a desperate, violent act of self-assertion to separate from the mother."[16] In the second group, of those abusing substances who became psychotic, a maternal threat to their masculinity was perceived. In the third group, they described men who were developmentally disabled/ neurologically impaired, had assaultive histories or became enraged. Campion and colleagues noted "An individual in crisis acquires the compulsion to carry out a violent act that has symbolic significance in addition to its apparent meaning."[17]

Finally, Bourget and colleagues completed a study of coroners' files of 56 perpetrators who had killed their parents (n = 64) in Canada.[18] This study is particularly important because it includes not only those who required psychiatric hospitalization after the murder (as most of the other studies do) but also those who committed suicide after the murder and those who were found guilty and incarcerated. They found that matricides were committed by children aged 14 to 58, with a mean age of 30.3.[19] The bulk of the matricides occurred in the family home, where the majority of the perpetrators were living with their mothers. Over a quarter of the cases had a homicide-suicide dynamic. Two-thirds of those who committed matricide evidenced a psychotic motive. As far as the perpetrator's diagnosis, most common was schizophrenia (54 percent) followed by depression (17 percent).

Parricide Research

Though the research literature regarding the killing of one's parent no matter the gender is still somewhat limited, more studies have focused on parricide (murder of either parent) than have focused on matricide alone. This may occur to increase the sample size in this, fortunately, unusual and rare crime.

Statistics from North America and Europe indicate that overall 4 percent of homicides are parricides.[20] Strikingly, 20–30 percent of homicides committed by people who are psychotic are parricides.[21]

In a Canadian sample of 39 adult sons and daughters found Not Guilty by Reason of Insanity for killing their parent, almost 90 percent were a single-victim single-offender situation.[22] There was an almost even split of fathers and mothers killed (22f vs. 19m). Over half of the perpetrators suffered from paranoid schizophrenia, while over a quarter merited a personality disorder diagnosis. Over half had persecutory delusions associated with the parricide and almost one-quarter had grandiose delusions with a religious theme. Most of the offenders were unemployed (74 percent), single (85 percent), and male (92 percent). A variety of methods of murder were used, but the majority (57 percent) killed with a knife. Marleau and colleagues noted: "many are certainly financially dependent on their parents and/or trapped in a difficult hostile/dependent/love relationship."[23]

In reviewing the limited studies of juveniles who killed their parents, West and Feldsher[24] found that perpetrators were often adolescent males who generally did not suffer from schizophrenia. They murdered spontaneously after a lengthy period of abuse by their parents and expressed relief after the murder. Heide proposed three categories of those who kill their parents: severely abused, severely mentally ill, and dangerously antisocial.[25] The severely abused type was most often seen among adolescent parricide offenders, whereas the severely mentally ill type was most often seen in adults.[26] Based on a study of news reports, juveniles who killed their parents were likely to be severely abused or dangerously antisocial, rather than mentally ill.[27]

Whether Grant Morris was aware of the literature regarding matricide and parricide or not, he included many of the common elements in Amadeus Arkham's character dynamics. Firstly, there was an unusual dependency dynamic between Amadeus Arkham and his mother in the context of an absent father. The mother, through her impairment from her illness, was indirectly controlling and potentially emotionally scarring to Amadeus. At the time of the murder, Amadeus was in late young adulthood (~28–30, the age Batman is traditionally represented in most continuities). In his psychotic state, Amadeus believed that he could see his mother's hallucinations (which for storytelling effect, took the form of a bat). When the murder occurred, Amadeus Arkham was not abusing substances, but also was not in treatment and was not on medication. According to Amadeus' journal, the reason for the murder was altruism; however, it should be noted that Elizabeth Arkham's death did free Amadeus Arkham to return to Metropolis to further his career and to be with his own family.

Dissociation and Murder

Van der Kolk and Fisler define trauma as "the experience of an inescapable stressful event that overwhelms one's existing coping mechanisms."[28] They further note that "trauma can lead to extremes of retention and forgetting: terrifying experiences may be remembered with extreme vividness, or totally resist integration."[29] Both of these features were found in Amadeus Arkham's story, depicted in ways that only a graphic novel or cinema could.

Amnesia after a traumatic event may last for years. "Generally, recall is triggered by exposure to sensory or affective stimuli that match sensory or affective elements associated with the trauma."[30] This too, we will see in Amadeus Arkham's case.

How accurate our memories are depends on how accurately they were laid down (which in turn depends on our emotional state at the time). In various traumatic experiences, amnesia for events occurs—such as people victimized by abuse and those in combat. Even some of those who have committed murder have reported experiencing amnesia.[31] In cases of murder, there is also the complicating factor that one may claim amnesia to try to avoid criminal prosecution or some other type of repercussion. In the case of Amadeus Arkham, it does not seem likely that he is malingering the amnesia since no mention of possible criminal charges or other repercussion of murder are discussed in his journal.

"Dissociation refers to a compartmentalization of experience: elements of the experience are not integrated into a unitary whole, but are stored in memory as isolated fragments consisting of sensory perceptions or affective states."[32] One of the four types of dissociation is known specifically as "peritraumatic dissociation" and includes depersonalization and derealization during the trauma itself. Depersonalization occurs when one feels detached from one's own bodily experiences, such as an out-of-body-experience or feeling like one is watching it happen from above. As well, one may feel lack of control of one's own actions. Perceptual distortions may also occur, such as time going fast or slow, or objects or sounds seeming closer or farther away than they really are. Derealization occurs when other people seem unreal or distant.[33]

"Peritraumatic dissociation" is a risk factor for developing Post-Traumatic Stress Disorder (PTSD)[34] and has also been suggested to predict amnesia.[35] Although Amadeus Arkham reported he did see the bat, nothing about the journal entry or the graphic illustration suggests he experienced any depersonalization or derealization at the time. If anything, the text suggests almost consciously forgetting or repressing the trauma—the notion that his memory was trying to protect himself. This is further supported by his ability to clearly recollect what happened later when his memory (for lack of a better word) was recovered.

Van der Kolk and Fisler's study of traumatic memory found that "it is in the very nature of traumatic memory to be dissociated, and to be initially stored as sensory fragments without a coherent semantic component."[36] Further, "traumatic experiences in people with PTSD are initially imprinted as sensations or feeling states that are not immediately transcribed into personal narratives."[37]

A recent review of juvenile parricide research perpetrated by abused children found that, "the youth is often stressed to the point of dissociation during the homicidal incident and the parent's death is frequently perceived as a relief to the offender and to the surviving family members."[38] While Amadeus Arkham was in his late twenties when he killed his mother, there was no evidence that he was physically abused by his mother as a juvenile. One could argue that seeing your mother eating beetles (in a psychotic state) might be a form of emotional abuse but given the mother's mental health state and likely lack of intentional harm it is better thought of as just emotionally traumatic.

Amnesia is reported by perpetrators of almost one-third (31 percent) of homicides.[39] Those who report amnesia are more likely to have an extreme emotional arousal in the homicide, to lack premeditation, and to have used alcohol or drugs prior to the murder. We can expect that Amadeus Arkham experienced extreme emotional arousal and did not premeditate his mother's murder; there was no suggestion of substance use before the murder.

Another recent study of defendants, who were referred to a court psychiatric clinic for forensic evaluation after allegedly committing felonies, found that substance use disorders were the most commonly diagnosed mental health issue among those who claimed amnesia for their offending.[40] Of note, these *pre-trial* defendants, who claimed lack of recollection of the offense, were often charged with violence against strangers.[41] Those who are pre-trial may present a different picture because of a greater motive to exaggerate their deficits in hopes of a better trial outcome.

Many of the classic concepts of dissociative amnesia related to a traumatic event could apply to or explain Amadeus Arkham's actions and revelations. For example, Amadeus Arkham's dissociation or repression does not start to break down until after he is exposed to the intense stimuli of treating the particularly violent and deranged killer of his wife and daughter. Initially it was not a full revelation but just a remembrance of his home as a child when first exposed to Mad Dog Hawkins. After meeting Hawkins, the journal notes that Amadeus dreamed of a Tunnel of Love amusement park ride and being with his father, only to awake with a feeling of "as though I'm back where I belong. Back in the old house"[42] (e.g., dissociative flashback).

There are episodes of depersonalization and full dissociative amnesia after Amadeus learns of his family's gruesome murder. For example, after he finds his daughter's decapitated head in a doll's house, Amadeus puts on his mother's wedding dress and comments "It all seems perfectly rational"[43] (e.g., derealization) before fully dissociating, with his next memory being vomiting in the lavatory with no remembrance or explanation of what happened in between. The journal then describes that Amadeus believes he may be ill, but it does not specify if his concern is physical illness or mental illness.

Initially there is a question if Amadeus Arkham had killed his own wife and daughter for "altruistic" reasons since the pages in the graphic novel preceding his family's murder discussed his daughter's state of health, her suffering with nightmares, and Amadeus' wish that "she need never grow up."[44] Considering the symbolism in the graphic novel— with disrupted sleep and nightmares often serving as symbolic representations of troubled emotional states—it is possible that Amadeus' daughter may be beginning to suffer from mental illness in ways similar to Amadeus Arkham and his mother. However, the journal does clearly note that "[Mad Dog] delights in recounting to me every detail of the atrocities he inflicted upon Constance and Harriet."[45] So, assuming the journal entry is not another repressed dissociative rationalization, like when it was stated that the mother committed suicide, it does appear Hawkins is the killer.

It is only after Amadeus' mental and emotional state further deteriorates due to prolonged frustration over not being able to cure Hawkins that the memory of Amadeus killing his mother is revealed. In a situation like his mother's death, Amadeus again "altruistically" commits murder by electrocuting Hawkins to protect society from an untreatable killer. This time, though, Amadeus does remember the act. The journal notes that Amadeus' motivation for opening the Asylum was "[to] contain the presences that roam these rooms and narrow stairways. I shall surround them with bars and walls and electrified fences and pray they never break free."[46] Shortly after the murder of Hawkins, Amadeus has symptoms of insomnia, hallucinations, and bizarre delusional beliefs regarding magic and has started to experiment with psychedelic substances. It is in this crazed and frantic state that the full memory and circumstances of his mother's death are revealed. It is unclear how long Amadeus was able to continue to function as a doctor after Mad Dog's death on April 1, 1922, but it is noted that in 1929 he tried to murder his stockbroker—which resulted in his commitment to the Asylum he had started.

Other examples of Matricide/ Parricide, both fictional and based on real events

Many of the themes in Grant Morrison's *Arkham Asylum* appear to be influenced by Alfred Hitchcock's *Psycho*. Similarities include both protagonists' killing their mothers with edged weapons, continuing to live in the ancestral home, wearing their mother's clothes to symbolize their emotional distress, and unusual relationships with their mothers. Not only that, but Norman's mother-personality overtakes his own personality and, according to Dr. Fred Richmond (the psychiatrist in the film), his dissociative reaction is the explanation for the murder.[47] Although there is no indication that Amadeus Arkham took on his mother's personality, he did develop and share his mother's psychosis of being pursued by a bat *(folie à deux)*. Given the overwhelming symbolism of the bat in the *Batman* mythology, this was probably done more for artistic effect than to provide clues about what the mind or disease state of Amadeus Arkham was.

Heavenly Creatures, an early Peter Jackson film, focused on the real-world Pauline Parker-Juliet Hulme case. In 1954, in Christchurch, New Zealand, a teenage girl, along with the help of her female friend with whom she was very close, plotted to kill Parker's mother. The girls engaged in vicious over-kill. After convincing Parker's mother that they were going on a girls' day trip including tea and a day hike, they hit her repeatedly on the head with a brick. The two were caught due to diary entries about their planning of the murder. Parker's relationship with her mother had been somewhat fraught, and she had believed that with her mother out of the way, she'd be free to travel the world with Hulme. Both girls spent five years in prison. Many years later, it was revealed that Hulme changed her name to Anne Perry and became a world-renowned mystery author. Although there was likely little about this real-life murder that influenced Morrison's take on Amadeus Arkham, there is the distinct coincidence (even though it was most likely just a narrative tool in the graphic novel) that both matricides were discovered due to journaling. Phantasmagorical imagery was used in *Heavenly Creatures,* like the hallucinatory bats in Amadeus Arkham's world. Finally, although Arkham did not plan to run off after the murder, his mother's death did free him up to return to Metropolis to be with his family.

In Showtime's *The Affair,* the male protagonist, Noah, reveals that he had killed his mother. His mother suffered from multiple sclerosis and he had been caring for her. When he won a full scholarship to college, he claims she wanted to kill herself so that caring for her would not hold him back, but she had been unable to open the medication to take an overdose. He spent a loving day with her and then fed her crushed pills in her food. While Noah and Amadeus Arkham's putative motive of "altruistic" matricide may be the same, the event played out quite differently with Amadeus' mother's execution being far bloodier.

Just as in real life, cases of patricide (murder of the father) are more often seen in film and theater than are matricides. In *Star Wars: The Force Awakens,* for example, many of the common characteristics of sons who kill their father (or either parent) are demonstrated by Kylo Ren (a.k.a. Ben Solo).[48] In murdering his father, Han Solo, Kylo Ren acts alone and uses excessive violence to kill (including both the lightsaber and the fall into oblivion). In addition, Kylo Ren is a single adult male with some psychotic-like features (grandiose ideas, communication with his grandfather's helmet), an addiction to the Dark Side (an allegory for drugs) and has a history of poor impulse control resulting in violence when frustrated or disappointed. Finally, Kylo Ren demonstrates relief rather than remorse in the film after the killing, similar to real-world offenders who report experiencing feelings of freedom. Since almost nothing is known about Amadeus Arkham's father except that he is dead, it is hard to draw parallels to either fictionalized or real-life cases of patricide, although this may become fertile grounds for future tales where the fate of Arkham's father is discussed in greater detail (perhaps also killed by Amadeus Arkham? killed by Elisabeth Arkham? died of natural causes?). This could occur since other Arkham relatives such as Amadeus' nephew, Jeremiah Arkham, is an established character in the *Batman* lore, indicating there is an extended Arkham bloodline (as well as aspects of Amadeus' history being part of the *New 52 All Star Western* 2011 story line). It would not be hard for future authors to expound upon the relationship Amadeus Arkham had with his father.

Conclusions

It is clear, after reviewing the literature on matricide (and to a certain extent parricide more generally) and traumatic amnesia, that this information does better flush out Amadeus Arkham's character and potential motivations. He was indeed a man with a long and complicated relationship with his widowed mother, where he was controlled by her need to have him as a caretaker. Although his exact age at the time of the murder was never given in the graphic novel, it would appear he was in his late twenties. He did not appear to have any drug or alcohol issues. However, there was indication of him suffering from psychotic symptoms around the time of his mother's murder that resolved (or lay dormant) until the murders of his wife and daughter. His motivation, like many classic tragic heroes, was initially altruistic but eventually became more self-destructive. It is the similarities and, ultimately, the differences from Batman that make Amadeus Arkham an interesting *Batman* character and surrogate. Part of the fun of reading a *Batman* comic (especially ones with a lot of moral ambiguity) is wondering if Batman will fall off that razor-thin edge between being a vigilante with a moral code—or becomes a deranged psychotic killer that many in his universe turn into.

Notes

1. Grant Morrison and David McKean, *Arkham Asylum: A Serious House on Serious Earth 15th Anniversary Edition* (New York: DC Comics, 2004; 1990).
2. *Ibid.*
3. *Ibid.*
4. S.A. Clark, "Matricide: the Schizophrenic Crime?" *Medicine, Science and the Law* 33 (1993): 325–328.
5. Kathleen M. Heide and Autumn Frei, "Matricide: a Critique of the Literature," *Trauma, Violence, & Abuse* 11 (2010): 3–17.
6. Kathleen M. Heide, "Matricide and Stepmatricide Victims and Offenders: an Empirical Analysis of U.S. Arrest Data," *Behavioral Sciences and the Law* 31 (2013): 203–214.
7. *Ibid.*
8. S.A. Clark, "Matricide: the Schizophrenic Crime?" *Medicine, Science and the Law* 33 (1993): 325–328.
9. Christopher M. Green, "Matricide by Sons," *Medicine, Science and the Law* 21 (1981): 207–214.
10. *Ibid.*
11. *Ibid.*

12. Susan Hatters Friedman and Phillip J. Resnick, "Child Murder by Mothers: Patterns and Prevention," *World Psychiatry* 6 (2007): 137–141.
13. Christopher M. Green, "Matricide by Sons," *Medicine, Science and the Law* 21 (1981): 207–214.
14. John Campion et al., "A Study of 15 Matricidal Men," *American Journal of Psychiatry* 142 (1985): 312–317.
15. *Ibid.*
16. *Ibid.*
17. *Ibid.*
18. Dominique Bourget et al., "Parricide: a Comparative Study of Matricide Versus Patricide," *Journal of the American Academy of Psychiatry and the Law* 35 (2007): 306–312.
19. *Ibid.*
20. Jacques D. Marleau et al., "A Comparison of Parricide and Attempted Parricide: a Study of 39 Psychotic Adults," *International Journal of Law and Psychiatry* 26 (2003): 269–279.
21. *Ibid.*
22. *Ibid.*
23. *Ibid.*
24. Sara G. West and Mendel Feldsher, "Parricide: Characteristics of Sons and Daughters Who Kill Their Parents," *Current Psychiatry* 9 (2010): 20–38.
25. Kathleen M Heide and Autumn Frei, "Matricide: a Critique of the Literature," *Trauma, Violence, & Abuse* 11 (2010): 3–17.
26. Kathleen M Heide and Autumn Frei, "Matricide: a Critique of the Literature," *Trauma, Violence, & Abuse* 11 (2010): 3–17.
27. Kathleen M. Heide and Denise Paquette Boots, "A Comparative Analysis of Media Reports of U.S. Parricide Cases with Officially Reported National Crime Data and the Psychiatric and Psychological Literature," *International Journal of Offender Therapy and Comparative Criminology* 51 (2007): 646–675.
28. Bessel A. van der Kolk and Rita Fisler, "Dissociation and the Fragmentary Nature of Traumatic Memories: Overview and Exploratory Study," *Journal of Traumatic Stress* 8 (1995): 505–525.
29. *Ibid.*
30. *Ibid.*
31. Andrew Moskowitz, "Dissociation and Violence: a Review of the Literature," *Trauma, Violence, & Abuse* 5 (2004): 21–46.
32. Bessel A. van der Kolk and Rita Fisler, "Dissociation and the Fragmentary Nature of Traumatic Memories: Overview and Exploratory Study," *Journal of Traumatic Stress* 8 (1995): 505–525.
33. Andrew Moskowitz, "Dissociation and Violence: a Review of the Literature," *Trauma, Violence, & Abuse* 5 (2004): 21–46.
34. Bessel A. van der Kolk and Rita Fisler, "Dissociation and the Fragmentary Nature of Traumatic Memories: Overview and Exploratory Study," *Journal of Traumatic Stress* 8 (1995): 505–525.
35. Andrew Moskowitz, "Dissociation and Violence: a Review of the Literature," *Trauma, Violence, & Abuse* 5 (2004): 21–46.
36. Bessel A. van der Kolk and Rita Fisler, "Dissociation and the Fragmentary Nature of Traumatic Memories: Overview and Exploratory Study," *Journal of Traumatic Stress* 8 (1995): 505–525.
37. Bessel A. van der Kolk and Rita Fisler, "Dissociation and the Fragmentary Nature of Traumatic Memories: Overview and Exploratory Study," *Journal of Traumatic Stress* 8 (1995): 505–525.
38. Kathleen M. Heide and Autumn Frei, "Matricide: a Critique of the Literature," *Trauma, Violence, & Abuse* 11 (2010): 3–17.
39. Andrew Moskowitz, "Dissociation and Violence: a Review of the Literature," *Trauma, Violence, & Abuse* 5 (2004): 21–46.
40. John Preston Shand et al., "And Then I Woke Up in Jail: Amnesia Claims in Evaluations," (poster presented at American Academy of Psychiatry and the Law annual meeting, Coronado, California, October 2013).
41. *Ibid.*
42. Grant Morrison and David McKean, *Arkham Asylum: A Serious House on Serious Earth 15th Anniversary Edition* (New York: DC Comics, 2004; 1990).
43. *Ibid.*
44. *Ibid.*
45. *Ibid.*
46. *Ibid.*
47. Susan Hatters Friedman et al., "Horror Films and Forensic Psychiatry," *Newsletter of the American Academy of Psychiatry and the Law* 42 (2017): 11.
48. Susan Hatters Friedman and Ryan C.W. Hall, "Star Wars: the Force Awakens Forensic Teaching About Patricide," *Journal of the American Academy of Psychiatry and the Law* 45 (2017): 726–732.

Murderous Minds, Arkham Villains and Real (Not Reel) Life Movie Massacres[1]

SHARON PACKER, M.D.

It has often been said that life mirrors art as much as art mirrors life. It has also been said that fact is stranger than fiction. The James Holmes *Batman* movie massacre in Aurora, Colorado, confirms those old adages—but it is unlike other calamities in one respect.

Typically, critics scapegoat the media in attempt to explain away heinous human acts. Or the blame entertainers for being bad examples. The public (and perpetrators' defense counsels) implicate adverse external influences that turn supposedly innocent citizens into soulless, cold-hearted criminals. How else can a secular society believe that such random acts of evil occur? Few of us blame Satan or sorcery, although those explanations were popular in the past and in some circles.

If we look closely (or not even closely), we find many parallels between *Arkham Asylum,* the Batman universe and Holmes' behavior at the time of his mass murders. There are also crossovers between Holmes' case and pressing medico-legal concerns, including the insanity defense (NGRI) or diminished capacity; coerced (or voluntary) treatments in psychiatry; and the ability to stand trial. Despite these obvious connections, next to no one blamed the Batman universe for turning this troubled neuroscience graduate student into one of America's worst mass murderers. And there was good reason to avoid this otherwise obvious media scapegoat.

Batman himself is so popular among the public and the *Batman* franchise so successful and so long-standing that even the most brilliant attorneys or journalists would be hard pressed to explain how hundreds of millions of fans have never displayed the bizarre behavior of *Batman* fan James Holmes. Considering that Batman has enjoyed his status as the world's most popular superhero for over three-quarters of a century, the usual media critics and pop culture blamers would need to conjure up a credible explanation for the lack of influence elsewhere.

We are equally hard-pressed to ignore the striking parallels between Holmes and *Arkham Asylum* characters, especially since the neuroscience graduate student identified himself as the Joker when confronted by police outside the theater. Before we explore those similarities and find links to pressing medico-legal issues in psychiatry and con-

Batman action figure designed by Hot Toys and based on *Batman: Arkham City* (2011) game. Wearing his signature scowl and black leather cowl and cape, the heavily-muscled Batman assumes a fighting stance. In the original video game, Batman is lured into Arkham Asylum by Joker, who threatens to blind a young artist unless Batman takes her place among his hostages. In a later iteration, the incarcerated Batman loses touch with reality and believes he is psychotic.

troversies and misconceptions about the insanity defense, let's look at the specifics of that sad summer night in July 2012.

The Dark Knight Rises *Movie Massacre*

When a man slipped out of the shadows, with a gas mask hiding his face and body armor covering his neck, groin, limbs, and torso, it struck spectators as a gimmick, akin to William Castle–style 1950s special effects.[2] Few people believed that the scene was real—not staged—when they saw the gunman point and shoot. As smoke spiraled from gas canisters rolling down the aisles, it seemed even more gimmicky than before. Then chaos erupted when reality set in.

It was opening night of the movie. Twelve people died, including a child. A pregnant woman lost her baby—and permanent use of her legs. What motivates a man to shoot women, children, family men, a teenage boyfriend, a mother's son? We may never know the whole truth or perhaps it will be parceled out, in bits and pieces, should the murderer so choose.

According to psychiatrist William H. Reid, M.D., the court-appointed psychiatrist who evaluated Holmes and who recently published a book entitled, *A Dark Night in Aurora: Inside James Holmes and the Colorado Mass Shootings* (2018), "some of those currents will probably never come to light because they're locked inside Holmes mind, and even Holmes isn't aware of them."[3] For now, we know that convicted mass murder James Holmes pled not guilty because of insanity (which might have made him eligible for Arkham Asylum for the Criminally Insane, had this occurred in the fictional Batman universe). In the real world, the jury refused his plea, despite his psychotic appearance, disorganized speech and his well-documented history of psychiatric treatment. Holmes did not meet legal standards for NGRI (not guilty by reason of insanity) or even for "diminished capacity" (which spared Harvey Milk's murderer from the death penalty in San Francisco, thanks to the much-mocked "Hostess Twinkie Defense"). Holmes' mental capacity was intact, according to legal standards, because he planned the massacre for so many months and so methodically. Holmes actions were anything but impulsive.

So, Holmes was convicted and sentenced like any other criminal—although he was spared the death penalty, perhaps because of his psychiatric history. He is currently serving a life sentence without the possibility of parole. Unlike some criminal trials, there were no controversies about coerced psychotropic medications that could make him eligible to stand trial—since he was deemed capable of standing trial at the start.[4]

Court documents later confirmed that his one-time psychiatrist, Lynn Fenton, M.D., had warned campus police of Holmes' homicidal thoughts, and of his wish to "kill as many people as possible." However scary those statements sound, they did not meet the standards for the "Tarasoff Act," which requires mental health professionals to breech patient confidentiality and warn intended victims to protect themselves or to inform the police or to take other measures to protect potential victims if their patient reveals plans to harm a specific person via a credible means. (Voodoo dolls and Santeria spells do not qualify as realistic ways to cause harm.)

Holmes' threats were too vague to invoke the Tarasoff Act. He did not identify specific victims. Still, Dr. Fenton followed college policy and alerted campus police of Holmes' attempts to intimidate her, his threats against her, and her belief that he was potentially dangerous. That occurred about a month before the shooting and after Holmes' treatment with Dr. Fenton had ended. By then, he had left his school program and was no longer eligible for services through Student Health.[5] He was never involuntarily admitted to a psychiatric ward.

His psychiatrist would stand a different trial in a malpractice case (and in the court of public opinion). Families of the deceased alleged that her prescriptions for sertraline (a Prozac-like selective serotonin reuptake inhibitor type of antidepressant used to treat obsessive-compulsive disorder as well as depression) sent this graduate student spiraling into a state of psychosis and a disinhibited murder spree. After all, he had no prior arrest record. Many psychiatric professionals questioned her decision to postpone involuntary hospitalization and the anti-psychiatry activists, who always seem to be lurking in corners, readying themselves for the occasion to diss psychotropic drugs, could not complain about psychiatry's function as an arm of the state, prepared to use police power, because just the opposite occurred.

The media emphasized that Holmes initially identified himself as the Joker, Batman's historic archenemy. The Joker wears signature green and violet and has an over-sized grin that recollects Conrad Veidt's facial scars in a film entitled *The Man Who Laughs*

(1928). At the trial to determine the shooter's sanity, we learned that he filled his rented room with Batman memorabilia and that he literally was a "die-hard" Batman fan.[6] He also rigged his apartment with explosives set to go off upon entry.

In a strange twist of fate, the shooter sent a package to his former doctor. It included details about his mass murder plans. Sadly, the university mail system failed on that fateful day, and his package of deadly plans was not delivered until the event ended. We do not know if he hoped she would halt him and hospitalize him—or if she would join him, like Harley Quinn.

In an earlier *Batman* blockbuster starring the since-deceased Heath Ledger, the Joker ditched his customary costume, dressed in drag, and donned a nurse's uniform (crisp pointy white cap and

In Fritz Lang's *Metropolis* (1927), an early full-length SF feature film, Rotwang (Rudolf Klein-Rogge) stares ahead, his eyes open wide, looking like the proverbial mad scientist as he stands alone in his workshop, having just completed his human-machine replica of Maria (not seen). Mad scientists were once the most common movie villains. They abound in Arkham Asylum. The actor who played Rotwang became a villain himself by joining the Nazi party, while Fritz Lang, director of *Metropolis,* fled for his life, in what sounds like an action-adventure story.

all). He strolled through hospital halls, pushing his way through packed wards before exiting the hospital, and pressing a hand-held remote control to ignite explosives that he hid inside the building. He glances back as he walks away, while the building blows up in the background. Curiously, the mother of the Colorado shooting suspect is also a nurse. Even more curiously, she showed no surprise when authorities arrived at her door and suggested that her son might be a murderer.

We know that the troubled young neuroscience student planned and plotted for months, ordering weapons, ammunition, and combat apparatus to prepare for his attack. Those who know more about the expansive Batman universe—which exists in comics, film, TV shows, cartoons, graphic novels, video games, children's toys, Halloween costumes, school lunch boxes, pencil cases, and much more—should know that many sinister psychiatrists and deranged neuroscientists pepper Batman stories. It is easy to understand how an unstable person might gravitate to stories about powerful but pernicious mental health specialists, especially if he is studying neuroscience himself.

In psychiatric practice, we sometimes encounter someone who develops a "psychotic identification" with fictional characters. Their ego boundaries blur, leaving them incapable of separating their already hazy sense of self from well-defined fantasy roles. While most people can draw a line between themselves and imaginary roles seen on-screen, and can "suspend disbelief" only temporarily, returning to reality once the credits roll, a person who is descending into psychosis may not be able to shift gears, and might go so far as to say that he is "the Joker."

In the hours that followed the summer shootings, press reports (and photos) emphasized the suspect's orange hair, reporting this fact as confirmation that Holmes merged his own identity with the fictional Joker. They forgot—or never knew—that the Joker has green hair. No one mentioned the red-headed Mad Hatter, the psychotic and malevolent neuroscientist in the Batman universe. A sex worker whom Holmes frequented insisted that Holmes imitated her red hair.[7] Apparently, the worker looked in the mirror more often than she looked at comics.

Although the Joker is neither a psychiatrist nor a neuroscientist, the Joker has multiple links to psychiatry and psychosis, largely because he had extensive contact with mental health professionals and institutions (including a dalliance with one-time Arkham psychiatrist Harleen Quinzel a.k.a. Harley Quinn). After each arrest, the Joker is remanded to Arkham Asylum for the Criminally Insane, where is sprung by an attractive young psychiatrist who is assigned to treat him, but falls in love with him in the process, even though he chokes her and mistreats her, and even though professional ethics forbid romantic encounters between doctor and patient. Quinn joins the Joker on his crime spree, but later attempts to abandon her evil ways by joining a team of high-powered and high-minded female superheroes.

Psychiatric reports from the trial were released to the public in July 2018, yet even the court-appointed psychiatrist who spent hours, if not days, interviewing Holmes, and who authored a book on the topic admits that "much remains unknown." At present, we can only speculate about the dark recesses of James Holmes's mind.

Facts About the Fictional Arkham Mythos

To avoid falling down the rabbit hole that results from unsupported speculation, let us return to the imaginary Batman universe, where comic book pages appear in print, and are quotable, rather than hypothetical. Some comics show a scheming medical student who steps up after Harley Quinn departs. That aptly named student is Alyse Sinner. Her name is sometimes spelled Alice Synner. Appearance-wise, the plain-looking Alice/Alyse is no *femme fatale,* but mentally, her mind is as dark as the darkest shadows from 1940s-era *film noir.*

While working at Arkham Asylum for the Criminally Insane, Alyce befriends Dr. Jeremiah Arkham, a direct descendent of the deranged clan that started the Elizabeth Arkham Asylum for the Criminally Insane. He becomes her mentor. Alyse and this older psychiatrist become romantically entangled. Jeremiah is secretly known as Black Mask II, head of a collective called The Ministry of Science. Alyse encourages his evil activities as he rounds up The Reaper, Dr. Hugo Strange, Dr. Death, and Fright (Dr. Linda Friitawa), an albino geneticist who has lost her medical license in response to her unethical human experiments.

This "Ministry of Science" should not be confused with Fritz Lang's German Expressionist-influenced noirish classic, *Ministry of Fear* (1944)—even though Batman's creators were strongly influenced by *noir*'s aesthetic and by Fritz Lang's *Metropolis* (1926). Batman creator Bob Kane based Gotham City on the *Metropolis*'s towering Art Deco edifices, where dark shadows cast by sky-high high rises carve out deep caverns in the cityscape.

Batman's Ministry of Science contrasts sharply with DC comics' Justice League or Justice Society, where superheroes join forces to help humankind and improve society.

Some Ministry of Science scientists are starkly psychotic, while others, such as The Reaper, were deceived by evil-minded Ministry members. The Reaper is a rageful Holocaust survivor who is so preoccupied with his past that he becomes easy prey for villains who want to reel him into their ranks. Most other Ministry of Science members are stereotypical science fiction "mad scientist" villains, reminding us that mad scientists were the most common science fiction villains until the mid–20th century.

Mad Scientists and Murderous Mental Patients: Facts and Fictions

Those stereotypical mad scientists fell out of favor as the 20th century progressed, and as scientific advances became less frightening and more acceptable to the public. Education increased among Americans, thanks in no small part to the GI bill that sent veterans to college and to more advanced science classes. Television science shows for children, such as *Mr. Science*, demystified science. From the 1950s and 1960s, Sputnik and the Race to Space, Dr. Jonas Salk's miraculous polio vaccine, and TV broadcasts of the Cape Canaveral space launch turned scientists into kindly creatures to be admired, even emulated, rather than feared. Most importantly, the successes of Alfred Hitchcock's *Psycho* (1960) and John Carpenter's *Halloween* (1978) starred murderous mental patients who were scarier than earlier iterations of mad scientists.[8] *Batman* stories offered an admixture of both new and old-style villains.

As the asylums emptied in the late 1950s, thanks to the introduction of Thorazine (chlorpromazine) along with financial pressures to cut costs, many mental patients headed home. Until Thorazine's invention, the seriously mentally ill seemed destined to spend their lives locked inside state hospitals. After Thorazine stopped the disturbing and sometimes dangerous voices and visions of schizophrenia, the floodgates opened and the need for long-term institutionalization faded away—or so it seemed at the start.

The push for "deinstitutionalization" gained momentum. Institutions now aspired to send patients home—but not everyone had homes, and not everyone had neighbors who welcomed them back. Consequently, many ex-mental patients headed for the street or the shelters. Many meandered in public parks after being rejected by parents or siblings or returned to uncaring relatives or fractured families. Deinstitutionalization was eventually deemed a naive move, but its impact remained, both in public mental health policy and in popular movie themes.

Fears of being attacked by a "maniac"—or an escaped mental patient who left the wards before being completely cured—seemed more realistic than ever before. The ever-perceptive *Batman* writers tapped into these fears and created ever more villains. They turned science fiction's time-honored mad scientists into escaped psychiatric patients, locked in the wards of Arkham Asylum for the Criminally Insane, until they wrangled their way out of those confines, and managed to menace society again. A prime example is the Joker, who seduced his psychiatrist and convinced her to orchestrate his escape from Arkham.

Batman story arcs reflect these fears and parallel other shifts in psychiatric theory and practice. Two decades earlier, in the late 1930s, electroconvulsive therapy (ECT) arrived in America and introduced machine-mediated neuropsychiatric care. (Hydrotherapy as depicted in a charming 1909 Georges Méliès movie[9] cannot correctly be classified as mechanical or technical, even though its apparatus resembles primitive Jacuzzis.) Shock therapy uses dramatic and potentially dangerous machinery. The invention of the electroencephalogram (EEG) that traces brain waves made ECT possible. ECT machinery appealed to gadget geeks like Bruce Wayne and Alfred, and to mechanically minded comics fans who follow their escapades. Decades earlier, the fictional Dr. Amadeus Arkham allegedly murdered his murderous patient with ECT, apparently unaware that ECT or even EEG apparatus had not yet been invented.

Brain machines proliferate in *Batman*, and understandably so. In a 1990s cartoon, Dr. Hugo Strange uses brain machines to extract memories and steal identities. The War II–era *Batman* serials show "Japanazi" Dr. Daka as the "Yellow Menace" who drains brains via brain machines that physically resemble contemporary transcutaneous magnetic stimulation (TCMS), which have very different functions. Daka turns his brain-drained victims into zombies. Japanese wartime medical atrocities committed with Asian victims had not yet come to light, so it's unlikely that Dr. Daka represents reality-based events but likely that he is an American stereotype. Premonitions of modern-day neuroscience in 70-year-old *Batman* serials are eerie.

Characters such as Skulldugger, Riddler, Mad Hatter, and even aliens have access to brain machines. When aliens extract Bruce Wayne's memories, they reexperience his "screen memories" of his parents' murders. These aliens cannot tolerate the emotional angst of losing one's parents in such a manner and so they begin to self-mutilate, like real-life persons with borderline personality disorders who often experienced severe personal trauma in their past, along with inappropriate or inadequate parent-child relationships.

Batman comics revolve around Bruce Wayne, who inherited his family's wealth after he was orphaned as a boy. With Alfred's help, the youthful Bruce perfects skills needed to fight crime, and spends his money on crime-fighting gadgets, such as the Batmobile. The orphan theme holds special appeal for children, even though children are no longer *Batman*'s prime audience. Orphan stories address children's fears of abandonment, as they wonder if their missing parents will return. Those themes also allow "rehearsal space" to reconcile children's wishes to outdo their parents, so they will no longer need them when they become independent, versus the respect that they are expected to show parents. Orphan imagery mirrors fears about metaphorically killing off one's parents as children grow up and become more independent.

Oedipal overtones permeate almost all orphan stories. They reference Freudian theories about boys who wish their fathers dead, so that they can possess their mothers. In *Arkham Asylum,* the reverse occurs when Amadeus murders (or euthanizes) his mother yet calls out for his mother when stressed.

In Bruce's case, this "unresolved Oedipal complex" leaves Bruce unable to leave the nest and impairs his ability to establish adult relationships with women. Bruce is doomed to live his life in prepubescent fashion, essentially entombed in a family mansion with Alfred the Butler, and later reliant upon a boyish companion named Robin, who himself was orphaned when his parents were murdered while performing as circus acrobats.

In the *Gotham* TV series, Bruce's dalliances with Selina Kyle, a homeless and penniless runaway (or castaway) and possible prostitute, show his preference for "bad girls" from society's underbelly over his social or economic peers.[10] Whether or not Freudian theories are accurate is unimportant; what is important is that this motif reflects the cultural currency and mirrors the broader social concerns of the era in which it was created—the World War II–era.

Batman stories are known for their colorful villains who function as foils for the agile—and altruistic—hero who is sometimes misunderstood and mistaken for a villain himself. Villains add texture to the stories, making them more dramatic and multidimensional. The age-old appeal of "good versus evil" permeates *Batman* motifs and superhero stories in general.

The Joker is not the only villain to pass through the pages of *Batman* comics, but he is the best known and one of the earliest. Historically, *Batman* villains attracted Hollywood's most talented actors. The first Joker was a buffoon, played by a jovial Cesar Romero in the TV series. Then a petulant Jack Nicholson made his mark in Tim Burton's movie versions of *Batman*. Most recently, the drug-addled Heath Ledger portrayed the most diabolical Joker ever. Unfortunately, Ledger ended his life with a drug overdose before he could collect the Oscar he posthumously won for Best Supporting Actor in Christopher Nolan's dark interpretation of *The Dark Night*.

One trend among *Batman* villains deserves more mention here. True, most of these villains are motivated by deep psychological wounds and unresolved personal traumas, as would be expected of villains invented soon after Freud died in 1938, when psychoanalytically informed story structures gained greater cache.[11] Some characters (Two-Face, in particular) reflect Jungian depth psychology theories, which point out that masks and public faces (personas) and false personalities can conceal private psychological identities. In contrast, Dick Tracy comic strip villains, which premiered in 1931, are physically disfigured and easily identifiable by spectators and comics characters, but those villains are not necessarily psychologically maimed and need not carry invisible psychological wounds.

In *Batman,* psychiatrist-villains and neuroscientist-villains are especially prominent and stand out among the standard-brand "mad scientists" from science fiction stories. The presence of scientists is not so surprising if we recall that superhero stories are a subgenre of science fiction, and that early superhero authors fell under the spell of Hugo Gernsback's "scientific fiction" [sic] magazine, *Amazing Stories* (1926), which promoted the emerging genre of SF.

Geneticists are also common, and presumably merited extra attention when the Nazis controlled Germany, when *Batman* began. The Nazis based their "racial purity" policies on spurious eugenics theories that justified their genocide. *Batman* began just after World War II erupted in Europe, after Nazi Germany annexed Austria, and invaded parts of Czechoslovakia and Poland. *Batman* premiered in 1940, in the same year that the Reich launched "Operation T-4," with killing centers for mental patients, cognitively impaired persons and chronic alcoholics. Those centers became training grounds for SS officers who would soon run death camps.[12]

For the most part, German psychiatrists were the henchmen for theoretically oriented German geneticists. So, it makes sense that 1940s-era *Batman* geneticists morphed into practicing psychiatrists when the time was ripe. Psychiatrists personally chose which chronic mental patients and inveterate alcoholics led "lives not worth living" and decided whom to send to gas chambers built specifically for mental patients. In short order, those gas chambers would be repurposed for the annihilation of Jews and gypsies. The first commandant of Treblinka was a psychiatrist. He was the only physician to command a Nazi death camp. He gained necessary "expertise" through his experience as superintendent of Brandenburg Psychiatry Hospital.

Unlike the skillfully concealed mass murders of the Jews and gypsies, Nazi plans for the wholesale destruction of mentally and physically handicapped persons became

84   Section II: Forensic Psychiatric Controversies

public knowledge. These plans inspired so much protest from clergy and others that the process was halted—but not until 200,000 lives were lost. *Batman*'s Nazi-like scientists and diabolical "Japanazi" mind doctors (such as Dr. Daka in 1943 serials) eerily anticipate disclosures about human medical experiments of Unit 731, conducted by the Japanese Imperial Army in Manchuria during the Second Sino-Japanese War (1937–1945) of World War II. Experimental subjects were mostly of Chinese ethnicity, but some other Asian people were recruited as well.

As for neuroscientists, several exist in the Batman universe, including the orange-haired Mad Hatter, who is adapted from the *Alice in Wonderland* story. Author of *Batman Arkham Asylum: A Serious House on Serious Earth* credits Carroll's *Alice* for inspiration and opens and ends his graphic novel with excerpts from *Alice in Wonderland*.

More to the point, Mad Hatter's flame-colored tresses correspond to James Holmes's orange hair far more than the green-haired Joker. Even their professional aspirations coincide. Holmes is an itinerant neuroscientist and Jervis is an actual (albeit fictional)

Hugo Strange action figure by DC Direct Secret Files, *Batman* Rogues Gallery. Dr. Strange is one of *Batman*'s earliest villains and should not be confused with the mystical Marvel superhero, Dr. Stephen Vincent Strange, who was a haughty neurosurgeon before his disabling accident. Dr. Hugo Strange functions as both psychiatrist, administrator, and laboratory scientist in the *Arkham* mythos. He conducts horrific human experiments in his Indian Hill hideaway beneath Arkham Asylum and eventually releases his murderous monstrosities on Gotham City, so they can wreak havoc on the city and its inhabitants (photograph by George Higham).

neuroscientist. Mad Hatter uses dream machines to steal dreams or insert dreams. He hypnotizes some victims with pop-up eyes. He implants brain chips in others to wield control. He later dabbles in biological warfare in attempt to avenge the accidental death of his sister.

In his recent incarnation for *Gotham* television series, the otherwise malevolent and mentally unstable Jervish Tetch (Mad Hatter) appears as the loving and devoted but overly controlling brother of Alice Tetch. He desperately tries to save his sister from dying from her rare blood disease which can cause psychosis if injected into others and which can be weaponized for biological warfare. Ironically, she falls from a ledge and dies while attempting to escape Jervish. According to some story arcs, Alice acquired her illness from experiments conducted by Dr. Hugo Strange at his Indian Hill facility hidden beneath Arkham Asylum.

Some latter-day psychiatrist-villains began their comics' careers as neuroscientists, and transformed into psychiatrists only later, when *Batman* writers attempted to retaliate against one psychiatrist, Fredric Wertham, M.D., by discrediting psychiatrists in general. In contrast to the conflation of psychiatrists and psychologists found in many films and earlier comics, and even in clinical situations to this day, *Batman* writers knew that Dr. Wertham was an M.D. and so made a point of vilifying psychiatrists specifically, rather than denouncing all mental health professionals. In fact, clinical psychologists who treat patients—rather than just administer tests—had not entered practice when Dr. Wertham began his anticomics crusade in the 1950s.

Dr. Wertham labored to bring down the comics industry, testifying before Congress, hosting anticomics academic conferences, and writing a best-selling book about the evils of superheroes. The title of *Seduction of the Innocent* (1954) plays off the New Testament theme of the "massacre of the innocents," when King Herod ordered the murder of newborn baby boys.

Wertham vilified gruesome horror comics from the 1950s, and lampooned many superheroes, but he attacked Batman more than others, singling out the Batman-Robin "man-boy love" relationship and denouncing Bruce Wayne as a pedophile. For what it's worth, Wertham also called Superman a "fascist." Wertham was empowered by Eisenhower-era conservatism and McCarthy-era paranoia of the 1950s, compounded with Victorian-era values instilled in his youth, when he was born and reared in late 19th century Europe. Wertham reached conclusions that sound quaint today, if not outright offensive or patently illegal. In recent decades, Wertham's crusade against Batman and Robin inspired comedy spoofs (*The Ambiguously Gay Duo*) on the Dana Carvey Show and *Saturday Night Live* (*SNL*). Yet Wertham's attitude toward race was more progressive than his peers. He testified on behalf of desegregation in *Brown v. Board of Education* and opened a first-of-its-kind mental health clinic for Harlem residents who were denied services elsewhere.

Still, some very bad doctors appear in early *Batman* comics before Wertham's time. Dr. Hugo Strange appears shortly after the Joker's 1940 debut. Dr. Hugo Strange should not be confused with Marvel's 1960s-era superhero, Dr. Stephen Vincent Strange, the disabled neurosurgeon who travels to Tibet, studies magical medicine, sheds his pre-existing narcissistic personality traits and money-grubbing business practices, and does good works upon return.

DC Comics' Dr. Hugo Strange begins as a geneticist and not as a psychiatrist per se. Yet he trolls psychiatric institutions in search of subjects for his strange studies. He experiments on asylum inmates, turning them into monsters and releasing them into society where they can cause greater havoc. By the 1960s, Dr. Strange morphs into a full-fledged psychiatrist who is enlisted to conduct psychological stress tests of Wayne Enterprise employees. Hoping to confirm his suspicions about Bruce Wayne's secret life as Batman, Dr. Strange exposes Bruce to hallucinogens prior to conducting his psychiatric interview of Bruce.

We later learn that Hugo Strange was abandoned as a child and reared in state-run homes, where he was mistreated. Hugo's childhood contrasts with Bruce Wayne's upbringing. Bruce also lost his parents at a young age, but he was accidentally orphaned (rather than intentionally abandoned). Bruce has unwavering social support from his butler and finds a mission in life that enables him to become a hero, rather than a villain, like Hugo Strange.

Another early psychiatrist is Dr. Crane, who goes by the name "Scarecrow." Invented in 1941, Dr. Crane began his career as a psychology professor who studies phobias and the psychology of fear. After he fires a gun inside a crowded classroom and wounds a student—somewhat like the neuroscience graduate student who opened fire in a crowded movie theater—Professor Crane loses his job. To avenge his job loss, Crane murders professors who recommended his termination. He proceeds to lead a life of crime. In a film version, this retired professor (Cillian Murphy) heads Arkham hospital, where he mistreats mobsters. Television's *Gotham* fleshes out Jonathan Crane's youthful traumas and shows scenes where his biologist father subjects young Jonathan to psychedelic experiments that land the son in mental hospitals. This experience molds Jonathan's later life professional activities after he becomes Dr. Crane. In other words, the abused becomes the abuser, or "like father, like son."

Comics stories can be confusing and contradictory, *Batman* comics included. There are several versions of Dr. Crane's encounters with young Tommy Elliot, the Wayne family's neighbor who starts as a child murderer before becoming a surgeon. According to one version, Dr. Crane is asked to evaluate Tommy when Tommy is still a young boy. Tommy has attempted to murder his parents. Intrigued by the developmental process of evil children, and unconcerned with moral conduct or professional responsibilities, Dr. Crane, a forensic psychiatrist, clears Tommy for release from the mental hospital so that Crane can monitor his maturation.

This evil boy goes on to become an equally evil surgeon who goes by the name of "Hush." Dr. Elliot/Hush has a life-long "sibling rivalry" with his neighbor Bruce, another only child without siblings. Hush has plastic surgery, so he can impersonate Bruce and assume Bruce's identity. He is obsessed with Batman and struggles to uncover Batman's identity.

The Arkham clan of psychiatrists is arguably even more evil than their predecessors. The Arkhams are later inventions, mentioned only in passing in a 1974 comic. Len Wein later adds to the Arkham story arc, but the Arkham mythos is not fully fleshed out until Grant Morrison's 1989 graphic novel came about. The video game about *Arkham Asylum* (2009) expanded our knowledge of Arkham, its origins, and its twisted hospital staff. The elder Dr. Arkham opened the Arkham Asylum for the Criminally Insane after he euthanized his psychotic mother, who suffers from a nondescript neurodegenerative disorder that left her permanently hospitalized at the then-Arkham Hospital. His mother already transmitted her "degenerative" genes to her progeny, who staff the asylum and torture patients with shock therapy. Some Arkham psychiatrists drug patients and turn them into zombies that follow their doctors' evil instructions.

The stories about sinister psychiatrists and nasty neuroscientists in *Batman* are

This scene shows Caucasian actor J. Carrol Naish standing to the right of Dr. Martin Warren (Gus Glassmire), as he plays evil "Japanazi" Dr. Daka in Chapter 3 of the 1943 *Batman* serial. Dr. Warren's head is encased in a glass-topped contraption that will turn him into a mindless zombie. The Asian American actor B.D. Wong, who plays the diabolical Dr. Hugo Strange in the *Gotham* TV series, evokes memories of the evil Dr. Daka from 40s-era *Batman* serials. Dr. Daka's character has not yet appeared among the many doctor-villains in the *Arkham* franchise.

always evolving and show no signs of fading away. In February 2013, yet another sinister and psychotic psychiatrist appeared in *Batman* comics. Dr. Meredith commands his patients to kill, behaving in much the same way as Dr. Caligari did in the 1919 German Expressionist classic. Dr. Meredith abhors the insanity defense and dreads hospitals for the criminally insane, which include the Elizabeth Arkham Asylum for the Criminally Insane. Meredith is devastated when an even crueler court psychiatrist declares him psychotic and sentences him to Arkham Asylum.

In yet another eerie premonition, earlier *Batman* story arcs anticipated events that would occur in the James Holmes story. Or perhaps James Holmes's murder spree was an homage to a psychotic mélange of *Batman* characters. We may never know for sure what motivated the movie massacre, but even if Holmes cannot recount the thought processes that made him a mass murderer, we can be certain that the ever-inventive *Batman* creators will add more interesting arcs. Maybe some of those future stories will be as prophetic as ones mentioned above.

Notes

1. For earlier discussions of this evolving topic, see Sharon Packer and Jody Pennington, eds., *A History of Evil in Popular Culture: What Hannibal Lecter, Stephen King, and Vampires Reveal About America* (Santa Barbara, CA: ABC-Clio, 2014).

2. When home TV sets became increasingly common, Castle found ways to compete against television and bring viewers back to movie theaters. for more details on William Castle's 1950s-era horror film gimmicks, see Sharon Packer, *Movies and the Modern Psyche* (Westport, CT: Praeger, 2007); Sharon Packer, *Cinema's Sinister Psychiatrists: From Caligari to Hannibal* (Jefferson, NC: McFarland, 2012).

3. The Associated Press, WTOP.com, August 5, 2018; revised August 25, 2018. Accessed August 25, 2018.

4. Sam Quinones, Kim Murphy, and Joe Mozingo, "Aurora Suspect's Profile Grows Murkier," *Los Angeles Times*, July 23, 2012, http://articles.latimes .com/2012/jul/23/nation/la-na-colorado-shooting-sider-20120723 (accessed February 17, 2013).

5. *USA TODAY,* April 5, 2013. Accessed August 25, 2018.

6. Richard Esposito et al., "Aurora 'Dark Knight' Suspect James Holmes Said He 'Was the Joker': Cops," Video, http://abcnews.go.com/Blotter/auroradark-knight-suspect-joker-cops/story?id = 16822251 Accessed February 2013.

7. Kate Sheehy, "Redheaded Hooker Says Theater 'Gunman' James Holmes Copied Her with Hair Dye," *New York Post*, July 30, 2012, http://www.nypost .com/p/news/national/joker_hooker_hairdo_AzlVI3vR1wET qaiQG9AojN (accessed February 17, 2013).

8. Andrew Tudor, *Monsters and Mad Scientists: A Cultural History of the Horror Movie* (Cambridge, MA: Basil Blackwell, 1989). Tudor chronicles the shifts in protagonists in American horror films.

9. See Georges Méliès' *Hydrothérapie Fantastique* (Méliès, 1909).

10. In comic book *Batman* #50, "The Wedding of Batman," Bruce Wayne is about to marry Selina Kyle until she halts the wedding, realizing that making Bruce happy will ruin his motivation for being Batman.

11. Wieder D. Sievers, *Freud on Broadway: A History of Psychoanalysis and the American Drama* (New York: Cooper Square Publishers, 1970).

12. Rael D. Strous, "Nazi Euthanasia of the Mentally Ill at Hadamar," *American Journal of Psychiatry* 163, no. 1 (2006): 27.

SECTION III
Medical-Ethical Controversies

Anti-Psychiatry and the Arkham Asylum

Fernando Espí Forcén, M.D.

During the decades of the 1950s through 1970s, citizens of the Western world began to demand societal changes congruent with their new values and beliefs. These decades were marked by the beginning of the civil rights movement, the disapproval of military intervention and the fight for gender equality. Psychiatry, the field of medicine that studies human behavior, was also not immune to criticism. A new bulk of thinking known today as the anti-psychiatry movement challenged the current diagnostic methodologies, psychiatric treatments, and the whole conception of mental illness. This approach is currently called "critical psychiatry" and still attracts the attention of philosophically oriented psychiatrists, psychologists, and philosophers.

Background

The approach to and management of mental suffering and erratic behavior has been dynamic and congruent with societal values and thinking throughout the centuries. For example, with the popularity of Christianity within the Roman Empire, demonic possession became a valid construct to explain spiritual and subsequently mental suffering.[1] According to the Gospels, Jesus performed exorcisms to relieve suffering caused by tormenting demons. Following Jesus' example, throughout the centuries, priests and the devout performed exorcisms to help alleviate mental illness. Therefore, in a Christian-dominated society, exorcisms were an approved tactic to deal with mental illness. Nonetheless, demonic possession was not the only accepted theory to explain mental illness. Followers of Hippocratic medicine also believed that alterations in the four humors of the body could cause madness, such as the bite of a rabid dog. During the late Middle Ages, people gradually abandoned the rural areas to migrate to the cities. Citizens became wealthier, in part, due to the birth of the bourgeoisie, trade, and commerce. In parallel, friars abandoned the rural monasteries to preach in the cities against usury or to promote other Christian values. In 1409, in Valencia (modern day Spain), a priest named Joan Gilabert Jofre saw a mentally ill person repeatedly kicked in the street. Indignant, Jofre preached a sermon denouncing the physical and sexual abuse that men and women with mental illness suffered in the streets; he asked for funding to build a hospital that could

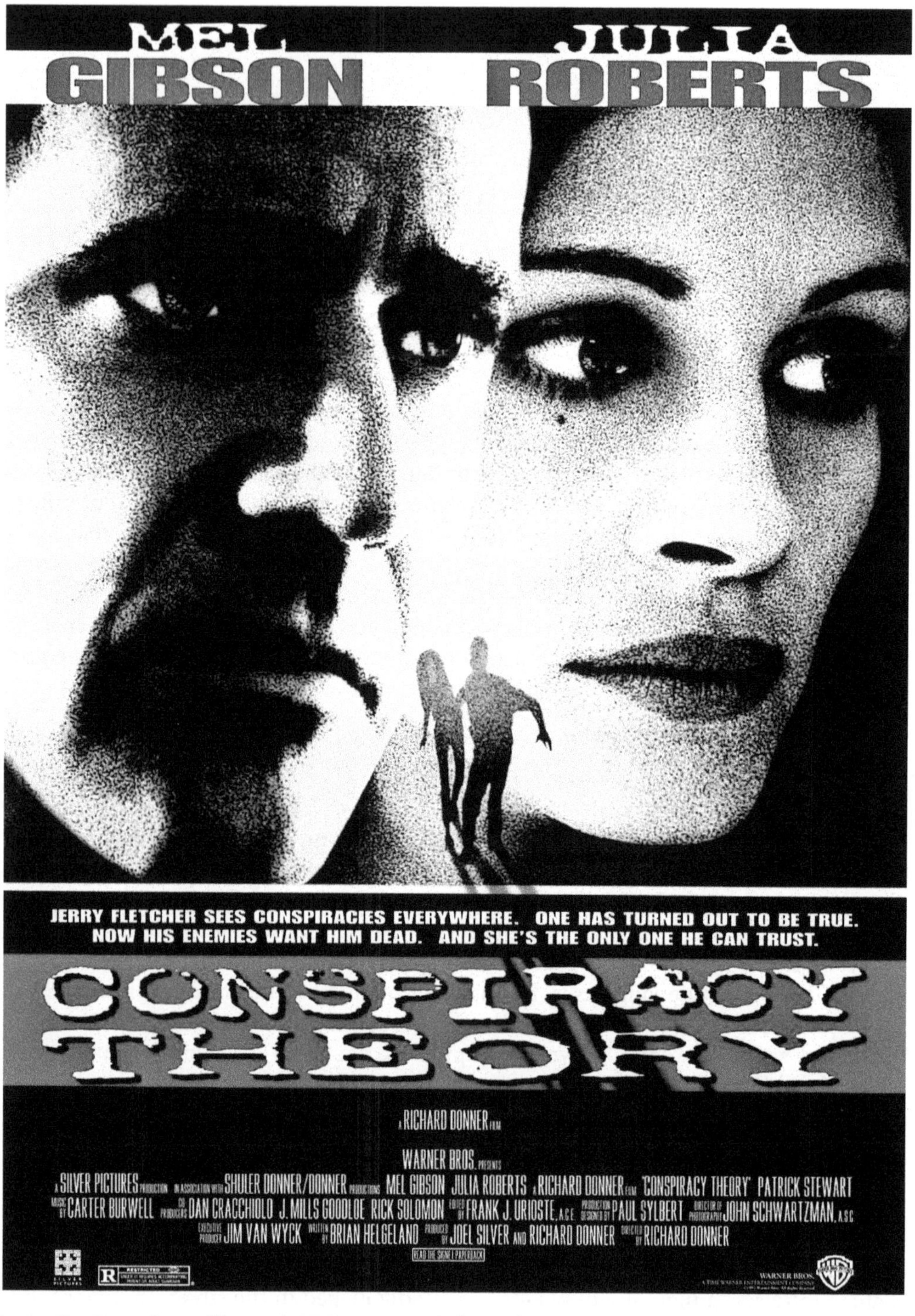

Poster for *Conspiracy Theory* (1997), starring Julia Roberts as romantic interest of Mel Gibson, who was subjected to botched experiments of CIA psychiatrist (Patrick Stewart) (not shown). The hallucinogenic experiments in this film are strikingly similar to CIA-sponsored hallucinogen experiments and parallel Dr. Jonathan Crane's hidden hallucinogens in *Arkham Asylum* stories (photograph by George Higham).

provide them with shelter and refuge. Jofre's efforts worked. Saint Mary of the Innocents Hospital was completed in 1409. Doctors there were pioneers for occupational therapy and rehabilitation; soon after, other hospitals with similar characteristics were built in Barcelona, Toledo, and Saragossa. Remaining active for centuries, Saint Mary of the Innocents Hospital inspired Philippe Pinel who visited the facility prior to developing Moral Treatment during the Enlightenment.[2] Congruent with the changes in thinking during the 18th century, Pinel advocated for a more humane treatment for mental illness, proposing unique communities where they could live, learn the rules of community life, and work before reintegrating into society. Pinel preached against purging, bloodletting, and other less humane treatments and confectioned one of the first classifications of the different types of mental illnesses. The innovative approach that he called Moral Treatment established the type of asylum care that dominated psychiatric treatment until the deinstitutionalization that resulted from the anti-psychiatry movement in the 1970s.

Pinel proposed that both staff and patients should live together in the same hospital. His pupil, Esquirol, preached these ideas all over France. In the United States, the first Asylum with similar characteristics was built in Utica, New York, in 1846. During the second decade of 19th century, Dr. Thomas Kirkbride in Philadelphia proposed that asylums should be constructed under his new architectural plan. He suggested these hospitals should have a central building for administration and staff with adjacent buildings on both sides where the patients would reside. This design would allow more air and light to enter the rooms, features that were considered therapeutic. Kirkbride proposed that these buildings should be constructed in rural areas so that patients could be in closer contact with nature and with farmlands so that they could work the land as part of their occupational therapy and rehabilitation. City planners and politicians welcomed Kirkbride's ideas, and during the second half of the 19th century, multiple asylums were built following this architectural design in the then popular Victorian Style. The new model of care that had started at the end of the 18th century became standard psychiatric treatment; fortunately, many patients with developmental and intellectual disabilities, psychotic disorders, neurosyphilis, and severe mood disorders were being transferred to these newly designed hospitals. At the end of the 19th century and the beginning of 20th century, asylums suffered significant budget cuts; consequently, quality care became scarcer. Moreover, in the field of psychiatry, psychoanalysis emerged as the new trend. Psychiatrists became less interested in working in asylums and started opening private practices in the cities to provide care for anxiety neuroses, stemming from urban life. Still, the demand to transfer the severe mentally ill to asylums continued in the same years that witnessed the gradual abandonment and neglect of these institutions. Asylums became overcrowded and the physicians working there were disconnected from academic centers and the emergent bulk of science surrounding neuropathology. In first half of the 20th century, the physician-patient ratio could well have been 1:1000. The catastrophic decline of the once successful asylum care model was an imminent reality.

During the 20th century, new somatic treatments in psychiatry emerged outside of the traditional treatment. In 1927, in response to the theory that sleep could be beneficial to treat mental illness, and in response to his personal observations while treating persons with addictive disorders, Austrian psychiatrist Manfred Sakel introduced insulin coma therapy which consisted of giving patients large doses of insulin to induce a hypoglycemic coma for several weeks. After recovering from the coma, up to 50 percent of patients showed improvement in mental symptoms. However, insulin coma therapy carried significant medical risks such as death from hypoglycemia or brain damage. In 1934, Ladislas Medula in Hungary thought that convulsive seizures could be therapeutic based on neuropathological observations that people with epilepsy had more glial cells (cells that nurture the neuron) than average, and people with schizophrenia had fewer than normal glial cells. He used a chemical to cause seizures in several patients with psychoses (9 out of 11 had catatonia) and saw a significant improvement in these patients. However, the two major problems were the difficulty to induce seizures and the lack of tolerance of the side effects these chemicals caused. In 1938, Italian neurologist Ugo Cerletti proposed the use of electricity to induce seizures. Through electrical currents it was easier to induce the seizures, and this therapy was more tolerable for the patient. That was the birth of electroconvulsive therapy.

Another somatic treatment that evolved in the first half of the 20th century was psychosurgery. In 1935, Portuguese neurologist, Antonio Egas Moniz, with the help of neurosurgeon, Pedro Lima, performed ablation of the white matter in the prefrontal cortex of patients with melancholy and obsessive-compulsive disorder. They coined this procedure "frontal leucotomy." Moniz believed excessive function and abnormalities in the prefrontal cortex caused excessive ruminations. In the United States, neurologist Walter Freeman performed the same procedure at George Washington University in 1936 with the help of neurosurgeon James Watts. After that, Freeman had a new idea to decrease the cost of this type of surgery with the goal of making it available to patients living in asylums. Using an ice pick from his kitchen, he was able to access the frontal lobe through the orbit of a pig's head. He called this new procedure "transorbital lobotomy" and began traveling in his van (which he called the "lobotomobile") to asylums across the states. The practice of the lobotomy rapidly declined with the introduction of chlorpromazine. Initially manufactured as an anesthetic, chlorpromazine was found to have an important effect in patients with psychosis and agitation, to everyone's surprise. These new somatic treatments were incorporated as part of the asylum care during this century and were the subject of intense criticism in the advent of the anti-psychiatry movement.

The Anti-Psychiatry Movement

In the decade that followed World War II, the United States saw an improvement in the economy. Houses and cars became more affordable, and people started abandoning the cities to buy land with more space in the suburbs. As a result of the increase in GHP and wealth, not to mention the development of the automobile industry, consumerism became a standard way of life leading to sedentary lifestyles and obesity. But this crass materialism was rejected by those who embraced the new Eastern traditions, sexual liberation, racial equality, and experimentation with psychedelic substances. This free-thinking segment of society would deeply impact society at large in the following decades. The civil right movement, the hippie generation, feminism, and psychedelia marked the counterculture of the 1960s and 1970s. This new generation of thinkers became critical of traditional values and the old authority. Psychiatry, a discipline that was often viewed as a tool of the government for behavioral control, did not escape criticism.

The anti-psychiatry movement started almost simultaneously in Europe and the United States, led by psychiatrists dissatisfied with the methodologies and treatments of the time. Following World War II, Europe blamed humankind (rather than God) for the disasters and calamities, and a new philosophy arose called "existentialism" which dominated the thinking of society in the 1950s. For the existentialist, it was important to rethink the role of humans in future societies. French philosopher Jean Paul Sartre is one of the leading thinkers in existential philosophy. Sartre's key maxim is that existence precedes essence. Therefore, humans have absolute freedom to define what they are and, consequently, each human would contribute to the definition of humanity. Sartre recognized that only humans could reflect about themselves as objects, and therefore the experience of "being" human is unique in the natural world. This capacity to reflect leads humans, according to Sartre, to impose a meaning on existence. Another existential philosopher, Karl Jaspers criticized the then diagnostic and treatment methodologies in psychiatry and proposed a biographical method to understand a patient's symptoms including much more personal information to understand the person's unique experience of the symptoms. Regarding psychoses, Jasper distinguished between primary delusions that were often not understandable versus secondary delusions that were congruent with the person's background. Silvano Arieti, an Italian immigrant in New York City, argued that, unlike other medical diseases, mental illness could not be understood in terms of Virchowian cellular pathology. He stated that while most scientists were still interested in the identification of a biological substrate of mental illness, he identified more with a psychological approach, a minority view. In *Interpretation of Schizophrenia* (1955), Arieti views the disorder as an unrealistic way to represent the self and the world and attempts to explain schizophrenia from a psychodynamic point of view.[3]

In the midst of the emerging anti-psychiatry movement, existentialism gave birth to existential psychiatry which significantly influenced the generation of European psychiatrists in the 1950s. In 1960, Scottish existential psychiatrist Ronald David Laing published *The Divided Self*. In this book, he theorized that the insecurity about one's experience (ontological insecurity) prompts a defensive reaction in which the self splits into separate components, thus generating the psychotic symptoms that characterize schizophrenia. Laing, however, differed from Jaspers in that he believed primary delusions could also be analyzed and understood from the person's experience. Laing was opposed to the standard treatments available for patients with schizophrenia at the time, such as electroconvulsive therapy and traditional asylum care. As a result, he created a new innovative institution called Kingsley Hall. In this facility patients could enter and leave the hospital at their will. Patients were treated with kindness and respect, and the model of care was largely influenced by Eastern philosophies and Shamanism. There was a room for meditation and patients were encouraged to express their artistic talent and creativity. Additionally, patients could even experiment with LSD and DMT. Laing also published literature on relationships and mental illness. He believed the relationship between a person and his or her family members (as well as larger society) could explain mental illness. David Cooper, a South African psychiatrist, moved to the United Kingdom and collaborated closely with Laing. Cooper considered himself an existential Marxist. Concomitant with the consolidation of communism in Russia and China, some sectors in Europe embraced the ideas of Karl Marx to explain problems in society and even mental illness. Cooper believed that mental illness could result from a mismatch between one's true identity and the identity society imposes. He believed that revolution could be the solution to the problem. He highly criticized the state of psychiatry in *Psychiatry and Anti-psychiatry* (1967), a book that named the incipient movement.[4] Moreover, Cooper argued that the family was an oppressive system that restricted freedom and autonomy. To deal with that oppressive system, Cooper argued that a person should break free from their families in a radical way, not only beyond geographical separation, but also by stopping all relations and even disconnecting from one's own family past.[5]

During the 1960s, the asylum model of care was highly criticized. Between 1955 and 1959, French philosopher and historian Michel Foucault wrote *Folie et déraison: Histoire de la folie à l'âge classique* (Madness and Civilization). In this book, Foucault analyzed the role of the mentally ill in society during the Renaissance, the Enlightenment and Modern times. Foucault noticed that during the Renaissance people with mental illness were depicted as wise in paintings and therefore had a place in society. In contrast, during the Enlightenment, when different societal behaviors were depicted rationally, the mentally ill were seen as outcasts along with the homeless, beggars, and prostitutes. According to Foucault, the Modern era was marked by the creation of confinement institutions supervised by physicians with a double purpose: to exclude these undesired members from society and to cure them while keeping them away from families that could not afford the treatments. For Foucault, psychiatry was a government tool for behavioral control in society.[6] In 1961, Canadian sociologist Erving Goffman wrote *Asylums* in which he discussed his theory of "total institution." Based on his observations working as a physical therapist at a mental institution in Washington, D.C., Goffman observed that once patients are admitted, they go through a process of institutionalization that can be as powerful as the cure process. Thus, accepting their new role and function as mental patients can be as important as their cure.

Franco Basaglia was an Italian psychiatrist fond of the theses of Sartre, Jaspers, Foucault, and Goffman; while working at the asylum of Gorizia, Basaglia criticized the treatments offered there such as ice packs, straitjackets, and isolation rooms while demanding more humanitarian care. Like Goffman, Basaglia agreed that asylums served as oppressive, locked, total institutions where staff inflicted recurring punishments when patients displayed undesirable behavior. Therefore, he proposed the deinstitutionalization of the inmates living in asylums and their return to the community. His efforts resulted in the entire reform of the Italian health system regarding psychiatric care. The Italian Mental Health Act of 1978, also known as Basaglia Law, closed all asylums in Italy; as a result, patients gradually returned to the community. One of Basaglia's pupils, Giorgio Antonucci, has, to this date, carried on Basaglia's legacy.[7]

Perhaps the greatest opponent to psychiatry was Thomas Szasz, who led the anti-psychiatry movement in the United States where he became the icon of psychiatric criticism. Szasz was born to a Jewish family in Budapest in 1920 and in 1938 migrated to the United States where he graduated from medical school at the University of Cincinnati. After finishing his residency, Szasz spent five years at the Chicago Psychoanalytic Institute and then joined SUNY Upstate as faculty. Szasz considered mental illness a disease only in the metaphorical sense. In 1961 he published *The Myth of Mental Illness*. In this book he discussed that the word "disease" denotes a demonstrable biological process that affects the body. For Szasz, the term "mental illness" referred instead to the undesirable thoughts, feelings, and behaviors of persons. Thus, classifying thoughts, feelings, and behaviors as diseases was a logical and semantic error. Szasz believed that individuals with mental illness had no problem in their brains unlike individuals with diseases in other organs. As such, he criticized the classification of mental illnesses as diseases, the lack of science in psychiatry, the use electroconvulsive therapy, psychopharmacology, pharmacotherapy, psychotherapy, involuntary hospitalization and the insanity defense. For him, psychiatry was to control mood, thought, and behavior. Hence, like the political practice of separating church and state, Szasz proposed that psychiatry too be separated from the state.

The Anti-Psychiatric Aesthetic in the Arts and the Arkham Asylum

The anti-psychiatry movement impacted the art and literature of the Beat generation and the counter-culture. Ken Kesey, who had participated in an LSD study led by the CIA, published *One Flew over Cuckoo's Nest* in 1962. This novel narrates the story of a man with behavioral problems who is committed to an asylum. At the asylum, a psychopathic nurse recommends electroconvulsive therapy and a lobotomy for punishment and behavior control. The novel was a commercial success and in 1975 Miloš Forman directed the film with the same name, which won best picture from the Academy Awards. During the decades following the anti-psychiatry movement, several films reflected on this fear of losing one's mind and being committed to a psychiatric hospital where electroconvulsive therapy and sedative medication were the standard treatment. These fears were especially present in horror films such as *Don't Look at the Basement* (1973) or the more recent TV Show *American Horror Story: Asylum* (2012–2013).[8]

Actors William Redfield, Sydney Lassick, Jack Nicholson, Christopher Lloyd, Vincent Schiavelli, William Duell (left to right) play patients who lounge around the psych ward in *One Flew Over the Cuckoo's Nest* (1975), just before the chaotic "I want my cigarette scene." *Arkham Asylum: A Serious House on Serious Earth* mirrors the anti-psychiatry attitudes cemented by Miloš Foreman's film adaptation of Ken Kesey's novel. *Arkham*'s knife-wielding, self-mutilating character, Victor Zsasz, recollects arch-anti-psychiatrist Thomas Szasz, M.D., a Hungarian transplant who held an academic psychiatry post in SUNY upstate medical school.

Anti-psychiatry has left its print in the arts, music, cinema, literature, and comics. In Batman's Arkham Asylum, for example, the hospital is depicted as a locked institution for involuntary confinement. Patients are not allowed to leave the institution; the facility resembles a prison more than a care center. Both patients and staff members can succumb to insanity if they stay there. As such, the Arkham experience follows the pattern of Goffman's "total institution" theory. According to Batman comics, the treatments implemented are not effective and patients' mental health deteriorates even more after questionable psychotherapeutic interventions. In Arkham, electroconvulsive therapy is practiced as punishment and revenge. That is the case of Dr. Amadeus Arkham, who uses electroconvulsive therapy on the villain Mad Dog, electrocuting him to death, a punishment the doctor administers to avenge the death of his wife and daughter.

The depiction of Arkham Asylum follows the model of the Kirkbride architectural model. The hospital has a central building for administration with small stairs and an entrance. Attached are the different pavilions of the hospital designed in a wing shape plan to allow air and light, as well as symbolically resembling a bat. The facade and structure resemble the Victorian style. This architectural style was named after Queen Victoria of Great Britain who reigned during the second half of the 19th century. During the Romanticism that characterized the 19th century a new interest in medieval themes grew in society. Congruent with that, Victorian style is characterized by a Medieval Gothic revival combined with other styles. The Parliament of Westminster and the Saint Pancras Station in London are good examples of this Gothic revival. The Gothic elements and tower of the building, together with the influence from German expressionism in the representation of Arkham Asylum, give a special tenebrous aspect that enhances the inhospitable atmosphere of the care center. Also, loyal to this Kirkbride construction, Arkham is located in the deep suburbs of Gotham City, separated from the urban center.

Throughout the Batman comics there are multiple references to psychoanalytic Freudian and Jungian concepts. The assassination of Elizabeth Arkham has interesting parallels with that of Norman Bates in *Psycho* (1960). Additionally, the comics have direct references to the leaders and writings of the anti-psychiatry movement. The clearest example is the villain Victor Zsasz whose name has an interesting resemblance with that of the most prominent anti-psychiatry leader in the United States, Thomas Szasz. According to the Batman comics, Victor Zsasz was born to a wealthy family and at the age of 25 he was leading the family's international corporation. One day, both of his parents died in a boat accident. After that, Zsasz fell victim to gambling and other vices. One night he lost everything to the Penguin, became depressed, and felt that his existence was meaningless. As a result, he decided to take his life by jumping off the Gotham Bridge but was interrupted by a homeless man who tried to assault him with a knife. Zsasz grabbed the man's arm, stared into his eyes, suddenly understanding that not only his own life but all life was meaningless and that nothing mattered. Taking the man's knife, Zsasz killed him to liberate the man from his pointless existence. After that murder, Zsasz murdered others to liberate them too. Zsasz suffered several incarcerations at the Arkham Asylum and was labeled insane but frequently broke out to continue killing. At the asylum, Zsasz is treated by Jeremiah Arkham, the nephew of Amadeus Arkham, who inherited the asylum. Zsasz is able to manipulate Jeremiah to use him as a henchman. The parallels between Victor Zsasz and Thomas Zsasz are loose and no more than a similarity in name. But one key similarity beyond the names is that the fictional character and the psychiatrist lose their faith in something they had invested in for years; and both attempt to destroy it. Victor Zsasz, however, seems to believe in existentialism, the philosophy that impacted the beginning of the anti-psychiatry movement. He lost his parents and his wealth, hardships which led him to feel that he was alone in the world and that existence was pointless and meaningless. Zsasz's attitude toward life reflects the nihilistic ideas of Arthur Schopenhauer who was a defender of suicide as a legitimate response to a meaningless existence. In Batman, another comic story arch with an anti-psychiatry association is *Death of the Family* (2012), a reference to *A Death in the Family* (1988) in which the Joker assassinates James Todd. These titles as well match David Cooper's *The Death of The Family* (1974).

Aftermath

When asylum care declined, and society demanded more autonomy and freedom, the criticism that came with anti-psychiatry carried important measures intended to bring patients more humanitarian treatment and to respect their autonomy. New community-based care models arose involving social workers, visiting nurses, and other care professionals. Still, the somatic treatments of the first half of the 20th century prevailed and continue to be valid treatments in the scientific community. Chlorpromazine, and other neuroleptic medicines developed from it, continues to be prescribed for psychosis, delirium, and mood disorders. Electroconvulsive therapy continues to be an empirically effective standard treatment in catatonia and refractory mood disorders. Though psychosurgery has been largely abandoned, minimal ablation of neurological sites with laser surgery continues to be exceptionally practiced in specific institutions. Moreover, new invasive therapies such as deep brain stimulation can be indicated in pain, neurological, and some psychiatric disorders such as obsessive-compulsive disorders. Although no specificity for the phenomenology of psychiatric disorders has been found, advances in neuroscience have shown inflammation, neurological, and genetic abnormalities in patients who suffer severe mental illness. Now more than ever, an argument for a biological genesis of psychiatric disease can be made. Psychiatry, nonetheless, continues to be the subject of criticism in our current society. Several intellectual and leaders in the field have challenged the current practice of limited-time appointments, involvement of the pharmaceutical industry, and the excessive reliability on a drug-centered paradigm of care. A new form of residential treatment is needed for patients with severe mental illness who end up becoming homeless or incarcerated. Our society now demands a more balanced biopsychosocial model to understand mental illness, its treatment, and the re-integration of psychotherapy as part of the regular model of patient care. In a constructive, critical manner, the spirit of anti-psychiatry must continue.

Notes

1. Carlos Espí Forcén and Fernando Espí Forcén, "Demonic Possessions and Mental Illness: Discussion of Selected Cases in Late Medieval Hagiographical Literature," *Early Science and Medicine* 19 (3) (2014): 258–79.
2. Fernando Espí Forcén, "A Hospital for the Mentally Ill in the Middle Ages—Psychiatry in History," *The British Journal of Psychiatry* 208(2) (2016): 103.
3. Silvano Arieti, *Interpretation of Schizophrenia: Second Edition, Completely Revised and Expanded* (New York: Basic, 1974).

4. D.G. Cooper, *Psychiatry and Anti-psychiatry* (Oxon: Routledge, 2007).
5. David Cooper, *The Death of the Family* (Harmondsworth: Penguin, 1980).
6. Michel Foucault and Richard Howard, *Madness and Civilization: A History of Insanity in the Age of Reason* (Abingdon, Oxon: Routledge Classics, 2009).
7. Franco Basaglia, *L'instituzione Negata* (Torino, Italy: Einaudi, 1973).
8. Fernando Espí Forcén, *Monsters, Demons and Psychopaths: Psychiatry and Horror Film* (Boca Raton: CRC, 2017); Susan Hatters Friedman et al., "Horror Films and Psychiatry," *Australasian Psychiatry* 22(5) (2014): 447–49.

Harley Quinn and the Joker
Pitfalls of Doctor-Patient Romances

Sharon Packer, M.D.[1]

Several daytime television soap operas featured steamy stories about doctor-patient romances and other sundry hospital-based adventures (or misadventures). *General Hospital* was one of the longest running of those soaps but surely not the only one of its ilk. The soaps were extremely popular with some of the public, especially before reality TV overshadowed those fictional scripts. Yet the soaps had already lost much of their traditional female audience base when women entered the workforce and left home en masse, even before arrival of reality TV. Until then, the soaps left many loyal fans glued to their TVs day after day. These cliff hangers were compelling, so much so that some hospitalized patients begged to postpone their morning doctor visits, so they could complete their soap story arc, uninterrupted, instead.

Yet those shows were misleading. As much as those memes appealed to their devoted fan base and added needed plot twists to potentially anemic doctor dramas, doctor-patient romances or sexual encounters depart from medical ethical and medicolegal standards. Strict legal and ethical taboos against romantic relationships between doctors and patients exist across the U.S. Sexual contact, even when consensual, is off-limits. These professional standards have become more stringent—not less stringent—in recent decades, even though society's overall acceptance of non-marital sex and non-heterosexual sexual preferences and its awareness of non-binary gender identities has broadened dramatically since the heyday of the soap operas. Psychiatrists and gynecologists are especially intolerant of such behavior and express more condemnation than other medical specialists.

Despite the many potential pitfalls that await those who disregard such standards, those standards are violated time and time again, not by all physicians and not even by most physicians but by a very small minority who commandeer a disproportionately large press. Sometimes, even by those who should "know better" skirt these unwavering standards. When highly placed professionals break those boundaries, they become fodder for hospital cafeteria small talk before their antics turn into tabloid news and catalyze even more extreme consequences.

"Boundary breaking" is psychiatric jargon for breaking *any* boundaries that protect patients against exploitation by health care providers who hold greater power, be it sexual, financial, professional, or emotional. Physicians who bypass boundaries risk legal and administrative charges. Civil lawsuits and criminal charges and sometimes even convictions await them. Licenses are lost or limited, and lawsuits ignited, in response to such entanglements.

Out-and-out accusations of sexual harassment or sexual exploitation—or even rape—can occur and in fact have been made after the fact by divorcing spouses who married the offending physician years earlier. Allegations of "unprofessional behavior" sound vague but reports to the state medical board can carry very concrete consequences. Medical boards, which operate under their own jurisdictions, unsupervised by civil and criminal courts, are not subject to the same standards of evidence. They are reputed to have even lower tolerance and to impose higher penalties than criminal courts or civil proceedings. The recent #me too movement embodies this anti-sexual exploitation sentiment but is late to the party by over a century; these events have been reported for the longest time and were topics of discussion among early psychoanalysts.

The film *A Dangerous Method* (Cronenberg, 2011)[2] capitalized on titillating stories about *Jungenfrau* (Carl Jung's women) by depicting the torrid romance and kinky sex that allegedly took place between psychoanalyst Carl Jung and his youthful patient (and future psychoanalyst), Sabina Spielrein. The Swiss-born and based Jung was Freud's one-time heir apparent until their bitter falling out. Jung was the son of a Zwingli Protestant minister while Spielrein was a wealthy young Russian Jewess who was admitted to the Bergholzi, a long-term Swiss psychiatric hospital. Spielrein eventually recovered from her psychiatric ailments and went on to study medicine and practice psychoanalysis herself for many years after her hospital discharge—before ultimately dying at the hands of the Nazis. Jung, in the interim, racked up a reputation as a womanizer and as a mystic (and cult leader, according to Richard Noll[3]).

Curiously, medical malpractice insurance carriers do not defend doctors against charges of sexual misconduct since such behavior does not fall within the scope of "professional practice" that their policies insure against. Should a civil lawsuit follow, damages may be difficult to prove and even harder to collect on, given the lack of support from malpractice insurance. Even if accusations do not convince a "jury of peers," or hold up in civil court (where strict standards of proof apply), such allegations shatter professional reputations and personal bonds while the acts themselves likely leave permanent scars on patients' psyches.

Standards have not always been so strict, but standards existed nonetheless and were articulated over a century ago. In the early days of psychoanalysis, Freud spoke of possible breeches. He admonished his acolytes against over-familiarity with patients (even though he invited some of his own patients to tea or even supper and treated patients as they reclined on a couch in his living room). He advised his trainees "not to let patients drive them crazy." Freud commented on transference and countertransference that occur when the patient develops intense emotional ties to the therapist (or vice versa, in the case of countertransference, where the therapist experiences his or her own emotional reactions to the patient).[4] Freud published a paper on "Recommendation to Physicians Practicing Psycho-analysis" in 1912 but he restricted related publications to analysts, hoping to hide details from the prying (and prurient) eyes of the public.

While many professionals and members of the public do not agree with much of what Freud wrote, most would agree that Freud had good reason for concern about possible sexual boundary breaking during psychoanalysis. For some of his most prominent acolytes indulged in such transgressive sexual behavior. In addition to Jung, who fell out of Freud's favor shortly after publication of the 1912 paper, albeit for very unrelated reasons, early psychoanalytic luminaries such as Wilhelm Stekel, Sandor Ferenzi and Ernest Jones became embroiled in unacceptable sexual conduct, sometimes with patients and sometimes in their personal life.

Since then, specifics about such breeches—and ways to avoid them—have filled entire academic books. This topic typically attracts attentive audiences at psychiatric conferences and at times fills lecture rooms beyond capacity, with listeners spilling into the halls. Gabbard's 1995 research on *The Early History of Boundary Violations in Psychoanalysis* chronicles those early 20th century events that tainted Freud's circles. Gabbard explains how the nascent psychoanalytic movement struggled to circumscribe professional boundaries, even though psychoanalytic circles and theories were still ill-defined and still evolving and best described as "embryonic."

A psychoanalyst himself, as well as a psychiatrist and a film scholar, Glenn Gabbard, M.D., examines "boundary violations" (the current euphemism) in his 1995 collaboration with Eva Lester, M.D., entitled *Boundaries and Boundary Violations in Psychoanalysis*.[5] Gabbard's shorter article on "Patient-Therapist Boundary Issues," published in *Psychiatric Times* on October 1, 2005,[6] summarizes salient issues, while his collaboration with forensic psychiatrist Thomas Guthiel, M.D., appears in an article entitled, "Boundaries in Clinical Practice," published in *American Journal of Psychiatry* (April 2006, online).[7] The already lengthy list of must-read articles on the topic grows longer over time. The names of some researchers appear repeatedly in this list.

The growing attention to such issues does not seem overblown and is not merely a reflection of publicity-hungry journalists who seek "clicks" to survive at a time when the ranks of employed reporters shrink as more populist social media gains steam. More recently, the chair of a large New York medical school psychiatry department stood accused of sexual improprieties with a patient. He attempted suicide after details of the affair came to light via a lawsuit. In the summer of 2017, the off-campus sexual antics of an esteemed medical school dean became public and cost him his academic position and professional standing. Far less illustrious practitioners have faced similar charges, but their situations do not stir such publicity or public commentary and often go unknown to anyone outside of their immediate communities.

In a book about *Psychiatry and the Cinema*, 2nd edition (APPI, 1999),[8] Gabbard and Gabbard dissect the depictions of female physicians and psychiatrists in film. The Gabbards note that the female cinematic psychiatrists typically get involved in romantic, if not also sexual, trysts with their celluloid patients. This recurring movie trope stands contrary to fact—yet it mirrors the comic book depiction of Harley Quinn's unsavory relationship with her patient-turned-consort and eventual partner-in-crime, Joker. Pop culture stereotypes reify one another.

In film, female psychiatrists are likely to be sexualized. Sometimes those fictional film psychiatrists even become entangled with female patients, as seen in *Side Effects* (Soderbergh, 2013),[9] whose storyline was inspired by a practicing Bellevue psychiatrist who assisted in the film's production. Every so often, those female psychiatrists are sexually exploited by sadistic men they encounter, as depicted in *Jade* (Friedkin, 1995), a film that is noteworthy largely because it was directed by the same man who won Academy Awards for *The French Connection* (1971) and the iconically frightening film, *The Exorcist* (1973), as well as the controversial gay crime film and sadomasochistic sensation, *Cruising* (1980). Like *Cruising, Jade* revolves around S&M and prostitution, as practiced by an otherwise reputable married female psychiatrist who is ultimately rescued by her amazingly understanding and successful but voyeuristic husband.

In real life, as opposed to reel life, female psychiatrists are much less likely to be charged with sexual boundary breaking than are male psychiatrists—but sensationalized cases occasionally come to light because they include extreme or unusual behavior that wavers far from the norm. When that happens, the events often make front-page news, especially when serious injuries or deaths follow. That was the case when a Boston-based, Harvard-affiliated psychiatrist sent provocative selfies to a young male medical student whom she treated but who subsequently suicided. In the summer of 2018, the bizarre behavior of a psychiatrist who headed a "Christian counseling" practice made headlines and discussion topics on Sermo.com after she stood accused of whipping her patients, berating them, and referring to them as "mules."

Only 20 percent of sexual boundary breaking accusations are leveled against female psychiatrists. Those accusations may include either men or women. (It is unclear if these numbers control for women's lower representation among practicing professionals.) Twenty percent of all accusations against men or women involve same sex dyads, as seen in *Side Effects*.

The dalliance between the Joker and the fictional Harleen Quinzel, M.D. (Harley Quinn), a one-time psychiatrist who began her career at Arkham as a psychiatrist-in-training (also known as a psychiatric resident) contradicts the stereotypical doctor-patient love-sex interlude in several respects. At the same time, it reinforces recurrent themes in film and television. It makes its point partly because it is so over-the-top and because the usual roles are reversed, with Harley ultimately becoming the victim. The fictionalized case of Dr. Harleen Quinzel (Harley Quinn) is even more exceptional because she is a young female, whereas most physicians involved in such activities in real life are late middle-aged males. Harleen has just started her first hospital job at Arkham Asylum when her more sophisticated and anti-social patient sensed her vulnerabilities and exploited her inexperience and preyed on other pre-existing personality problems.

Harley Quinn the character debuted well before the *Arkham Asylum* video game franchise emerged. Originally a cartoon character, Harley began in "Batman: The Animated Series," a 1992 TV show written by Paul Dini and Bruce Timm. Her character, as voiced by Arlene Sorkin, was popular enough to translate into a DC comic book and a graphic novel entitled *Mad Love* (1994), also written by Dini and Timm. *The New Batman Adventures* (1999) adaptation aired seven years after Harley's first appearance in the Batman universe, mainstreaming her character and moving her away from a peripheral role as the Joker's helper and henchwoman.[10]

The New Batman Adventures elaborates on Quinn and the Joker's early encounters. Prior to the publication of the graphic novel *Mad Love* (1994), audiences know only that she was a psychiatrist who "went crazy"[11] and fell in love with the Joker while he was her patient. Soon enough, The Joker abuses Harley, but that does not distance her from her forbidden lover. Just the opposite occurs—she becomes even more attached to him, as explained in *Mad Love* (1994). Curiously, this pattern often occurs with victims of IPV (intimate partner violence) in real life. The on-and-off affection, with intermittent positive reinforcement, conditions the victim to return to her abuser, since "intermittent irregular reinforcement" conditioning patterns, which are unpredictable, and erratic, are the most enduring, according to experimental psychologists.

Harley Quinn's irreverent attachment to the Joker is expanded in an episode entitled, "The Laughing Fish" (1993),[12] aired in *Batman: The Animated Series*. The Joker drops a toxin into Gotham City's harbors, turning all fish into "laughing fish" that bear the Joker's grin. After Detective Bullock refers to the Joker as a "demented abusive psychotic maniac," Quinn sighs and says, "Yeah, I'm really gonna miss him." In the animated series, Quinn explains her attraction to the Joker, noting that he was the first person to listen to her.

Over time, DC writers responded to fan demand (as is standard in the development of comic book plotlines). They added the increasingly popular Harley Quinn into more TV episodes. She appeared in the short-lived *Birds of Prey* (2002–3), a television series about several female superheroes, Black Canary included. Black Canary is a reformed criminal turned crime-fighter. Black Canary has a complicated and often contradictory but always intriguing backstory.[13]

Harley Quinn has an equally elaborate back-story, as is typical of comics characters. Before beginning her medical training and her career as a physician, Harley was a high school gymnast. She retains her athletic abilities into adulthood and uses them to great avail as the acrobatic accomplice to the Joker. With her paramour, she literally jumps in and out of trouble, dressed as a harlequin. The love-smitten couple embarks on criminal caper after caper.

When known as Dr. Quinzel, Harley enters residency training in psychiatry. Audiences follow her progress (and downfall) after she qualifies for a staff appointment at Arkham Asylum's unique hospital setting. Arkham Asylum is an institution for the criminally insane. Harley Quinn's encounters with the Joker began in a most ordinary way, if we consider a stint at an asylum for the criminally insane as "ordinary." Arkham administrators assign her to treat this arch-criminal, who was deemed insane and in need of psychiatric treatment rather than criminal punishment.

We watch her transformation from physician and psychiatrist-therapist to villain and the Joker's moll. In cartoons that began in the early 1990s, and that introduced fans to Harley Quinn, Dr. Quinzel sits by the Joker's bedside, taking copious notes as he talks about his childhood. Dr. Quinzel wears a standard issue white hospital jacket, the hallmark of a medical professional and a vestige of the days when "the men in the white coats" carted emotionally disturbed persons (EDP) out of their homes and into locked hospital wards.

Dr. Quinzel listens intently. Tears pour from her eyes and drip down her cheeks as the Joker recounts heartbreaking stories of abuse. "My father used to beat me up pretty badly," he states, as he reclines on the proverbial psychoanalytic couch. She sits upright in a nearby chair. The Joker continues, "There was only one time that I really saw Dad happy. He took me to the circus. We saw the clowns, running around and dropping their pants."

Even before he utters this provocative line about clowns who drop their pants, and drops hints about his sexual intents, the Joker has set the stage for Harleen's seduction. A few minutes earlier, he told her that he "likes [her] name: 'Harlequin.' It's a name that puts a smile on my face … makes me think that this is someone I can relate to." She dismisses his comment about her name, noting that she has heard that line about "harlequin" before. She sidesteps the sexual innuendo implicit in his comments and makes no comment herself.

As a trained psychiatrist, Dr. Quinzel should instantly connect The Joker's fond memories of his father at the circus with her sound-alike name (and with the name that she will soon adopt) and perhaps interpret this tale as "transference" (even if it turns out to be outright deception and fabrication). In some versions, she is even forewarned by a supervising psychiatrist. She also overlooks his reference to his "smile." (We can excuse her ignorance of Paul Leni's 1928 German Expressionist film, *The Man Who Laughs,* which inspired the Joker's smile, but we cannot excuse her failure to protect her boundaries better, nor can we accept her apparent inability to link her patient's memories of the past to important people in the present.) She does not consider the possibility that the sociopathic Joker is playing her and perhaps even tailoring his history to tell her what he believes she wants to hear.

He convinces her that she alone possesses the unique qualities and abilities to cure him. She does not question his credibility or wonder if he fabricated this heart-rending story to engage her and to make her like him better or to tempt her to break boundaries. In this way, Dr. Quinzel is opposite of the street-savvy FBI Agent Starling (Jody Foster) in *The Silence of the Lambs* (Demme, 1991).[14] Agent Starling speaks to the psychotic and sociopathic psychiatrist Dr. Hannibal Lecter from behind locked bars and can see through his attempts to enmesh her even as he reveals impressive insights about her past experiences and possible motivators in the present.

Dr. Quinzel begins to muse about the Joker in her off-hours, jotting down notes at all hours. She justifies his bad behavior, framing her insights in psychiatric jargon. She writes that, "It soon became clear to me that the Joker, often described as a homicidal madman, was an injured child, determined to make the world laugh." Dr. Quinzel falls in love with her dangerous patient, doodling hearts in her notebook rather than recording process notes, as is standard procedure. In the cartoon, the two eventually trade places, with the Joker sitting at the helm, and Harleen lying on the couch, confiding in him, rather than the other way around. The roles have reversed, and he is in charge. Like other fictional psychoanalytic sessions in cinema, the Joker's treatment goes on fast-forward, and moves far faster than real life analytic sessions.

As is typical of persons with anti-social personality disorder (ASPD), the Joker is charming and engaging. Instinctively, he knows just what to say. He appeals to the opposite gender. Persons of the same gender typically dislike patients with ASPD, and this distinctive "counter-transference"—the subjective reactions of the treatment team— often raises suspicions of the diagnosis in clinical settings. Forensic settings or courtroom testimony require more formal testing to confirm such a diagnosis, but these split reactions on the part of psychiatric hospital staff may signal the presence of previously undiagnosed anti-social personality traits. Once she becomes enamored of her patient and paramour, Dr. Harleen Quinzel is easily persuaded to spring the Joker from Arkham Asylum for the Criminally Insane. The two elope and leave the prison-like institution. Dr. Quinzel leaves all vestiges of respectability and professional decorum behind. She throws off her white coat, sheds her professional identity, dons seductive harlequin costumes and becomes the acrobatic accomplice to the Joker. She is now known as Harley Quinn, her new alter ego. She joins the ranks of evil clowns and tricksters who pepper historical fact and fiction.[15] Like most female figures in superhero comics, Quinn's exaggerated body contours sexualize her and objectify her. She is fetishized by her fans.

For example, in writing for *The DC Comics Encyclopedia: The Definitive Guide to the Characters of the DC Universe* (2004), Scott Beatty describes Quinn as "the Joker's moll, slinking around in a sexy jester's costume." He nicknames her "the giggling gangstress."[16] Beatty claims that "she still finds places to hide weapons of mass distraction," even before her wardrobe shifts. In the animated series and in her original comic book appearances, her costume was form-fitting but not revealing, with a black and red full-body jumpsuit. When she is redesigned, she has "multi-colored hair and a grab-bag wardrobe," wears skimpy shorts and tight tops that barely conceal her ever more prominent and overly accentuated bosom.[17]

Shortly before the publication of Beatty's book, Harley Quinn appears in a short-lived television show, *Birds of Prey* (2002–2003). Due to popular demand, she joins other female superheroes in a series that begins after Batman has abandoned New Gotham City and left for self-imposed exile. In this revamped universe, Huntress (Helena) and Oracle (who was born as Barbara Gordon and who subsequently became Batgirl) assume responsibility for crime-fighting capers that had been the purview of the now-absent Caped Crusader. As the daughter of Batman and Catwoman, Huntress appeared to have inherited her mother's meta-human catlike abilities as well as her father's cunning and conviction to combat crime.

Oracle (Barbara Gordon) is the daughter of Commissioner Gordon, the one-time policeman who rose through the ranks while hunting down the Joker and other Gotham criminals. In the *Gotham* TV series (2014–2019), which was aired by Fox, directed by Danny Cannon and developed by Bruno Heller, we encounter Gordon as a police rookie who is promoted to detective, then captain and lieutenant. Later on, he heads the station house (with dramatic detours along the way). Before becoming Oracle, Barbara Gordon was raped, beaten and crippled by The Joker in retaliation against her crime-fighting father. This dreadful story is recounted in *The Killing Joke* (1988), a graphic novel by Alan Moore. *The Killing Joke* attracted a cultlike fan base that apparently applauded the horrific assault. Detractors expressed their disdain, appalled by the misogynistic plotline that leaves Barbara paralyzed and wheelchair-bound, doomed to staring at a computer screen that forecasts the fates of able-bodied superheroes.

In the *Birds of Prey*, which survived a mere 13 episodes, Harley supposedly reforms and denounces her bad behavior—yet she clandestinely masterminds criminal plots that will be combated by Huntress and Oracle at other points in the Batman universe.[17] Played by Mia Sara for twelve of those episodes, Dr. Quinzel resumes her career as a psychiatrist. She treats Helena, The Huntress, who proclaims that "This whole thing is gonna send me straight to my shrink."[18] The Huntress intentionally withholds secrets from her psychiatrist, Dr. Quinzel, but the series does not last long enough to unravel the consequences of this deception.

As time goes on, Harley Quinn's character becomes popular enough to earn her a starring role in a video game version of *Arkham Asylum* (Rocksteady Studies, 2009), which itself became popular enough to spawn an entire *Arkham* franchise. In the same year as the original *Arkham* video game, Harley is featured in the comic book version of *Gotham City Sirens* (2009). She does not remain completely criminal in this rendition but becomes morally ambiguous. She eventually stars in the comic book series of *Suicide Squad* (2014), which was made into a movie by the same name: *Suicide Squad* (2016). Images of the revamped (and even more vampish) Harley star in the promotional posters for the 2016 film.

Harley Quinn's appearance was redesigned when DC Comics restarted the classic series in 2011 and redesigned almost everyone on board.[19] In the *Arkham* video games, Harley Quinn wears corseted tops or short skirts that look like X-rated Halloween nurse costumes sold at seedy Sixth Avenue stores in NYC's pre-gentrified Greenwich Village.

This provocative look parallels broader trends in DC Comics overall and has specific implications for Harley.

Harleen Quinzel's fall from grace, and her spiraling downward from promising young staff psychiatrist to passive recipient of IPV (intimate partner violence) and partner in a Bonnie and Clyde-like crime couple rings a warning bell to those who defy ethical standards. Her popularity with the public suggests that there is an unconscious—perhaps even conscious— need to witness the downfall of such boundary-breaking professionals. Even though Harley Quinn garners many fans as she pursues these underground activities, she inherently reminds spectators of the pitfalls of breeching accepted standards and of the dangers of becoming infatuated with patients without referring them to alternative and unbiased treatment resources.

Harley Quinn reminds us of the hapless professor in Josef von Sternberg's proto-noir, German Expressionist classic, *The Blue Angel* (1930), which catapulted Marlene Dietrich to near-mythic status. The career of Professor Rath (Emil Jannings) careens downward after he becomes enamored with cabaret performer, Lola-Lola (Marlene Dietrich). He is spotted at the café by students who already resent his authority. Disgraced, Rath loses his teaching position and then accompanies his mistress on stage, dressed as a clown. Even more of his former students fill the audience to jeer at the one-time prim and proper educator. Harley Quinn similarly becomes an object of caricature as she dresses as a circus performer after forfeiting her professional status.

Even sadder still, Dr. Quinzel is acutely aware of her transgression but appears helpless to overcome her emotions. Speaking to herself in a film noir-style voice-over, she blurts out, "Yes, I admit it, as unprofessional as it sounds, I've fallen in love with my patient."

The parallels between Harley Quinn subplots and German Expressionist classics is no coincidence; German Expressionism influenced early *Batman* creators as well as film noir. The dark-tinged tragedies cum comedies of the 1920s have been updated for the animation audience. Their stories of human frailty recur over time, despite changes in setting, language, or era.

Notes

1. My thanks to Gracie Friedman-Lifschutz for supplying several comics references.
2. *A Dangerous Method* (Cronenberg, 2011).
3. Richard Noll, *The Jung Cult: The Origins of a Charismatic Movement* (Princeton, NJ: Princeton University Press, 1994).
4. Sigmund Freud, "Recommendation to Physicians Practicing Psycho-analysis," in *The Standard Edition of the Complete Psychological Works of Sigmund Freud, Volume XII*, 1911–13, ed. J. Strachey. http://www.Bgso.edu. Accessed online July 8, 2018.
5. Glenn O. Gabbard, M.D. and Eva P. Lester, M.D., *Boundaries and Boundary Violations in Psychoanalysis* (Arlington, VA. American Psychiatric Association Press, 1995).
6. Glen O. Gabbard, M.D., "Patient-Therapist Boundary Issues," *Psychiatric Times* 12: XII, October 1, 2005.
7. Thomas Guthiel, M.D. and Glen Gabbard, M.D., "Boundaries in Clinical Practice" in *American Journal of Psychiatry* (April 2006, online).
8. Glen O. Gabbard and Krin Gabbard, *Psychiatry and the Cinema*, 2nd Ed. (Arlington, VA: American Psychiatric Association Press, 1999).
9. *Side Effects* (Soderbergh, 2013).
10. Paul Dini et al., "Harlequinade," *Batman: The Animated Series* (1994). Reference supplied by Gracie Lifschutz.
11. Paul Dini and Bruce Timm, *The Batman Adventures: Mad Love*. (New York: DC Comics, 1994).
12. Paul Dini et. al, "The Laughing Fish," *Batman: The Animated Series* (1993).
13. A live-action film about the "Birds of Prey" collective is in production and is tentatively entitled,

Birds of Prey (and the Fantabulous Emancipation of One Harley Quinn). It is scheduled to be released in 2020 and is directed by Cathy Yan, who is touted as the first Asian American female director of a superhero film.

14. *The Silence of the Lambs* (Demme, 1991).

15. Adam W. Darlage, "From Pogo to Pennywise: the Rise of the Evil Clown in American Popular Culture Since 1978," *A History of Evil in Popular Culture: What Hannibal Lecter, Stephen King, and Vampires Reveal About America,* eds. Sharon Packer and Jody Pennington (Santa Barbara, California: Praeger, 2014).

16. Scott Beatty, Alastair, Jimenez, *The DC Comics Encyclopedia: The Definitive Guide to the Characters of the DC Universe* (New York: DK Publishing, 2004), p. 140. My thanks to Gracie Freeman-Lifschutz for this reference.

17. More films about Harley Quinn in her various incarnations are in production.

18. It is doubtful that the proverbial *Ship of Fools* existed in actuality, even though Foucault's much-read anti-psychiatry writings treat it as a concrete entity, analogous to a floating prison.

19. Daniel Wallace, *DC Comics Super-Villains: The Complete Visual History* (San Rafael, California: Insight Editions, 2014).

Unethical Experiments in Arkham and Elsewhere

SHARON PACKER, M.D.

Dr. Strange's Strange Experiments and Even Stranger Events in History

In Arkham Asylum, psychiatrist Dr. Hugo Strange conducts experiments that churn one's stomach. He is a latter-day Dr. Moreau and maybe a Dr. Mengele wannabe. Dr. Strange's Project Chimera takes place beneath Arkham Asylum proper, in Indian Hill's hidden halls and locked cells. This is not his first hideaway for hideous experiments; it is simply his most recent. Dr. Strange hybridizes humans and creates monsters in the process. He also raises the dead, which is more than we can say for Moreau or Mengele but not entirely unexpected in a superhero story that is as much fantasy as science fiction.

In the *Gotham* TV series, his efforts are uncovered by Ed Nygma (The Riddler). Before that happens, Dr. Strange experiments upon arch-criminal Penguin, then mayor of Gotham who was once infatuated with—but spurned by—Nygma. Strange turns the beak-nosed Penguin into a polite and mild-mannered person. His methods vaguely remind us of the Ludovico technique from Stanley Kubrick's *Clockwork Orange* (1971), where behavioral conditioning and paired associational learning reform a hardened criminal by creating an aversion to antisocial impulses, and to Beethoven's music, in the process.

In the television version, Dr. Strange is played by a bearded B.D. Wong, a versatile Chinese-American actor with a dual-edged legacy and a long resume of doctor, psychiatrist, and evil experimenter roles (along with acclaimed Disney animation voiceovers and appearances in *M. Butterfly* on Broadway). Wong's performances in the *Jurassic* franchise anticipate his horrific Dr. Strange performance. His portrayal of the level-headed, soft-spoken, well-respected and respectful FBI agent/psychiatrist on *Law & Order: SVU* contradicts his stereotyped casting in *Jurassic* and elsewhere, although *SVU*'s Dr. Huang and *Batman*'s Dr. Strange are both brilliant scientists and psychiatrists.

Dr. Strange's penchant for performing unsavory experiments on his psychiatric patients is hardly unique to the *Arkham* universe. It's not even unique to Dr. Strange in Arkham. For example, Dr. Linda Friitawa, the albino geneticist, lost her medical license because of her unethical human genetic tests. Both Drs. Arkham take liberties with their patients, turning them into mindless zombies who do their bidding without questioning.

Evil experiments have been seen on screen so many times in the past. Until *Psycho* (1960) paved new paths by substituting a murderous mentally ill person for the stereotypical mad scientist, mad scientists were cinema's preferred villains. Evil scientists starred in literature long before the celluloid screen appeared at the fin-de-siècle and long before the invention of video games or graphic novels. Science fiction welcomed stories about evil experimenters. Superhero stories, as a subgenre of science fiction, abound in tales of sinister scientists who disregard the humanity of their human subjects (or the dignity of their animal subjects) and instead pursue their perverted science experiments, often expecting to prove their brilliance to the world at large and to justify their previously unappreciated genius (which others dismiss as megalomania or worse).

To find examples of unethical or evil experiments in fiction, let us start with an American silent film from 1919, Victor Fleming's *When the Clouds Roll By*. In that same year, but across the Atlantic, Robert Weine completed a film that would become a German Expressionist classic: *The Cabinet of Dr. Caligari*. Dr. Caligari lives on in our memories, while Fleming's early foray into film has been forgotten by the public, even though Fleming's more mature films are among the best-remembered.

IMDB (www.imdb.com)[1] notes that American audiences found Dr. Metz's tongue-in-cheek attempts at human experimentation funny. The psychiatrist-protagonist tries to drive an innocent and unsuspecting person to suicide by inducing bad dreams via bad food. Parallels with the Biblical Job are apparent but unmentioned.

The English language inter-titles describe the details:

"Guinea pigs and rabbits are often sacrificed for scientific purposes.... Before a clinic of mystery, Dr. Ulrich Metz propounds a fantastic theory of evil design."

A hand holding a skull appears as Dr. Metz says, "I mean to take a human life in the cause of science, but this must remain a professional secret with us."

"Other scientists experiment with animals, but I have selected a human being—as my work concerns the human mind."

Fantastic imagery flashes across the screen, like Hieronymus Bosch paintings. Surrealistic turnips and radishes dance on human legs. This fantasy film anticipates Fleming's directorial genius twenty years later, exemplified by the *Wizard of Oz* (1939).

Today, virtually no one disagrees about Victor Fleming's directorial skills, but virtually no one in our era laughs about human experimentation. This over-the-top trope seemed funny in 1919, soon after World War I ended, but if it premiered today, it might launch protest marches, congressional hearings, even worldwide summits, like the one in Finland, which produced the Declaration of Helsinki about Ethical Principles for Medical Research Involving Human Subjects in 1964. Sensibilities changed as time proved that humans are capable of unspeakably inhumane acts, doctors included.

Definitions of "ethical experimentation" versus "unethical experimentation" shifted over time. Those changes can be seen on screen—or in courts of law, in professional debates about medical ethics, in journalistic exposés about violations of those laws, and even in book choices made by the American public and best-seller lists. Consider the many years that *The Immortal Life of Henrietta Lacks* (2010) spent on that list. That condemns the ethics of using dead and discarded cells that were cultured from a tumor that required removal. No experiments were performed on patient HL, who expired long ago.

Yet many consider the use of lab tests made from those cells to be unethical.

It's safe to say that most members of the public are morbidly afraid of being conscripted into unethical experiments. Many are wary of all medical experiments, even when others demand newer and better treatments and even when special interest groups condemn the F.D.A. for its slow approval process. Apart from bureaucratic red tape, approvals of new medications may be delayed because of difficulties in recruiting participants for controlled studies needed to confirm the benefits (and weigh the risks). Interestingly, researchers report that some cancer patients are more frightened by the prospect of being assigned to the "control group" with dummy pills rather than the experimental medication, concerned that they might miss the chance for promising, but unproven and possibly dangerous, treatments. It is not surprising that people with no other options left—and who might die without different treatments—are more willing to take chances on experimental methods offered by reliable and respected sources.

Recipients of psychiatric care may have even more fears about unethical experimentation—and for good reason. The idea that doctors stealthily select patients for secret studies in locked laboratories sounds paranoid, and persons with pre-existing paranoia may express such ideas without prodding and without basis. Books, plays and films about Dr. Moreau or Dr. Jekyll sowed seeds for such fears long ago. Recent revelations about brain damage caused by clandestine microwaves are even scarier and are likely to spur more apprehension and promote innovative ideas about diseases.[2] An even more recent Netflix release, *Maniac* (2018), presents this theme as a dark comedy.

Promotional photograph of Victor Zsasz from *Batman: Arkham Asylum* (2009) video game, dir. Sefton Hill. Zsasz is a minor player in this video game but his namesake, the Hungarian-born Thomas Szasz, M.D., was a major player in the antipsychiatry movement of the 1960s. Szasz' book on *The Myth of Mental Illness* (1960) remains a mainstay of the anti-psychiatry movement today. Because the serial killer Zsasz carves tally marks into his skin for each of his victims, his body is covered with self-mutilation scars. Zsasz debuted in *Batman: Shadow of a Bat* #1 (June 1992).

Before dismissing such fears outright and seeing them as evidence of psychiatric illness, and nothing but, we should consider historical facts. Enough ignominious events have occurred in American history—and not just in Nazi Germany—to give us pause. Articles in *JAMA* (*Journal of American Medical Association*), and *New England Journal of Medicine* and elsewhere catalogue those occurrences.[3]

Why would persons receiving psychiatric treatment (voluntarily or involuntarily) have special concerns? Recall that people who are deemed to be dangers to themselves or others, or who are unable to care for themselves, can generally be admitted to mental institutions against their will, and held for one to three days, with variations from state to state. Involuntary (non-consenting) commitment to a psychiatric ward is still possible.

In the distant past, people could be committed to asylums for fewer reasons and for longer time periods. Not that long ago, some people never returned after they entered a state hospital, as cemeteries on abandoned hospital grounds attest. Some countries, such as Peoples' Republic of China (PRC) or the FSU (former Soviet Union), were accused of incarcerating political prisoners in psychiatric asylums. Such practices have been attacked by the APA (American Psychiatric Association) and similar organizations.

In our current era, we rightfully worry about pharmaceutical companies that fund experimental studies, paying research teams and universities directly, perhaps adding extra incentives under the table. We quiver when we read about Harvard-based psychiatrists who do not disclose million dollar-plus payments from drug companies. What else are they hiding, from the public, from patients, and from other professionals?

Given such continuing concerns in contemporary society, it makes sense that "unethical experimentation" is a recurring theme in *Arkham* and elsewhere. This topic is popular enough in horror films to merit a separate subgenre: "medsploitation." As its name suggests, many (but not all) such films are low-budget, straight-to-video releases.

Literary Classics: Dr. Jekyll, Dr. Moreau, Dr. Frankenstein

Unethical experimentation is not the sole province of horror films or Grade B melodramas or even the pulp pages of comic books. This topic holds a hallowed place in literary history. Some of the 19th century's most enduring tales concern unethical experimentation. Dr. Moreau, Dr. Frankenstein, and Dr. Jekyll and Mr. Hyde remain favorites more than a century later. These fictional beings lived second, third, maybe even twenty or more lives in movies and TV, video games, toys, lyrics and plays of the 20th and 21th centuries. The names of Dr. Moreau, Dr. Jekyll, and Dr. Frankenstein may be better-recognized today, in our media-saturated 21st century, than in the 19th century.

Each of these fictional characters dabbled in areas related to brain chemistry, brain anatomy or brain-based behavior. Dr. Jekyll was a compassionate doctor who prioritized the treatment of poor patients in London's charity clinics over the care of the affluent paying patients (to the chagrin of his future father-in-law, whom he unwittingly murders when he transforms into the bestial Mr. Hyde).

Dr. Jekyll was a humanitarian, but he also used experimental elixirs to change brain chemistry and unleash libidinous, animalistic instincts that lay buried beneath social demands and Victorian etiquette. Dr. Jekyll references Darwinian evolutionary ideas when he regresses to an ape-like appearance after ingesting neuroactive chemicals from his vials. He also spoofs Victorian society, with its strict social and sexual mores. He dramatizes the dangers inherent in complete repression of animal instincts (or libido). He anticipates Freudian theories about the "observing ego" and its ability to mediate the id.

Dr. Jekyll also acts as a morality tale against self-experimentation. Even though he uses his experimental potions on himself, and does not distribute them to patients, one of his patients indirectly meets her maker because of his experiments. That lady sang in disreputable dancehalls and was sexually provocative (at least in the definitive film version). She was polar opposite of Dr. Jekyll's polished and proper lady love. She brought out the beast in Dr. Jekyll, literally and metaphorically, so that he turned into the hideous Mr. Hyde as he tended to her injury. Mr. Hyde then strangles this seductress.

In the last scene of Mammoulian's 1931 version, Dr. Jekyll's confidante, who previously objected to Jekyll's self-experimentation, realizes that Dr. Jekyll has assumed the appearance of Mr. Hyde. The other doctor shoots Jekyll/Hyde. In a dramatic ending, the dying Mr. Hyde morphs back to his original physical form as the good Dr. Jekyll.

Although many, many, many versions of *The Strange Case of Dr. Jekyll and Mr. Hyde* have appeared on stage and screen over the years, Robert Mamoulian's 1932 version is considered the classic, with Fredric March winning an Oscar for his portrayal of the handsome and refined Dr. Jekyll as well as his course and ugly counterpart, Mr. Hyde. Ingenious theatrical lighting techniques revealed different make-ups by changing filters on the lights, turning one character into another, long before computer animation.

According to Henri Ellenberger's 1981 magnum opus about *The Discovery of the Unconscious: The History and Evolution of Dynamic Psychiatry*,[4] Stevenson's 1886 novella foreshadowed Freud's century-shaping theories about ego, id, and superego and so holds an important place in the histories of psychoanalysis and psychiatry. It also reflects currents in medical ethics.

Dr. Moreau's morality bears little-to-no similarity to Dr. Jekyll's, who was a good man before bad drugs turned him into a bad humanoid, as his misguided intentions turned into terrible mishaps. Dr. Moreau has no higher aspirations for humanity although he has a high regard for himself and his scientific acumen. Moreau experiments on animals, and trains them to act more human. His operations make them more human-like and impart abilities to speak and to stand upright. He also causes extreme pain to his subjects, as he disrupts the natural order and disregards the inborn tendencies of his menagerie. Moreau's operating room is the aptly named "House of Pain."

Dr. Moreau's fictional story is retold in *The Island of Lost Souls* (1932), directed by Erle C. Kenton. Kenton's film premiered one year after Mamoulian's definitive version of *Dr. Jekyll* (1931) and one year before Hitler became Chancellor of the Third Reich. In a strange foreshadowing of the future, Dr. Moreau's inhumane experiments on his remote island mirrored experiments that the Nazi doctors would soon conduct on humans. Don Taylor directed another movie version of *The Island of Dr. Moreau* (1977) in 1977. Two decades later, in 1996, John Frankenheimer (*The Manchurian Candidate; Seconds*) filmed another remake, starring Val Kilmer as Montgomery and an aging Marlon Brando as Dr. Moreau.

One film that pulls no punches about medical experimentation is the remake of *House of Haunted Hill* (1999), directed by William Malone. William Castle's original 1959 *House of Haunted Hill* stars horror-meister Vincent Price. Two years later, Stanley

Kramer's film about *Judgment at Nuremberg* (1961) made the public aware of the horrors of the Holocaust, as did the Eichmann Trial, which was televised worldwide from Jerusalem in that same year.

And so, mass media peaked interest in the Nuremberg Trials that prosecuted Nazi war crimes from 1945 to 1946, shortly after World War II ended. Baby Boomers and their parents and perhaps their grandparents were the prime audience of these early Sixties' films and documentaries, but Boomers were either toddlers when the actual trials were held or had not yet born. It is unclear how many Americans knew that the Doctors' Trial was the first of twelve Nuremberg Trials in post-war Germany, but the number is likely to be low. Two-thirds of millennials don't know of the Holocaust as of 2018, according to Julie Zauzmer of the *Washington Post*, on www. washingtonpost.com.

The Doctors' Trial included twenty-two men and one woman. Twenty were physicians, with one female physician who worked at Ravensbruck, a women's camp. Eighty-five witnesses testified. Almost 1,500 documents went into evidence. Sixteen doctors were found guilty. Seven were executed. Some who were found guilty of crimes against humanity were subsequently recruited for the CIA's Operation Paperclip.

The original *House on Haunted Hill* was produced by William Castle, who remains one of the most memorable horror masters of all times. His cute-but-corny touches included paper skeletons that floated through movie theaters. The remake is the first film produced by Dark Castle Entertainment, which went on to make remakes of other horror classics, such as *House of Wax*, which starred Vincent Price in the original. The remake is a far cry from the cuteness and corniness of the first film.

The second *House on Haunted Hill* film draws on Nazi war crimes and medical experiments that were exposed during the Doctors' Trial at Nuremberg and alluded to in *Judgment at Nuremberg* in 1961. The second film adds Hollywood touches and spices up true tales with psychiatrist seduction subplots and sensational "shock schlock" scenes.

With its ghoulish special effects and a cadre of dislikable characters that includes a philandering psychiatrist, a murderous millionaire and a deceptive spouse, plus psychiatric treatments that function as torture techniques, this supernatural horror cinema incorporates historical fact and tacitly comments on that history. The backstory about human experimentation that had been clandestinely conducted in psychiatric asylums— and in Nazi medical experiments— deserves serious attention. However, mixing these scenes with supernatural visitations softens the historical truth, leading spectators to believe that these unethical psychiatric experiments were as unreal as the ghost story.

In the remake, the action unfolds in an abandoned asylum known as the Vannacutt Psychiatric Institute for the Criminally Insane. The name alone reminds us of Arkham Asylum for the Criminally Insane. Many murders were committed the Vannacutt asylum, mostly in the 1920s, when the asylum's chief, Dr. Richard B. Vannacutt, performed grotesque experiments on patients. Many died as a result. Coincidentally (or not), the refurbished and rededicated Arkham Asylum opened its doors in those very same years.

According to the film, the hospital in *House on Haunted Hill* was closed in 1931, a few years before Hitler took power in 1933. In 1931, Vannacutt's patients escaped after killing most staff and burning the hospital to the ground. The abandoned building became known as "The House on Haunted Hill." The asylum lay idle until an amusement park mogul leases it for a lavish Halloween party, with plans to murder his hateful wife.

Although the amusement park mogul is well-versed in spook house special effects, which he will use at his party, he is unaware that ghosts inhabit the old asylum. Those ghosts tampered with his guest list and invited five complete strangers, hand-picked because the ghosts knew that these would-be guests were descendants of the old asylum's original sadistic staff. The guests start dying gruesome deaths, post-slasher style. The remaining guests struggle to escape from the old asylum, stumbling through a basement filled with remains of patients who are strapped to tables, gyrating in agony, as they endure unimaginable experiments. Knowing that they are just ghosts of the original patients, rather than real, living people, does not make the viewing any easier.

Spectators who have seen photographs from concentration camps, or early documentary films such as *After Mein Kampf* (1961), are reminded of Dr. Mengele's horrific twin studies, of Nazi surgeries performed without anesthesia, and Dachau hypothermia experiments on concentration camp inmates. Like a PTSD (post-traumatic stress disorder) flashback, we are forced to recall German psychiatrists who decided which mental patients did not lead "lives worth living" and which were "hereditary degenerates" who deserved to die (according to Nazi standards). Those unfortunates were shunted to gas chambers that were built specifically for such eugenics purposes. Those very same gas chambers would be repurposed, and used for Jews and gypsies, after Christian clergy from around the world protested the murders of mental patients.

It is disturbing to believe that doctors participated in such events, but additional documentation of the willing participation of physicians and psychiatric physicians appears in Robert J. Lifton's book about *The Nazi Doctors* (1986), and in the U.S. Holocaust Memorial Museum archives on Nazi pseudo-science and racial hygiene. The *New England Journal of Medicine* published a succinct review of this subject.[5]

Bans on Nazi-like experiments on non-consenting humans or on humans who are incapable of providing informed consent gave rise to the Nuremberg Code for medical research ethics. The Nuremberg Code bears the name of the city that hosted the Nuremberg Trials where these horrific medical experiments were brought to light. This code was subsequently revisited and expanded in the Declaration of Helsinki (1964).

Inexplicably, inhumane experiments that violated the Nuremberg Code persisted in America, and some were sponsored by the government-run Public Health Service. Some studies continued in the same years as the Nuremberg Trials. Studies on residents of homes for the mentally retarded, mental hospital inmates, prisoners, nursing home patients, black men from Tuskegee, Alabama, or Guatemalans, ran through the early to mid-seventies, for reasons to be explained below.

The 1972 *Luke Cage* comic book and, to a lesser extent, the *Luke Cage* Netflix series based on the Marvel comics, alludes to unethical prison experiments that persisted through the mid-seventies. The original story appears in Marvel's Blaxploitation tale of a black man who is convicted of a crime that he did not commit, and sentenced to prison, where he consents to participate in medical experiments in exchange for early parole.[6]

Until then, let's consider the fact that hepatitis studies were conducted on profoundly retarded residents of the Willowbrook School between the years of 1956–1972. The details of those studies came to light in 1972 and became even better known because former Beatle John Lennon performed a benefit concert for the victims. Lennon was inspired by Geraldo Rivera's groundbreaking investigative reports about Willowbrook. When the comic book character Luke Cage asks his doctor if he is about to be "injected or infected," he reminds readers of Willowbrook.

Dr. Beecher had called attention to the Willowbrook research in his *New England Journal of Medicine* article in 1966,[7] using far less flamboyant speech than John Lennon or Geraldo Rivera. The *NEJM* article reached scholarly medical audiences. Perhaps it also infiltrated the cultural currency of the counter-culture that was percolating in 1966. The Beecher article made a political point, but it was dispassionate and avoided placing blame on "the establishment" exclusively. The article informs us that the children's parents signed away the rights of their retarded [sic] progeny and allowed them to be infected with hepatitis so that vaccine studies could be conducted on them.

Some parents later claimed that they felt coerced into consenting, fearing that their children would be denied a place in the residence if they refused to participate. Others suggested that children whose parents pre-signed consents for experiments were granted preferential admission to the Staten Island school. Whatever the truth may be, this experiment, and other experiments conducted on psychiatric patients who lacked the ability to provide informed consent, opened a whole new avenue of ethical inquiry. If a retarded child or a demented adult cannot understand the purpose of an experiment, can that person provide properly informed consent? Of course not. But who can, if anyone?

This question turned out to be relevant in other ways in the same years. In Illinois, psychotic patients housed in state hospitals were used as test subjects. In sixties' era Brooklyn, doctors injected live cancer cells into demented geriatric patients, in hopes of learning about cancer transmission. These subjects had no ability to consent or dissent.

The most widely publicized "episode" of unethical human experimentation that came to light in those years was the Tuskegee syphilis study, which was conducted on black men in Tuskegee, Alabama. The study focused on neurosyphilis, which causes severe psychiatric symptoms, among other things, so it can be counted among the "unethical experiments" conducted in the name of neuropsychiatry.

In this now-shameful episode in public health history, poor black men who were known to be infected with syphilis were not informed about curative treatment that became available after 1947, when penicillin was proven to be effective against syphilis. Researchers observed their subjects over a course of years, collecting data about the natural progression of untreated syphilis. They dutifully recorded their findings, without sharing the news of effective and usually safe treatments on the frontier.

Untreated subjects—as well as some wives of the subjects and the children born to those women—developed a wide range of cardiac, cardiovascular, visual, bone, neurological and dermatological problems. Some became blind or psychotic. Death rates were higher than expected, which might not have happened with early intervention.

Those studies were stopped in 1972, after the *New York Times* published a front-page article on studies conducted by an agency that exists to protect the public. Articles in *The Washington Post* appeared soon after. But there was a glitch: the study that was stopped in 1972 had had a forty-year run. When asked to defend their actions in the aftermath of the Nuremberg Code (which came about around the same time that penicillin was proven to stop syphilis' progression), the American public health doctors in question claimed that they thought that the Nuremberg Laws against prisoner experimentation applied to German doctors only. Their shallow defense was disturbing.

Equally amazingly, data from 2010 and 2011 show that Guatemalan men were used in related American-sponsored studies, with the difference being that their plight did not become known for another forty years. *New York Times* articles about these events did not create the same stir that occurred in the early 1970s, when the Youth Culture reigned.

The uproar that resulted from revelations about the experiments on poor black men in Alabama resulted in increased scrutiny of the already-suspect prisoner studies. Most prisoners did not fare as well as the fictional comic book character of Luke Cage, who developed iron-hard muscles that broke through bars, because of an experimental error.

Most states stopped prisoner studies soon after the Tuskegee studies were revealed, especially since a disproportionate number of American prisoners were black. By 1976, prisoner medical experiments—such as the kind that Luke Cage underwent—were banned in federal institutions. Luke Cage's imagined experiences were relics of the past.

But that does not mean that all unethical psychiatric experiments stopped forever after? Quite the contrary. Other ongoing government-sanctioned studies about psychopharmacology and behavior modification gained steam in this era. Congressional committees and speeches by Robert Kennedy addressed these issues by 1977.

Even the Canadian government proved to be complicit in some unauthorized LSD studies. Dr. Cameron, the Scottish-born psychiatrist who once headed the World Psychiatric Association, and who had been president of both the Canadian Psychiatric Association and the American Psychiatric Association, and who was at the top of his profession, was implicated in some of the most notorious studies. A 2011 article in *Psychiatric News,* a monthly newspaper published by the America Psychiatric Association, commented on Cameron's studies and on the shifts in ethical standards.[8]

Not everyone reads *Psychiatric News,* but many people watch movies. Some movies publicize important issues that might otherwise be known only to select scholars. Richard Donner's *Conspiracy Theory* (1997) is a film that serves this function—even though it also functions as an action-adventure film with a light romantic subplot.

Conspiracy Theory stars Mel Gibson as a pseudo-psychotic taxi driver. Curiously, Gibson's recorded racist rants recollect his unhinged character from *Conspiracy Theory.* Cleverly, the director had Gibson ad lib his conspiracy theories when he spoke with movie extras who posed as passengers in New York City yellow cabs.

The plot unfolds when Gibson's Jerry Fletcher meets Julia Roberts, a government attorney who spends her spare time investigating the unexplained death of her father. Sheer coincidence causes their paths to intertwine. Her father's murder is the MacGuffin of the movie, as is MKUltra, the once-secret government LSD brainwashing study.

If we knew nothing about the government experiments mentioned by the lead character, we would assume that the exciting chase scenes and daring escapes of this thriller are intended as light entertainment only. We would not expect this Cassandra-like cinema to tell untold truths. The fact that the cab driver is clearly psychotic makes him an unreliable narrator, in much the same way that the men who tell the story of *Caligari* discredit their tale after they reveal that they are inmates of the asylum that they deride.

However, many details about the CIA-run project MKUltra have become public knowledge, enough to make us rethink the cab driver's crazed conspiracy theories. Project MKUltra, or MKUltra, which is mentioned in the movie, was the code name for a covert, illegal CIA human research program, run by the CIA's Office of Scientific Intelligence. This official U.S. government program began in the early 1950s and continued through the late 1960s. Both U.S. and Canadian citizens were used as test subjects for studies on brain function, psychedelic drugs, hypnosis, and the manipulation of mental states. Sensory deprivation, isolation, verbal and sexual abuse were used to break down defenses and variably make subjects reveal sensitive information or cause psychotic behavior that discredited their political theories.

Project MKUltra attracted public attention in 1975 when the Church Committee and the Rockefeller Commission presented their findings to Congress. CIA Director Richard Helms ordered the destruction of all MKUltra files in 1973, forcing the investigators to rely on testimonies of participants and a few surviving documents. In 1977, 20,000 documents about project MKUltra were retrieved and subsequently presented at Senate Hearings. Information on MKUltra has since been declassified.

In 1977, Senator Ted Kennedy spoke on the Senate floor, specifically stating that "The Deputy Director of the CIA revealed that over thirty universities and institutions were involved in an 'extensive testing and experimentation' program which included covert drug tests on unwitting citizens 'at all social levels' ... Several ... involved the administration of LSD to 'unwitting subjects in social situations.' At least one death ... resulted from these activities." The death was Dr. Olson, who was one of many military and government scientists and doctors who received LSD surreptitiously. Dr. Olson jumped from a window while under the influence. Dr. Olson's wife contended that her husband was murdered because he had a change of heart about the experiments and threatened to expose them. The government never confirmed Ms. Olson's claims, but it admitted to administering LSD and paid out $750,000 for lawsuit.

Eventually, it was revealed that 44 American colleges or universities, 15 research foundations or chemical or pharmaceutical companies, including Sandoz (now known as Novartis) and Eli Lilly, 12 additional hospitals or clinics and three prisons had participated in MKUltra. Sandoz is better-remembered for Dr. Albert Hoffmann's discovery of LSD, and for marketing ergot-based precursors of LSD for migraines.

In *Conspiracy Theory*, taxi driver Jerry (Mel Gibson) sermonizes about conspiracies to his passengers. He shares his implausible ideas with attorney Alice (Julia Roberts). He claims that NASA is trying to kill the President and that its secret weapon triggers earthquakes. While walking down the street, he identifies random men as CIA operatives. He follows them into a building, where he is captured and rendered unconscious. He awakens in another building, but he is bound to a wheelchair with duct tape.

Psychiatrist Dr. Jonas (Patrick Stewart) enters the scene, tapes Jerry's eyes open, and injects him with so-called "Gravy for the Brain" (LSD). The water torture-assisted interrogations recollect *Marathon Man* (1976), where "White Angel" Nazi conspirator tortures Dustin Hofmann in a dentist's chair hidden below the Brooklyn Bridge.

When Jerry responds to his injection and sees scary cartoons and starts to mumble, Dr. Jonas moves closer, to hear details, but Jerry bites the doctor's nose, leaving a telltale mark that will prove Jerry's conspiracy theories true. Then Jerry makes a daring escape while still bound to the wheelchair. He shuttles down the stairs and drops into a laundry truck. The truck drives away, revealing a hidden "mental hospital" sign on the building.

While visiting Jerry in the hospital, Alice hears Jerry babble about the conspiracy and about biting someone's nose. Dr. Jonas appears in the hospital, his nose bandaged. Jonas says that his dog bit him, but Alice and audience are now convinced of Jerry's claims.

In real life, psychiatric patients (like Jerry), plus other vulnerable populations, are accorded extra protection under the National Institute of Health guidelines on research involving human subjects. A special section on "Research with Vulnerable Populations" mentions Pregnant Women, Human Fetuses and Neonates, Prisoners, Children, Persons at Risk for Suicidality, and Persons with Impaired Decisional Capacity.

Considering that serious breaches of the Nuremberg Code have occurred in the not so distant past, we can expect to hear more fears of unethical experimentation. Movies, novels, games and TV shows about unethical experimentation offer safe settings to experience such worries and hopefully feel relief when the game is over—if players and spectators believe that such events occur only in fiction. Sadly, that is not so. The unethical experiments in Arkham Asylum for the Criminally Insane exist on a continuum with similarly unethical and evil experiments in literature and cinema. They may be nothing more than another story arc, added for entertainment value, or they may include yet-unspoken truths that are waiting to be revealed.

Notes

1. https://www.imdb.com/title/tt0010879/

2. William J. Broad, "Microwave Weapons Are Prime Suspect in Ills of U.S. Embassy Workers," *New York Times,* September 1, 2018. Accessed via *NY Times* App, September 2, 2018.

3. Credible references in reputable medical journals are far too numerous to catalogue here and are found in specialist publications on medical ethics and history of medicine. the few citations included here represent but a tiny number of a vast body of literature. Preeti Malani, review of *Dark Medicine: Rationalizing Unethical Medical Research,* ed. Lafleur, W, G Bohme, S Shimazono. *JAMA* Sep 10, 2008; 300 (10):1217–1218; Jochen Vollmann and Rolf Winau, "Informed Consent in Human Experimentation Before the Nuremberg Code," *British Medical Journal* (December 7, 1996) 313: 1445; Thomas R. Frieden and F Collins, "Commentary. Intentional Infection of Vulnerable Populations in 1946–1948," *JAMA* 2010; 304 (18): 2063–2064. Accessed online October 11, 2010.

4. Henri F. Ellenberger: *The Discovery of the Unconscious: The History and Evolution of Dynamic Psychiatry* (New York: Basic Books, 1990).

5. Richard Hunt, review of *Hitler or Hippocrates: Medical Experiments and Euthanasia in the Third Reich* by Paul Hoedeman, *New England Journal of Medicine* (May 13, 1993) 328:1429; Michael Kater, *Doctors Under Hitler* (Chapel Hill, N.C.: University of North Carolina Press, 1989); Marcia Angell, "The Nazi Hypothermia Experiments and Unethical Research Today" (Editorial), *New England Journal of Medicine* 1990; 322: 1462–1464; R.L. Berger, "Nazi Science—The Dachau Hypothermia Experiments," *New England Journal of Medicine* 1990; 322:1435–1440. Accessed September 2, 2018.

6. Sharon Packer, "*Luke Cage* and Race-Based Unethical Medical Experiments," *History of Medicine* (December 2014).

7. Henry Beecher, "Ethics and Clinical Research," *New England Journal of Medicine* 1966; 274:1354–60.

8. Mark Moran. "When Ethical Lines Were Crossed in Service to the Nation." *Psychiatric News* 2011 (June 17, 2011) 46: 12.

Section IV

Big Screen Parallels

Arkham's Sinister Psychiatrists and the Continuum with Caligari

Sharon Packer, M.D.

Dr. Caligari remains the prototype and poster boy of cinema's evil psychiatrists. He is also the namesake for *Sinister Psychiatrists: From Caligari to Hannibal* (Packer, 2012).[1] That book, by this author, includes far more information on sinister psychiatrists than this essay can comfortably contain.

Dr. Caligari made it to the silver screen in 1919. The brainchild of two European screenwriters, Dr. Caligari retains high name recognition a full century later. Robert Weine's film, *The Cabinet of Dr. Caligari* (1919), still enjoys respect, no matter how outdated its cinematography may be. (In fact, some attribute part of its continuing charm to its styled sets and archaic camera work.) Its technology may lag far behind contemporary standards but its main motifs (and there are several) reverberate to this day. It is the exemplar of German Expressionism, an artistic style that has overarching historical significance because it emerged after the First World War but was denounced as "degenerate" by the Third Reich. The German Expressionist aesthetic also influenced *Batman*'s creator, Bob Kane.

The continuum between Arkham Asylum's odious psychiatric staff and Dr. Caligari, the charlatan asylum superintendent of silent cinema, is clear and continuous albeit complicated. The fragile line between sanity and psychosis remains as confusing today as it was in the days of *Caligari*. These deliberations pop up in court and stay in the public eye. This unanswered and often unspoken question drives the *Arkham Asylum* universe, where doctors become patients and where the mind doctors who treat the patients are typically as sick as their sickest charges, and sometimes sicker. It's a topsy-turvy world.

Over the decades, many sinister psychiatrists have graced—or disgraced—the silver screen. A few were restricted to the small screen of TV, which appeared in most American homes by the middle of the 20th century and so has been monitored more closely than the big screen. Video games are far younger than celluloid film or electronic tubes and so offer fewer examples of sinister psychiatrists than screen media. Yet one game, *Arkham Asylum*, and its spinoffs, abound in sinister psychiatrists. There are arguably enough examples of sinister psychiatrists in this single-story arc to compensate for the years that video games lack in experience or existence. One television series showcases Arkham Asylum for the Criminally Insane (the institution) better than any big screen *Batman* movie to date: *Gotham* (2014–2018).

124 Section IV: Big Screen Parallels

Dr. Caligari (Werner Krauss), in top hat, stands left of his somnambulist Cesare (Conrad Veidt), whom he turns into a murderer via hypnosis in *The Cabinet of Dr. Caligari* **(1919). Dr. Caligari became the "poster child" for sinister cinema psychiatrists, and for charlatan psychiatrists, but his evil deeds are overshadowed by** *Arkham* **psychiatrists and scientists who also command their patients to kill, turning them into zombies rather than Caligari-esque somnambulists.**

Directed by Danny Cannon and developed by Bruno Heller, *Gotham* is a police procedural based on DC Comics characters and aired by Fox Networks. It is still aired at the time of this writing and starts its fifth and final season in 2019. Its action in the fictional metropolis is set in the present day, nearly a century after the establishment of the asylum that memorializes Elizabeth Arkham, mother of Dr. Amadeus Arkham, circa 1920.

Arkham Asylum did not begin as Arkham Asylum, according to the mythos, and Dr. Amadeus Arkham of the Arkham clan was not the first sinister psychiatrist to run the asylum. *Arkham Asylum: A Living Hell* describes the asylum that existed before the Arkham family came to occupy the dilapidated Victorian structure. The mansion was named "The Gotham House of Madness and Ill Humors." Jason Blood, an occultist and owner of the property, housed the mentally ill on the grounds, and attempted to exorcise the evil spirits that inhabited those unfortunate souls. His efforts were consistent with the long-standing belief that demons and dybbuks cause psychosis. His cruel treatment of the human inhabitants and their inhumane chains and cages were also consistent with asylum practices that pre-dated reforms advocated by the likes of the American Dorothea

Dix, the British Quaker William Tuke and the French psychiatrist Pinel. Sadly, many of those abuses persisted far longer than they should have.

After the Arkhams take charge, at least two of the Arkham clan practice psychiatry at the asylum. Each is evil, to say the least. Dr. Amadeus Arkham, son of the asylum's namesake, shocks one patient to death, under the guise of delivering curative ECT (electroshock therapy). Admittedly, he had his reasons for his "outburst": "Mad Dog" Hawkins had raped and murdered Amadeus' wife and daughter, even though Amadeus offered Hawkins more humane care than other settings and viewed him as "mad" rather than "bad" and treated him like a patient rather than a prisoner. Dr. Arkham's exploitation of ECT as a torture device in a psychiatric setting is a tried and true technique which recurs many times over in movies, and even appears in famous action-adventure hospital chase scenes.

When Dr. Amadeus Arkham murders his mother in the first few pages of Grant Morrison's graphic novel, *Arkham Asylum: A Serious House on Serious Earth* (DC Comics, 1989), he may have been acting out of mercy rather than murderous intent. The text is ambiguous and allows the reader to add his or her own interpretation. Amadeus may have euthanized his demented mother who hallucinated bats and ate bugs and had become bedbound, although he told others that she suicided to escape her sorry state. His own dissociation blocked his recollection of this event until Mad Dog's acts triggered his memory.

Amadeus' nephew, Dr. Jeremiah Arkham, has no excuse for his bad behavior, other than the probability that he inherited the same neurodegenerative gene that afflicted his uncle and his late great-aunt. Jeremiah is so sinister that he organizes a Mafia-like group of scientists and other physicians—Ministry of Science—to aid and abet his evil acts. Among other things, the league turns patients into zombies who do their bidding and then exploits them as test subjects. They recruit unassuming and vulnerable scientists such as The Reaper, a Holocaust survivor whose judgment is impaired by his emotions. The albino geneticist Dr. Linda Friitawa, (aka Fright), is also drawn into the fold, partly because she has little recourse after having lost her medical license for unethical genetics experiments.

Successors and predecessors to the Arkhams are no better. Even Dr. Cavendish, the cross-dressing psychiatrist who presided over Arkham prior to the ascent of Amadeus Arkham, was evil to the core. Cavendish recollects the cross-dressing killer psychiatrist in Brian de Palma's *Dressed to Kill* (1980), not to mention the unforgettable Norman Bates of Hitchcock's classic, *Psycho* (1960), who wore his mother's wig and dress. Norman was not a psychiatrist, but he became the subject of a psychiatrist's summary as the film ended. This crossdressing scenes anticipates Amadeus' crossdressing after the murder of his mother, when he dons her wedding dress and parades before her mirror, in a twisted ritual that symbolizes his psychotic identification with his deceased mother, in the spirit of Norman Bates.

As time goes on, Dr. Hugo Strange and Dr. Jonathan Crane (also known as "Scarecrow") appear in Arkham Asylum, as does Dr. Alyse Sinner, the one-time medical student who befriended and presumably bedded Dr. Jeremiah Arkham and who eventually heads the asylum herself. Each of these demonic doctors is admitted to Arkham at some point in their careers. Dr. Harleen Quinzel, better known as Harley Quinn, did not begin with evil intent, like so many of her peers. Her chief flaws are professional ineptness, with an inability to control her "countertransference" reactions and overemoting in the presence of patients. Dr. Quinzel's colorful story about her dalliance with the Joker earned her a separate chapter.

Dr. Hugo Strange is among the worst of the lot. He experiments on unwitting inmates of Arkham and moves them to even scarier confines on Indian Hill. In the television series *Gotham,* we see Strange concoct strange combinations of humans and animals a la Dr. Moreau. He later lets these hardened criminals loose, so they can terrorize the city in their monstrous and sometimes superpowered forms.

Dr. Hugo Strange was not invented for *Arkham.* Rather, he is one of the oldest and longest-lasting villains of the Batman universe, created by *Batman* veterans Bill Finger and Bob Kane. Dr. Strange debuts in *Detective Comics* #36 in February 1940. He has many incarnations over the years, morphing from sinister scientist to sinister psychiatrist to asylum superintendent to psychology professor and more. Whatever his function within the fields of science, psychiatry or psychology, he is always evil.

In the TV series *Gotham,* Dr. Strange is played by a bearded B.D. Wong, who has a long resume of doctor, experimenter, and psychiatrist roles. His role as evil paleo-biologist Dr. Henry Wu in the *Jurassic* franchise (*Jurassic Park,* 1993; dir. Steven Spielberg); (*Jurassic World,* 2015: dir. Colin Trevorrow); (*Jurassic World: Fallen Kingdom* (2018: dir. J.A. Bayona) is consistent with his *Gotham* character. Yet Wong was also revered for his role as the dispassionate and omniscient psychiatrist and Special Agent Huang on NBC's *Law & Order: SVU* (Wolf: 1999–2018). Although he is a psychiatrist, Wong's *SVU* character is an FBI special agent, on temporary loan to NYPD. SVU is still aired, and is currently television's longest lasting drama, although Wong departed the series before Season 13 and before *Gotham* aired and cast him in a very different light.

At some point, audiences learn the backstory of Dr. Strange. Strange was "abandoned as a child, and reared in state homes," or perhaps in an orphanage on Gotham's Lower East Side, near the infamous "Crime Alley" in Gotham's "Hell's Crucible." Other early DC characters trace their origins to the LES or to Hell's Kitchen, and some of DC's early cartoonists also hail from LES Jewish environs near Delancey Street. Even as a youth, Hugo tinkered with genetic experiments. As an adult, his genetic engineering endeavors gain full steam, and produce frightening monstrosities in his *Arkham* outpost. He can also resurrect the dead, which conflicts with his credibility as a Mengele-like medical experimenter. We may never commiserate with Hugo, but this hardscrabble backstory helps us understand the path he chose.

Scarecrow, or Dr. Jonathan Crane, is also shaped by adverse childhood experiences, perhaps even more directly and more literally than Dr. Strange. In a memorable scene in *Batman Begins* (2005), Dr. Crane (Gillian Murphy) sprays his patients with fast-acting aerosolized hallucinogens, dons a monster mask that he hides in his briefcase, and convinces his Mafioso patients that they, not he, are "crazy."

In *Gotham,* we witness Dr. Jonathan Crane's lifelike flashbacks of experiments conducted on him as a child by his father, also known as Dr. Crane. The elder Dr. Gerald Crane is portrayed as a biology teacher as well as the proverbial mad scientist who uses his son as his test subject. The youthful Jonathan was drugged with fear-inducing serum and exposed to scary images of scarecrows that drove him psychotic and led to his hospitalization on an equally frightening psychiatric ward. Over time, Dr. Crane became as sadistic and sociopathic as his scientist-father and adopts the name Scarecrow almost as an antidote to the images that plagued him in the past.

These comic book-like characters are so over the top that it's hard to imagine their place in "serious cinema"—until we review cinematic history and find a string of sinister psychiatrists throughout film history, from the beginning. We find another recurring meme—that of the psychiatrist as psychotic.

Hypnotists, some of them doctors but most of them not, appear in silent shorts even before the 20th century. Evil experimenters debut early on, playing on the legacy left by 19th century literary figures, such as Dr. Moreau, Dr. Frankenstein, and Dr. Jekyll. Hypnosis was an important treatment technique in the late 19th century, when film and psychoanalysis emerged within a year of one another. Before inventing psychoanalysis, Freud used hypnosis to facilitate free association. He studied with Dr. Charcot in Paris, where artists also came to watch the neurologist demonstrate hypnotic trance on hysterics housed at the Salpêtrière in Paris. Primitive and silent cinema offers several evil hypnotists: *Svengali, Caligari, Mabuse,* for starters.

The Cabinet of Doctor Caligari, which was made in 1919 and which premiered in 1920, remains a classic, in spite of—or perhaps because of—its archaic cinematography and set design and costumery. The plot highlights the blurry line between sanity and insanity; between dream and delusion; between asylum inmate and asylum superintendent. In *Caligari,* two men sit on a bench outside the asylum, conversing and introducing us to the story of a carnival showman who doubles as a sinister asylum psychiatrist. The charlatan psychiatrist also works in a side show where he keeps a cabinet containing a somnambulist (hypnosis subject) named Cesare. Caligari commands Cesare to kill his rivals and anyone who offends him. When Caligari commands Cesare to kill the woman he loves, Cesare cannot comply. Instead, he collapses and dies.

The men tell an engrossing story but, as the film ends, it returns to the framing device that the director reportedly added to soften the story, over the objections of the screenwriters. The narrators reveal themselves to be inmates of the very same asylum that they have been discussing. Their credibility is lost when we learn that their sanity was lost. Yet we wonder if their tale is true, and we wonder who is sane and who is psychotic and how to tell the difference.

As is the case with Dr. Caligari, many memorable screen shrinks offer more than mere entertainment or escape. They may embed important messages about contemporary clinical controversies or they may comment on far-reaching social and political concerns. Specifically, the despotic Dr. Caligari, who commands his surrogate Cesare to kill, was compared to Hitler by an influential but controversial author, Kracauer, who wrote *From Caligari to Hitler* (1947).

Others see parallels between Dr. Caligari and physician-hypnotists, such as Drs. Freud, Charcot, and Janet or with the fictional hypnotist Svengali, who lived many lives in film and theater but never lived in real life. More recently, Dr. Caligari has been linked to the despised Austrian military psychiatrists who sent shellshocked soldiers back to the front after they fled the battlefields during the Great War (World War I). Those psychiatrists essentially commanded soldiers to kill, as if they were Caligari's surrogate, Cesare.[2] The doctors, along with the future Nobel Prize-winning psychiatrist and professor, eventually stood trial at the "Wagner-Jauregg Trial."[3]

Fritz Lang's *Doctor Mabuse* film followed on the heels of *Dr. Caligari* in 1922. Dr. Mabuse was always more popular in Europe than in America. *Mabuse* was reworked many times over before Fritz Lang died. Even after Lang died, Dr. Mabuse reappeared in spin-offs. Mabuse continues to inspire various German musicians, songwriters and even American authors. Mabuse earned a mention by the esteemed American writer,

David Foster Wallace, whose literary career was interrupted by psychiatric hospitalizations and shock therapy before he ultimately suicided.

Hannibal the Cannibal (Dr. Lecter) currently holds the record for repeat American films about sinister psychiatrists. To date, Hannibal Lecter has appeared in only half as many movies as Dr. Mabuse, but Dr. Hannibal Lecter is currently Hollywood's best recognized movie villain. He has surpassed Freddy, the child-molesting janitor from *Nightmare on Elm Street* (1984). The *Arkham Asylum* psychiatrists cannot compete with Hannibal's popularity, even though they appear in the world's best-selling video game to date (and elsewhere in Batman universe).

Hannibal the forensic psychiatrist shines a harsh light on forensic psychiatry, which took some beatings for the Hostess Twinkie defense used in the 1979 Harvey Milk murder trial in San Francisco. Harvey Milk was California's first openly gay elected official. The perpetrator of this double murder (which included SF's Mayor Moscone) attributed his "diminished capacity" to his junk food diet. The jury concurred. This defense made a mockery of insanity defenses. This lenient sentence outraged gay activists. The assailant suicided years later.

A few years later, John Hinkley, Jr., stood trial for his attempted assassination of then-President Reagan. John Hinkley, Jr.'s acquittal via the insanity defense (NGRI) in 1981 catalyzed the Insanity Defense Reform Act of 1984. The grievous gunshot wounds suffered by James Brady led to laws requiring background checks on gun purchasers and a 5-day waiting period.

Fictional Psychiatrist Stories and Their Function as Agents of Reform

Some of fictional psychiatrist stories tell truths about imperfections in the system that need improvement. Some remind us of bad conditions that existed in the past but have since been outlawed—and these films may offer relief from fears about psychiatric treatments or policies that no longer exist. A few films instigated undeserved fear, and one prompted anti–ECT legislation, even though ECT (electroconvulsive therapy) can be lifesaving under certain circumstances and is safer than most medications for persons with certain medical conditions.

The backstory of Amadeus Arkham, and his ECT assassination of Mad Dog, reflects the fear of ECT kindled by Jack Nicholson's electrifying performance as McMurphy in *One Flew Over the Cuckoo's Nest* (Forman; 1975). *Cuckoo's Nest* is etched into the annals of film history because it won all five major Academy Awards and earned a place in the Library of Congress.

Nicholson's character is a smalltime criminal who was arrested for statutory rape and sentenced to a prison farm. To avoid hard labor, he feigns psychosis to facilitate transfer to a supposedly "cushier" psychiatric hospital. There, he locks horns with Nurse Ratched, who retaliates against his rabble-raising on the ward and orchestrates his ECT and later a lobotomy.

Interestingly, this "sinister psychiatrist" is not a psychiatrist at all but is a nurse on a psychiatric ward. Some say that Louise Fletcher's Academy Award-winning (and Golden Globe and BAFTA-winning) portrayal of an embittered, power hungry and vindictive charge nurse commented on societal fears of women's empowerment and the growing feminist movement, which had begun in the late 1960s and had come to full flower by the mid–1970s. Nurse Ratched is even more venomous than Jeremiah Arkham, who considers lobotomy an unnecessary evil, but endorses the use of ECT.

We can identify interesting and important trends in the representation of psychiatric hospitals and psychiatric staff in recent years. Mental hospital movies are either set in the past, are supernatural, or involve prison psychiatry settings. The depictions of psychiatrists who work within those asylums or sanitariums or hospitals or institutions reflect their settings.

For our purposes here, the prison psychiatrist is most significant because *Arkham Asylum for the Criminally Insane* falls under this rubric. However, some aspects of Arkham Asylum overlap with another major trend and so it's worth reviewing each of them.

Most obviously, the supernatural films are removed from reality, and so the need for realistic representation of contemporary treatments or treaters or treatment settings is less essential. Spectators know that those plots exist in a parallel universe that lies outside of consensual reality. Yet supernatural psychiatric films often overlap with other memes.

Most commonly, asylum films are set in bygone eras. They become "period pieces." Many use antiquated treatments that have fallen out of favor and draw on the past for dramatic effect. Alternatively, some films are set in abandoned asylums (haunted or not), to remind us that most asylums were, in fact, abandoned when pharmacological treatments improved, and financial incentives changed. The remake of *House on Haunted Hill* (1999) reminds us of the latter trend, while Clint Eastwood's movie, *Changeling* (2008), chronicles a true tale about mental hospital abuse of women (and child abuse and mass murder) in the late 1920s through the 1930s.

We can posit that shortened hospital stays (courtesy of managed care restrictions, and, to a lesser extent, public health laws that guard against too liberal hospital admissions policies) led to a surge of period films that harp back to times when involuntary incarceration and indefinite hospital stays, and even ordinary inpatient treatment and state institutionalization, were far more prevalent than they are now. *Shutter Island* (2010) is one such film. The 50s-style fedoras of the lead characters shout "period piece," even if spectators don't know that "funny farms" (like the one seen in the opening scene on *Shutter Island*) belong to the distant past.[4] Almost all have been "shuttered" like the name of the island itself and the very few examples that persist charge exorbitant six-figure fees that are not subsidized by medical insurance or government programs.

In contrast to the closing of psychiatric wards, be they in community, university or state hospitals, prison psychiatric wards persist. The population seeking psychiatric care while incarcerated for criminal behavior has exploded. Those centers operate outside of the watchful eyes of managed care and answer to authorities in the criminal justice system, which funds medical care in jails and prisons. The systems themselves have shortcomings, but it is worth knowing that prisoners are the only persons in America who are guaranteed health care by law.

The public may not know that "insane asylums" or "men in white coats" are relics of long-gone eras, and that even "locked wards" or "involuntary admission" (commitment) are used only in extreme circumstances or for criminal confinement. But the public does know about school shootings, workplace massacres, hotel gunman, and shopping mall murders that occur with increasingly frequency in America. The knee-jerk reaction is to blame these tragic events on untreated mental illness and to hope out loud that prison psychiatry becomes more available.

130 Section IV: Big Screen Parallels

In *Shutter Island* (2010), a bald-headed psychiatrist Dr. Cawley (Ben Kingsley) speaks to a skeptical U.S. Marshall Teddy Daniels (Leonardo DiCaprio), as another "Marshall" (Mark Ruffalo) stands back. The opening scene shows an antiquated "funny farm," most of which have been shuttered, as the name implies. Arkham Asylum for the Criminally Insane stands in stark contrast to this placid sanitarium of the past, which also houses "criminally insane" persons like DiCaprio's character, Teddy Daniels, but treats them far better than Arkham's inmate-patients.

Yet we hear public outcry and news exposés about the shortage of prison psychiatrists willing to provide treatment to inmates who need it and want it. We hear about innovative telepsychiatry programs to ameliorate such shortages. We also hear about the penal system's inability to distinguish persons with genuine psychiatric or substance abuse problems from unrepentant sociopaths who are not expected to benefit from currently available treatments and who do not meet criteria for official psychiatric diagnoses. While we hear about escalating concerns about public safety, and about demands for gun control overall and especially among the mentally ill, we also hear diatribes about appropriate and available treatment for persons designated as SPMI (seriously and persistently mentally ill). In psychiatry newsletters and journals, we repeatedly read about the criminalization of the mentally ill, who are more likely to be incarcerated than hospitalized. Some consider that to be a crime, in the metaphorical sense.

Given these shifts, we can readily understand the uptick in entertainment related to prison psychiatry settings. Entertainment offers a safe distance from the realities of the day but allows a space to contemplate those upsetting realities as it masquerades as an escape. Admittedly, *Silence of the Lambs* (1991) cemented a trend when it won all major categories of Academy Awards (as did *Cuckoo's Nest* in 1975), and proved that criminal psychiatrists like Hannibal Lecter, as seen in a specially fortified prison cell, could be popular with the public. That alone could convince moviemakers and game designers to create similar settings or related characters. Yet prison psychiatry settings in cinema or games or TV editorialize while they entertain and remind us that long-term state hospitals have shut their doors or have revolving doors. Judging by the continuing expansion of the *Arkham* franchise, the end of this trend is nowhere in sight.

Fiction as a Reflection of Real-Life Concerns and Controversies

At present day, professionals worry more about the revolving door of mental hospitals than about persons who are "locked away" behind gated doors. We are concerned about patients who are released before their symptoms cease. In recent years, we have witnessed seemingly senseless murders committed by persons with schizophrenic symptoms. News reports tell of parents who pleaded with emergency room staff and begged them to admit their adult children to mental wards, only to see their progeny turned away or discharged too soon. And then they go on to commit unspeakable acts, as happened when a disturbed young man (Andrew Goldstein) pushed a young blonde woman onto a subway platform. That act inspired Kendra's Law, and New York State's practice of "outpatient commitment" to a psychiatric clinic (rather than a locked hospital).[5] Many wonder if the *Batman* movie massacre, perpetrated by a neuroscience graduate student, might have been prevented had Holmes been admitted to a mental hospital for closer observation and more intensive treatment, instead of continuing care through out-patient health service office appointments (which he could not access after withdrawing from school).

Sadly, the stories about "what could have been, what should have been, what might not have happened" have multiplied in recent years. There are too many stories to recount. We all heard about Adam Lanza, who was diagnosed with autism spectrum disorder or Asperger's syndrome, but who went untreated and unsupervised before accessing his mother's guns and shooting his mother and 20 schoolchildren and 6 staff at the school where his mother taught.

More recently, David Katz's name made headlines when the videogame champion opened fire at a videogame competition. Katz had a long history of schizophrenia and an impressively long history of attempted treatments, as well as a concerned mother who apparently tried everything she could. (Lanza's mother, in contrast, took her troubled son with her to the firing range, permitted him to shoot and never secured the cache of firearms she stored at home.)

These dangerous persons described on the nightly news make up only a small minority of all seriously mentally ill. But these tragic events remain etched in our memories, largely because of the extreme harm that results, and because of the extreme remorse, hand-wringing and second-guessing that follows in the wake of seemingly preventable deeds. These stories suggest that contemporary psychiatrists or psychiatric hospitals are not doing enough, rather than doing too much, by incarcerating persons inappropriately, as pictured in "sinister psychiatrist cinema."

Shifts in the Professional Prestige of Psychiatrists

Many condemn filmmakers or game manufacturers for producing films or video games that depict mental health care or mental patients so badly, and for exploiting the public's fears about psychiatric treatment and mental illness. Yet media's many "sinister psychiatrists" also recollect the prominence and prestige that American psychiatry enjoyed for a good part of the 20th century. Psychiatry enjoyed its highest status in the mid–1950s, when more people were in mental hospitals than ever before and ever since, and when veterans returning from World War II needed—and wanted—more mental health care.

Then times changed. Professional authority was challenged by "consumers," health insurance regulations, managed care administrators, Internet-based information sites and chat rooms, direct-to-consumer pharmaceutical advertising, and easier access to non-medical mental health training, with licensure laws that permit treatment by a wide variety of non-medically trained practitioners and by therapists who lack a doctorate degree (as required for clinical psychologists). The proliferation of "patient satisfaction" surveys contributed to America's current opioid epidemic by turning patients into "consumers" or even customers. Some say that the medical armor lost its luster a few decades earlier, when malpractice claims spiked, and attorneys without medical degrees challenged choices made by doctors (some of whom deserved it). While such disputes are bad for the accused M.D.'s, they are good for fiction—for they push the plot and combine courtroom drama with medical drama, peppered with tales of personal tragedy or triumph.

From Evil Scientists to Murderous Mental Patients

Before concluding this essay, it's worth examining an earlier shift in mental health care administration to understand how those sea changes translated into shifts in traditional fictional villains. In the early to mid–20th century, evil scientists took center stage. By 1959, the cultural climate changed. The mental patient became the most common film villain. That mental patient could easily be a disturbed psychiatrist like Dr. Caligari or any of the Arkham psychiatrists.

Superficially, we can attribute this shift to the success of Hitchcock's *Psycho* (1960). In Hollywood, nothing succeeds better than success, and moviemakers emulate the motifs and techniques of very well-received movies. Yet we can equally easily trace this shift to the deinstitutionalization movement that gained steam in the mid–1950s, after phenothiazines became available in America. Those new anti-psychotic medications stopped the haunting voices of schizophrenia and lessened the need for custodial care. These "events" occurred nearly simultaneously and so it is difficult to say which held greater sway—Hitchcock's enormously influential *Psycho* or the release of long-term mental patients from state hospitals.

Here is what happened: in the post-phenothiazine era, persons with serious psychotic symptoms no longer needed the same level of supervision that they needed prior to the invention of these so-called "chemical restraints." Or so it seemed. And so, they were set free, to a degree.

Deinstitutionalization began a decade or two earlier in response to rising costs even though the much-touted "deinstitionalization movement" did not begin full force until the mid–1950s, shortly before *Psycho*'s release. Anthony Perkins' terrifying portrayal of the soft-spoken and socially awkward motel clerk Norman Bates reified fears that the shy "boy next door" might be a seriously ill mental patient and a murderous one at that. By then, it was common knowledge that persons who had been locked away in so-called insane asylums or state hospitals had been released and sent home to a nebulous "community." This policy shifts justifiably ignited public anxiety, which they displaced onto portrayals of dangerous mental patients in movies.

Arkham Asylum goes many steps further. Not only does it house dangerous criminals who are too out of control to restrain in Blackgate Prison, and who repeatedly escape from both prison and from Arkham, but it is run by a string of psychiatrists who are more psychotic and sinister than their patients. Thus, the *Arkham Asylum* franchise represents more than the artistic and technical achievements of its creators and speaks to current concerns.

Consider these 2007 CDC (Center for Disease Control) statistics: half the American public seeks some form of psychotherapy at some point in their lives and almost 50 percent are diagnosed with a mental illness.[6] Twenty-five percent take prescription psychotropic medications. Antidepressants are the most commonly prescribed medications in America.[7]

Those numbers suggest that Americans feel the need for relief from psychiatric symptoms. Some value psychiatric treatment—while many fear treatments. They fear losing control over those symptoms and they fear abdicating control to persons who provide such treatment, whose qualifications and characters are enigmatic. So, they project their fears onto stories they see on screen, be it a video screen or a celluloid screen. Or they project such fears onto cheap pulp pages of comic books or onto glossy pages of graphic novels about Arkham.

In the end, it appears that the *Arkham* universe offers much more than mere fantasy stories about an unpleasant institution and its unpleasant inhabitants. It channels fears, and maybe it extinguishes some fears and maybe it ignites more, much like Grant Morrison's own magic spells. The franchise succeeds because it *speaks* to the anxieties of our era. And those anxieties are not limited to the "other" or the school shooter. That "other" may be you or me.

NOTES

1. Sharon Packer, *Sinister Psychiatrists: From Caligari to Hannibal* (Jefferson, NC: McFarland, 2012).
2. Anton Kaes, *Shell-Shock Cinema: Weimar Cinema and the Wounds of War* (Princeton, NJ: Princeton University Press, 2009).
3. The trial became known as the "Wagner-Jauregg Trial" not because Wagner-Jauregg was the only doctor on trial but because his name was so well-known in Austrian society and in scientific circles. He was but one of several psychiatrists accused of military crimes. Freud testified about hysteria at this trial and some say that Freud gained greater respect and recognition as a result.
4. A few farm-like residential treatments facilities remain in rural areas, and some drug rehabilitation residential programs include horse therapy, but these very pricey places are rarely reimbursed by insurance and so generally serve the very wealthy only.
5. Jonathan Gregg, "Will the Real Andrew Goldstein Take the Stand," *Time Magazine*, Friday, Mar. 03, 2000. http://www.time.com/time/arts/article/0,8599,40257,00.html#ixzz1bBYxafL0. Accessed online on October 18, 2011. *The* New York Times *ran Dozens of Articles on This Topic Over a Course of Years. Articles Include, but Are Not Limited, To: Julian Barnes: Judge Allows Lesser Charge in Trial of Subway Pusher,"* NY Times, *March 22, 2000; Julian Barnes, "Second Murder Trial Opens in Subway Shoving Case,"* NY Times, *March 4, 2000; David Rohde, "For Retrial, Subway Defendant Goes Off Medication,"* NY Times, *February 23, 2000; Michael Winerip, "The Nation; Behind One Man's Mind,"* NY Times, *December 26, 1999; Anemona Hartocollis, "Nearly 8 Years Later, Guilty Plea in Subway Killing,"* NY Times, *October 11, 2006; Anemona Hartocollis, "A Subway Nightmare Will Be the Focus of Yet a Third Trial,"* NY Times, *May 23, 2006. News of His Imminent Parole Did Not Attract the Same Public Reactions as the Trials Themselves.*
6. Non-commercially biased data is published on government-sponsored websites that include http://mentalhealth.gov/statistics; http://www.nimh.nih.gov/statistics; http://www.ptsd.va.gov/professional/pages/epidemiological-facts-ptsd.asp; detailed statistics about trends in pharmaceutical prescribing is also available through various financial websites, market research firms, and http:www.ProPublica.org.
7. www.cdc.gov/nchs/fastats/drugs.htm; http://articles.cnn.com/2007-07-09/health/antidepressants_1_antidepressants-high-blood-pressure-drugs-psychotropic-drugs?_s =PM:HEALTH, accessed October 16, 2011.

Haunted by Madness

*Horror and the Supernatural
in Arkham Asylum*

Michael Markus

When it was originally published in 1989, Grant Morrison's graphic novel *A Serious House on Serious Earth* constituted the first real attempt to fully flesh out the dimensions and properties of what had previously been a largely unexplored corner of DC Comics' Gotham City: The Elizabeth Arkham Asylum for the Criminally Insane.[1] The book's enormous success ensured not only that Arkham Asylum would become an increasingly visible location within the DC Comics universe, but that it would be one which immediately conjures a set of frightful associations. Of course, Morrison's depiction of Arkham Asylum as a frightening place did not, in and of itself, constitute a novel approach to the representation of a mental asylum. And indeed, for the most part, the fears which the asylum evokes in Morrison's book are precisely the types of fears which cultural representations of mental asylums have always evoked. However, Morrison did introduce, as well, a crucial representational innovation: Arkham Asylum, as it emerges in the pages of *A Serious House on Serious Earth*, is haunted. This essay situates Morrison's depiction of Arkham Asylum in a centuries-long history of the cultural representation of the mental asylum. I argue that the precise way Morrison deploys the supernatural in his depiction of the asylum has the effect, not of dispelling or displacing the standard asylum-related fears which the book evokes, but of transmuting and accentuating them.

The Image of the Asylum: Representation and Popular Anxieties

In his 1792 treatise *Observations on Maniacal Disorders*, the English physician William Parteger noted that "[t]he idea of a *mad-house* is apt to excite, in the breast of most people, the strongest emotions of horror and alarm; upon a supposition, not altogether ill-founded, that once a patient is doomed to take up his abode in these places, he will not only be exposed to very great cruelty, but it is a great chance, whether he recovers or not, if he ever more sees the outside of the walls."[2] Parteger's comment is highly suggestive of the pervasiveness in eighteenth century England of a cluster of popular anxieties regarding mental asylums. Given the fact that most people at the time would have had no direct contact with such places, it is reasonable to conclude that the presence of these broadly shared anxieties was the product, mainly, of cultural depictions of asylums—both visual and literary—which had been a part of England's cultural landscape from the early seventeenth century.[3]

As Parteger's observation indicates, some of these culturally evoked anxieties pertained to notions of the horrific conditions to which asylum inmates were popularly supposed to be subjected. The madhouse, as it emerged both in English literary and visual representations, was a place where mad people—forlorn, erratic, often naked and frequently dangerous—were confined in close quarters with one another. Manacles and chains limited their movement, while locked doors and barred windows ensured their complete segregation from the world of the sane. Worse still, savage violence, in the form of beatings and floggings, was frequently directed against the inmates by their keepers. In short, to be an asylum inmate was to be trapped in a world not only of madness, but of unfreedom, fear, and abuse.

Moreover, Parteger's comment is suggestive, as well, of the existence of a second set of anxieties which might be said to lie beneath the first. In noting the prevalence of the belief that the front door of the madhouse swings only one way, and that even a "recovered" patient—in other words, a *sane* person—might find it impossible to effect release from their confinement, Parteger touched upon popular anxieties regarding the involuntary confinement of sane people in asylums. And indeed, the relatively modest proliferation in the number of privately run, unregulated madhouses in eighteenth century England had quickly been accompanied by culturally expressed anxieties regarding the possibility that sane persons might *intentionally* be confined in such places by grasping relatives or powerful enemies who act in collusion with corrupt asylum-keepers.[4] Eliza Heywood's novella *The Distress'd Orphan; or, Love in a Mad-house* (1726), which features a heroine who is unjustly confined in a madhouse by a greedy uncle, provides an early example of a stock narrative which would recur frequently thereafter in literary representations of the asylum.[5]

A related anxiety—one which is at once more prosaic and more unsettling—sits closely beside this notion of the innocent falling victim to the machinations of the malicious: namely, the possibility that the long-term confinement of a sane person in an asylum might occur even in the *absence* of such malicious intentionality. Once confined in an asylum, might not a sane person (or, for that matter, a mentally ill person who had recovered their sanity) have difficulty in convincing even well-meaning and professional staff of their suitability for release? Mid-nineteenth century developments on both sides of the Atlantic—particularly the advent of governmental oversight of asylums, the "professionalization" of asylum management along avowedly "medical" lines, and the incredibly rapid increase in asylum populations—brought such anxieties to greater prominence. And of course, this anxiety surrounding the notion that "sanity" might be a difficult thing to *prove* is suggestive, in turn, of an even more fundamental and disquieting thought: that the line which demarcates the border between the realms of sanity and insanity might be far more faintly drawn than we would prefer it to be.[6] If it is difficult to tell the sane from the mad, then the reverse must also be true.

Closely connected with these anxieties surrounding the possibility of sane persons being involuntarily confined in asylums is the notion, clearly present from the eighteenth century onward, that such places can actually *cause* madness. For instance, Annilia, the heroine of Heywood's *Distress'd Orphan*, is terrified by the possibility that the horrific

conditions of the asylum in which she has been confined will literally drive her mad. And crucially, asylum doctors and staff have not been held to be immune from this danger. Monsieur Maillard, the asylum superintendent featured in Edgar Allan Poe's "The System of Dr. Tarr and Professor Fether" (1845) provides an early literary example of an asylum doctor who, like Dr. Amadeus Arkham in *A Serious House on Serious Earth*, ultimately winds up being confined in his own asylum. The prevalence of such anxieties even amongst asylum professionals is attested to by the words of the English asylum administrator John C. Bucknill, who, in his 1860 address to the Association of Medical Officers of Asylums and Hospitals for the Insane, lamented "the number of mental physicians who have suffered more or less from the seeming contagion of mental disease."[7]

Asylum Anxieties and the "Anti-Psychiatric" Turn

In the years immediately following World War II, respect for the psychiatric profession appears to have been at an all-time high. However, beginning in the late 1950s a host of new scholarly critiques of the modern mental institution began to appear, putting to rest any notion that these institutions might be evolving in such a way as to obviate traditional popular anxieties.[8] The most widely read and influential of these critiques was that penned by the sociologist Erving Goffman, whose 1961 study *Asylums: Essays on the Social Situation of Mental Patients and Other Inmates* had the practical effect of repackaging and reasserting traditional anxieties. Although his tone was cool and dispassionate, Goffman's argument suggested that asylum conditions were not only horrific, but intrinsically so. The state mental hospital, he argued, was a "total institution" which operated along the same lines as a prison or a Chinese re-education camp.[9] Most asylum inmates were confined involuntarily, and all of them experienced a complete deprivation of autonomy while so confined. And while floggings and beatings were by now a thing of the past, he contended that the "disciplinary use of medical practices" was commonplace.[10] "The use of electroshock, on the attendant's recommendation, as a means of threatening into discipline and quieting those that won't be threatened" was "widespread," he claimed, while the use of lobotomy for the same purpose was held in reserve "for a hospital's most incorrigible and troublesome patients."[11]

Furthermore, Goffman's study revivified the traditional fear that just about *anyone* might find themselves confined in such a place. The villainous role once assigned to the avaricious family member who sought to wrongly confine a relative was now being performed by society itself, which sought to isolate and contain social non-conformists.[12] The chances of a person finding themselves confined in an asylum, Goffman averred, had much less to do with mental illness than with simple bad luck: "[O]ne could say that ... [asylum] patients distinctly suffer not from mental illness, but from contingencies."[13]

Opposite: Poster for original *House on Haunted Hill* (1959), where an eccentric millionaire (Vincent Price) orchestrates the murder of his wife, who conducts an affair with a psychiatrist and party guest. The remake of *House on Haunted Hill* (1999) takes place in the Vannicut Asylum for the Criminally Insane and incorporates imagery of Nazi-like medical experiments. The fictional Vannicut Asylum opened in the same years as the fictional and refurbished Arkham Asylum. Like the haunted Vannicut Asylum, Morrison's Arkham Asylum is also inhabited by ghosts, and thus continues a long legacy of conflating mental illness and asylums with supernatural forces.

Worse still, once a person was confined in an mental institution, it was next to impossible for them convince anyone of their sanity. Alarmingly, he noted that "[t]he patient's very presence in the hospital is taken as *prima facie* evidence that he is mentally ill, since the hospitalization of these persons is what the institution is for. A very common answer to the patient who claims he is sane is the statement: 'If you aren't sick, you wouldn't be in the hospital.'"[14] Moreover, once confined in the asylum, every statement which an inmate makes, and every action which he or she takes, is interpreted through the lens of their putative mental illness. As Goffman put it, "[E]verything a patient is caused to do can be described as a part of his treatment or of custodial management; everything a patient does on his own can be defined as symptomatic of his disorder or his convalescence."[15] And finally, Goffman's study also served to reaffirm the traditional notion that it is difficult to *preserve* one's sanity in an asylum: "[S]ome attendants feel," he reported, "that prolonged exposure to mental patients can have a contagious effect."[16]

From the early 1960s, the asylum-related anxieties thus refurbished by Goffman and other critics began to find expression in popular culture at a seemingly unprecedented rate. Ken Kesey's novel *One Flew Over the Cuckoo's Nest* (1962) highlighted the notion that mental hospitals might employ painful and potentially devastating interventions such as ECT and lobotomy as punishment rather than treatment; and the enormously successful 1975 film adaptation brought this point home viscerally to an exponentially larger audience. The notion that asylums can *cause* mental illness was underscored in Samuel Fuller's film *Shock Corridor* (1963), which relates the story of an investigative reporter who goes undercover in a state mental hospital—only to succumb, by the end of the film, to catatonic schizophrenia. Traditional anxieties regarding the possibility of sane people being wrongly confined in an asylum and unable to obtain release were sensationalized in Howard Avedis' exploitation film *The Fifth Floor* (1978), which was based on a true story, according to advertisements.

The Impact of Deinstitutionalization

Ironically, these depictions were being produced at a time when the actual likelihood of anyone—mentally ill or not—being confined in a state-run psychiatric facility was declining precipitously. The "deinstitutionalization" of the mental health care systems of both the U.S. and the U.K. took place largely during the same time period: the early 1960s to the mid–1980s.[17] By 1985, the inpatient population in state mental hospitals in the United States was just one fifth of what it had been in the mid–1950s[18]; and under the new legal regime which accompanied deinstitutionalization, long-term involuntary confinement in a psychiatric ward had become a fate reserved almost exclusively for those who had been processed through the criminal justice system.

Although the impact of deinstitutionalization on cultural representations of the asylum appears to have been quite limited prior to the late 1990s, its influence since then has been pervasive.[19] Crucially, the developments associated with deinstitutionalization appear to have done little to dislodge or upend traditional asylum-related anxieties. Indeed, deinstitutionalization has led, largely, to the displacement, as opposed to the replacement, of these anxieties. This displacement has taken two main forms: displacement from the present to the past; and displacement from the realm of the natural to that of the supernatural.

As Sharon Packer has noted, in the wake of deinstitutionalization, films which strive for an aura of authenticity in their depictions of asylums must either be set in the past, when large state-run mental hospitals were still in operation, or they must be set in prison psychiatric wards, which have been relatively unaffected by the process of deinstitutionalization.[20] Films set in the past, such as *Changeling* (2008) and *Shutter Island* (2011), deftly exploit most of the asylum-related anxieties which have been noted, while at the same time comfortably displacing those anxieties onto a bygone era.

The displacement of traditional asylum anxieties onto the realm of the supernatural is a development which is closely connected with another important aspect of deinstitutionalization—namely, the fact that many the state mental hospitals which were abandoned during the process of deinstitutionalization were never re-purposed and fell into utter dilapidation. Such abandoned asylum sites have frequently become, themselves, sources of popular fascination, with the perhaps predictable result that they have often come to be seen as haunted locations.[21] However, as one sociological study has noted, the status of these abandoned asylum sites as "haunted" is related not merely to the physical decrepitude of the structures themselves, but, more importantly, to popular beliefs about what occurred in these structures during the era when they were operational: "While any abandoned building potentially raises curiosity about past use and occupancy, the particular mystique of madness and the long shadow of carceral care mean the abandoned asylum is an especially unsettling space."[22] In other words, their status as haunted places is, at least in part, a direct function of the persistence of traditional anxieties which the asylum has always evoked.

Detective Jim Gordon (and future Commissioner Gordon), as played by Benjamin McKenzie in TV's *Gotham* (2015–2019), stands outside of Arkham Asylum's massive gates that supposedly protect Gotham City citizens from the mentally ill and murderous inmates inside. Gordon himself was temporarily incarcerated in Arkham after being dishonorably discharged from GCPD. While still on the force, he was temporarily assigned to guard duty at Arkham.

Prior to the late 1990s, only a handful of films depicted asylums as being places where supernatural events might occur. Since that time, however, there has been a veritable explosion in the number of horror films which depict asylums as places characterized by ghostly presences (*The House on Haunted Hill* [1999]; *Gothika* [2003]), demonic spirits (*Silent Hill* [1999]; *Session 9* [2001]), or psychic phenomena (*In Dreams* [1999]). Even though some of these films depict *functioning* asylums, as opposed to abandoned ones, there can be little question that cultural awareness of deinstitutionalization has played an important part in instigating this trend. Indeed, the notion of the "haunted abandoned asylum" gave way quite naturally to the notion that functioning asylums, too, might be sites of supernatural activity.[23] Films such as these typically evoke many of the traditional asylum-related anxieties which have been noted, such as those regarding the abusive treatment of inmates or the possibility of sane persons being involuntarily confined. At the same time, these films displace those anxieties onto an entity—be it a ghost, demon, or psychic serial-killer—which is presented as being a far more pressing threat than the asylum conditions themselves. The overall effect of such displacement is to mitigate, to some degree, the asylum-related anxieties which the film has evoked.

Asylum Anxieties and the Supernatural in A Serious House on Serious Earth

Grant Morrison's *A Serious House on Serious Earth* was published in 1989—about a decade prior to these deinstitutionalization-related developments in horror cinema. Morrison's deployment of supernatural elements in his depiction of Arkham Asylum was highly innovative, coming as it did at a time when such elements had only rarely been utilized in *any* representations of mental asylums. Moreover, as we shall see, the role played by the supernatural in Morrison's depiction of Arkham Asylum differs substantially from that which it typically had played, or would in the future come to play, in other depictions of asylums.

A Serious House on Serious Earth employs a dual-narrative structure, with one narrative set in the past and focusing on the events surrounding Dr. Amadeus Arkham's establishment of the asylum in the 1920s, and the other set in the present and focusing on the events of a single evening during which Batman confronts the asylum inmates—led by the Joker—who have seized control of the institution. Significantly, much of the book's dramatic tension is leavened by Morrison's canny exploitation of virtually the full panoply of asylum-related anxieties which popular culture has been evoking for centuries.

For instance, the book touches upon longstanding anxieties regarding the abuse of asylum inmates—particularly in one memorable scene in which Dr. Arkham intentionally employs an ECT apparatus to electrocute one of his patients, the despicable "Mad Dog" Hawkins. Furthermore, the prospect of "present day" patients being severely harmed even by the seemingly benign treatments which they receive in the asylum is also highlighted. The well-intentioned and comparatively gentle psychotherapy which the inmate Two-Face has undergone, for example, has resulted in the crippling of his mind's executive function to the extent that he is completely unable to make any decisions whatsoever.

A Serious House on Serious Earth is also highly evocative of traditional anxieties surrounding the possibility of the involuntary confinement of sane persons in mental asylums. Indeed, the story of Batman's confrontation with the inmates of Arkham Asylum is, at bottom, the story of a (reasonably) sane man who finds himself involuntarily confined in a mental hospital. Batman enters the asylum unwillingly, doing so only because the Joker threatens to murder or mutilate hostages if he refuses; and once he is inside, the ongoing hostage threat is utilized to force him to undergo psychological testing, as well as to engage in a potentially deadly game of hide-and-seek. The theme of the sane person trapped in the world of the mad is underscored by the book's epigraph, which is taken from Lewis Carroll's *Alice's Adventures in Wonderland*:

> "But I don't want to go among mad people," Alice remarked.
> "Oh, you can't help that," said the Cat: "We're all mad here. I'm mad, you're mad."
> "How do you know I'm mad?" said Alice.
> "You must be," said the Cat, "or you wouldn't have come here."[24]

This exchange, which is redolent of the type of terrifying circular logic by which Erving Goffman claimed asylum inmates were kept imprisoned by their warders, hints as well at the unsettling possibility that the boundary between sanity and madness is an ill-defined and porous one.

That latter possibility, in turn, is intimately interrelated with another traditional anxiety which the book evokes—namely, the concern that mental asylums might actually *cause* madness. Both asylum administrators featured in the book—Dr. Amadeus Arkham, who founds the asylum, and Dr. Charles Cavendish, who is the administrator in the present—ultimately wind up hopelessly insane. Although the reader eventually discovers that Dr. Arkham's insanity is possibly hereditary, and that it began to manifest itself prior to the founding of the asylum, the same cannot be said of Dr. Cavendish. And of course, a central aspect of the book's plot is the profound deterioration of Batman's own mental health during his time in the asylum. Shortly after having had his nerves rattled by the rudimentary word-association test which the Joker has ordered Dr. Ruth Adams to administer to him, Batman begins to experience memory flashbacks to his childhood—flashbacks which are so intrusive and debilitating that he feels it necessary to thrust a shard of glass completely through his left palm in order to dispel them.

While *A Serious House on Serious Earth* thus evokes a host of standard asylum-related anxieties, Morrison also introduces what was, in 1989, a noteworthy innovation: the asylum-related anxieties which the narrative evokes are refracted through the lens of the supernatural. Specifically, *A Serious House on Serious Earth* adopts elements of a horror-genre convention which originally came to prominence in the 1960s and 1970s—a convention which Stephen King has referred to as the archetypal "Bad Place,"[25] and which literary scholar Dale Bailey refers to as "the contemporary haunted house."[26] The contemporary haunted house, as elucidated by Bailey, differs from traditional conceptions of the haunted house in that the house is not presented as being merely the *location* of a ghostly haunting or spiritual presence. On the contrary, the house is presented as being, *itself*, a living organism, "sentient and malign," possessing a will and a personality of its own.[27] A classic example of such a depiction is found in Shirley Jackson's *The Haunting of Hill House* (1959), the famous opening sentences of which breathe life into the notion of a man-made structure being a sentient organism: "No live organism can continue for long to exist sanely under conditions of absolute reality; even larks and katydids are supposed, by some, to dream. Hill House, not sane, stood by itself against its hills, holding darkness within; it had stood so for eighty years, and might stand for eighty more."[28]

As presented in *A Serious House on Serious Earth*, Arkham Asylum is also such a structure. The notion that the asylum is a living, sentient being is attested to by several the book's characters. Amadeus Arkham, for example, bluntly concludes that "the house is an organism, hungry for madness. It is the maze that dreams."[29] One of the inmates whom Batman encounters, the Mad Hatter, likens the asylum to a head—one which "dreams us all into being."[30] And Dr. Charles Cavendish's plot to murder Batman is rooted in his belief that it is Batman himself who is responsible for having "fed this hungry house" with "poor mad souls."[31]

Although the reader might dismiss such testimonials to the supernatural nature of the asylum as the ravings of madmen, the book provides less equivocal evidence as well. *A Serious House on Serious Earth* presents Arkham Asylum as being not merely a living organism which feeds upon madness, but also one which can generate temporally anomalous events. Within the walls of Arkham Asylum, the present is haunted not only by the past, but also by the future. In this regard, Arkham Asylum bears a strong resemblance to the malevolent Overlook Hotel depicted in Stephen King's novel *The Shining*, a place in which—as that novel's characters eventually come to realize—"all times are one."[32]

Throughout *A Serious House on Serious Earth*, Amadeus Arkham is haunted by events and personalities from the future. For example, both he and his mother Elizabeth live in utter terror of a seemingly supernatural bat-figure, the presence of which can be seen as just one instance of the way in which the asylum itself projects future occurrences (in this case, Batman's terrifying experience in the asylum) into the past.[33] April Fools' Day—which might be thought of as the Joker's special holiday—is the specific date which connects many of the horrific events which occur in the asylum. It is the date upon which Arkham's wife and daughter are savagely murdered; the date upon which he exacts his horrible vengeance upon "Mad Dog" Hawkins; and the date upon which (many decades in the future) Dr. Cavendish and the Joker will engineer the inmates' take-over of the asylum. Several months prior to the murder of his family, Arkham discovers a joker playing card (which, of course, is the calling-card of The Joker) on the floor of his daughter's room. Although Arkham is unaware of the (future) significance of this card, and assumes that it was simply dropped by "one of the workmen," the reader knows differently.[34] And when Arkham's wife presents him with a pair of Japanese clown fish, he experiences what he calls "an inexplicable frisson of déjà vu," and his mind is brought instantaneously to the subject of April Fools' Day.[35] The reader recognizes that, far from being an instance of déjà vu, what Arkham is experiencing is an uncanny presentiment of future events.

Of course, the book also presents Arkham Asylum as a place in which the past is supernaturally projected onto the present. In one early scene, the Joker leads Batman into the dining hall of the asylum amid a cacophony of voices. Among these voices is that of Amadeus Arkham's murdered daughter, Harriet, whose heart-rending plea for her father's assistance echoes across the decades: "Oh daddy, make him stop! He's hurting me! The dog's hurting me!"[36] Again, while the book's characters may be insensible to the meaning of this incident, the reader is not.

Ultimately, then, Morrison leaves the reader in little doubt that Amadeus Arkham's conviction that the asylum is "an organism, hungry for madness" is, in fact, a well-founded one. And crucially, this representation of Arkham Asylum as a malign sentient being which feeds upon madness has the effect of transmuting, as opposed to displacing, the asylum-related anxieties which the book evokes. In Morrison's hands, the various evils which have for centuries been associated with asylums are—rather than being displaced onto an outside entity such as a ghost or demon—personified, quite literally, by the asylum itself. As presented in *A Serious House on Serious Earth*, Arkham Asylum is very much like a ravenous spider, trapping anyone—mad or sane—who is unfortunate enough to venture too close to its web. Far from being a place where mental illness is cured, Arkham Asylum intentionally causes madness—for the simple reason that it is madness upon which it feeds. The various horrific events which occur within its walls are the natural consequence of its madness-attracting and madness-inducing properties.

In short, *A Serious House on Serious Earth* depicts Arkham Asylum in such a way that longstanding asylum-related anxieties—anxieties which have always been rooted, at least superficially, in empiricism and rational thought—are transmuted into fears which are even more unsettling precisely because they defy any attempt at rational analysis. For good or for ill, the book introduced an image of the mental asylum which was at once utterly novel and powerfully evocative. For this reason, it ought to be regarded as a seminal work—not merely in the history of comic books, but in the history of the cultural representation of the asylum.

Notes

1. Grant Morrison and Dave McKean, *Arkham Asylum: A Serious House on Serious Earth* (New York: DC Comics, 2014).
2. William Parteger, *Observations on Maniacal Disorders* (1792), 123; cited in Andrew Scull, *Madhouse: A Tragic Tale of Megalomania and Modern Medicine* (New Haven, CT: Yale University Press, 2005), 14.
3. Andrew Scull, *Madness in Civilization: A Cultural History of Insanity from the Bible to Freud, from the Madhouse to Modern Medicine* (Princeton, NJ: Princeton University Press, 2015), 106–7.
4. Ibid., 138–140.
5. Ibid., 138–140; 233–240.
6. For a discussion of the anxiety which accompanies the discovery that mental illness, see Sander L. Gilman, *Disease and Representation: Images of Illness from Madness to AIDS* (Ithaca, NY: Cornell University Press, 1988).
7. Scull, *Madness*, 231.
8. The genesis of the diffuse cluster of critiques—both of psychiatry in general and of the asylum-model of treatment—which began to appear in the late 1950s, and which are often lumped together under the heading of "anti-psychiatry," is helpfully explored in Michael E. Staub, *Madness Is Civilization: When the Diagnosis Was Social, 1948-1980* (Chicago: University of Chicago Press, 2011).
9. Erving Goffman, *Asylums: Essays on the Social Situation of Mental Patients and Other Inmates* (Chicago: Aldine Publishing, 1961), xiii.
10. Ibid., 382.
11. Ibid.
12. Ibid., 364.
13. Ibid., 135.
14. Ibid., 380.
15. Ibid., 206.
16. Ibid., 75.
17. Scull, *Madness*, 361–371.
18. Staub, *Madness Is Civilization*, 186.
19. Sharon Packer attributes the two-decade lapse between the process of deinstitutionalization and its acknowledgment in popular culture to the phenomenon of "cultural sedimentation" by which knowledge of the changes wrought only gradually filtered down from the realm of the specialist to that of popular perception. Sharon Packer, *Cinema's Sinister Psychiatrists: From Caligari to Hannibal* (Jefferson, NC: McFarland, 2012), 10.
20. Packer, *Cinema's Sinister Psychiatrists*, 11.
21. For this, see Graham Moon et al., *The Afterlives of the Psychiatric Asylum: Recycling Concepts, Sites and Memories* (Burlington VT: Ashgate, 2015).
22. Moon, *The Afterlives*, 156.
23. Since neuropsychiatric illness was attributed to demonic forces until the 19th century and fell under the purview of "doctors of the Church" rather than "doctors of Medicine," and is still linked to supernatural forces in some sects and in some cultures, it should not be surprising that cinema often links supernaturalism and psychiatric asylums.
24. Morrison, *A Serious House*, 1.
25. Stephen King, *Danse Macabre* (New York: Everest House, 1981), 252.

26. Dale Bailey, *American Nightmares: The Haunted House Formula in American Popular Fiction* (Bowling Green, OH: Bowling Green State University Popular Press, 1999), 5.
27. Bailey, *American Nightmares*, 6.
28. Shirley Jackson, *The Haunting of Hill House* (1959: Reprint, New York: Penguin Books, 1984), 3.
29. Morrison, *A Serious House*, 44.
30. *Ibid.*, 40.
31. *Ibid.*, 59.
32. Stephen King, *The Shining* (1977: Reprint, New York: Anchor Books, 2012), 447.
33. In a footnote to the "full Script" of *A Serious House on Serious Earth* which is published in the 25th Anniversary Deluxe edition, Morrison confirms that the image which haunts Elizabeth Arkham is that of "Batman's Rage and Confusion [which] Echoes Back Through Time to Haunt the Past[.]" Morrison, 54 n.
34. Morrison, 24.
35. *Ibid.*, 27.
36. *Ibid.*, 15.

Breaking Out

The Escaped Mental Patient in the Batman Universe

JEFFREY BULLINS

Lightning streaks across the sky, illuminating tall gothic spires. Rain pounds against the pavement as a dark vehicle speeds past a rusty iron gate towards the menacing structure. What horrors could be housed in such a building? Frankenstein's monster? Dracula? A vengeful ghost? While the introduction of this location could be something out of a classic horror film, this building is not an evil baron's castle but the Elizabeth Arkham Asylum for the Criminally Insane.

The connections between depictions of Arkham and horror genre tropes go beyond the menacing towers of the asylum. Mentally ill characters have a long-standing tradition in the horror genre from "mad" scientist Dr. Frankenstein to Norman Bates (*Psycho*) to Michael Myers (*Halloween*). It has also been noted that this theme began even in silent cinema. "An early film that served as a prototype for horror films, Weine's *The Cabinet of Dr. Caligari* (1919), is highly expressionistic and established a precedent for setting macabre murders in mental institutions."[1] Likewise, the "escaped mental patient" is a common villain in the genre. This trope allows for seemingly random, antisocial behavior without much explanation beyond "they're crazy." The popularity of mentally ill antagonists in the horror genre boomed after the success of Hitchcock's *Psycho* (1960). Unrealistic representations persisted in part due to the viewing public's lack of understanding about real mental illnesses. In a 2011 study, Hal Arkowitz found that "surveys show that 60 to 80 percent of the public believes that those diagnosed with schizophrenia, in particular, are likely to commit violent acts."[2]

The meme of the escaped patient was integrated with the "slasher" killer of the 1970s and 1980s. Interestingly, in 1979, the year after Michael Myers escapes Smith's Grove Sanitarium, Arkham Asylum becomes the official mental hospital in *Batman* comic books. The institution had been around for several years previously, however, referred to as "Arkham Hospital" or "Arkham Sanitarium." Some depictions of the asylum seem to closely borrow from the horror genre or even a specific film. For example, in the first episode of the animated series *The Batman* (2007), "The Bat in the Belfry," police arrive at Arkham to find patients wandering around the grounds. This bears close resemblance to Dr. Loomis' arrival at Smith's Grove at the beginning of *Halloween*.

For nearly 40 years since, Arkham Asylum has been the focal point for many of Batman's encounters with his foes. It is a catchall and "eventually, each *Batman* villain ends up, however briefly, in Arkham Asylum, Gotham's institute for the criminally insane."[3] To adhere to the convention of the *escaped* patient, all those bad guys must end up in the asylum so that they can actually engage in escape. This essay examines how various instances in the Batman Universe utilize this meme of the escaped mental patient. By borrowing and building on other genres, most notably horror, the image of escaped mental patients as dangerous villain is established and encouraged.

It is worth reiterating the time period at which Arkham Asylum is firmly established in the Batman universe. Following a glut of films in the wake of *Psycho* and amid the growing "slasher" horror subgenre, Arkham Asylum's image was built on existing fears and stereotypes. Before this point, mental illness was not the go-to reasoning for *Batman*'s rogue's gallery. In the television series starring Adam West, the villains were never referred to as "criminally insane" and "the flamboyant felons escape from Gotham State Prison, not Arkham Asylum."[4]

Characterizing *Batman*'s villains as "criminally insane" and moving them from prison to an asylum marks a point where the storylines become darker in tone. Instead of the colorful, campy "biff, pow" of Adam West's Batman, the dark halls of Arkham Asylum evoke feelings of fear and dread. In the documentary *Batman Unmasked*, the claim is made, "In the annals of superhero history, Batman's enemies are the most psychologically scarred. Walking definitions of dysfunction whose vicious deeds often evoke the violent and perverse acts of real-life criminals."[5] Furthermore, this is the stereotype perpetuated via the meme of the escaped mental patient. "Real-life" criminals are "psychologically scarred" and will commit "violent and perverse acts."

Transitioning from flamboyant, cartoonish supervillains to ones that are psychologically damaged is also in line with what was happening in the horror genre at the same time. Instead of a fantastic threat like a vampire, werewolf or ghost, escaped mental patients were "real" and "could actually happen." This emphasis on what is real builds upon the public's fears and makes for sensational storytelling. Lack of factual knowledge of mental illness and established misrepresentations in media fuels the fear of the uncertain and unknown. The walls of the asylum are the tenuous barrier between our organized society and potential disruption. What better way to strike fear in the hearts of Gothamites (and readers) than to unleash this torrent of chaos?

The first introduction of Arkham Hospital in *Batman* #258 involves an escape. In that issue, Arkham Hospital is described as "a polite name for an asylum which houses the criminally insane."[6] In this issue, Two-Face escapes, but the Joker is left behind after Two-Face's coin flip determines his fate. In an article for *Comic News*, Brian Cronin claims the first "full Arkham Asylum breakout," in which multiple patients escape, happens in *Batman* #400.[7] In this issue, Ra's al Ghul is responsible for setting loose the inmates of both Arkham and Gotham State prison. The asylum's walls are breached, letting loose villains who have "one common factor: hatred, seething... waiting to explode."[8]

Thus, escapes are what Arkham is made for. "This facility faces more escapes, infiltrations, riots, [and] assaults during Batman's career than some nations' entire penal systems see in a century."[9] So why exactly do so many patients escape from Arkham Asylum? One obvious reason is the apparent lack of security. Why after all these years does the city not build another wall or hire a few guards? In Gotham, the higher security institution

The Gothām Exāminer

SPECIAL EDITION — FREE — Thursday, June 9, 2016

JOKER ESCAPES

ASYLUM SECURITY UPROAR
MANIAC ON THE LOOSE AGAIN!

Arkham Asylum: The fugitive escaped by replacing himself with one of his complices in a cleverly hatched plot. The police and The Batman are currently investigating the case.

Crimefighter unavailable for comment

VICKI VALE // EXCLUSIVE

Arkham Asylum has been rocked by the audacious escape of highly dangerous serial killer and psychopath 'The Joker'. Police are currently investigating the situation and the institute is on high alert as security has been tripled overnight. It's been reported that this is not the first time someone has escaped the highly-guarded facility. The situation was discovered last night as 'The Batman' arrived at the institute to question the prisoner. Halfway through the interrogation, the man who was being questioned was revealed as an imposter who had been posing as the convict.

The man turned out to be one of The Joker's henchmen who had somehow managed to sneak into the asylum disguised as the prisoner and switched places whilst the real villain escaped. No more information was given on the case as The Batman refused to speak to reporters, seemingly wanting to leave as quickly as possible. His whereabouts are also unknown, but officials insist he's in pursuit of the missing prisoner and is confident The Joker will be apprehended imminently. Searches around and inside the building continue as there seem to be no sign of breaches or forced entry. Reports say that if nothing suspicious is found in the building, each member of staff is to be submitted for questioning to rule out any internal conspiracy or staff involvement in the escape. Officials from the Mayor's office are tonight denying that the Asylum is trying to cover up the mistake.

In the meantime, the citizens of Gotham are on high alert to stay aware that 'The Joker' is roaming the streets once again and may strike at any time. He still has many henchmen who lurk about the city and will be helping him out as much as possible.

Continued on Page 4

Faux newspaper promotional, dated Thursday, June 9, 2016. Joker's escape from Arkham Asylum makes front page news and commands large headlines in *The Gotham Examiner*, which states, in bold print, "JOKER ESCAPES"; "ASYLUM SECURITY UPROAR"; "MANIAC ON THE LOOSE AGAIN!" This event is yet another example of Arkham's infamous "revolving door" policy (which is strikingly similar to contemporary short-term hospital admissions in real life). If this paper had been printed in 1974, opposite headlines would have appeared on the front page: "Two-Face escapes Arkham Hospital"; "Joker left in lock-up"; "Deranged DA on rampage for revenge" because the once-handsome Harvey flipped his two-headed coin before deciding to leave Joker behind and absconding alone, with the General's help.

Blackgate Prison (evolved from Gotham State). This is where "sane" criminals are sent and the escape rates are much lower. Since locked-up criminals offer little drama, the chaotic exploits of escaped Arkham patients like the Joker, Riddler, and Scarecrow continue to sell comics. Thus, the vast majority of Batman's antagonists end up in the asylum one way or another. This happens so much that one critic feels other prisons are essentially nonexistent. "The villain goes to Arkham (there do not seem to be any prisons in Gotham anymore, since all the villains end up in Arkham)."[10]

This massive mix of inmate population in turn gives the public another fear in terms of escapees. Not only are unpredictable, dangerous mental patients pouring out of the asylum, but actual criminals as well. The corruption of Arkham's administration and of Gotham's psychiatrists and psychologists appear to be responsible for this. In *Batman Begins* (2005), Dr. Jonathan Crane (who later becomes Scarecrow) testifies in court that crime boss Carmine Falcone and his associates are "insane," thus sending them to Arkham instead of Blackgate.

Sending criminals to the lower-security Arkham instead of prison is an established convention both in the Batman universe as well as the television show *Gotham*. *Gotham* typically shows Arkham as a run-down, ineffective facility with the housed inmates wearing traditional black and white striped prison garb. Certainly, this is in line with depictions from the comic books. An interesting deviation occurs mid-way through the second season. In season two, episode twelve, "Mr. Freeze," Oswald "The Penguin" Cobblepot is transferred from a holding cell at the police department to Arkham. This is done not to place Penguin in a low security setting, but as punishment. When he asks where he is being taken, a police officer responds, "Arkham. You are insane, right?" Once Penguin is there, he tries to exert the same type of command he had as a gang leader. This attempt at leadership does not yield respect but rather results in the other patients mocking him, "I'm the king of Gotham!" As they chant, there is whimsical carnival music playing, which furthers the feeling of absurdity and chaos.

As an "institution" in the Batman universe, Arkham is featured throughout various types of media beyond comic books. In 2009, in *Batman: Arkham Asylum*, it is the focus of a video game. Adding to the mythology of the institution, the game plays with and breaks established conventions and expectations. The premise of the game is not Batman fighting escaped asylum inmates, but rather his journey through the asylum itself, which has been taken over by the Joker. Even though "escaped" patients are not the threat, the opening of the game recognizes this meme in the Batman universe. As the Batmobile speeds down a rain-slicked road to deliver an "easily" caught Joker to the asylum, it passes a sign reading, "Hitchhikers may be escaping patients." Security at Arkham is so bad they had to put up a sign.

References to the perpetual problem of escaped patients continue through the game. As the Joker is wheeled in on a stand-up gurney, Hannibal Lecter style, Warden Sharp comments, "I want him securely locked away this time. Another escape and I will lose support for my mayoral campaign."[11] The public's fear of escapees from Arkham is at the forefront of local politics. Furthermore, Sharp states, "Joker is our most challenging patient. Curing him will cement my reputation."[12] Thus, caring for patients is only a tool for political maneuvering. In referencing the problem of escapees and this ambivalence of the asylum administration, *Batman: Arkham Asylum* follows traditional representations of the asylum while using those conventions to create a new story experience for the audience.

Turing focus inward (figuratively and literally) is not new to this video game. The 1989 graphic novel *Arkham Asylum: A Serious House on Serious Earth* by Grant Morrison and Dave McKean follows Batman as he ventures into an Arkham that has been taken over by the Joker. The story "found him wandering the halls of the madhouse, tormented by the very criminals he put away, endlessly troubled by the possibility that his own damaged mental state might be indistinguishable from theirs."[13] In DC's 2011 "New 52" reboot of *Batman*, this concept is revisited in the "Death of the Family" storyline in which the Joker lures Batman into a booby-trapped Arkham. The Joker says regarding the hostages he forces to dance, "They dance to welcome you home! Home to Arkham Asylum." Batman also asserts that Arkham is his home and that he knows every corner of it.[14]

Batman: Arkham Asylum was successful and began the "Arkham series" of video games which includes *Arkham City* (2011), *Arkham Knight* (2015) (both sequels), *Arkham Origins* (2013) (prequel), *Batman: Arkham VR* (2016), and several comic and novel tie-ins. Unlike its predecessor, *Arkham City* branches outside the asylum walls, but only to an extent. While Arkham itself may embody frightened misconceptions about the dangers of the mentally ill, in *Arkham City*, it is deemed necessary to section off an entire portion of the city to put all the inmates from both Arkham Asylum and Blackgate Penitentiary. Thus, no differentiation exists between a mentally ill patient at the asylum and a convicted criminal at the prison.

Mayor Sharp won the election after the events in *Batman: Arkham Asylum* masterminded the "city." Yet it was later revealed that Sharp was under the influence of Dr. Hugo Strange.[15] Viki Vale asks the mayor about this new "prison," but he replies, "I prefer the term 'quarantine zone.'" Vale responds, it "is more akin to a wild animal park than a mental health facility."[16] This conversation reinforces the concept that those in Arkham are little more than dangerous, caged animals. Their escape is a constant fear and they can only hope to be contained, not cured.

Indeed, being cured does not really seem to be an option for those in Arkham Asylum. Time spent there rarely seems to improve anyone. "Inside its walls, the villain is treated, but treated in a way that is harmful to his mental state rather than helpful. Before long, the villain is released or escapes, only now he's more delusional, more deranged, and generally loonier than ever before."[17] Like the meme of the escaped patient itself, this point is in line with other media depictions of mental illness. One of the best-known examples is *One Flew Over the Cuckoo's Nest* (1975), in which Randle McMurphy is transferred from a prison to a psychiatric hospital. Through the course of the film, the treatment he receives seems to worsen his mental state.

Receiving such counterproductive treatment is a hallmark of Arkham Asylum. Patients are treated poorly, and as a result, become more dangerous when they break out of the asylum again. In the comic *Arkham Manor*, Batman comments after Arkham is destroyed, "When Arkham fell, the walls of the tumor burst, its sickness spreading into the arteries of the beast."[18] This metaphor suggests that mental illness is somehow transmittable and that the escaped patients will somehow drive others to madness. This also goes beyond the patients. "To survive your employment at Arkham, your best hope may be to become a masked villain yourself."[19]

Another revealing fact is that the institution itself was founded from an act of violence and mental illness. In Morrison's *Arkham Asylum*, the origin story of Arkham is told during interludes between Batman's encounters there. According to this history, founder Amadeus Arkham created the facility after watching his mother struggle with mental illness. It is revealed that he killed his mother and blocked out the memory. Later, his wife and child are murdered by one of his former patients, Martin "Mad Dog" Hawkins. Arkham, while treating Hawkins, murders him and is in turn incarcerated in his own asylum.[20] This tragic history of the institution continues to affect inhabitants. The asylum is "cursed," and the contagion of mental illness affects anyone there. The Mad Hatter exclaims in *Arkham Asylum*, "This house, it does things to the mind."[21] In a similar vein, the 1972 horror film *Asylum* features a patient, Dr. Starr, who was previously the head of the institution. In *House on Haunted Hill*, (1999) the titular building is a cursed former asylum and the characters are tormented by ghosts of mental patients who were abused there. *Gothika* (2003) follows the story of a psychiatrist who awakens to find herself a patient in the institution where she worked. Whether a place has a history as a mental hospital or is presently mistreating patients, negative influence persists.

Beyond the institution's founder, Dr. Hugo Strange is a notable "mad" doctor at Arkham. Originally appearing in *Batman #36* as "Professor" Strange, he is often seen as an administrator at Arkham who uses patients for experimentation. In the *Arkham* video game series he is the mastermind behind Arkham City. In the television show *Gotham*, he subjects the Penguin to "extreme treatment" to cure him of his criminal ways. The procedure is like that in *A Clockwork Orange* (1972) where anti-hero Alex is forced to watch disturbing images to become averse to violence.

This "brilliant but mad" doctor has roots in the "mad scientists" of classic horror films. Operating outside of law and society, mad scientists often create external threats. For example, Dr. Caligari has the somnambulist Cesare, Dr. Frankenstein has his monster, and Dr. Jekyll transforms into Hyde. Genre researcher James Burrell has noted the comparison between doctors and mad scientists in Canadian horror. He cites David Cronenberg's films as "introducing a mad scientist character, often in the form of an experimenting doctor who engages in some sort of deviant medical behavior."[22] A "mad doctor" such as Strange thus perpetuates threats from the mentally ill through counterproductive treatments. Once the patient inevitably escapes, he or she will be far more dangerous. Dr. Jonathan Crane (Scarecrow) is also sometimes seen working at Arkham and using patients as test subjects for his fear toxin. When released on the public, the toxin spreads "madness" by exaggerating phobias.

Arkham Asylum then falls in with the tradition of deficient mental health facilities that do more harm than good. In a breakdown of misconceptions about mental illness in the movies, Danny Wedding notes that "Psychiatric hospitals are dangerous places, or at the least, unhelpful; the patients are not sick, they are harmlessly eccentric or misdiagnosed."[23] *One Flew Over the Cuckoo's Nest* has been mentioned as a prominent example. Other instances include *King of Hearts* (1966), *12 Monkeys* (1995), and *The Jacket* (2005). In the case of *12 Monkeys*, we find the protagonist questioning his/her sanity after spending time in a mental hospital. Likewise, an episode of *Buffy the Vampire Slayer*, "Normal Again" (S6E17), finds Buffy in a mental institution questioning the reality of her being "the slayer." In *Batman #327*, the Dark Knight is restrained in Arkham by Professor Milo and almost convinced he is not actually Batman.

Regarding the ineffectuality of treatment, Otto Wahl notes, "There is also the frequent suggestion that those with mental illnesses do not get better with treatment—and thus they remain violent and dangerous."[24] The incorrigible Joker is the most notorious product of Arkham Asylum's ineffectiveness. Beyond the threat he poses as an escaped mental patient, his madness can potentially spread to others. In the animated film *Batman Beyond: Return of the Joker*, Tim Drake (Robin) is tortured by the Joker, forced to give information about Batman, and becomes a version of the Joker himself. While Tim (Robin) does side with Batman in the final battle, he subsequently suffers a complete mental breakdown. In the video game *Arkham Knight*, the 2015 installment of the series, the titular antagonist is revealed to be a former Batman ally who has been driven insane by the Joker.

Harley Quinn, a formidable *Bat*-villain in her own right, is also a product of the Joker's "contagious" madness. She was not originally introduced in *Batman* comics, but in *Batman: The Animated Series* television show. In the episode "Joker's Favor" (S1E22), Harley appears as the Joker's moll and accomplice, becoming a recurring character on the show. The story of her origin was featured in the "Mad Love" storyline of the comic book tie-in *The Batman Adventures*. As a student on a gymnastics scholarship at Gotham State, she studied psychology. It is suggested that she received high marks by engaging in inappropriate behavior with her professors. She also sought fame, and Alfred notes, "she was going to be one of those annoying pop psychologists."[25]

During her first day as an intern at Arkham Asylum, Harley is warned that the patients are "…Hard core psychotics. They'd just as soon kill you as look at you."[26] Despite the warning, she is immediately drawn to the Joker and the possibility of learning his secrets. She sympathizes and becomes enamored with him through the course of their therapy sessions. The Joker's magnetic personality calls to mind the charismatic nature of other villains such as Hannibal Lecter. After "that horrible week when he escaped"[27] during which Harley worried for the Joker's safety, Batman returns him to Arkham where Harley subsequently breaks him out again. Her role is an interesting twist on the meme of the escaped mental patient. During the second escape, Harley is the mastermind and drags the Joker along with her.

While "Mad Love" portrays Harley's infatuation with the Joker as a product of his charisma, the origin story portrayed in the 2016 film *Suicide Squad* is a bit darker. While Harley is somewhat smitten, the Joker subjects her to high levels of electricity with an ECT device (granted, Harley does seem somewhat willing). This manipulation is a shift from the idea that the Joker could simply drive someone to madness by talking to them, suggesting that some sort of trauma is the cause. Later in the film, Harley jumps willingly into the same vat of chemicals that caused the Joker's transformation. The origin story is told in flashbacks during the film with the main storyline following Harley and other villains who are forced by a government agency to go on a "suicide mission" against a supernatural enemy. Though Harley is consistently described as "crazy" throughout *Suicide Squad*, she is not held at Arkham. She and the rest of the squad are at Belle Reve Special Security Barracks where security is tighter. However, at the end of the film, the Joker, assumed to be dead, breaks Harley out, returning the favor.

The potential escape of any mental patient is a constant threat to Gotham City. The television series *Gotham* features Arkham Asylum prominently in several episodes in the first season when Detective Gordon is forced to take a position there, a punishment for him. In season two, Arkham becomes more of a threat when (secret) antagonist Galavan releases patients from the asylum to cause chaos in the city and position himself as the hero who stops them.

In the *Knightfall* comic book storyline, Bane releases inmates from Arkham. With Batman greatly weakened from fighting all of them, Bane defeats him by breaking his back. During the breakout, the Joker exclaims "Madness is the only freedom—and all the madness once restrained under [Jeremiah Arkham's] control will soon be free to run WILLLD!"[28] This speaks to the dangerous "wild animal" nature of the inmates and their sowing of madness and chaos in the city. Commissioner Gordon is also told "They're all loose….runnin' wild like a pack o' mad dogs."[29] Arkham's patients are presented as little more than caged animals waiting for a moment to escape.

This dehumanization is in line with another convention from the horror genre: physically deformed villains. Particularly in the slasher subgenre of horror films, villains often have a physical abnormality to reflect their evil nature. Most masked killers like Jason Voorhees or Leatherface are hiding a disfigured face. Wahl notes of this trope, "Those with mental illnesses are recognizably different from others in both manner and appearance, they stand out as deviant and bizarre."[30] This physical difference allows the reader or viewer to distance him or herself from the villains and to avoid identifying with them. Thus, escaped patients are threats, not individuals.

When thinking about physical abnormalities, several specific Batman villains might come to mind: Penguin, Two-Face, and Bane. However, Penguin is often cited as one of

Two-Face's two-headed 1922 Liberty Dollar prop replica is used by the physically and mentally scarred Harvey Dent, the former District Attorney who cannot make decisions without the coin. One side of the coin shows smooth skin, while the other side, also a head, is scarred, like Harvey. When Arkham Hospital was introduced to *Batman* universe in 1974, Two-Face's coin flip determined Joker's fate; Two-Face escapes but leaves Joker behind. Hoping to wean Dent off his two-headed coin, Arkham Asylum therapist Dr. Ruth Adams substitutes dice and then Tarot cards for this coin but added options make Harvey worse rather than better (photograph by George Higham).

Batman's more "sane" opponents. Indeed, Penguin is a calculating, powerful crime boss (though he sometimes shows up in Arkham). Prior to his accident, Two-Face was Harvey Dent, but "driven mad" when his face was disfigured. Like Penguin, Bane is often presented as being rational and calculating. Originally, Bane infused a serum that gave him abnormal size and strength. In *The Dark Knight Rises* film, he retains only a breathing apparatus necessary after a violent prison assault.

The physical abnormalities of these characters externalize their internal evil. Such is the case for many inmates at Arkham Asylum. The Joker has been marred by falling in a vat of acid. Mr. Freeze is confined to an apparatus that keeps his body temperature low. Clayface is a former actor who can change his misshapen form. Victor Zsasz is a serial killer who intentionally carves tally marks into his own skin.

It is easy to identify the bad guy through outward appearance. One of the more unhuman villains is Waylon "Killer Croc" Jones, a veteran *Bat*-foe and resident of Arkham. Born with a condition that causes him to become increasingly reptilian, the comic *Batman Arkham: Killer Croc* notes, "When facing the Croc, the Dark Knight isn't just dealing with madness, he's fighting a creature that is more beast than man."[31] In the issue of *Joker's Asylum II* that focuses on Croc, Commissioner Gordon visits Arkham after Croc bites his own hands off, kills a doctor, and escapes. He comments, "This is what rehabilitation gets us…"[32] Gordon perpetuates the idea of the futility of treatment at Arkham. Batman concur, stating, "Jones belongs in a cage. Not in Arkham being 'treated.'"[33] This quotation calls to mind Dr. Loomis' assertion in *Halloween* that Michael Myers is "pure evil" and cannot be cured.

These tropes further increase the dangerous image of the escaped mental patient. Treatment is ineffective. Even those who work in the institution will be driven to madness. Security is lax, and escape is inevitable. When those patients do escape, they will "spread insanity." By incorporating the meme of the escaped mental patient, Arkham Asylum situates itself in the tradition of depicting the mentally ill as malevolent and dangerous. Collecting *Batman*'s villains in the asylum is an easy way to have them ready for conflict; the potential for escape is both a constant threat and storyline starter. Since the sensationalized representations of mental illness predictably fill theater seats for horror films, the meme of the escaped mental patient in the Batman Universe will remain a primary source of villainy.

NOTES

1. Danny Wedding et al., *Movies and Mental Illness 3: Using Films to Understand Psychopathology* (Cambridge: Hogrefe Publishing. 2010), 6.
2. Hal Arkowitz, "Deranged and Dangerous?" *Scientific American Mind*, July 1, 2011, 1.
3. Steven Smith, *Batman Unmasked: The Psychology of the Dark Knight* (Prometheus Entertainment, 2008), DVD.
4. Travis Langley, *Batmen and Psychology: A Dark and Stormy Knight* (Hoboken, NJ: Wiley and Sons, 2012), 12.
5. Smith, *Batman Unmasked.*
6. Dennis O'Neil, "Threat of the Two-Headed Coin," *Batman* #258 (NY: DC Comics, October 1974).
7. Brian Cronin, "Drawing Crazy Patterns," *Comics News Comment.*
8. Dough Moench, "Resurrection Night," *Batman* #400 (NY: DC Comics, October 1986).
9. Langley, *Batman and Psychology*, 130.
10. Pau Lytle, "The Madness of Arkham" in *Batman Unauthorized*, ed. Dennis O'Neil and Leah Wilson (Dallas, TX: BenBella Books, Inc., 2009), 110.
11. Paul Dini, *Batman: Arkham Asylum* (Rocksteady Studios, 2009), video game.
12. *Ibid.*
13. Mitch Frye, "Seminar on the Purloined Batarang," in *Riddle Me This, Batman: Essays on the Universe of the Dark Knight*, ed. Kevin K. Durand and Mary K. Leigh (Jefferson, NC: McFarland, 2011), 93.

14. Scott Snyder, "Knock, Knock." *Batman* #16 (NY: DC Comics, March 2013).
15. Paul Dini, "Ruins," *Batman: Arkham City #1* (NY: DC Comics, July 2011).
16. *Ibid.*
17. Lytle, "The Madness of Arkham," http://www.paullytle.com. Accessed July 10, 2018.
18. *Arkham Manor #1.*
19. Langley, *Batman and Psychology*, 35.
20. Grant Morrison, *Arkham Asylum: A Serious House on Serious Earth*, 15th Anniversary Edition (NY: DC Comics, 2005).
21. *Ibid.*
22. James Burrell, "The Physician as Mad Scientist: a Fear of Deviant Medical Practices in the Films of David Cronenberg," in *The Canadian Horror Film: Terror of the Soul* (Toronto: Toronto University Press, 2012), 233.
23. Wedding, *Movies and Mental Illness 3*, 225.
24. Otto Wahl, *Media Madness* (New Brunswick, NJ: Rutgers University Press, 1995), 58.
25. Paul Dini and Bruce Timm, "Mad Love," *The Batman Adventures: Mad Love #1* (NY: DC Comics, February 1994).
26. *Ibid.*
27. *Ibid.*
28. Dough Moench, "The Freedom of Madness," *Batman* #491 (NY: DC Comics, April 1993).
29. *Ibid.*
30. Wahl, *Media Madness*, xvii.
31. Gerry Conway et al., *Batman Arkham: Killer Croc* (NY: DC Comics, 2016).
32. Mike Raicht, "Beauty and the Beast," *Joker's Asylum II: Killer Croc #1* (NY: DC Comics, August 2010).
33. *Ibid.*

The Suicide Squad

From Bad to Good and Back Again

JAQ GREENSPON *and* RASA GREENSPON

In 1965, E.M. Nathanson's novel *The Dirty Dozen* took a rag tag group of hardened criminals and turned them into a fighting force designed to be expendable in the face of life-threatening danger. The film, which followed two years later, is considered a classic and the formula has oft been repeated. So, when DC Comics invited John Ostrander to bring his talents to the fold, he could think of nothing better than to reimagine the general conceit of the film,[1] only with supervillains, which was entirely Ostrander's concept from the beginning.[2] To accomplish this, Ostrander knew he would need a suitable cadre of villains and ne'er-do-wells, with the only caveat being that they could not be major players in anyone else's stories. The primary reason for this caveat was the "by definition" nature of the team's title: Suicide Squad. Characters had to be expendable, to be killed off (by Ostrander) if need be. What good is a "Suicide Squad" if their success, or more importantly, their survival, is assured? So, the initial compliment of members included B-list villains and second stringers who would not be missed from others' series.

From the beginning, though, Ostrander chose to distance himself from the rest of the DC Universe where his characters reside. Instead of basing the operations of the Suicide Squad out of the better-known Elizabeth Arkham Asylum for the Criminally Insane, which is the subject of this book and is an institution dedicated to both the treatment and confinement of persons who are too psychotic to be held legally responsible for their felonies, Ostrander instead created the more peaceful sounding Belle Reve Penitentiary. As a reference to the ancestral home of the DuBois sisters from Tennessee William's play *A Streetcar Named Desire*,[3] the Belle Reve [Beautiful Dream] Penitentiary is firmly placed in the real-world swamps of Terrebonne Parrish, Louisiana, far from the fictive universe of Gotham. This appears to be a conscious and practical choice, even though several rotating members of the Squad have, at one time or another, resided in Arkham Asylum and one member (Harley Quinn) practiced psychiatry there. Substituting Belle Reve for Arkham allows for important plot twists: characters declared "not guilty by reason of insanity" (NGRI) and thus incarcerated by order of the judge (who acts on at the recommendation of psychiatrists or psychologists), would have to remain until they are "cured," or, more likely, until they escape—for the escape record of Arkham is woefully abysmal. By eliminating Arkham Asylum for the Criminally insane from the equation, those characters are subject to the legal system only, without the confounding contribution of the psychiatric system.

The prison-only setting, albeit one "designed not only to incarcerate convicted super-powered felons but to also act as a holding facility,"[4] allow for the necessary incentive for recruiting Squad members, namely, commutation of their current penal sentence. There is no concern with curing their psychiatric symptoms, as there would be in Arkham Asylum. Naturally, there are strings attached, as laid out in the following exchange from Suicide Squad #1 (1987):

> RICK FLAG: Plastique, I just want to make sure you and Mindboggler understand the deal being offered.
> PLASTIQUE: You take this mission and your sentence gets changed to time served. Provided, of course, that you survive and you keep your trap shut afterwards.
> CAPTAIN BOOMERANG (*sotto voce*): The gag is they don't expect you to survive, Luv. Wanna watch yer backside with this lot.[5]

As this is the first issue, the expectation of exposition is fulfilled at this point, with the team's organizer, Mrs. Amanda Waller, watching this exchange through the relative safety of a two-way glass. She works with Marnie Herrs and Dr. Simon LaGrieve, the onsite psychiatrist for the Squad. Waller provides the reader with backgrounds of newer group members. Several important pieces of information are revealed about unsavory characters who may not be known to the comics readership at large. The two highest profile villains of the lot, Floyd Lawton, aka Deadshot, a Batman adversary, and "Digger" Harkness, aka Captain Boomerang, an Australian and member of The Flash's *Rogues Gallery*, are still considered lesser adversaries who are not capable of carrying a book on their own. The Squad is filled out with Bronze Tiger and The Enchantress, making a total of seven members to lead off their series. Harley Quinn (who began comics life as psychiatrist Dr. Harleen Quinzel) may be the best-known of all of them.

The introduction of Amanda Waller herself is most important, for it is she who will provide the most insight into the group dynamics throughout its continued run, now surpassing thirty years. Waller is one of the few constants within the ever-changing roster and it is through her that the squad is founded. Interestingly, as its visionary and de facto leader, one could say she is the guiding principle, although, she in turn reveals a stunning lack of morality that puts her in the same, or even worse, position as those amoral characters over whom she presides. Waller brings the proverbial concept of the "inmate running the asylum" to the foreground. Such reversal of roles accounts for the longevity of the Suicide Squad, and not only in the comic universe. This twist makes it understandingly appealing for crossing over into the filmed worlds of the CW's *Arrowverse* as well as 2016's *Suicide Squad* feature film.

Amada Waller makes her first appearance in *Legends* #1, alongside the present-day incarnation of Rick Flag, two issues before the appearance of the Squad. We are privy to their first meeting. From their initial introduction, Ostrander makes clear not only who is in charge, but he also sets the tone for most of the next thirty years' worth of stories.

Flag, the archetypal action-figure hero, enters, bedecked in military uniform. He immediately sets off his boss by questioning her authenticity ("—this *isn't* exactly what I was expecting!") and her authority ("Come *on*—you can't be serious! Are you out of your cotton-picking mind, lady?"). Still nothing more than an unseen, well-manicured hand, Waller responds calmly ("Well, life is just full of little surprises, Colonel"), offering

Screenshot of former psychiatrist Harley Quinn in nurse-style costume embellished with leather from the first *Batman: Arkham Asylum* video game (2009). Previously known as Dr. Harleen Quinzel, Harley Quinn tapped her high school gymnastics skills when she joined Joker in criminal capers, performing acrobatics and dressing like a harlequin. As her patient at Arkham, Joker says that Harley's name evokes happy memories from his childhood visits to the circus.

the officer a way out, which he doesn't take. Instead, he shows his surprise and disbelief with his second statement.

By turning the comic book page, the reader finally gets to see Waller's face. Even in this close-up, she is an overweight, out-of-shape African American. She is the opposite of everything Flag represents (and is very different from her svelte and stylish incarnation in television's *Gotham*). After reaffirming her seriousness, Waller confronts the casual racism inherent in Flag's statement, and possibly, by extension, in the whole military complex, admonishing him that "if you ever again call anything about me '*cotton-picking*,' mister—I'll stuff those bright shiny eagles on your shoulders so far up your butt, they'll be able to nest in your skull!" By the time the reader's eyes drift to the following panel, where both Waller and Flag are shown in a classic two-shot, head to toe, it is noticeable that Waller is not just overweight, but clinically obese. She stands at least a head and a half shorter than Flag. Physically, she is no match for him but as a good soldier, Flag understands the chain of command perfectly well and knows that, in this case, it begins and ends with her—and he accepts it immediately. The upshot of these few panels is that no matter what the dialogue or future considerations may bring, the power struggle has already been fought and won and Flag will always be subservient to Waller.[6] As will be shown later, this dynamic plays itself out in various ways over the course of the Squad's history and adventures.

When the whole Squad is introduced two issues later, the same scene plays itself out a second time, with Captain Boomerang in the Flag role. This time, Boomerang has an exaggerated, elongated form, making him tower over a diminutive Waller; Boomerang excitedly asks for "any chance o' me speakin't' the gent in charge" (about the return of his weapons of choice). In the following panel, Waller grabs him by the cravat[7] and pulls him down to her level, reminding the supervillain that "for the last time, I am the 'gent in charge'—and the name is Mrs. Waller!"[8] She not only expects respect, but demands it as well. In fact, throughout the series, only a few people ever use her first name, instead referring to her by her chosen sobriquet of Mrs. Waller.[9]

The final bit of information needed to fully comprehend how Waller operates happens in the four panels after her dressing down of Boomerang. She first explains the rules, "that if he accepts the mission, and somehow manages to survive the mission—all current criminal charges against him will be dropped."[10] Again, this could not happen if Ostrander had set his tale in Arkham, since he needs criminals awaiting release, not patients awaiting relief of symptoms. This rule, however, will be broken in one specific instance as the series morphs into its modern incarnation when Harley Quinn is added.

Boomerang, for all his sarcasm and bravado, is not stupid and figures out quickly (as beautifully illustrated by John Byrne) that what he is seeing is the carrot only and not the stick. As soon as he brings it up, though, Waller is right there with an answer—slapping an explosive bracelet on his wrist with a resounding "Klakt!" It becomes apparent that all incarcerated members of the Squad carry the same fashion accessory, designed to detonate if the wearer decides "to wander away from Colonel Flag during this mission."[11]

This inaugural mission, complete within nine pages of a six-issue mini-series detailing a plot wherein DC villain mainstay Darkseid attempts to take over the world, does more than set-up Ostrander's basic premise of The Squad: it sets the stakes implied in the title. When the team goes after one of Darkseid's minions, the lava-based creature Brimstone, who is described as a "monstrous man-brute," is killed in action.[12] When the reality of his demise sets in, it is once again up to Boomerang to make sense of the situation. "I don't believe it!" he intones. "Except for poor Blockbuster we're all still alive!" And that is when the pieces fall into place. He admonishes Flag that they were, in fact, "a Suicide Squad—just so much cannon fodder!" and that they were all supposed to die on the mission. Flag, who knows his role in the proceedings, explains that the "all" to which Boomerang alludes includes himself, that "everyone on this mission was considered expendable." At this point the penny drops and Boomerang, along with the reader, understands exactly what Ostrander was striving for—that no one is safe.

While the reader can understand the message from title and circumstance, even before Boomerang's voicing of the revelation, that all characters are expendable, it is not until half way through the first issue that the reader begins to understand the stakes with which Waller is playing. The psychological debriefing provided by Doctor LaGrieve to ensure the Squad is "psychologically fit for the mission" provides more insight into Amanda Waller than into any of her charges.

When LaGrieve explains that Rick Flag "took leadership of the former squad trying to ameliorate feelings of guilt stemming from the death of his father.... Sooner or later, he's going to need counseling to cope with it," Waller responds "Then make it later. Right now, we need him and he's operational." "Operational" for Waller is a fluid term. She requires her soldiers to be upright and able to complete the mission, regardless of the psychological and emotional cost. For some, like Floyd Lawton, the death promised by the mission would be more welcoming than the mind games Waller has no problem playing.

In fact, Lawton may prove to be the most complex character of the lot. He is the next to be diagnosed, this time by Marnie Herrs who explains that Lawton has a "strong self-destructive urge. He may be looking for a way to die and thinks the Suicide Squad will provide one." Then she continues, in the same panel, "yet, there's another side to him, I think, that wants to be well, and doesn't know how!"

This concept recurs with other characters. As the rest of the crew is introduced, the reader is told about some mental damage they incurred in the past; part of their acceptance of Squad membership is to help their recovery from the trauma. Yet Waller is callously unconcerned.

> LaGrieve: The point is they are all "bruised personalities," including Flag. Some of them should be institutionalized.[13] They can probably do what you want but I am concerned... as to what it will do to them!
> Waller: That doesn't bother me much.

One would be hard pressed to find out if it bothers her at all, especially when we see what she has waiting in store for Flag. On page 19 of that same first issue, Dr. LaGrieve prepares the reader for the final shock of the issue when he asks Waller if she told Flag "about the newest member to join the ground crew?" Waller responds, "It must have slipped my mind."

> LaGrieve: Hrumph! Not Likely! Hardly a good time to spring this kind of surprise on him.
> Waller: All surprises from here on are gonna be nasty. If he can't hack this one, he can't hack what's up-coming. And I want to know that!

The nature of the surprise is irrelevant.[14] Instead, it shows that Waller not only keeps her own council (Remember, she had brought in LaGrieve to determine the psychological fitness of the Squad) but her "mission at any cost" attitude which will come to mark her (and land her, albeit briefly, in Belle Reve herself) is in place from the beginning. She is running her own private war, only slightly restrained by government oversight.[15]

Ostrander's initial run lasted 66 issues,[16] until June 1992. But the concept was too good to keep down for long and in 2002, a 12-issue run was written by Keith Giffen. This series replaced Waller (although she still makes several appearances) with Sgt. Rock as the head of the Squad, which has been renamed *The Injustice Squad*, perhaps to highlight its contrast with the benevolent "Justice League." Rock, while just as single-minded as Waller, instead wraps himself in the flag and so can always fall back on his earnest patriotism and love of country. Waller, in contrast, is simply immoral and enjoys the privilege and power her position provides.

Ostrander reclaims his characters and his initial concept in 2007 for an 8-issue, single story-line run. On page 4, he reestablishes who is in charge, literally and figuratively, by once again putting Waller in the forward position and having her confront Jackson Jones, a minor villain (he was initially caught by Aqualad) called Puma, who is leading an inmate revolution. He wants Waller (whom he calls Fat Lady) to open the gates.

At this point, Jackson seems like a prime candidate for the Squad itself: low level, not very bright, full of attitude, and easily controlled by Waller. But Ostrander changes the rules a bit to affect the Squad going forward. Waller explains, "You got a small explosive device inserted into the base of your skull" and then threatens to blow his "damn head off" if he does not back down. This is a bit more on the nose than the Waller readers have come to expect, but then, the world has changed in the 20 years since she was first introduced. The events of 9/11 make the *threats* of violence useless without their execution. The following quotation illustrates this a bit further:

> PUMA: Who're you kiddin'? I heard all about you and your squad and the wrist bracelets that're supposed to blow somebody's arm off. But I ain't never worked on your squad and nobody said nothin' about no head bombs. Get 'er!

At which point Waller, indeed, blows his "damn head off."

Ostrander is clearly not fooling around with subtleties this time. This new Waller, who, on the following page declares she is "fat, black, cranky, and menopausal!" is not the same self-assured Waller we have seen before. There is an edge to her which indicates that even though her moral compass may be just as adrift as it ever was, the calm reserve which assured the reader nothing could phase her is wearing thin at the edges.[17] Eventually, this wavering of confidence will lead to a secondary leader of the Squad, who will assume the position with a moral compass, and since the immorality is coming from outside, the righteousness will come from within.

And it starts with the other change Ostrander makes with his reintroduction to the series. In this storyline, Waller is effectively putting the band back together to rescue Flag, who has gotten himself into trouble. To do this, she needs Lawton, who is no longer a prisoner at Belle Reve, but now is a resident at Arkham Asylum, a psychiatric facility for the criminally insane.

By opening up Arkham, Ostrander paves the way for its future use, of which later writers will take full advantage. Meanwhile, over the course of the eight-issue run, Lawton gradually becomes the moral center of the group, a process which will come to completion in the *Suicide Squad* film. By 2011, the Squad had left Ostrander's control and was taken over by Adam Glass who detours and re-envisions Waller not only as a soldier, but thin (and, yes, sexy) and scrappy, a fighter.[18] Yes, she is still just as amoral and conniving as ever, but her motivations and the original thrust of her character has been wiped, turning her into just another generic figure. In fact, the only thing Glass' version of the Squad changes, and again, not for the better, is bringing Arkham Asylum into a more central role, specifically with the addition of famed *Batman* villain Harley Quinn as a team mainstay. This changes the dynamic and dilutes the effectiveness of the Squad even within the fictive world he inherited.

As an inmate of Arkham, Quinn needs to be "broken out" during missions which, with the already mentioned lax security at Arkham notwithstanding, certainly does not do much for keeping the secretive nature of the team. Additionally, it lessens Waller's control since now the only reason her team is working towards a common goal is to avoid the threat of death, a simplistic approach compared to the much more psychologically complex characters and motivations Ostrander initially created.[19] Plus, with Quinn in the mix, she is such a big star that the reader can rest assured she is never going to fulfill the Squad's titular promise. It is, however, mostly Glass' version of the Squad which has persisted to the present day and which was adapted to the 2016 movie, which also coincided with yet another reimagining of the Squad, this time in *Suicide Squad: Rebirth*, written by Rob Williams.

By this point in their evolution, the Squad in both *Rebirth* and film, is fully embracing its less than stellar origins along their journey to become bona fide heroes. Quinn is still among the regulars, as are Captain Boomerang and Deadshot, and still ostensibly led in the field by Rick Flag. Waller is back to being her "fat, black, cranky, and menopausal" self. Now, however, the role reversal is complete. Waller, the "free" one, is completely compromised by her own ambitions while Deadshot finally steps into the position of moral guidance counselor. In the inaugural installment of *Rebirth*, in addition to getting yet another origin story, this time with Waller getting her authorization from President Obama, the book ends with the team riding off into battle, guns blazing, while Flag yells, "Let's save the world."

The transformation is complete. They are no longer the anti-heroes Ostrander had wanted them to be, but complete, world-saving good guys, no matter what we are told about them; in this case their actions speak far louder than words. By issue #8 of the series, they team up with the Justice League[20] for a 10-issue crossover which not only sees the Squad come out on top, but leads to the following exchange between Waller and Batman:

> BATMAN: I may have ... misjudged your.... Suicide Squad. There's room in the world for both of our teams.
> WALLER: You're saying that you.... Batman ... were wrong?[21]

With the film,[22] all the pieces do, indeed, come together to finally give us the full journey for both Waller and Deadshot, who have been on a collision course since Ostrander first brought them together. In fact, Ostrander himself has nothing but praise for the two performers and their performances, gushing that "Amanda Waller was my creation and Viola Davis embodied her to perfection. I was happy when she was cast, I was delighted when I saw her in the trailers, and I was ecstatic when I saw her in the film. Davis has Amanda's voice, her look, and her attitude." And while he did not necessarily see Smith's Deadshot performance as being exactly in line with the way he originally conceived his version of the character, he still saw him as "intense, cynical, with a weak spot for his daughter,"[23] which is where the circle has led us.

The reader has been told since the beginning that Lawton "does not care if he lives or dies."[24] And yet he has survived for 30 years, and now it is finally revealed he *does* care—and always has. He has a daughter who fully accepts him ("I know you do bad things," she tells him. "I still love you."[25]), but the viewer believes this because Deadshot has been the one member of the team who *earns* his respect, both by being a good leader and fully embracing who he is. He is even given a line directly out of the Squad/JLA crossover which was originally spoken by Batman.[26] No higher praise can be given. Waller, meanwhile, has used her ambition and drive to place herself in mortal danger, referring to herself as "the voice of God" when she represents the devil who always has a deal ready to be made.

As the Suicide Squad continues, it remains to be seen if these characters' resting places hold or if new creators will come along to put their own spin on the stories. If it is done right, though, the moral dichotomy of Waller and Lawton will forever circle each other, one balancing the other. And while other members may come and go, the reader should never doubt that, if Lawton is on the ground, looking out for the team, that the toast will always be, "Here's to honor among thieves."[27]

NOTES

1. The original Suicide Squad was a military based series which premiered in *The Brave and the Bold* #25, September 1959. While there were no super villains present, the squad was still referred to as *Task Force*

X led by Rick Flag, albeit later revealed to be the father, not the son (although future writers will play fast and loose with this relationship, using the logic of comic book timelines to often conflate the two), two pieces of nostalgia which would carry over into the new series. (Kanigher and Andru 1959).

2. John Ostrander, *Ostrander Reviews the Suicide Squad!* 2016.

3. The introduction of the penitentiary in *Suicide Squad* #1 seems to allude to this directly when journalist Vicki Vale is touring the facility and notes that "…the Prison Was Built on the site of an Old Southern Plantation."

4. Ostrander and McDonnell, *Suicide Squad #1*, 1987.

5. Ibid.

6. Ostrander et al., *Legends #1*, 1986.

7. Captain Boomerang, created in 1960 by John Broome and Carmine Infantino, originally wore a knee length jerkin covered with a boomerang motif topped off by a cravat around his neck in favor of a tie. Later incarnations would adjust the costume into a more rough and tumble leather-based pieces. (Infantino and Broome 1960).

8. Ostrander, *Legends #3*, 1987.

9. The complete history of Amanda Waller is told to then President Ronald Reagan by way of qualifying her to start up and lead *Task Force X,* specifically, the Suicide Squad division. This is all revealed in *Secret Origins* #14, which was published immediately after the *Legends* series and two weeks before (to act as a lead in to) the eponymously titled *Suicide Squad* series.

10. Being a serialized story, this bit of information will be repeated often to ensure the casual reader understands the rewards being offered.

11. This will change over time from an observable, explosive bracelet to a subdermal micro-explosive implanted in the neck, and from a proximity detonator to a more deliberate device controlled ostensibly by Flag and/or Waller to allow more flexibility for the wearer and allow Waller to inflict more terror.

12. Ostrander, *Legends #3*, 1987.

13. Again, Ostrander understands his need for Arkham in his mythos, as well as why he cannot make use of it.

14. It is the reappearance of Flag's ex-lover, whom we find out was in the hospital and Flag was told to stay away to aid in her recovery. She, of course, sees it differently.

15. In *Secret Origins* #14 (May 1987), she receives initial approval for the reactivation of *Task Force X* and the Suicide Squad from President Reagan and then again, almost as a reboot, in *Suicide Squad- Rebirth* #1 (October 2016) from President Obama. in both cases, Waller is given reprimands and refusals but by the end of the conversations, she once again has tentative permission to run her own militia.

16. Issue #67 was produced in 2010 as a link-in to the DC crossover event "Blackest Night."

17. This is exacerbated by the knowledge revealed two panels later that she herself has a neck explosive implanted "case I Ever Got Captured." the Waller of twenty years prior would never even have considered that possibility. (Ostrander and Pina, Suicide Squad—Raise the Flag #1 2007).

18. Glass and Dagnino, *Suicide Squad—New 52 #0*, 2012.

19. Glass, *New 52 #1*. 2011.

20. In this incarnation including Superman, Batman, Wonder Woman, the Flash, Cyborg, and Jessica Cruz's Green Lantern.

21. Williamson and Porter, 2017.

22. Ayer, 2016.

23. Ostrander, *Reviews the Suicide Squad!* 2016.

24. Williams and Tan, 2016.

25. Ayer, 2016.

26. In both Justice League vs. Suicide Squad #3 and the Suicide Squad movie, there is a point where a character (Batman or Deadshot, respectively) is boasting about something, ostensibly to a guard. When the guard refutes the claim, the response, in both cases, is "I Wasn't Talking to You, I Was Talking to Your Boss," wherein the character speaking references Waller. Williamson and Merino, Justice League vs. Suicide Squad #3 2017 and Ayer 2016.

27. Ibid.

Section V

Small Screen Parallels

Animated Arkham

*Television and Children's Perceptions
of Psychiatric Treatment*

KRISTI ROWAN HUMPHREYS

"Arkham ... the one place where costumed delusional personalities can receive compassionate help." When Dr. Bartholomew, the psychiatrist treating Batman in the episode "Dreams in Darkness" from *Batman: The Animated Series*,[1] makes this assertion about Arkham Asylum, he characterizes the facility as a place where mentally ill individuals receive the care—the compassionate care—they need. Taken out of context, it would seem that, via statements such as this, these cartoons convey the notion to a child audience that Arkham Asylum and mental health facilities, in general, are trustworthy institutions where people receive proper psychiatric attention. However, as with similar claims in the series, Dr. Bartholomew's statement is followed by a scene where orderlies struggle to wrestle Batman to the ground and Arkham guards attempt to shoot him with tranquilizer guns. Whereas Dr. Bartholomew asserts compassion, the subsequent actions instill fear.

This essay examines episodes from the cartoon programs *Batman: The Animated Series* (1992–1995), *The New Batman Adventures* (1997–1999), and *The Batman* (2004–2008), investigating how these shows, which were largely targeted to child audiences, included animated depictions of violence and abuse between trained Arkham staff and patients—violence that seemed to send a clear message: psychiatric treatment is something to be feared.

Batman: The Animated Series originally aired on Fox Kids, a programming block on the Fox network with time slots on Saturday morning and weekday afternoons. As a continuation of that series, *The New Batman Adventures* ran on the WB (Warner Bros.), a network primarily featuring adolescent programming, and *The Batman* ran on Kids' WB. All time slots indicate that the general viewing audience comprised mainly children and adolescents. In the book *Children and Television*, Barrie Gunter and Jill McAleer identify television as a pervasive medium and a possible source of social learning for children. "Characters on television can provide role models whom children may strive to emulate," they claim. "Even if they do not directly copy their favourite characters, children may acquire certain values, attitudes or rules from them."[2] Aletha C. Huston et al. find that this is particularly true of work that is unfamiliar to them. In the chapter, "From Attention to Comprehension: How Children Watch and Learn from Television,"

166 Section V: Small Screen Parallels

they discuss a child's ability to judge reality concerning occupations, such as psychiatry, that are largely unfamiliar to them:

> When occupations are unfamiliar … children use both factual and fictional TV as a source of information. In one experiment, we showed children documentaries or fictional stories about unfamiliar occupations. When asked what people in that occupation do, they responded with the actions they had seen. Those who had seen documentaries were a little more likely to think the content was accurate, but those who saw fictional content often thought it presented a realistic view of the occupation.[3]

In another study, Aletha Huston Stein, Lynette Kohn Friedrich, and Fred Vondracek examine the effects specifically of the *Batman* cartoons on young children's behavior.[4] *Batman* is chosen for the study because it is regarded as a common show for children to watch that features human characters exhibiting aggressive behavior. The authors address the debate over whether cartoons can have the same effects on viewers as programs featuring live actors. "Although many writers have asserted that cartoons are less influential than 'real-life' presentations because children perceive them as being less realistic, there is little evidence on this point."[5] In other words, despite being animated, children seem to perceive the characters and actions in these cartoons as being representative of reality. In the study, 92 children, ages 3 to 5, are repeatedly shown 6 episodes of *Batman* cartoons[6]

Gateway to Arkham Asylum, as featured in the animated show aired on daytime television and directed toward children. A long and winding path, replete with cast shadows and a sense of desolation, leads to the fortress-like asylum that sits on a hilltop, recollecting haunted houses of horror films. The crosses atop the "Arkham Asylum" signage are similar to double crosses seen on tuberculosis sanitoriums of the 1960s, which were also isolated from the community to prevent spread of this once-deadly and debilitating contagion. Mental illness was once viewed as contagious, and mental patients were also swept aside, far from the community.

in a preschool setting for 4 weeks, and their behaviors are observed before and after. The results include the following: "For children of both sexes who were above average in initial interpersonal aggression, exposure to aggressive television programs led to higher levels of interpersonal aggression than similar children showed under neutral conditions."[7] Even though this essay does not address aggression in children, it is fair to assume that if *Batman* cartoons influence children's behavior, as this study indicates, these programs could also influence their perceptions of the things they encounter in reality, such as mental illness and psychiatric treatment.

These studies suggest that children regard fictional depictions, such as those encountered in the following *Batman* episodes, as realistic representations of what happens inside of an asylum or a mental health facility, in general—an institution that is likely unfamiliar to many young viewers. From these depictions, kids can develop an early perception that straitjackets and tranquilizer guns are the norm for individuals seeking psychiatric treatment, even if these perceptions evolve as children mature.

In the aforementioned episode "Dreams in Darkness" from *Batman: The Animated Series*, Batman has been exposed to a fear gas that Scarecrow (Professor Crane) plans to use to infect Gotham's water supply. The fear gas causes Batman to hallucinate, and Batman narrates the scene, saying, "Some thought I went mad, so they put me where they thought I belonged." He is placed in Arkham Asylum under the care of Dr. Bartholomew, and the opening scene begins with the doctor, a nurse, and an orderly approaching Batman's room. Dr. Bartholomew asks, "Has the new patient quieted down?" The orderly responds, "Yes, doctor. His hallucinations seem to have stopped." Dr. Bartholomew replies, "Such a pity really, to think after all he's accomplished that he should end up here like this." The doctor peeks through the small window in the door to the room and sees Batman sitting on the floor in the dark, subdued by a straitjacket. "Yes, he does seem calmer," says Dr. Bartholomew. "You can turn on the lights. It's all right Batman. I'm Dr. Bartholomew, your psychiatrist." Batman immediately asks, "Did you contact Commissioner Gordon and Doctor Wu?" "Calm yourself. Everything is under control," responds the doctor. Batman rushes to the door, asking, "Haven't you listened to anything I've told you?" Dr. Bartholomew then says to the orderly, "He needs more time. See that he's not disturbed." Batman yells, "We don't have any more time," and the doctor replies, "Now, now, there's always time to heal." The scene ends with the doctor leaving the room, muttering, "Such a pity."

Dr. Bartholomew reiterates his feeling of pity for Batman and expresses a desire to be patient with his healing. However, he also implies that one's placement in Arkham is an end to a life of accomplishment; on the one hand, the doctor anticipates healing for Batman, but on the other, he perceives this as a pitiful finale to an impressive life. These interpretations may not be ones an audience of children would make, but a child might perceive the more concrete and fear-inducing aspects of Batman's treatment, such as the use of a straitjacket and absolute darkness in the room.

In the next Arkham scene, Dr. Bartholomew tries again, pulling up a chair and saying to Batman, "It's time we had another chat, Batman, so tell me again about this supposed gas?" Batman responds, "I've already told you. When the gas is poured into Gotham's water supply, the entire city will be affected. Why won't you believe me?" The orderly tries to calm Batman, saying, "Easy," and the doctor asks, "How could such a complex plan be implemented without attracting attention?" "I think this may be just another delusion, and deep down, you believe so too. Otherwise, why come to Arkham?

The one place where costumed delusional personalities can receive compassionate help." Batman says, "I didn't come here for help. I came to find the criminal behind all this."

Batman is presenting the situation clearly, but his hallucinations have rendered him unreliable according to the doctor. Also, by asking "Why come to Arkham," the doctor implies that Batman's placement in the asylum, and the placement of other Arkham patients, is optional. This statement is inconsistent with the methods used to restrain and contain these individuals—methods signifying the idea that placement in the asylum is mandated and maintained by force, not merely allowed and treated via therapy.

The next Arkham scene occurs the following day. Batman is alone in his locked room, still wearing the straitjacket. The doctor walks in with two orderlies and says, "I hope I'm not disturbing you." Batman replies, "Isn't that why I'm here? Because I'm disturbed?" Indicating that he is making an effort to believe Batman's claims, Dr. Bartholomew reveals, "I asked an orderly to look in on Professor Crane." Batman replies, "And he was gone." Batman then asks about the location of Gotham's water supply, and upon hearing it is underground, he demands to go there. Dr. Bartholomew responds, "In your state? I can't allow that. You're staying here." The doctor begins to back away and allow the two orderlies to ambush Batman, who is still in a straitjacket. Batman springs over them, but the orderlies ultimately wrestle him to the ground. Dr. Bartholomew begins filling a large hypodermic needle with a substance, saying, "You're still very ill, Batman. This will make you feel better. Don't worry. The police will handle Professor Crane." Batman kicks the needle out of his hand and throws an orderly to ground, proceeding past the others. The doctor triggers the Arkham alarm, and guards begin loading guns with tranquilizer darts. The guards pursue Batman with baseball bats and shoot darts at him, eventually missing Batman and hitting another guard in the chest with a dart.

This type of scene is at the crux of this essay's argument. The doctor's dialogue involves statements suggesting compassion: "I can't allow that in your state." "You're still very ill." "This will make you feel better." These statements, however, are juxtaposed with acts of violence, thus distorting perceptions of psychiatric treatment for child audiences. The disorienting integration of tolerant and benevolent dialogue with pugnacious and violent actions fosters the interpretation that psychiatric care must take ferocious and brutal forms when necessary, even when the patient is regarded as "very ill."

In the same series, the episode "Lock-up"[8] presents Lyle Bolton, the Chief of Security at Arkham, hired to serve as the main form of protection for the asylum. Following some recent strange behavior by Bolton, he is brought before a panel of Arkham doctors, administrators, and Bruce Wayne. They begin asking patients, which include Harley Quinn, Scarecrow, and the Ventriloquist, if they have been mistreated by Bolton. Each one takes a moment to look at Bolton before answering, and their faces reveal their fears, as they hesitantly tell the panel that Bolton has always been kind to them. Dr. Bartholomew re-assures them, saying, "I promise you can speak freely here." Then, when Bruce Wayne proposes that they extend Mr. Bolton's contract for another 18 months, the patients become agitated and panic-stricken. Ventriloquist yells, "No, You can't! You don't know what he is doing to us!" Harley Quinn says, "It's all true! If we don't speak up now, we'll never get the chance! He threatens us, takes away our privileges even when we are good!" Scarecrow shouts, "He says scum like us must be kept in line. That's why he chains us down at night and electrifies our doors!"

Orderlies begin to restrain the patients but then turn to restrain Bolton, who is now attacking fellow asylum staff. Bolton shouts at the patients, "You are all scum! You should all be beaten within an inch of your misbegotten lives." He then turns to the panel, saying, "Before I got here, Arkham was a revolving door for every maniac in Gotham. I kept them in. Me. Now, I realize I was wrong to punish those pathetic miscreants. They're only symptoms. You're the cause: the gutless police, mindless bureaucrats, and coddling doctors."

This scene presents an example of the asylum attempting to act in the best interests of its patients, first by hiring Bolton to secure the facility and then by taking the proper steps to investigate him when his behavior becomes suspect. However, the scene also reveals a history of brutality in the psychiatric care and protection of the patients. In front of the panel, patients are forced to expose the Arkham reality that "protection" within the walls of a mental health care facility includes chains and electrified doors.

Furthermore, the episode ends with Bolton returning to Arkham, this time as a patient. As other patients, formerly terrorized by Bolton as an Arkham staff member, witness him being taken to his own room within the asylum, they heckle him. Harley says, "Look, the big shot is back." Scarecrow mutters, "Now, you shall learn new lessons in fear." Bolton responds under his breathe, saying, "They thought they could trap me in a world of lunatics, but I showed them. Now, I shall keep an eye on everyone. They will never slip by me again." In this final scene, Scarecrow's words are particularly telling, as "fear" is precisely the sentiment Arkham inspires throughout these depictions. Moreover, this scene, in particular, conveys another confounding message regarding psychiatric institutions: psychiatric treatment, although therapeutic, can result in fears of both the care provider and the fellow patient. Incidentally, as the previous scene notes, Bolton refers to Dr. Bartholomew as a "coddling doctor"—a moniker that construes even Dr. Bartholomew's compassionate moments as overprotective rather than therapeutic.

The episode "Mad Love" from *The New Batman Adventures*[9] provides the history of the character Harley Quinn, a psychiatric intern who becomes an asylum patient in this episode. The episode begins with Arkham psychiatrist Dr. Joan Leland meeting intern Dr. Harleen Quinzel (Harley Quinn). Dr. Quinzel asks Leland to call her "Harley," and Dr. Leland reveals her surprise that Harley would choose to intern at Arkham. Harley replies, "I have always had an attraction for extreme personalities. They're more exciting, more challenging." Suspecting other motives, Dr. Leland asks, "And more high profile?" Harley responds, "You can't deny there's an element of glamour to being a super criminal." "I'll tell you right now, these are hard core psychotics," says Dr. Leland. "If you are thinking of cashing in by writing a tell-all book on them, think again. They eat a novice like you for breakfast." Harley is assigned to treat Joker, and she begins to fall in love with him. During therapy sessions, she listens to him describe his abusive father who "favored the grape," and he begins sending her notes and flowers. After a while, Harley reveals, "It soon became clear to me that Joker, often described as a raving homicidal mad man, was actually a tortured soul crying out for love and acceptance, an injured child trying to make the world laugh at his antics. As unprofessional as it sounds, I had fallen in love with my patient." Harley eventually breaks into Arkham and uses various explosive weapons to enable Joker's escape.

Like the episode involving Lyle Bolton, in these cartoon series, Arkham is repeatedly depicted as an institution that struggles to hire competent individuals—individuals capable of providing professional psychiatric attention and appropriate protective care. Compassionate statements such as "tortured soul crying out for love and acceptance" and "injured child" are juxtaposed with therapy sessions utilizing unprofessional and psychologically abusive methods. These depictions suggest that psychiatric care has the potential to involve a doctor falling in love with a patient and then using violence to free the patient from the very institution that is deemed the appropriate measure for treating "hard-core psychotics." Whereas Arkham is but one example of a mental health care facility in popular culture, it is likely one of few examples directed at children, and repeated scenes that emphasize Arkham's inability to provide adequate, professional, non-violent psychiatric care has the capacity to shape how young minds interpret psychiatric treatment in general.

In the episode "Meltdown," from the series *The Batman*,[10] the history of the character Clayface is revealed. In the first Arkham scene, a suspicious-looking orderly is pushing a cart, presumably containing medications, down the hall, amidst the sounds of whispers and dripping water. The orderly arrives at Joker's room, finding him restrained in a straitjacket and seated on the floor in a sealed, furniture-less chamber featuring padded walls and only a small barred window in the door. The orderly enters the room and tells Joker it is time for his medication, and Joker responds, "But 'Flunky,' you left the meds outside." The orderly morphs into the monstrous character Clayface, stating angrily "Not the kind of medicine I had in mind." Joker replies, "Either I'm crazy, or you're melting." Clayface growls, "It's payback time Joker. You're going to suffer for making me what I am." Clayface begins wielding arms of flails and spikes, as he attempts to ambush Joker, who is still wearing the straitjacket. Later, another orderly removes his uniform, reveals himself as Batman, and tells Clayface that he is there to help Clayface get the help, namely psychiatric help, he needs.

Regarding psychiatric treatment, this episode sends mixed messages on multiple levels. Not only does it imply to child viewers that psychiatric patients commonly need to be fearful of their care providers, much like patients were of Lyle Bolton, but the scene also underscores the possibility of suspected hallucinations being reality. Clayface is superhuman, and he takes the form of an orderly—an individual whom patients are urged to trust—in order to gain access to Joker, with the intention of destroying him. Like Bolton and Harley Quinn, Clayface is in need of psychiatric treatment himself, yet the episode places him in a position of authority and trust, a position to provide treatment, even without the mental stability and fortitude to do so. Images such as this have the potential to cause child viewers to develop early misunderstandings of the realities of psychiatric treatment and mental-health care providers, even if those misperceptions are clarified later with maturity and education.

The role of Arkham administrators is dealt with explicitly in the episode "Topsy Turvy" from *The Batman* series.[11] Dr. Bagley, the head psychiatrist and administrator at Arkham, believes he is speaking on the phone with a reporter from *The Gotham Gazette*, when he says the following: "Well I'm always delighted to speak to the press, particularly *The Gotham Gazette*. Actually, I don't consider myself merely a top criminal psychiatrist here at Arkham. I view my role as the last line of defense between Gotham and psychopaths." Bagley defines his position outright. His primary function is to contain the "psychopaths," not necessarily to see that patients receive proper care and treatment. This episode also furthers the idea that all members of Arkham staff are incompetent care providers. When city officials assume that Joker is wreaking havoc in Gotham again, Batman is told it could not actually be Joker because he has been in his "cell" in Arkham the entire time. Once Batman captures "Joker," the poser is revealed to be an Arkham orderly, who says, "Don't hurt me." Batman asks, "Who are you?" "Nolan," he says. "I'm an orderly.... Joker said he would 'do me in' unless I helped him with his plan. He gave me the keys to his place to bring him stuff." Nolan provides another example of the incompetence of the Arkham psychiatric staff.

The Batman series also addresses psychopharmacology in Arkham Asylum. In the episode "The Bat in the Belfry,"[12] Joker checks himself into the asylum, claiming he is feeling a bit "screw loose." He is attempting to use the asylum as his new hideout to develop and administer a gas that will paralyze the inhabitants of Gotham. After vanquishing the orderly, Joker releases all of the Arkham patients from their "cells," and the patients are seen wandering the streets like zombies. These patients are slowly shuffling along, hunched over and unaware of their directions or surroundings. When the police cars arrive on the scene, the patients are unable to recognize the danger or remove themselves from the street. All patients are depicted as being heavily sedated, under the influence of substances that prevent them from ascertaining their surroundings.

This episode furthers two common misconceptions regarding the role of medicine in psychiatric treatment: that medication is overprescribed and that it turns patients into zombies. First, the Arkham patients are exhibiting the same "drug-induced" state, implying that all patients, regardless of condition, are on a similar medication that dulls their senses and inhibits their behavior. Second, the patients seem incoherent, implying that they have been given medicine that has stripped them of their individual personalities and identities, thus making them appear more like "zombies" than humans. Images such as these have the potential to cause children to be fearful and perhaps critical of psychopharmacology, in general.

Animated depictions of Arkham Asylum reveal opportunities for discussion regarding television and its ability to shape childhood understandings of mental illness and psychiatric treatment. In addition to the larger issues of fear and distrust discussed in this essay, Claire Wilson et al. find that even the basic vocabulary used to describe mental illness in children's television programs is central to the discussion. In creating a list of potentially stigmatizing terms used in children's programs to describe the mentally ill, terms that include "crazy," "loony," and "nuts," for example, these authors conclude that "even if children's understanding of terms related to mental illness should vary from that of adults, an acquaintance with these terms exposes them to the language and images that are a part of adult vocabulary."[13] In other words, when children are exposed to stigmatizing terms for mental illness, they are introduced to an adult conversation that uses these terms. According to the episodes examined in this essay, Arkham Asylum is home to mentally ill individuals who are referred to as "lunatics," "scum," "maniacs," "disturbed," and "pathetic miscreants," among other terms. These terms, along with the disorienting combination of violent measures and compassionate dialogue, likely leave child viewers with a distorted view of the mentally ill and psychiatric treatment—a view that, without guidance, can instill in young viewers an element of fear rather than the reality of hope.

NOTES

1. *Batman: The Animated Series*, Season 1, "Dreams in Darkness," Aired on Fox, November 3, 1992, written by Judith and Garfield Reeves-Stevens, directed by Dick Sebast.
2. Barrie Gunter and Jill McAleer, *Children and Television*, 2nd edition (London: Routledge, 2005), 72.
3. Aletha C. Huston, David S. Bickham, June H. Lee, and John C. Wright, "From Attention to Comprehension: How Children Watch and Learn from Television" in *Children and Television: Fifty Years of Research*, eds. Norma Pecora, John P. Murray, and Ellen Ann Wartella (Mahwah, NJ: Lawrence Erlbaum, 2007), 54.
4. Aletha Huston Stein, Lynette Kohn Friedrich, and Fred Vondracek, "Television Content and Young

Children's Behavior," *Television and Social Behavior: Reports and Papers, Vol II, a Technical Report to the Surgeon General's Scientific Advisory Committee on Television and Social Behavior*, eds. John P. Murray, Eli A. Rubenstein, and George A. Comstock (Rockville, MD: National Institute of Mental Health, 1972), 202–317.

5. Stein, "Television Content," 206–207.

6. Children were shown episodes of *Batman* in addition to episodes of *Mister Roger's Neighborhood* and *Superman*. the *Batman* and *Superman* programs were used to assess aggressive behavior, and *Mister Roger's Neighborhood* was used to assess prosocial behavior.

7. Stein, "Television Content," 249.

8. *Batman: The Animated Series*, Season 2, "Lock-Up," Aired on Fox, November 19, 1994, story by Paul Dini, teleplay by Marty Isenberg and Robert N. Skir, directed by Dan Riba.

9. *The New Batman Adventures*, Season 1, "Mad Love," Aired on Warner Bros., January 16, 1999, written by Paul Dini, story by Paul Dini and Bruce Timm, directed by Butch Lukic.

10. *The Batman*, Season 1, "Meltdown," Kids' Warner Bros., June 25, 2005, written by Greg Weisman, directed by Seung Eun Kim.

11. *The Batman*, Season 1, "Topsy Turvy," Kids' Warner Bros., January 1, 2005, written by Adam Beechen, directed by Seung Eun Kim.

12. *The Batman*, Season 1, "The Bat in the Belfry," Kids' Warner Bros., September 11, 2004, written by Duane Capizzi, directed by Seung Eun Kim.

13. Claire Wilson, Raymond Nairn, John Cloverdale, and Aroha Panapa, "How Mental Illness Is Portrayed in Children's Television: a Prospective Study," *British Journal of Psychiatry* 176 (2000): 440.

The Fine Line Between Sanity and Madness in *Star Trek*'s "Whom Gods Destroy" and *Arkham Asylum: A Serious Place on Serious Earth*

DARREN HARRIS-FAIN *and* ERIC J. STERLING

Both Grant Morrison's *Arkham Asylum* and the *Star Trek* episode "Whom Gods Destroy" feature heroes confronting insane criminals who have taken over their respective asylums. In these asylums, both Batman and Captain Kirk must hold on to—and rely upon—their heroic identities while walking the blurred line between sanity and madness. In the asylums, the social order has been inverted, leaving the audience unsure of what is sane and what is not. The lack of a firm demarcation between sanity and madness and between reality and fantasy is manifest when characters seamlessly transform into other characters. This essay explores how these works, similar in plot, present different approaches to the relationship between rationality and mental illness and how their respective heroes confront their true selves in the midst of their struggles.

"Whom Gods Destroy" (1969) aired in the third season of the original *Star Trek* series. Written by Lee Erwin based on a story by Erwin and Jerry Sohl, the episode derives its title from Henry Wadsworth Longfellow's "The Masque of Pandora" (1875). In the Longfellow poem, Prometheus warns his brother Epimetheus, who loves Pandora because the gods have given her the gift of beauty, "Whom the gods would destroy, they first make mad."[1] In Greek mythology and Hesiod's *Works and Days*, Zeus orders Hephaestus and Athena to create a human female, Pandora ("Pandora" is Greek for "all gifted"), to punish humankind for Prometheus's theft of fire. Pandora's "gifts" deriving from the gods turn out to be curses because they lead to destruction. In this aptly named *Star Trek* episode, Garth (Steve Ihnat) receives a gift (shapeshifting), but it turns out to be a curse, for it leads to his madness. Madness is indeed central to the plot of "Whom Gods Destroy": Captain James T. Kirk (William Shatner) and First Officer Spock (Leonard Nimoy) beam down to Elba Two, a prison planet with a poisonous atmosphere used by the Federation to hold insane criminals. They bring a medicine that can cure the inmates, but as they are led through the facility by its director, Governor Donald Cory (Keye Luke), one of the inmates, Marta (Yvonne Craig), warns Kirk and Spock that their guide is not really the asylum administrator Cory. When they see the actual director in a cell, they realize she is telling the truth and find themselves at the mercy of a former starship captain named Garth, who learned from an alien race to change his physical form. Aspiring to become "Master of the Universe," Garth attempts to gain access to the *Enterprise* through his shapeshifting ruses, cajolery, Marta's seduction, and torture. Yet he is routinely thwarted by Kirk's foresight and self-mastery, as well as Spock's supposedly well-timed rescue of Kirk from Marta's murderous attempted seduction, and finally outwitted by Kirk and Spock's logic. An intriguing aspect of Garth's criminal insanity is that it involves uninhibited ambition and a concomitant attempt to show intellectual mastery over Kirk. Instead of merely tricking Kirk with his shapeshifting, Garth instructs Marta to warn him in advance that he is being deceived, that the asylum director is an impostor. Thus, Garth attempts to demonstrate his superiority over Kirk by successfully deceiving him despite giving the *Enterprise* captain a warning. Furthermore, Garth attempts to trick Kirk into divulging the code necessary to be beamed aboard the *Enterprise*. He arranges for Marta to pretend to try to stab Kirk to death[2]; when Kirk struggles with Marta for control of the knife, Spock intervenes, gaining Kirk's trust; however, the captain demonstrates his own intellect by not falling for the ruse, suspecting that the Spock who supposedly saved his life is actually the shapeshifting Garth himself. Such great action and intellectual stimulation in such *Star Trek* episodes very likely influenced comics writer Grant Morrison.

Two-Face bobblehead toy by NECA spoofs Harvey Dent's latter-day incarnation as Two-Face, the persona assumed by the once-handsome and law-abiding District Attorney after Dent is disfigured by Joker's bomb (or by a mobster's acid attack, in an earlier comics iteration). Harvey Dent's double-face invites Jungian interpretations that distinguish the external *persona* shown to the world from the inner soul and the "shadow self" that harbors unacceptable ideas. Anniversary edition annotations to *Batman Arkham Asylum: A Serious House on Serious Earth* mention visits to Jung, and images of "Professor Jung" appear in the text (photograph by George Higham).

In *Supergods* (2011), his semi-autobiographical study of superhero comics, Grant Morrison said, "In my formative years, I'd bought wide-eyed into *Star Trek* and the promise of an Aquarian revolution of space travel, head trips, free love, and superscience."[3] Although he has not said that the plot of "Whom Gods Destroy" influenced his graphic novel *Arkham Asylum: A Serious House on Serious Earth* (1989), the similarities between the two are striking. It too features a facility for the criminally insane, the asylum of the title, that has been taken over by the inmates, and it too involves a hero, in this case Batman, finding himself surrounded by insane villains who lord their newly acquired power over the protagonist, whose own sanity is challenged through his ordeal.

Both Morrison's graphic novel and "Whom Gods Destroy" contain many inversions. The primary inversion occurs when the inmates imprisoned in a facility for the criminally insane assume control over the asylum and take the administrators hostage. In *Arkham Asylum*, the Joker takes control of the madhouse and seems to imprison Dr. Cavendish, a psychiatrist and Arkham's administrator, and Dr. Ruth Adams, a therapist (although it appears later that Cavendish allows this upheaval to occur). In "Whom Gods Destroy," while delivering the serum, Kirk and Spock are captured by madman and former Starfleet captain and hero Garth of Izar. These upheavals seem like inversions, with the inmates (the Joker and Garth) seizing control of the asylum and the sane (Batman, Cavendish, Adams, Kirk, and Spock) becoming inmates. As the Joker triumphantly declares to Batman, "YOU'RE IN THE REAL WORLD NOW AND THE LUNATICS HAVE TAKEN OVER THE ASYLUM."[4] When Batman enters Arkham Asylum from the streets of Gotham City, he seems to be venturing from one insane asylum to another.

Such inversions, including elements of the grotesque in both stories, evoke the carnivalesque reversals described by Mikhail Bakhtin in his 1965 book *Rabelais and His World*. In the realm of carnival, according to Bakhtin, the low are elevated and the mighty are mocked, demonstrating that "established authority and truth are relative."[5] Carnival, says Bakhtin, "celebrates temporary liberation from the prevailing truth of the established order; it marks the suspension of all hierarchical rank, privileges, norms and prohibitions."[6] But one might also consider the possibility that instead of a dissolution or suspension of an established order, a hierarchy is still present yet inverted, because the Joker seems to exercise power over Batman and Garth demonstrates his hegemony over Kirk. Suspending and creating an upheaval of the hierarchy are both carnivalesque because they represent a form of disorder and misrule. Carnival imagery is also present in both stories in the sense that the insane inmates who seize control are depicted as clownish figures. Garth possesses Napoleonic ambitions with an ego to match, and his connections to the French emperor are emphasized by the planet's name (Elba was the site of Napoleon's 1814–1815 exile) and by his habit of placing only one arm within his coat, evoking Napoleon's portraits in which one arm is less visible since his hand is placed inside his waistcoat. However, Garth is insane, and thus his Napoleonic gestures also call to mind the trope in popular culture of crazy characters thinking they're Napoleon.

Garth's clownish nature is also signaled by another part of his attire: his boots, which are different colors. Although these colors match the rest of his ensemble, the impression conveyed is that of a medieval jester in motley. Garth's clownish behavior is reinforced by the juxtaposition with his delusions of grandeur: the more spectacular and superhuman he considers himself, the more absurd his Napoleonic complex and motley appearance seems. Likewise, the Joker in *Arkham Asylum* takes his very name from the playing card image of the jester or fool, and in other Batman comics he is often called the Clown Prince of Crime. Moreover, the action of *Arkham Asylum* takes place on April Fool's Day, and he refers to Batman's tests, such as hide-and-go seek, within the asylum as a game.

However, unlike the harmless pranks played on April 1, the Joker's game is deadly serious, as is Garth's desire to rule the universe and his ruthless treatment of Marta. In contrast to Bakhtin's description of carnival, where misrule is temporary and contained within the dominant social order, in both "Whom Gods Destroy" and *Arkham Asylum*, the forces of chaos and insanity threaten to overwhelm the forces of order and sanity, in part by blurring the boundaries between the two. An intriguing aspect of both works is that the asylum is part of the real world, and life inside and outside the asylum are intertwined and indiscernible. For instance, the Joker tells Batman to come to Arkham Asylum because he belongs there, for he too is mad: "WE WANT YOU. IN HERE. WHERE YOU BELONG."[7] Batman confesses to Commissioner Gordon that his adversary is possibly correct: "THE JOKER MAY BE *RIGHT* ABOUT ME. SOMETIMES I … *QUESTION* THE RATIONALITY OF MY ACTIONS…. AND I'M AFRAID THAT WHEN I WALK THROUGH THOSE ASYLUM GATES… IT'LL BE JUST LIKE COMING HOME."[8]

Morrison suggests that the initial demarcation between the Joker and Batman might not be as rigid as one thinks. Batman seems to suffer from mental illness, partly because as a child he witnessed the murder of his parents. As Morrison noted in his annotations for the fifteenth anniversary edition of the graphic novel, the Batman of *Arkham Asylum* is "damaged,"[9] and must "integrate his psychological demons" in order to "emerge stronger and more sane."[10] The reader has no clue what caused the Joker's mental illness, and readers should recognize that their empathy for Batman in his clash with the Joker derives partly because Morrison presents the action largely from the superhero's perspective. Yet Adams also says that the Joker possesses "super sanity," suggesting that he is saner in a way than everyone else, again blurring the line between sanity and madness. Likewise, Amadeus Arkham initially seems like a psychologically stable man whose mother suffers from mental illness. In fact, he created the asylum partly in her honor, but he either is also mentally disturbed or he becomes so after his wife and daughter are murdered and after caring for his mother—and ultimately becoming her. Also, Cavendish seems mentally stable and even serves as the director of the asylum, yet he, like Arkham, transforms into a madman and into Arkham's mother. Thus, the blurring of gender boundaries parallels the blurring of boundaries between sanity and insanity. Throughout the Batman comic books, the Joker has always been considered male, but in *Arkham Asylum*, he seems to have transformed into a female or at least to possess female characteristics, and there are also verbal and visual allusions to Norman Bates from the Alfred Hitchcock film *Psycho* (1960), whose male protagonist also assumes a female persona.

Similarly, shapeshifting is a prevalent theme in "Whom Gods Destroy." Garth of Izar has learned to transform himself physically into various people, such as Governor Donald Cory, Kirk, and Spock. It is his shapeshifting that allows him to invert the social order, transforming from an asylum inmate to a governor and leader of the asylum and from a prisoner into a Starfleet ship captain. As with *Arkham Asylum*, in the *Star Trek* episode, it becomes unclear to the audience and to the characters who is a criminally insane inmate, who needs to be locked up, and who is a sane leader who belongs on the outside of the asylum. However, in the case of Dr. Cory and perhaps Cavendish and Adams, the asylum administrators live inside the mental institution, blurring the distinction between those who are considered sane and those who are considered mentally unstable. The supposed leader of the asylum is actually insane. Dr. Donald Cory is actually Garth, who has shapeshifted himself to resemble Cory, and Dr. Cavendish believes that he is carrying out the work of Amadeus Arkham and Arkham's mother, both of whom believed they saw bats. Arthur Asa Berger notes that Batman "is a figure closely related to shadow and mystery; the bat is a symbol of something deadly and strange, a nocturnal beast associated with vampirism and the occult."[11] It is unsurprising, then, that the mental illness of Amadeus Arkham and his mother would manifest itself in a fear and hallucination involving bats. Garth assumes the disguise of Cory and Cavendish as Amadeus Arkham's mother, complete with her wedding dress.

It is clear, though, that the antagonists of both "Whom Gods Destroy" and *Arkham Asylum* are in fact criminally insane. In particular, both works share three aspects of the so-called criminally insane: the quest for power, the thirst for revenge, and the desire to play games. The Joker and Garth of Izar suffer from delusions of grandeur and a wish to seize power. The Joker has often attempted to usurp control of Gotham City, and in this graphic novel, he garners control over Arkham Asylum (which serves as a microcosm of Gotham City) and the bodies and minds of the inmates and hospital staff. Garth gains power on Elba Two and attempts to seize control over the *Enterprise* so that he can employ the ship and crew for intergalactic conquests and destruction. Their criminally insane minds incite them to strive for power at all costs, disregarding the feelings and lives of those who stand in their way or who can be used as weapons, such as the staff member whom the Joker threatens to stab in the eye to lure Batman to Arkham, and Marta, whom Garth blows up with a bomb in "Whom Gods Destroy." Garth feels no animosity towards Marta when he murders her; he merely considers her expendable and indifferently blows her up to make a point to Kirk regarding his power. The two works link the criminally insane mind not only with an obsession with power but also with a concomitant egocentrism. The Joker and Garth exhibit symptoms of Antisocial Personality Disorder— "Reckless disregard for safety of self or others"[12]—and Narcissistic Personality traits: "Lacks empathy: is unwilling to recognize or identify with the feelings and needs of others."[13]

Both the Joker and Garth want revenge, in their insanity projecting their imprisonment onto their enemies rather than accepting responsibility for their mad actions. The Joker seeks vengeance on Batman for all the times his crime-fighting nemesis has triumphed over him. He wants to hurt Batman and imprison him in Arkham Asylum just as Batman has sent him to prison and the asylum. Garth attempts to destroy the inhabitants of the planet Antos in a psychologically misguided effort to exact revenge on the people who saved his life and taught him shapeshifting; his anger against the Federation and his desire to seek vengeance upon it stem not only from their imprisoning him on Elba Two but also from his crew preventing him from carrying out his insane genocidal attempt against Antos. It is true that both Kirk and Batman use violence in subduing their opponents, and that Batman's mission is driven by a hatred of criminals rooted in his parents' murder, but in both cases, they are impelled by a sense of law and justice rather than vengeance, and are, unlike the murderous Joker and Garth, loath to use lethal force.

A lack of empathy and an inflated sense of self also relate to the villains' treatment of their conflicts as if they were games. The Joker and Garth enjoy playing games even though they realize (but don't care) that they are playing with people's lives. The Joker sends the inmates to kill Batman, calling it a game of hide-and-seek. Even the stabbing of the staff member in the eye is a game because it turns out to be a ruse to compel Batman to enter the asylum. Garth attempts to trick and force Kirk to give him the password so that he can seize control of the Enterprise; ironically, the password is a move in a chess game. And Garth temporarily detours from his mission to seize control of the Enterprise in order to test whether Spock can pick the correct Captain Kirk; he transforms into Kirk so that Spock cannot discern which man is truly the captain; he says, "This could be most amusing" because it is a game to him.[14]

Yet despite their many similarities, "Whom Gods Destroy" and *Arkham Asylum* present very different approaches to their depictions of heroes battling insane villains on their own turf. One difference concerns the very nature of that turf, the respective settings of these stories. The prison for the criminally insane in the *Star Trek* episode is a clean, well-lighted place. It may be on a planet with a toxic atmosphere to deter escape, but it nonetheless gives the impression of a humane approach to treating the mentally ill—an impression supported by Dr. Cory's benign intentions and the Federation's supplying a serum that can cure the inmates. In contrast, Arkham Asylum is a dark, hellish place, and McKean's impressionistic art suggests a disturbed hallucinatory state very different from the filmed reality of "Whom Gods Destroy." The very name of the institution reinforces Arkham's depraved nature, alluding as it does to the work of H.P. Lovecraft, who wrote about a fictional town called Arkham where dark, disturbing things happen.

Similarly, the two stories differ in their treatment of mental illness. Just as the physical appearance of the Elba Two prison suggests a kinder attitude toward the mentally ill, so the faith in science and technology conveyed throughout *Star Trek* suggests that we may one day develop a cure for even criminal insanity, revealing an Enlightenment optimism about progress and the value of human life. Steven Schlozman believes that in the optimistic world of *Star Trek*, social problems, predispositions, and internal causes of mental illness have been eradicated, so characters "may become *psychotic* (experiencing serious loss of contact with reality), but they are psychotic with clearly explicable *etiologies* (origins)" such as energy surges and exposure to environmental contaminants.[15] Garth's psychosis derives not from a predisposition to mental illness, but rather from his engagement in shapeshifting. On Elba Two, there are but a few "remaining criminally insane humans and aliens who have not been cured by the otherwise harmonious state of the Federation.... [T]he patients, whether dangerous or not, are treated with dignity and compassion."[16] Such optimism, as noted above, inspired Morrison's enjoyment of the show in his youth and derived from real-life scientific accomplishments of the late 1960s, in particular the moon landing of 1969.[17] But the realities of life in Morrison's native Scotland in the 1970s dimmed his earlier optimism: "...I was being offered instead of Starfleet a bleak tomorrow of fuel shortages, urban decay, and economic and social unrest."[18] A sense of gloom, he adds, likewise fell over superhero comics in the 1970s and 1980s, and *Arkham Asylum* is very much a manifestation of this. Here, instead of the bright Enlightenment feel of *Star Trek*, we have the dark sensibility of the Gothic, with its emphasis on crime, passion, and the irrational. In the world of *Arkham Asylum*, madness is not depicted as an illness capable of being cured; it is a condition that, if anything, is a natural response to reality. While "Whom Gods Destroy" concludes with the serum injection instantly healing of the mentally ill, including the formerly villainous Garth, *Arkham Asylum* ends with the criminally insane really no different than they were at the start of the book. Indeed, Batman even seems to accept their madness, for instance restoring Two-Face's coin and thus in a sense condoning Harvey Dent's criminal fixation on duality. Batman's returning of the coin is an improvement upon Adams's treatment of providing Two-Face with dice and Tarot cards, which had rendered her patient more indecisive and consequently more psychologically unstable. According to Marc Singer, "Rather than demonizing the inmates for their deviance, *Arkham Asylum* reconciles Batman with the manifold modes of deviance he battles every night on the streets of Gotham City."[19]

However, if the villains of *Arkham Asylum* remain uncured, Batman himself has passed through a kind of dark (k)night of the soul. As Singer says, the combination of McKean's art and Morrison's script presents Batman's night in the asylum as "an initiation rite in which he faces his deepest fears and darkest impulses, personified in the forms of his worst enemies."[20] Each of Batman's criminally insane foes in the asylum represents a characteristic within the superhero's psyche. Richard Reynolds agrees, stating, "The great *Batman* villains all mirror some key point in Batman's character, a point of reference which gives their villainy special purchase within the metatext of the *Batman* myth.... The Joker epitomizes the dark and negative side of the personal obsessions which fuel Batman's crimefighting career; the Joker is a constant reminder that strength, which derives from traumatic experience, can be turned toward evil as easily as good."[21] Batman's struggle in the graphic novel is not so much against his foes as it is against his own tortured psyche. This struggle is symbolized not only by the plot but also by McKean's art. As James F. Wurtz notes, "*Arkham Asylum* realizes its complexity through, and derives its energy from, its spatialization and visualization of sanity and insanity."[22] Not only are details difficult to discern in McKean's dark artwork, paralleling the difficulty in the graphic novel in distinguishing between sanity and madness, but also the physical spaces of the asylum are hard to figure out, both in terms of layout and in the ways McKean plays with depth and distance. Likewise, "McKean's Batman," says Will Brooker, "is a devil-eared shadow rather than a concrete human figure, while his Joker, all swirling fluorescent hair and gleaming white face, remains a blur who refuses to be pinned down."[23] Indeed, despite Morrison's initial desire that *Arkham Asylum* be drawn by Brian Bolland, known for his clear lines and realistic renderings, Brooker argues that McKean's jagged painterly style perfectly complements the book's "often blurred, obscure, literally 'dark' vision of the Batman's physical and emotional journey through the asylum."[24]

On the other hand, *Star Trek* exults in its elevation of reason over the passions, in its characterization as well as in its setting and plot. It is a commonplace observation that the three major leads of the original *Star Trek*—Kirk, Spock, and Dr. Leonard "Bones" McCoy—correspond to Sigmund Freud's theories of the self, with McCoy as the passionate id, Spock as the hyper-rational superego, and Kirk as the ego that unifies the competing forces of passion and reason while containing elements of both. In "Whom Gods Destroy," though, Kirk and Spock both must rely on their reason when confronting the shapeshifting, unbridled id of "Lord" Garth. Indeed, Garth's ploy of using the Orion woman Marta to try to seduce Kirk, after she has already displayed her feminine charms and considerable flexibility in an erotically charged dance, is nearly as much a test of Kirk's resolve as his later torture. By the third season of the show, viewers were well aware of Kirk's love of the ladies, so him resisting Marta shows his efforts to keep his wits instead of giving in to his passions. Aided by the ever-logical Spock, he needs his wits, of course, in trying to outsmart the devious Garth. The two of them use reason to counteract Garth's deceptions, very much in contrast with Batman's highly emotional responses to the criminally insane of *Arkham Asylum*.

Thus "Whom Gods Destroy" and *Arkham Asylum*, despite their similar plots and themes, present rather different attitudes toward the hero in relation to criminals who are mentally ill. The *Star Trek* episode favors reason and order; Morrison's graphic novel, for much of the book, seems to embrace the irrational and the chaotic. The former places its trust in science and the dream of progress, while the latter casts doubt on the idea that our problems can be completely bested. In both stories, though, the hero is the figure who can look madness in the face and defeat it without succumbing to madness himself.

Notes

1. Henry Wadsworth Longfellow, "The Masque of Pandora." in *The Masque of Pandora and Other Poems* (Boston: Osgood, 1876), 33.
2. Marta pretends to try to kill Kirk; Garth comprehends that if she slays Kirk, Garth cannot extract the code from him.
3. Grant Morrison, *Supergods: What Masked Vigilantes, Miraculous Mutants, and a Sun God from Smallville Can Teach Us About Being Human* (New York: Spiegel & Grau, 2011), 160.
4. Grant Morrison, *Arkham Asylum: A Serious House on Serious Earth*. Art by Dave McKean. 15th Anniversary Edition (New York: DC Comics, 2004), 14.
5. Mikhail Bakhtin, *Rabelais and His World*. Translated by Hélène Iswolsky (Cambridge, MA: MIT Press, 1968), 10.
6. *Ibid.*, 109.
7. Morrison, *Arkham Asylum*, 6.
8. *Ibid.*, 8, first ellipsis in text.
9. *Ibid.*, 61.
10. *Ibid.*, 66.
11. Arthur Asa Berger, *The Comic-Stripped American: What Dick Tracy, Blondie, Daddy Warbucks, and Charlie Brown Tell Us About Ourselves* (New York: Walker, 1973), 161.
12. American Psychiatric Association, *Diagnostic and Statistical Manual of Mental Disorders*, 5th ed. (Washington, DC: American Psychiatric Association, 2013), 659.
13. *Ibid.*, 670.
14. Lee Erwin, "Whom Gods Destroy," *The Star Trek Transcripts—Episode Listings*, 3 Jan. 1969, http://www.chakoteya.net/StarTrek/71.htm, Accessed 15 May 2017.
15. Steven Schlozman, "What Happened to Mental Illness by the 23rd Century?" in *Star Trek Psychology: The New Frontier*. Edited by Travis Langley (New York: Sterling, 2017), 126–27.
16. *Ibid.*, 130, 131.
17. Morrison, *Supergods*, 160–61.
18. *Ibid.*, 161.
19. Marc Singer, *Grant Morrison: Combining the Worlds of Contemporary Comics* (Jackson: University Press of Mississippi, 2012), 66–67.
20. *Ibid.*, 64.
21. Richard Reynolds, *Super Heroes: A Modern Mythology* (Jackson: University Press of Mississippi, 1992), 68.
22. James F. Wurtz, "'Out There in the Asylum': Physical, Mental, and Structural Space in Grant Morrison and Dave McKean's 'Arkham Asylum: a Serious House on Serious Earth,'" *Amerikastudien / American Studies* vol. 56, 4 (2011), 556.
23. Will Brooker, *Batman Unmasked: Analysing a Cultural Icon* (London: Continuum, 2001), 272.
24. *Ibid.*, 271–72.

SECTION VI

Video Screen Parallels

If Walls Could Scream

*Embedded Narratives and Mazes
of Madness in the Virtual Space
of Arkham Asylum*

Shawn Edrei

As a narrative medium, one of the most significant innovations offered by video games is the possibility of actively traversing fictional spaces. Where other platforms restrict access to the fictional world to the "eye" of the camera (as seen in film and television) or are dependent upon the reader's cognitive reconstruction of said world (as with textual literature), the virtual environments of today's video games allow—and, in fact, almost always require—real-time navigation of its internal diegesis, a differentiation established by Janet Murray nearly twenty years ago: "The new digital environments are characterized by their power to represent navigable space. Linear media such as books and films can portray space, either by verbal description or image, but only digital environments can present space that we can move through."[1] The environments in question are not worlds the audience projects or imagines: visual representation is consistent with the filmic standard, in that the "text" effectively maps out specific segments of the fictional world in which the plot takes place. However, as Bob Rehak points out, the added components of digital embodiment and active participation have a direct impact on how game narratives are consumed:

> video games have evolved toward ever more complex simulations of corporeal immersion, subsuming economic, social, and technological determinants under an overarching goal: to confront players with detailed and lifelike "doubles." As the avatar took on character, history, and presence within increasingly detailed story worlds, the coded representation of sensory immersion epitomized by the FPS brought video games into dialogue with the dominant representational system of Hollywood filmmaking.[2]

This immersion, in turn, enables authors of virtual narratives to manipulate conventions of storytelling in new and fascinating ways. One such technique involves implanting "sub-narratives" within the world, a process that according to Elana Gomel has become increasingly common in contemporary fiction: "as the chronotope of embedding develops through the twentieth century, writers begin to join it to other narrative techniques. As its narrative sophistication increases, embedding becomes increasingly used for metafictional purposes: figuring the process of constructing the storyworld."[3]

Batman: Arkham Asylum, a game published by Eidos Interactive in 2009, serves as an apt demonstration of this process of embedding, particularly in terms of how the technique has been adapted to serve a new narrative medium. Based on the infamous mental institution in DC Comics' *Batman* serials, the game casts the player in the titular role of Gotham City's vigilante hero, now trapped on Arkham Island by the Joker and his followers. As Batman, the player is tasked with navigating the asylum's labyrinthine passages and exploring the rest of the island in order to prevent the escape of the imprisoned supervillains, many of whom are explicitly portrayed as dangerously unstable. Though *Batman* has been a part of American pop culture since 1939—and Arkham Asylum similarly part of the mythos since 1974, appearing in almost every film and TV adaptation since—the prospect of actively exploring this fictional setting is entirely new. Past depictions would rely on clear visual cues to communicate Arkham's foreboding status in the fictional world: the Gothic architecture, the solitary positioning of the Asylum as the only structure on a barren and deserted island, its consistent representation in perpetual nighttime and so on. But these variations keep the audience at a distance due to the nature of their respective media, and the passive process of observation mandated by both text-based and cinematic narratives. By assembling a simulacrum of Arkham Asylum in a virtual environment, via a medium which requires active participation on the part of the player, the game's developers ensure that even those deeply familiar with the source material will be confronted with an entirely new narrative experience, one Murray claims serves a dual purpose: "The adventure maze embodies a classic fairy-tale narrative of danger and salvation. Its lasting appeal as both a story and a game pattern derive from the melding of a cognitive problem (finding the path) with an emotionally symbolic pattern (facing what is frightening and unknown)."[4]

Understanding the significance of the exploratory powers wielded in *Arkham Asylum* is key to defining the spatially inscribed stories within. While the foreboding edifice was initially conceived as a matter of plot convenience—an answer to the question of where Batman could imprison his defeated superhuman nemeses—it has gradually become an active part of the diegetic landscape. One of the most significant texts dedicated to a more complete examination of the institution is the DC graphic novel *Arkham Asylum: A Serious House on Serious Earth* by Grant Morrison and Dave McKean, which in many ways serves as a direct template for the Eidos video game. The Morrison/McKean project, originally published in 1989, begins with a premise very similar to that of the game published two decades later: the dangerous inmates of Arkham Asylum, led by the Joker, have seized control of the facility and are demanding Batman's presence in exchange for their hostages. However, the graphic novel does not begin in the present day; rather, the frame story is a 1901 excerpt from the journal of Amadeus Arkham, the asylum's founder, discussing his mother's mental illness: "But even then, I understood that Mother had been born again, into that other world. A world of fathomless signs and portents. Of magic and terror. And mysterious symbols."[5] While Arkham's description of his mother's psychosis may seem overly romantic and mysticized, it does fall in line both with the generally simplistic depictions seen in the *Batman* series and the sublime terrors typically invoked in the works of H.P. Lovecraft. Indeed, the *Arkham Asylum* graphic novel has much to say about madness, and whether Batman is himself a victim of mental illness—when another inmate demands that the Joker unmask Batman to reveal his true face, the Joker responds: "Oh, don't be so predictable, for Christ's sake! That is his real face."[6] Batman's present-day wanderings through the Asylum and encounters with his enemies are intercut with additional entries from Arkham's founder, detailing his own descent into vengeful insanity following the murder of his wife and daughter; his narration overlaps with Batman's struggles, creating a further parallel between the two. Upon reaching the heart of the institution, Batman learns that one of the Asylum's doctors freed the criminals and instigated the entire scenario: "Now listen, I only did what had to be done. You read the book on the table beside you and you'll see. Go on. It's Amadeus Arkham's journal."[7] Arkham's last entry reveals that, in his delusional state, he imagines the very concept of insanity as an enormous bat.

As previously mentioned, most of the Morrison/McKean graphic novel is given over to Batman's journey through the maze of the Asylum. But by the very nature of the medium in question, said journey is both passively received by the reader and segmented into pages and panels per Morrison's script and McKean's page layouts. According to Espen Aarseth, any cognitive or emotional impact is therefore limited: "A reader, however strongly engaged in the unfolding of a narrative, is powerless. Like a spectator at a soccer game, he may speculate, conjecture, extrapolate, even shout abuse, but he is not a player.... He cannot have the player's pleasure of influence: 'Let's see what happens when I do this.'"[8] Thus, the release of Eidos' *Arkham Asylum* video game makes the notion of wandering through the most notorious madhouse in American fiction more than a mere thought experiment. In this, J.P. Wolf's system of categorizing phenomena in virtual environments is a most useful set of standards for analyzing the transmedia shift and its implication:

> Elements occurring in video games can be divided into four general categories: those indicating the player's presence in the game (the player-character); those indicating the computer's presence in the game (computer-controlled characters); objects that can be manipulated or used by game characters; and the background environment that generally serves as the setting and is not manipulated or altered by any of the characters during the game.[9]

In the case of *Arkham Asylum*, the player's presence is embodied in the role and function of Batman himself: the famous superhero's every physical movement is determined by the player's consistent input, and Batman will succeed or fail in his task based solely on the player's aptitude, reflexes and skill at mastering the game's mechanics. The computer's presence is evident in the presence of every other character in the game world not controlled by the player, whether these be police officers or dangerous madmen. Usable objects correspond to Batman's famous arsenal of tools and tricks, which the player may use practically at will. But it is the background environment that is most relevant here, as it is the platform upon which the developers of the game attempt to mimic the structure of the Morrison/McKean novel by inscribing a secondary narrative onto the surface of the virtual space itself.

The game's official guide describes one recurring element in the Asylum as follows: "These are strange writings and symbols that have been found around Arkham Island and deciphered by Batman. They must have been left for a reason. What story do they tell? ... The messages are uncovered in sequential order, regardless of the order you find them in the game."[10] These twenty-four text pieces, attributed to an entity referred to as "The Spirit of Arkham," are scattered throughout the island, and most are concealed from plain view—thus, the Spirit's story may only be pieced together if the player is determined to explore every nook and cranny of the game world. Though there is no mandatory obligation to do so, the Spirit's first message is explicitly designed to create a sense of intrigue: "I am the spirit of Amadeus Arkham. Through my actions, I have saved this

Dr. Hugo Strange from *Batman: Arkham City* (2011) video game, dir. Sefton Hill. Dr. Strange stands in militaristic pose and garb, rather than in laboratory coat or asylum administrator's suit. He is flanked by two armed, masked and uniformed men, standing before a backdrop of fascistic slogans, such as "Obey Obey," and the word "Arkham" pasted across a large letter "A." This scene recollects the villainous North Korean psychologist in *The Manchurian Candidate* (1962), who hypnotizes and brainwashes unsuspecting servicemen, led by Frank Sinatra's Major Marco.

cursed city, though my own curse is to forever remain in the shadows. My story is carved into the very soul of Arkham and will only be revealed to those dedicated enough to discover it."[11] These writings serve a dual purpose: from a gameplay perspective, the Spirit's messages are "collectibles," one of several sets of virtual items to be gathered via exploration and participation in the game; typically, completing such sets reward the player with similarly virtual trophies which openly display their achievements to other players. From a narrative standpoint, however, assembling this fragmented first-person account is far more significant; indeed, the text itself is considerably more complex than the original upon which it is based. The first few messages discovered by the player follow the familiar story of Amadeus Arkham: his mother's illness, his belief that Gotham City itself is a breeding ground for insanity, the murder of his family at the hands of his patient, and Arkham's torturous revenge upon said patient. However, as more fragments are discovered, the player gradually becomes aware of a chronological inconsistency. The Spirit's thirteenth message reads: "The Gotham police dragged a new patient to the island. They said he was responsible for the disappearance of hundreds of the city's vagrants. As I looked at his disgusting body, all scales and teeth, my mind ran free, dreaming of delicious punishments to break this monster."[12] Though no explicit parallel is drawn, the Spirit's description of this new patient bears some similarities to Killer Croc, a present-day enemy of Batman—one who lives nearly a century after Amadeus Arkham's death.

Given the many monsters Gotham City produces on a regular basis, it is within the realm of possibility that a precedent to Croc may have existed in the time of Amadeus Arkham; yet the seventeenth message allows for no such ambiguity: "I watched in silence as he brought in the woman. Her skin now a venomous green, the wanton creature no longer looked like a human being, much less a woman. The Bible says, 'Suffer not a witch to live,' yet he has once again delivered this female atrocity to our care. Once I have dealt with the monster, I think it will be time to see if green wood does, in fact, burn."[13] This entry leaves no doubt as to the identity of its subject, as the Spirit describes both Batman (as the "he" who brings the inhuman criminals to the Asylum) and longstanding supervillain Poison Ivy, whose unique appearance and plant-based affinities are the result of a particular set of circumstances. At this point, it is clear to the player that the game has played a trick on them: the Spirit cannot be Amadeus Arkham himself, despite the initial reiterations of the doctor's biography; rather, it is someone in the present, an individual with access to all levels of the Asylum and the island beyond, where these writings have been dispersed. Further entries describe the Joker's seduction of Harley Quinn, the presence of Jonathan Crane (also known as the Scarecrow), and the breakout which led to the opening scenes of the game. Tellingly, the official guide does not reveal the contents of the final entry:

> The mysterious raconteur who left these timely messages wished to leave his identity as the final puzzle. Reread the messages here for clues and head to the last place Batman had seen the person who you believe the Spirit of Arkham to be. For those who need a little more assistance, we've hidden the name of the room where the final message has been hidden somewhere in this chapter. The twenty-fourth Chronicle of Arkham appears on no maps in the game, nor in this book, but you will know it when you see it. Good luck![14]

Only players most dedicated to complete exploration of the virtual landscape will uncover the final text, which lays bare the identity of the author: "My name is Quincy Sharp, the spirit of Amadeus Arkham. You have done well to decipher my story and I pray it has helped on your path. I trust that through my writings you will do what is right. Please, I implore you, continue my work. This city deserves a savior; continue my work!"[15] Quincy Sharp is, in fact, the Warden of Arkham Asylum; his writings reveal him to be as unhinged as his patients, believing himself to be possessed by the murderous founder of the institution and seeing the violent eradication of the mentally ill as a form of holy crusade. Two components stand out in Sharp's final message: the first is that its phrasing suggests a dual addressee—Batman, as the diegetic figure who has fully deciphered the texts; and the player, who has led their avatar through a rigorous investigation and probed every corner of the Asylum to do so. The second, and most significant, is that by the time the final message can be discovered, Sharp is beyond the player's access; the game allows (and expects) Batman to defeat his enemies at every turn, whether these be faceless henchmen or the most iconic names in the mythos, yet the Warden remains tantalizingly out of reach. This is an intriguing limitation, given Evan Skolnick's assertion that video games are inextricably tied to action and activity: "Core game designs and mechanics are always directly linked to what the player character can *do* … the verbs she is able to express within the confines of the game space."[16] Here, then, both Batman and the player are confronted with an opponent that cannot be defeated within the set framework of *Arkham Asylum*.

The lack of closure concerning Warden Sharp evokes a similar problem faced by the graphic novel as well: for all that it has proven an enduring and critically lauded tale in the long-running *Batman* oeuvre; its format restricts to some extent its ability to communicate its central metaphor. The reader may only observe Batman's traversal of the Asylum at a distance, and has no direct output on the course of his journey; at the same time, the medium of comics cannot conceal information as such: panels may be composed in such ways as to obscure details (and indeed, McKean's art presents images all the more unsettling for their amorphous and unfocused appearance), yet these may be studied and analyzed as part of the process of narrative consumption. The video game medium, on the other hand, is defined primarily by player input: the environment may be pre-programmed, the layout set in stone (or its digital equivalent), yet the player must choose to step outside the bounds of linear narrative progression to solve the mystery of the Spirit. The revelation of Sharp's madness is not a core component of *Arkham Asylum*'s narrative presentation, but an optional addition designed to provide further texture and complexity to the storyworld. In fact, William Uricchio notes that the game's deviations from the Morrison/McKean template, and any inconsistencies that may be generated from the player's choice to prioritize exploration over story progression, has no effect on the aggregate construct that is Arkham Asylum: "Gotham is a space where the variant renderings of decades of multi-authored Wayne Towers or Arkham Asylums do not so much compete with one another as inconsistencies but rather cohere together as an experimental *bricolage*. It is a space whose dynamic flux is the source of its vitality."[17] Rather than detract from the mythic status of Arkham Asylum, the titular game only further enhances its potency in the minds of its audience.

The narrative significance of the Spirit of Arkham subplot is that it plays into the central allegory of Arkham Asylum in all its transmedia incarnations: namely, that the structure itself represents mental illness in all its myriad forms, with Batman's navigation a metaphor for psychological treatment (making sense of twisting passages, piecing together incomplete stories, imposing a sense of order, and so on). The allegory originates with the graphic novel, in which Batman's successful campaign into the heart of the labyrinth grants him access to Amadeus Arkham's journal; with a clearer and more complete understanding of the Asylum's origins and purpose, he proceeds to break down the front doors, announcing to the inmates: "You're free. You're all free."[18] This phrasing clearly implies that Batman's triumph parallels the course of successful treatment—the root cause of the inmates' torment (the corrupt doctor) has been neutralized, the riot quelled, order restored. Yet the Joker's reply reminds the reader that even in the cartoon world of the superhero, solutions to mental illness are rarely so complete and definitive. In response to Batman's proclamation, the Joker holds up a straitjacket and asks: "Oh, we know that already. But what about you? Have you come to claim your kingly robes? Or do you just want us to put you out of your misery, like the poor sick creature you are?"[19] Lacking any permanent solution to the problem, Batman leaves Arkham to the inmates, who show no interest in leaving—the Joker's parting words, referring to the outside world as an asylum, leaving no ambiguity as to why. Metatextually speaking, the conclusion of the graphic novel demonstrates a broader impasse in these representations of mental illness: according to Danny Fingeroth, the superhero genre is by its very nature poorly equipped to portray any process (such as psychological treatment) which may result in a changed status quo:

> The comics industry spent thirty-five years establishing a set of values—cultural, political, and religious—that pretty much reflected the status quo blandness served up by the rest of popular culture. It's spent the three decades since then trying to reevaluate and reinterpret those values to reflect the diversity of the culture it both reflects and influences.[20]

This deadlock, produced by the genre's inability to fully deconstruct its own foundations, translates in-text to Arkham becoming a place of perpetual and paradoxical insanity:

Batman's enemies are sent to a facility that cannot treat them, let alone rehabilitate them, as the ontological and generic laws of the setting will not allow it. Morrison's denouement is, in essence, an admission of defeat in the face of an ironclad, culturally reinforced status quo, as learning the story of Amadeus Arkham provides the hero with no real solution to or insight into Gotham's current-day plights. The game echoes this inability to present a decisive conclusion, bound as it is by the same narrative conventions; having quelled the uprising and defeated the Joker, Batman is now free to further explore the island and the Asylum: "Completing Story Mode unlocks the Armored Batman character for use in Challenge Mode. In addition, you can continue the story with free run of Arkham Asylum and solve any of The Riddler's Challenges that you haven't yet cracked."[21] Tellingly, restoring order to Arkham has no visible effect on the environment, save for the lack of combat opportunities; the madmen have been locked away again, and that is the most the player-as-Batman can accomplish on that front. No new possibilities for treatment are presented; Warden Sharp, the

Image of the knife-wielding Victor Zsasz from Rocksteady Studio's first *Batman: Arkham Asylum* (2009) videogame, directed by Sefton Hill and voiced by Danny Jacobs. The fictional Zsasz was born into wealth but developed a gambling addiction after both parents died in a boat accident. The scar-ridden, chain-wearing, sword-wielding Zsasz murdered a man to liberate him from his pointless existence and was incarcerated in Arkham after continuing this killing spree. "Zsasz" plays upon the name of psychiatrist Thomas Szasz, M.D., author of *The Myth of Mental Illness* (1960), which became America's anti-psychiatry "sourcebook" in those radical years.

Spirit of Arkham, remains beyond the player's grasp; any faceless, nameless guards or asylum staffs are replaced by others just as anonymous; and Arkham Island itself becomes a form of virtual playground for the player.

In this, the post-endgame section of *Arkham Asylum* iterates its primary mission statement far more effectively than the graphic novel: to perpetuate the representation of navigation and exploration as allegories of mental treatment. While the environment itself is freely and fully accessible—as it must be, to permit the player to backtrack and explore further—the hard-coded boundaries of the virtual world restrict access to all but the Island itself, a tacit admission that as a chapter in the ongoing narrative of *Batman*, this scenario can neither innovate nor alter the static nature of the world and its inhabitants. Later games in the series would indeed expand the scope of the setting: for example, the subsequent release, *Arkham City*, details Sharp's plan to transform an entire section of Gotham City into a no-man's land given over to the former residents of the Asylum, essentially spilling the practically contagious madness of Arkham into an urban space. This leads to a sharp increase in psychopathy, obsessive-compulsive disorder, dissociative identity disorder and other psychological phenomena in the city; but the attempt to superimpose the Asylum's nature on a wider, more open environment is ultimately less pronounced than its claustrophobic predecessor. The enforced futility of treatment in this storyworld ensures that when all challenges have been overcome, all fragmented narratives have coalesced, and Arkham has no further mysteries to offer, the player is ultimately able to accomplish the one thing both Batman and his enemies never will: to exit the Asylum.

Notes

1. Janet Murray, *Hamlet on the Holodeck: The Future of Narrative in Cyberspace* (Cambridge: MIT Press, 1998), 79.
2. Bob Rehak, *The Video Game Theory Reader* (London/New York: Routledge, 2003), 156.
3. Elana Gomel, *Narrative Time and Space: Representing Impossible Topologies in Literature* (New York/London: Routledge, 2014), 102.
4. Janet Murray, *Hamlet on the Holodeck: The Future of Narrative in Cyberspace* (Cambridge: MIT Press, 1998), 130.
5. Grant Morrison and Dave McKean, *Arkham Asylum: A Serious House on Serious Earth* (New York: DC Comics, 1989), 13.
6. *Ibid.*, 39.
7. *Ibid.*, 89
8. Espen Aarseth, *Cybertext: Perspectives on Ergodic Literature* (Baltimore/London: John Hopkins University Press, 1997), 4.
9. Mark J.P. Wolf, *The Video Game Theory Reader* (London/New York: Routledge, 2003), 79.
10. Doug Walsh, *Batman: Arkham Asylum Signature Series Guide* (Indianapolis: Bradygames, 2009), 210.
11. Paul Dini, *Batman: Arkham Asylum* (London: Eidos Interactive, 2009).
12. *Ibid.*
13. *Ibid.*
14. Doug Walsh, *Batman: Arkham Asylum Signature Series Guide* (Indianapolis: Bradygames, 2009), 211.
15. Dini, *Batman: Arkham Asylum*.
16. Evan Skolnick, *Video Game Storytelling: What Every Developer Needs to Know About Narrative Techniques* (Berkeley: Watson-Guptill Publications, 2014).
17. William Uricchio, "The Batman's Gotham City™: Story, Ideology, Performance," in *Comics and the City: Urban Space in Print, Picture and Sequence* (New York: Continuum International Publishing Group, 2010), 130.
18. Morrison, *A Serious House*, 106.
19. *Ibid.*, 106.
20. Danny Fingeroth, *Superman on the Couch: What Superheroes Really Tell Us About Ourselves and Our Society* (New York/London: Continuum International Publishing Group, 2004), 155.
21. Doug Walsh, *Batman: Arkham Asylum Signature Series Guide* (Indianapolis: Bradygames, 2009), 175.

Excavating Arkham
The Mental Asylum as Horrible Homecoming

Brenda S. Gardenour Walter

In American popular culture, the insane asylum serves as a locus of dread and horror, a haunted place, dangerous for the living to enter. From paranormal investigation shows such as *Ghost Adventures* (2008-present) and horror films such as *Session 9* (2001) to the graphic worlds of the Batman universe, to step across the threshold of a sanitarium is to risk bodily and psychological transformation. This experience of being swallowed and transformed is intensified in survival-horror games such as *Batman: Arkham Asylum* (2009), *Outlast* (2014), and *The Evil Within* (2014), all of which feature hungry asylums and mental hospitals, at once dead and alive, silently waiting for human prey. This perception of the mental asylum as a dangerous and digestive space stems, in part, from its ability to collapse categories. Within the asylum's walls, the boundaries between body and mind, self and other, present and past become slippery, fluid. Stay too long and it might become a prison, both physical and psychological, from which the unwary visitor might never escape.

The transformative nature of the insane asylum as an architectural structure is rooted in its very history. From the Enlightenment forward, architectural theorists argued that properly designed institutions such as asylums, prisons, and hospitals could not only control human behavior but also cure mental, physical, and sociological diseases.[1] For example, the early nineteenth-century architect Guillaume Abel-Blouet designed Mettray, an institution "for the regeneration of young delinquents."[2] At Mettray, boys wore uniforms, meals were taken in silence, and daily activities were regulated with military precision. The stated goal was to create an iron-fisted patriarchal family to reform wayward boys into obedient and strong men. The architecture at Mettray supported this regimen of absolute discipline, going so far as to incorporate cells for solitary confinement for those in need of intense "rehabilitation." Émile Gilbert took such ideas even further in his design of Charenton, an enormous insane asylum that sorted patients into wards according to classification of illness and provided numerous isolation cells. The buildings at Charenton were cold machines, stripped bare of ornamentation, lest "contrasts of light and shade ... stir or trouble the imagination."[3] Similar approaches were taken in the design of prisons such as Pentonville in London, Mazas in Paris, and the Eastern State

192 Section VI: Video Screen Parallels

Image of Dr. Strange from the second video game of the franchise, *Batman: Arkham City* (2011), dir. Sefton Hill. Sporting a lab coat and hospital badge, Dr. Strange stands in an ambiguous space that suggests his Indian Hill hideaway beneath Arkham Asylum, where he conducts inhumane experiments on human inmates. Dr. Strange previously headed a secret laboratory in an expansive mansion in upstate New York, financed by the Wayne family prior to their deaths, and unbeknownst to Bruce until several seasons in the television version of *Gotham* (2015–2019).

Penitentiary in Philadelphia, all of which were focused on the merciless psychological, behavioral, and physical reform of the human mind and body through uniformity, discipline, and intense isolation.

For Foucault, insane asylums and prisons were not places of healing or help, but institutions designed for the confinement of individuals labeled deviant and inconvenient by "normative" society.[4] Those confined to institutions lived in exile, often never to return to their family homes. But what if the insane asylum *is* home, or more aptly put, the family home is an insane asylum? This is one of the questions posed by Grant Morrison's 1989 graphic novel, *Arkham Asylum: Serious House on Serious Earth*, which details the strange history of Gotham's most shadowy institution.[5] Morrison's Arkham is a space of utter collapse, a structure that is at once a Victorian family home and an enormous asylum, a place where the realms of maternal domesticity, psychological manipulation, corporal punishment, and solitary confinement are one and the same.[6] Through intertwining narrative arcs, Morrison invites the reader into Arkham, a leaky and monstrous locus of slippage where past and present mingle seamlessly and where a return to childhood and the family home is one of madness and horror. To enter the Arkham house-asylum is to embark on a pilgrimage into the inner sanctum of the mind and memory, to regress into the child-self, and to return to the mother and the primal scene—the womb—the ultimate transformative structure. This horrifying return to origins and the subsequent loss or recovery of identity informs the core narrative of *Batman: Arkham Asylum*, a digital game released in 2009. A similar construction of the asylum and the human experience within it pertains across several horror-survival games, from the American game, *Outlast* (2014) to Japan's *The Evil Within* (2014), all of which feature the horrifying exploration of mental institutions and the ultimate rediscovery of self as truly horrifying homecomings.

Arkham Asylum: The Digestive Womb

Grant Morrison's 1989 graphic novel, *Arkham Asylum: Serious House on Serious Earth*, reveals the shadowy history of the Arkham institution for the criminally insane. The asylum was founded by a fin-de-siècle mentalist, Amadeus Arkham, who transformed his family home into a sanitarium after the death of his mentally ill mother. The story of the building's transformation from a middle-class home to a place of abject horror unfolds through two intertwined narrative arcs. In the first arc, The Joker lures Batman into Arkham Asylum, and the reader follows him as a third person who makes semiotic sense of what unfolds.[7] This present-day narrative is punctuated by Amadeus' journal entries, which are narrated in the first person. This split-personality narrative gives the reader an experience of uncanny slippage, not only of personal identity but also of time and space. As the reader journeys deeper into the asylum with Batman and into its past with Amadeus' ghost, Arkham Asylum emerges as a multifaceted entity, at once alive and dead, caring and malicious, a space of total collapse.

Morrison's foundation myth peels back the layers of Arkham's past, revealing the structure's irrational multiplicity as both an asylum and a family home, a haunted space filled with a "gloom that smells of dust and childhood" where the rules of time no longer apply.[8] This disassembly of time is signified by an image of a broken pocket watch, its gears and springs scattered about its corpse, a motif echoed throughout the book.[9] To cross Arkham's threshold, to walk its dusty hallways and explore its myriad rooms, is to enter a disordered world of invisible spirits and horrifying memories buried within the self.[10] Amadeus recalls that as a child he felt like "an insignificant ghost" who was trapped in the family home, "haunting its corridors" as he nursed his dying mother, disconnected from the world of the living.[11] After his mother's murder, Amadeus determines to convert his family home into a treatment facility; with this decision, he re-enters the haunted house where "time becomes strange."[12] "That night" he writes in his journal, "I dream I am a child again."[13] He has been drawn back into the past and trapped in the family home, an asylum-prison from which he will never escape.[14]

For Amadeus and, later, Batman, stepping into Arkham is "just like coming home," a Freudian return to maternal origins. In his dreams, Amadeus' childhood home is not a place of nurturing and love, but of horror and perversion. It is a "funhouse" where he is afraid that his father will force him into the Tunnel of Love, where his mother vomits forth beetles.[15] As both family home and insane asylum, Arkham is a projection of mother Elizabeth's embodiment—beneath its composed physical façade lurks corruption, distortion, and toxicity. "The house is an organism," Amadeus writes, "hungry for madness."[16] In Morrison's text, to enter Arkham's bloody maw is to re-enter Elizabeth's building-body—to return to the hungry womb of the mother. For example, as Batman pushes deeper into the asylum, he has a flashback of his mother being shot, much like a scene from Walt Disney's *Bambi*. Just as his father and the gunman's phallic-shaped bullet penetrated his mother, so too does Batman penetrate himself with a long shard of glass. Blood drips from his hand and splashes across subsequent panels. Batman's childlike utterance, "Mommy?" is followed by an image of Norman Bates crying, "Mother! Oh God, Mother!" as well as a madman chanting, "Blood! Blood!" and an image of mother moon, round and full.[17] In a later hallucination, Batman confronts the mother-dragon that haunts not only Arkham's halls but also his own mind; as he penetrates her with his spear, she penetrates him, both of them bleeding around the same rigid shaft. Like Attis, Christ, and Odin, Batman hangs shamed before his mother, his bloody pudenda open for all to see.[18] In that moment of horror, he realizes that he cannot discern between his mother and himself; they are one, their bodies bound forever in blood and flesh.

Arkham promises the horror of regression and transformation. For Amadeus and Batman, crossing Arkham's threshold means not only returning to childhood, but ultimately fetus-hood. It is a Freudian return to the womb as a prison, a place of creation and destruction. Re-entering the womb-asylum, Amadeus becomes someone new while devolving into his origins, in this case, becoming one with his mother and her madness. The primal scene is writ large in Amadeus' discovery of his daughter's raped and mutilated body in her room—which he describes as a "nursery abattoir"—a place of bloody birth and death.[19] Just as his daughter's severed head has been thrust into her dollhouse, so too is Amadeus split from reality and thrust into his mother's house-womb, now a prison from which he cannot escape. In this moment, Arkham loses his adult male identity. "Slowly, methodically" he puts on his "mother's wedding dress" and kneels down, in effect taking a vow to his mother as his mother, becoming one with her again at last.[20] Amadeus' transformation is foreshadowed in a discussion of the zebra fish; "when a dominant female dies," he notes, "one of the men in her entourage will actually change sex and assume her former role."[21] This fluidity between son and mother, male and female, is echoed in the character of Zeus Arrhenothelus, "part man, part woman, electricity enflames my brain….the AC/DC Altar awaits!"[22] Having metamorphosed into the mother, into the past, Arkham must confront his true identity as the "other," a madwoman and murderer. In becoming her, he has become himself—a horrible homecoming at last.[23]

The transgressive power of Arkham Asylum affects not only those who enter her walls, but also Gotham city writ large. In transforming his family home into an asylum, Amadeus originally sought to bring order to chaos, to usher in a "triumph of reason over the irrational" for the benefit of all. Despite his intentions, he is transformed into his worst nightmare, reduced to beetle vomit, while his home-asylum becomes a leaky and transgressive facility, a source of infection for the greater community.[24] Even in his madness, wearing his mother's bloodied wedding dress, Arkham realizes the need to "contain the presences" that roam Arkham's hallways. This will require "bars and walls and electrified fences," thereby collapsing home into madhouse into prison.[25] And yet, like Elizabeth's body, madness and decay ooze from the building's locked doors, dark windows, and hidden passages deep in the soil. On the edge of Gotham, it reaches out, begging for its sickness to be touched, to share its disease, for the unwary to touch its stickiness.[26] The criminals captured by Batman and confined to Arkham are never rehabilitated, but become increasingly insane and routinely escape to plague the good citizens of Gotham. Having entered the asylum, confronted his past, and battled his family demons, Batman maintains his identity and can enter the asylum when necessary. But like a madman, he returns again and again in a futile attempt to keep the contagion of madness contained within Arkham's leaky and pestiferous walls.

Digital Arkham

Morrison's construction of the home-asylum as a dangerous and transformative place of slippage provides the foundation for *Batman: Arkham Asylum*, a survival-horror digital game released by Rocksteady Productions in 2009 for multiple platforms. Entering Arkham through the pages of Morrison's graphic novel is terrifying, but there is distance between the reader, who can control the pace of the narrative's unfolding, and the images on the page. Dropping into the digital version of Arkham removes this distance. Both alongside *and as* Batman, the player navigates the asylum as a three-dimensional space; despite third-person perspective, the player has limited sightlines. The experience is disorienting as hallways lead into rooms and courtyards with shadowy corners and gruesome remains, the detritus of violence. This sense of slippage is intensified by eerie effects such as ambient noise, moaning, and the sound of footsteps played against dead silence. These auditory cues reverberate through the player's real-world environment; experienced through headphones, one is left to wonder if the player is in the game, or the game is in the player.[27] Ensconced in a narrative driven by digital Arkham, the player can pause the game if it becomes too intense; upon resuming gameplay, however, the asylum once again drags the player deeper into the dark past, swallowing them whole.

Like its graphic counterpart, digital Arkham is as space of collapse marked by an impossible architecture. On the surface, Arkham is like many other abandoned asylums, both real and fictional. It features the crumbling Victorian architecture of a central Kirkbride building with a wrought iron gate, complete with shrouded figures holding lamps. The gate and high fence, both electrified and fitted with razor wire, signify a sacred boundary. In gameplay, the theme of transgression is reinforced as Batman steps across Arkham's threshold and passes through several security checkpoints leading into the very bowels of the building. Once inside, the building shifts shape; while it retains Victorian elements such as gargoyles and a gothic cemetery, it morphs into a hybrid haunted space that claims to be a mental hospital but is in reality a maximum-security prison-cum-abattoir. Despite signage throughout the building that describes the inmates as patients, they are almost always chained like beasts. The asylum is populated not by doctors but instead by armed guards with permission to "shoot to kill" any patient who refuses to "return ... to its cage." Duality and slippage reign at Arkham. What was once meant to be an institution with the power to restore order to chaotic minds has become a locus for violent irrationality, a factory that produces madness. Arkham was designed to "clean the arterial blood of Gotham City." Instead, the asylum has become Gotham's dark heart—corrupt to the core—that pumps infection in the form of insane criminals far beyond its leaky walls.[28]

As in Morrison's graphic novel, digital Arkham is a transformative space, a locus for a horrible homecoming. As the Joker says, "It's always nice to return to my ha-ha-hacienda." Once inside, Batman begins to lose touch with the outside world, just beyond the asylum's gate. His only link with "reality" is Barbara Gordon, the Commissioner's daughter, who speaks to him through his bat helmet. She is the voice in his head, guiding him through the asylum and out to freedom. Despite her calming presence, Batman is penetrated by the asylum and its inmates. Under the influence of Scarecrow's toxins, he hallucinates that the corpses of his parents speak to him. As the sound of a music box chimes in the background, Batman opens each body bag to hear his father and mother admonish him for not being man enough to save them. Later, he relives the night of his parents' murders, their disembodied voices leading him through a seemingly endless Victorian corridor to the dark Gotham alley where they died. In that moment, he is transformed into his childhood self, bent over their bodies, alone until he meets the voice of Commissioner Gordon, his surrogate father. For Batman, this return to the past is a horrible homecoming; in return for this willingness to face his fears, he gains the power to fight off contamination by Scarecrow and ultimately return the Joker and Arkham to order, if only temporarily. Batman remains un-warped. Not all who enter the asylum are so lucky.

Arkham: Beyond Batman

The deep structures of Arkham pertain beyond the Batman Universe. The haunted and hungry mental asylum that threatens to regress and transform those who step within its leaky walls serves as a setting for many survival-horror digital games. In *Outlast*, for example, the player takes on the role of Miles Upshur, an investigative reporter charged with discovering the true nature of the Mount Massive Asylum. High in the mountains of Colorado and far from cell service, the asylum sits at the end of a winding road in complete isolation.[29] From a first-person perspective, the player approaches a wrought-iron gate beyond which lies a ponderous Victorian institution, its spires reaching menacingly into an evening sky streaked with orange. From a distance, the building seems to be an orderly and rational space, ponderous and authoritative; squeezing through the gate, however, Miles finds abandoned military vehicles and debris strewn across the institution's grounds. Slipping through the window, he enters a realm of chaos, with peeling paint, broken furniture, and shifting shadows. Descending deeper into the structure, he discovers increasing decay, including the mutilated bodies of the dead and dying, blood and viscera splattered on every surface, and evidence of torturous "medical" experimentation. The only constant is the glow of computer screens in the gloom, promising the presence of a centralized intelligence hidden somewhere in the building.

Once inside, Upshur's mental and physical transformation begins. Exposed to horrifying scenes, stalked by a juggernaut of an inmate, Upshur—and through him, the player—become traumatized. He explores much of the institution through the lens of his hand-held video camera, which records his erratic breathing, shakes when he is terrified, and ultimately becomes cracked, much like his mind. While the camera lens serves to mediate between Upshur and his environment, the experience of shifting between unmediated reality, the basic camera lens, and night vision contributes to his dissociative experience. Ambient electronica, sound effects, distant moans, and screams echo throughout gameplay, further contributing to the feeling of being surrounded by madness. Upshur's mental unraveling is compounded by his physiological breakdown; he is chased, wounded, tied down, forcibly injected with serum, has two fingers severed, and ultimately limps his way to the game's conclusion. The asylum has subsumed him, transformed him into its own corrupt and deformed likeness, much like the "forgotten lunatics" left within its walls. In notes discovered on different desks, Upshur discovers that no one is safe from the asylum's transformative power. Records indicate that employees of the asylum succumb to "psychopathological proximity stress disorder," a condition in which they contract insanity from the patients and begin to see their delusions. Another memo indicates that the institution was once shut down completely because of a "catastrophic security failure… with imminent danger of environmental contamination." Even in its remote location, the madness within the institution might infect the greater population beyond its gates, much like Arkham releasing its poisons into Gotham City.

Unlike Arkham Asylum, Mount Massive did not begin as a family home. Nevertheless, it retains some of the most horrifying elements of family dysfunction. The patients who enter Mount Massive lose their autonomy and are subjected to corporal punishment by an overbearing father figure, Dr. Werner, who is himself an agent of a larger paternalistic organization, the Murkoff Corporation. As "children," the patients are confined to a house of horrors, a prison that binds them ever closer to their toxic family. Like Arkham, Mount Massive is a space not only of paternal domination but also maternal transformation, a theme magnified in *Outlast: Whistle-blower* (2014). In this two-hour expansion pack, the player takes on the role of Waylon Park, a computer specialist who is forcibly confined to the asylum. In a pivotal scene, Park witnesses a mad doctor known as "The Groom" who traps patients and slices through their genitalia with a table saw, all in an attempt to transform them into women. Ultimately, the player as Park is stripped naked and strapped splay-legged to the saw-cum-gynecology table. The doctor—truly a father gone mad—strokes the player's bare thighs and explains that is his going to create a "soft place to welcome my seed." Much like Arkham, Mount Massive is a horrible home devoid of a mother's love. Ultimately, Park escapes but he has seen the shredded bodies of men "mutilated and bent to mimic or mock the moment of birth. The kind of thing a man cannot see without changing in some irreparable way." In returning to the primal scene, Park has been transformed—a process that cannot be undone. Park realizes that he cannot "leave the way I came." No one does. To enter Mount Massive is to lose one's identity completely, to be forcibly subsumed into a collective known as the Walrider—a mad family, bound for all eternity, from which there is truly to escape.

Arkham's legacy is also imprinted on The Beacon Asylum, the hungry structure

B.D. Wong plays the villainous Dr. Hugo Strange in television's *Gotham* series (2015–2019), where he experiments on inmate-patients in a secret hideaway in Indian Hill, sequestered beneath Arkham Asylum and accessed through a secret elevator. His sterile white lab coat hides a dark heart that recollects the screen's long string of sinister psychiatrists and scheming scientists. B.D. Wong's persona evokes his evil scientist roles in the *Jurassic* franchise, but also reminds us of his earlier law-abiding FBI psychiatrist stint in TV's long-running *Law & Order: SVU*. His presence invites comparisons with the Japanese game and film about asylums, *Silent Hill* (2006).

that serves as the setting for the Japanese survival-horror game, *The Evil Within* (2014). Released by Tango Gameworks and directed by Shinji Mikama, the creator of the *Resident Evil* franchise, *The Evil Within* tells the story of Sebastian Castellanos, an alcoholic homicide detective with PTSD who is called to investigate a massacre at The Beacon. With him are two colleagues, Joseph Oda and Juli Kidman, both of whom appear and disappear throughout the game. Like Arkham and Mount Massive Asylum, the Beacon is a menacing structure with a Victorian façade and central tower containing a light, the very source of its name. Unlike a traditional lighthouse that guides ships safely through the darkness, however, this Beacon draws men to their destruction and projects darkness out into Krimson City. It is also a digestive space, a hungry building that devours humanity. As Castellanos spreads the front door open, he notes that "it smells like blood." Stepping inside, he suffers a concussion and awakens in a kitchen "abattoir" with humans hanging from meat hooks and cooking in pots, all while classical music plays softly in the background, suggesting a Hannibal-esque domesticity. Castellanos slides down a blood-gutter filled with human offal until he drops into a massive cistern of fetid blood—a horrifyingly literal return to the womb. Desperate to escape the asylum, he investigates increasingly impossible spaces, sometimes endless decaying corridors within the asylum, other times dreamscapes beyond it. This asylum is unbound. Probing the building's bloody viscera, Castellanos discovers the rotten brain at its core—a machine called STEM that is linked to the diseased mind of Ruvik, a young man with a tragic childhood. Through STEM, Castellanos experiences a slippage of time and space as well as the collapse of his own identity. Much as inmates at Arkham enter into Amadeus' traumatic past and become infected by his demons, so too do visitors to Beacon partake in Ruvik's family traumas. And like Arkham, the horrors within the Beacon Asylum do not remain confined. Instead, they leak out of its walls and windows, travel with inmates who ultimately escape, and haunt the minds of those who step over its threshold and are forever transformed.

In digital Arkham and beyond, individuals such as Batman, Park, and Castellanos confront the past and emerge with their own identities intact; many others, however, remain captives of the asylum collective, drawn ever closer to the hungry mother, forever trapped in the toxic womb of the family home. Over time, they have little choice but to become beetle vomit, trapped in a cycle of birth and decay. "Madness and inhumanity rule this place" Welcome home.

Notes

1. Carla Yanni, "The Linear Plan for Insane Asylums in the United States Before 1866," *Journal for the Society of Architectural Historians* 62 (1) (2003), 24.
2. Robin Middleton, "Sickness, Madness and Crime as the Grounds of Reform," *AA Files: Architectural Association School of Architecture* 25 (1993): 17. See also John Ramsland, "Mettray: a Corrective Institution for Delinquent Youth in France, 1840-1937," *Journal of Educational Administration and History* 2 2(1) (1990): 30–46.
3. *Ibid.*, 23.
4. Michel Foucault, *Madness and Civilization: A History of Insanity in the Age of Reason* (New York: Vintage, 1988). See similar concerns, including the power of architecture to govern human behavior, in his *Discipline and Punish: The Birth of the Prison* (New York: Vintage, 1995).
5. Grant Morrison, *Arkham Asylum: Serious House on Serious Earth* (Burbank, CA: DC Comics, 1989).
6. On Victorian architecture, decay, and the collapsing of time, see Sarah Burns, "Better for Haunts: Victorian Houses and the Modern Imagination," *American Art* 26 (3) (Fall 2012): 2–25.
7. Eduardo Neiva and Carlo Romano, "The Semiotic Immersion of Video Games, Gaming Technology and Interactive Strategies," *The Public Journal of Semiotics* 1 (2) (2007): 31–49.
8. Morrison, *Serious House*, 19.
9. *Ibid.*, 7.

10. "Morrison Explains That 'the Construction of the Story Was Influenced by the Architecture of a House." the narrative, both in text and structure, is rooted in the journey from room to room. Morrison quoted in James F. Wurtz, "Out There in the Asylum: Physical, Mental, and Structural Space in Grant Morrison and Dave McKean's Arkham Asylum: a Serious House on Serious Earth," *Amerikastudien / American Studies* 56(4) (2011), 558.

11. *Ibid.*, 9.
12. *Ibid.*, 74.
13. *Ibid.*, 23.
14. *Ibid.*, 75.
15. *Ibid.*, 24.
16. *Ibid.*, 69. Amadeus knows the building's true nature; on his return he declares that he will exorcise the Devil within, that he "will Bring Light to Those Dismal Corridors of My Childhood…open the Locked Doors…fill the Empty Corridors." Morrison, *Serious House*, 38.
17. *Ibid.*, 50–51.
18. For a Jungian interpretation, see Wurtz's "Out There in the Asylum."
19. Morrison, *Serious House*, 56–7.
20. *Ibid.*, 57.
21. *Ibid.*, 43.
22. *Ibid.*, 71–2.
23. On the parallel mothers, see Sarah K Donovan, "Under the Mask" *Batman and Philosophy: The Dark Knight of the Soul*, eds. William Irwin, Mark White, and Robert Arp. (Hoboken, NJ: Wiley Press, 2008), 135-6 [129–55].
24. Morrison, *Serious House*, 58.
25. *Ibid.*, 90.
26. *Ibid.*, 59; on stickiness, see Robin Longhurst, *Bodies: Exploring Fluid Boundaries* (London: Routledge, 2001), 30–32S.
27. See Isabella Elferen, "Sonic Descents: Musical Dark Play in Survival and Psychological Horror," *The Dark Side of Game Play: Controversial Issues in Playful Environments*, eds. Torill Elvira Mortensen, Jonas Linderoth, and Ashley ML Brown (London: Routledge, 2015), 226–41.
28. Bradley J. Daniels, "Arkham Asylum: Forensic Psychology and Gotham's (not So) Serious House," *The Psychology of Superheroes*, eds. Robin Rosenberg and Jennifer Canzoneri (Dallas, TX: SmartPop Books, 2008), 201–11.
29. The winding road might be imagined as a vaginal canal and the asylum a horrible place of gestation. to emerge from the asylum would then be to be reborn into the world.

SECTION VII

Literary and Artistic Influences

Bizarro Arkham, Bizarro World
The Looking Glass Looks Back

Aaron Barlow

When newspaper comic strips first appeared toward the end of the nineteenth century, they provided a fractured vision of the quotidian world. This began a tradition that would continue unending in the funny pages and, notably, one that spread to include entities like *Mad* magazine and, in the movies and on television, through *Loony Tunes*, *The Rocky and Bullwinkle Show* and beyond even *The Simpsons* and *The Boondocks*. This tradition harkens back to Lewis Carroll's *Alice in Wonderland* and even before, of course, but it was the comics that gave it its first popular-media focus. For several reasons (including fear of the impact of the comic books of the 1930s and 1940s on impressionable youth), by the eve of World War II, another thread had joined the weave, one of superheroes whose quest was to right the world, to take the strange and smooth it into the usual and the moral. David Hadju (2008) describes the perspective of those who saw the depravity of the comic-book industry:

> Imbued with gallantry, righteousness, physical strength, and patriotism, the bright, kinetic fabulism of superhero stories took the comics far from the tawdry chaos of the early funny pages. *Action* [*Comics*] and its ilk were not so much outlets for the errant impulses of their artists, writers, and readers, or vehicles for them to challenge social convention or authority, as blunt credenda of virtue and testaments to the goodness of America. With Superman, the comics assimilated.[1]

These, though, could not completely dominate the older pattern of parody and offbeat humor, the insanity that *Mad*, in its early days in the 1950s, would still manage to call "humor in a jugular vein." Eventually, the creators of the new sort of comics even came to discover ways to embrace the genre's past (*Mad* itself was one of those ways), partly as a reaction to negative views of their art (and the older comics art).

Just as comics were a contrast to "high" art, so too did comics create worlds that contrasted with the "real" world. Early villains in the superhero comics tended to reflect the stereotypical enemies of other entertainment media—but the superhero comics quite quickly began to develop strange, even bizarre, villains who provided even greater contrasts to the straight-laced, rather humorless new protagonists. Of the dozens of these created for DC Comics' *Action Comics* is the Joker, Batman's *bête noire* memorably played by Heath Ledger in the 2008 film *The Dark Knight*. Another of the many is Bizarro, an opposite to Superman who, like creators of the comics themselves, "builds" his own world.

The Bizarro world grew out of a character created by Alvin Schwartz in the late 1950s as an opposite to Superman. "Yes," to him, means "no." From this character grew an entire world of htraE which Bizarro has created, one that evolved into a comical parody of the world of the "real" Superman. Not quite the same, though it relates to it, is the world of *Emperor Joker*, where Bizarro is again a character and the world shares a shape with htraE.

Comics, even superhero comics, never shy away from recognition that the worlds they present are concocted. All of the worlds created *within* the worlds of comic books are implicit commentaries on the worlds created *for* comic books, which are, of course, commentaries on *our* world—going back to a time long before Superman was even conceived. The comics always contained an element of parody, something that continued even as they drew deadly serious, as they did with the coming of World War II and of attacks on them as immoral constructs. The introduction of Bizarro (like the introductions of quite a few Batman villains, not to mention other Superman villains) brings into the comics a resurgent, almost nostalgic, vision of an early comics age as well as a rebuke to the censors.

Bizarro can change over the decades after his introduction. In worlds that, on face value, are fake, there's no reason to strive for a foolish consistency. Especially while a character is being embraced by the world of the reader, it makes sense to further tailor the character to the readers' perceived desires. If that's done successfully, the character can become part of popular culture, his/her life taking a position far beyond the comic pages. That has happened, of course, with Superman and Batman, but, in another fashion, it has also happened to Bizarro.

It could even be said that "Bizarro" has invaded our physical world. In just two days in October of 2017, "Bizarro" showed up in news stories from major newspapers at least three times, in a column in *The Washington Post* ("the defining moment of this Bizarro, alternate reality we're living in today"[2]), in the sports section of *The New York Times* ("'It was a Bizarro world,' Cubs Manager Joe Maddon said"[3]) as the description of a quince[4] in *The Los Angeles Times*. Obviously, the word Bizarro has become a commonplace in contemporary America.

"Bizarro" was not invented by anyone at DC Comics even though its popularization comes through DC publications. It was used by Sir Walter Scott in the 1830s as the nickname he claims to have heard for a bandit of "wily but inexorable temper."[5] He started a book about a fictionalized version of this man, but it was not published until 2008, having been incomplete at the time of his death. The brigand, Scott notes in his journal, murders his own child to keep it quiet so that capture can be evaded—and is murdered in turn by his outraged wife.

That use is a fitting ancestor for today's broader usage and it points to something not noted nearly often enough about American comics from their earliest iterations: they dip into entertainment traditions often much older and far removed from the popular and kitschy funny pages and books. When they hold distorting mirrors to society, they often have created those mirrors in sophisticated and even startling ways and out of knowledge of the past. Is it any wonder that references (including the character Jervis Tetch, the Mad Hatter) to Lewis Carroll's works populating the *Batman Arkham* books, among others?

Literary references and antecedents aside (for the moment), comics still lie at one end of the spectrum that Clement Greenberg, writing in the *Partisan Review* on the eve of World War II (just a year after Superman was introduced) called "avant-garde" and "kitsch." The avant-garde includes art for art's sake and arises out of the leisure of the upper classes while kitsch is a rearguard of "popular, commercial art and literature with their chromeotypes, magazine covers, illustrations, ads, slick and pulp fiction, comics, Tin Pan Alley music, tap dancing, Hollywood movies, etc., etc."[6] Ultimately, kitsch uses "for raw material the debased and academicized simulacra of genuine culture."[7] Though this distinction has been eradicated through (among other things) postmodern sensibilities, it weighed on the psyches of some of the writers and artists of Greenberg's time and on the succeeding generation.

When Greenberg, a keeper of the asylum of art, called the avant-garde culture one of "the imitation of imitat*ing*,"[8] some of the creators of comics must have been rather confused: through their kitsch, that is exactly what they were sometimes doing. Greenberg tries to explain: "If the avant-garde imitates the processes of art, kitsch, we now see, imitates its effects."[9] But the comics creators were doing even more than that. In a way, they were (and are) like talented squirrels, collecting and hiding away all sorts of shiny objects and nuts to copy and warp for their own later purposes, some of which had nothing to do with any aspect of either the avant-garde or kitsch but were, in fact, postmodern even before postmodernism was born.

The recognition by comics' creators of the duality Greenberg created (and that they would have liked to doubt) made them more aware of, and more likely to use, dualities of a variety of other questionable sorts, too. These included that of sane versus insane, even making duality of newly constructed superhero conventions which contrast to the older comics and literary culture. They were always raising the question, which is sane and which insane. In a way, they were artists without the constraints of the avant-garde, freed by being called "kitsch."

Though much of what Greenberg wrote is headscratchingly peculiar to 21st-century aesthetics (especially when he gets into the relationships of politics to art), some of the points he made do describe the methodology and attitude of the comics artists of the time. He writes that kitsch would be impossible without "the availability close at hand of a fully matured cultural tradition, whose discoveries, acquisitions and perfected self-consciousness kitsch can take advantage of for its own ends."[10] What Greenberg didn't fully comprehend was that those ends could include an avant-garde that not even its creators were yet in a position to recognize, a postmodern avant-garde that could slip a word like "Bizarro" into common usage without many even noticing. An avant-garde deliberately (or not) constructed to be a Bizarro imitation of his own and, thus, far more avant-garde than any other—even in Greenberg's own terms.

Surrounded by the high-profile presence of serious artists and critics, the creators of comics had to question their own positions. They were not stupid or naïve or unaware; they knew what was being said about them. Even those who might have had the experience and exposure to defend what they were doing must sometimes have had doubts in face of the overwhelming general condemnation of their creations. Just as some of the characters they created would start to raise questions—especially when finding themselves in bizarre reflections of their own worlds (as the comics creators themselves must sometimes have felt, on looking around) or confined in asylums like the infamous (especially in Batman's Gotham City) Arkham.

"Arkham." It is another word common to the DC universe. It is the name of a family and of a mental institution in Gotham and, in at least one instance, in a Bizarro world of the sort that sometimes figures into Superman's universe. "Arkham" has specific literary antecedents (the name is taken from a town in the fiction of H.P. Lovecraft), but the word has never quite made it into the popular culture the way "Bizarro" has. In a way, this is too bad, for "Arkham" represents that very type of turnabout "Bizarro" does, but in a more nuanced fashion (until, that is, the two are combined), becoming a deft examination of just who belongs on the inside, who out—or even who belongs between comic covers and who should be the reader. In a distant fashion, it can even be a commentary on the fluid distinctions between avant-garde and kitsch. The world of the asylum (for that's what Arkham is, in the DC universe) is one of a conflation of evil, difference and insanity—with the question of just who is insane always left slightly unanswered.

This is an old conceit, of course, as we shall see, but it is used in comics in a particular way. Even though, by the time of *Batman: Arkham Asylum*, the reputation of comics—or "graphic novels," as some had come to be called—had improved and the avant-garde/kitsch distinction had, to some degree, evaporated, the suspect reputation of the comics had not completely receded. Few were willing to call them "real" art. The arbiters of taste, the keepers of the asylum, had never really reached the point where they admitted that they could be wrong in their diagnosis. The continued use of questions—not just about who runs the asylum, the inmates or the guards, but about who *should* run the asylum—illustrates that the story creators of the comics worlds still sometimes see themselves as inmates or, at best, barely tolerated outsiders.

In the Bizarro world, things as we know it are turned around ("Earth" becomes "htraE," for example) and the opposite from the expected can result. In Arkham, the twists are never so simple—as we see in *Batman: Arkham Asylum*. Making sense of either world/reflection/asylum is difficult enough; the real problem comes when they are combined, as they are in *Superman: Emperor Joker* (which title carries the resonance of Eugene O'Neill's *The Emperor Jones*, another work set in a surreal world and, for a time, controlled by an insane ruler).

The literary backgrounds for Arkham and Bizarro Arkham are obvious enough but are worth exploring. They can be found in Raymond Chandler's *Farewell, My Lovely*, a 1940 novel where narrator Philip Marlowe speaks to the head of the asylum where he has awoken:

> "I had a nightmare," I said. "Silly idea. I dreamed I was tied to a cot and shot full of dope and locked in a barred room. I got very weak. I slept. I had no food. I was a sick man. I was knocked on the head and brought into a place where they did that to me. They took a lot of trouble. I'm not that important."[11]

He escapes, though, and his words call to mind Superman's condition when he awakens each day in the "Arkham" of *Emperor Jones* only to escape and be captured and returned. The doctor responds:

> "You have been a very sick man, Mr. Marlowe. I think I shall have to insist that you go back to bed."[12]

Insist. That's what the sane do when confronted with the insane. But it is also what the insane do, especially the megalomaniacs and the psychopaths. How, Superman asks himself each day, do we know one from the other? And that, of course, is the core question at the heart of Ken Kesey's *One Flew Over the Cuckoo's Nest*. One of the other patients explains the situation as he sees it to central character McMurphy, a purportedly sane man who has had himself committed in order to avoid a jail term. Is the cure worse than the putative disease?

"Oh, yes; I forgot to add that I noticed your primitive brutality also this morning. Psychopath with definite sadistic tendencies, probably motivated by an unreasoning egomania. Yes. As you see, all these natural talents certainly qualify you as a competent therapist and render you quite capable of criticizing Miss Ratched's meeting procedure, in spite of the fact that she is a highly regarded psychiatric nurse with twenty years in the field. Yes, with your talent, my friend, you could work subconscious miracles, soothe the aching id and heal the wounded superego. You could probably bring about a cure for the whole ward, Vegetables and all, in six short months …"

Instead of rising to the argument, McMurphy … finally asks in a level voice, "And you really think this crap that went on in the meeting today is bringing about some kinda cure …?" "What other reason would we have for submitting ourselves to it my friend? The staff desires our cure as much as we do. They aren't monsters. Miss Ratched may be a strict middle-aged lady, but she's not some kind of giant monster of the poultry clan, bent on sadistically pecking out our eyes. You can't believe that of her, can you?" "No, buddy, not that. She ain't peckin' at your eyes. That's not what she's peckin' at."[13]

That is at the heart of Superman's situation, too, which even includes a Lois Lane who is effectively emasculating him. In many other cases, the situation is one of well-intentioned caretakers inadvertently making the situation worse, instead of sadistic keepers enjoying such work. The former is the case in Charlotte Perkins Gillman's "The Yellow Wallpaper":

"The repairs are not done at home, and I cannot possibly leave town just now. Of course, if you were in any danger, I could and would, but you really are better, dear, whether you can see it or not. I am a doctor, dear, and I know. You are gaining flesh and color, your appetite is better, I feel really much easier about you."

"I don't weigh a bit more," said I, "nor as much; and my appetite may be better in the evening when you are here, but it is worse in the morning when you are away!"[14]

The doctors and nurses don't always know what they are doing, as in "The Yellow Wallpaper" where they are driving the central character crazy rather than sane—or they do know, but don't care. In the DC universe, the rulers of Arkham are generally every bit as insane as their inmates—even if outside authorities do not understand this. We can bring that back home: the arbiters of taste in *our* world are no different from comics' creators—except in position. They just don't know that it may be they who are crazy.

Sometimes, the insane are able to turn this about, especially when the rulers, in fact, have gotten as crazy (or wrong) as the inmates, as in Ray Bradbury's "Usher II," where a turnabout leaves the crazy person in command of the (also crazy—though it's really the society that is crazy) authority:

"For God's sake, what are you doing?" shouted Garrett, rattling about.

"I'm being ironic. Don't interrupt a man in the midst of being ironic, it's not polite. There!"

"You've locked me in chains!"

"So I have."

"What are you going to do?"

"Leave you here."

"You're joking."

"A very good joke."

"Where's my duplicate? Don't we see him killed?"

"There's no duplicate."

"But the *others*!"

"The others are dead. The ones you saw killed were the real people. The duplicates, the robots, stood by and watched."[15]

Doubt. That is what could have saved Garrett, but he was too certain of society's image of sanity, so walked into a trap. That's what the institutions and taste mavens lack but foist upon the individuals beyond them, the ones they have power over, be they McMurphy or Superman or a writer or artist of the comics. Doubt runs many ways, from many sources, as we see in Fyodor Dostoyevsky's *The Idiot*, where a supposed newspaper article is quoted:

> Six months ago—that is, last winter—this particular scion returned to Russia, wearing gaiters like a foreigner, and shivering with cold in an old scantily-lined cloak. He had come from Switzerland, where he had just undergone a successful course of treatment for idiocy (*sic!*). Certainly Fortune favoured him, for, apart from the interesting malady of which he was cured in Switzerland (can there be a cure for idiocy?) his story proves the truth of the Russian proverb that "happiness is the right of certain classes!" Judge for yourselves. Our subject was an infant in arms when he lost his father.... The orphan was brought up by the charity of a very rich Russian landowner.... P— brought up the orphan like a prince, provided him with tutors and governesses (pretty, of course!) whom he chose himself in Paris. But the little aristocrat, the last of his noble race, was an idiot.... At last P— was seized with a strange notion; he imagined that in Switzerland they could change an idiot into a man of sense.... [After his benefactor's death, he] had scarcely arrived in St. Petersburg, when a relation of his mother's (who was of bourgeois origin, of course), died at Moscow.... Aristocrat, millionaire, and idiot, he has every advantage![16]

This bit of topsy-turvy fits well with American visions of aristocracy and with the popular disdain for the avant-garde, which was the toy of the elite. It also resonates with the backgrounds of both Superman and Batman, both of whom had also lost their parents early.

More specific to Arkham (and, in a way, to the Bizarro world) is Edgar Allan Poe's "The System of Dr. Tarr and Prof. Fether," a short story where, not surprisingly, the inmates are running the asylum, though the narrator has yet to catch on:

> "There is no accounting for the caprices of madmen; and, in my opinion as well as in that of Dr. Tarr and Professor Fether, it is never safe to permit them to run at large unattended. A lunatic may be 'soothed,' as it is called, for a time, but, in the end, he is very apt to become obstreperous. His cunning, too, is proverbial and great. If he has a project in view, he conceals his design with a marvelous wisdom; and the dexterity with which he counterfeits sanity, presents, to the metaphysician, one of the most singular problems in the study of mind. When a madman appears thoroughly sane, indeed, it is high time to put him in a straitjacket....
>
> "For example: not a very long while ago, a singular circumstance occurred in this very house. The 'soothing system,' you know, was then in operation, and the patients were at large. They behaved remarkably well-especially so, any one of sense might have known that some devilish scheme was brewing from that particular fact, that the fellows behaved so remarkably well. And, sure enough, one fine morning the keepers found themselves pinioned hand and foot, and thrown into the cells, where they were attended, as if they were the lunatics, by the lunatics themselves, who had usurped the offices of the keepers....
>
> "The keepers and kept were soon made to exchange places. Not that exactly either- for the madmen had been free, but the keepers were shut up in cells forthwith, and treated, I am sorry to say, in a very cavalier manner."
>
> ...
>
> "And the treatment- what was the particular species of treatment which the leader of the rebels put into operation?"
>
> "Why, as for that, a madman is not necessarily a fool, as I have already observed; and it is my honest opinion that his treatment was a much better treatment than that which it superseded. It was a very capital system indeed—simple—neat—no trouble at all—in fact it was delicious it was... "[17]

Here, the inmates have not righted a situation but are making it worse, much as Joker as authority does in both *Batman: Arkham Asylum* and *Emperor Joker*.

In *Emperor Joker*, Superman daily repeats his escape from Arkham only to be defeated and returned by Bizarro. Though we do not know it until later in the story, Batman is suffering an even worse version of the same fate, dying each day and coming to life the next—only to die again. Superman has lost all faith in himself due, in large part, to the fact that no one around him has faith in him at all, seeing him as the deranged killer of Lex Luthor. An imp, Mxyzptlk, who is somewhat responsible for the situation and regrets it, manages to reveal a bit of the truth to Superman, starting him on the road to recovering his confidence and, eventually, to defeating the Joker who seems to have complete control of the universe.

The Joker, of course, can be a stand-in for all sorts of things. Looking at him in terms of the history of comic books, he is the ruler of the art world, the guardian of the avant-garde. What he doesn't understand, and that Superman learns, is that he needs kitsch (in this case, personified by Batman) in order to survive. This is the saving grace, too, for the comics' creators. They may be crazy and locked away from the mainstream, but none of the rest, in their view, could exist without them.

The looker, in this case, cannot survive without the looking glass.

Comic creators have the luxury of working in a medium where rules and conventions can be subverted without rocking the genre, something they owe to the very history of the genre and to the way it has been treated by the society at large. They can be the inmates running the asylum if they want because few have ever expected much more from them. Because of that, they have had a freedom to explore that has been much more real than even that of the old avant-garde, which was limited by conventions its members weren't even aware of. The freedom of art today owes a great deal more to the comics than is generally acknowledged, for it is the comics that inked in at least some of the bars around art that had previously been invisible.

Who was it, after all, who really needed to break out of Arkham in the first place? Who was really living in the Bizarro world?

It was never the comics' creators.

Notes

1. David Hajdu, *The Ten-Cent Plague: The Great Comic-Book Scare and How It Changed America* (New York: Picador/Farrar, Straus and Giroux, 2008), 31.
2. Petula Dvorak, "A Black Man Charged in His Own Beating, and Charlottesville's Lasting Hatred," *The Washington Post*, October 12, 2017. Accessed July 10, 2018. https://www.washingtonpost.com/local/a-black-man-charged-in-his-own-beating-and-charlottesvilles-lasting-hatred/2017/10/12/ba474e5a-af5d-11e7-a908-a3470754bbb9_story.html?utm_term = .a713f4bb9e76.
3. James Wagner, "Cubs Add a Chapter to Nationals' Painful Postseason History," *The New York Times*, October 13, 2017. Accessed July 10, 2018. https://www.nytimes.com/2017/10/13/sports/cubs-nationals-nlds.html?_r = 0.
4. Noelle Carter, "Beets Are in Season. We Have Recipes," *The Los Angeles Times*, October 13, 2017, Accessed July 10, 2018. http://www.latimes.com/food/dailydish/la-fo-farmers-market-report-beets-recipes-20171014-story.html.
5. Walter Scott, Journal, April 1832, Accessed July 10, 2018. http://www.online-literature.com/walter_scott/journal-of-scott/58/.
6. Clement Greenberg, "Avant-Garde and Kitsch," *Partisan Review, 39*.
7. *Ibid.*, 40.
8. *Ibid.*, 37.
9. *Ibid.*, 44.
10. *Ibid.*, 40.
11. Raymond Chandler, *Farewell, My Lovely: A Novel* (Philip Marlowe Series Book 2) (New York: Knopf Doubleday Publishing Group, 2002), 178. Kindle edition.
12. *Ibid.*, 179.
13. Ken Kesey, *One Flew Over the Cuckoo's Nest* (New York: Penguin Publishing Group), 50–51. Kindle edition.

14. Charlotte Perkins Gilman, "The Yellow Wallpaper," *The New England Magazine*, January 1892, 652. Accessed July 10, 2018. https://www.nlm.nih.gov/exhibition/theliteratureofprescription/exhibitionAssets/digitalDocs/The-Yellow-Wall-Paper.pdf.

15. Ray Bradbury, "Usher II," *The Martian Chronicles* (Garden City, NJ: Doubleday, 1958), 44–45.

16. Fyodor Dostoyevsky, *The Idiot*, 162–163. Kindle edition.

17. Edgar Allan Poe, "The System of Dr. Tarr and Prof. Fether," *Graham's Magazine*, Vol. XXVIII, No. 5, November 1845. http://xroads.virginia.edu/~hyper/poe/system.html.

The Neo-Expressionist Agony of Arkham Asylum

Rosa JH Berland

At first consideration, it offers little food for analysis. It is, unmistakably, a scene of torture. To repeat the usual account, a band of criminals has broken into a dwelling and there, in the attic, has proceeded at its leisure to commit unspeakable villainies upon the inhabitants. Nobody, of course, will take this incident at face value. The grotesque exaggeration of brutality and pain, above all the dreamlike peculiarities of its details, make it obvious that Beckmann meant in some sense to paint us an allegory of the human condition"—Beckmann's *Nacht*, Franciscono[1]

In much of historic artistic depiction, the asylum reflects the inner state of the patient or prisoner and at the same time mirrors the problematics of the outside world, including society's understanding of deviance, pathology, medicine, criminality, religion, and even gender. One such place is the fictional insane asylum Arkham, featured in *Batman* stories in various embodiments: filmic, graphic novel, animations, and more recently as a video game. Like Max Beckmann's horrific expressionist painting *Nacht*, the story takes places in the confines of a nightmarish off-kilter interior, where terror reigns.[2] This dungeon-like institution appears in many plot lines, sometimes moralistic, veering into the supernatural realm, and most often blending horror and science fiction. This nocturnal realm—claustrophobic, vertically distorted—evokes both a sense of entrapment and abuse of authority. Faces of the mentally ill and criminal appear ghoulish and stylized, dramatically outlining the concept of criminality and mental illness, and a convergence of the two "characteristics."[3] In the imaginative theater of the asylum we find many things: sanctity and refuge, safety for both inmate and the public pledged through imprisonment and cure. So much is promised in the asylum and so many things lost, broken, destroyed, and violated.

In graphic novels, contemporary narrative visualizations express a distilled impression of post-war mistrust of asylums, radical psychiatry, and the eventual drive to shutter state asylums.—It is not possible to discuss every iteration of the narrative, and so this essay will focus on two graphic novels, *Arkham: A Living Hell*, 2004, and *A Serious House on Serious Earth*, 1998, with special attention given to intertextuality and the relationships with Expressionist theater and art, however fluid or distilled.[4]

Poster for *The Thousand Eyes of Dr. Mabuse (1960)/Die 1000 Augen des Dr. Mabuse (1960)*, Fritz Lang's last *Mabuse* movie. Lang made this low budget, West German horror film after leaving Hollywood and returning to his native Europe. The subject of many films, Dr. Mabuse is far better-known in Europe than in the U.S. The Arkhams continue the tradition of evil screen psychiatrists such as Mabuse, while Bob Kane incorporated German Expressionist aesthetics in his *Batman* comics and especially appreciated Fritz Lang's SF film, *Metropolis* (1927).

An Expressionist Concern

The critic Lotte Eisner characterized the German Expressionist approach as "concerned solely with the images in the mind." This may be true in part, but Expressionists were also concerned with contemporary societal concerns and misdeeds, the occult, psychiatry, and human sexuality. Both Expressionist art and theater and contemporary neo-expressionist graphic novels visualize societal problems, with a narrative in which science fiction meets mysticism. This approach depicts the confrontation of medicine and mental illness and criminality: illness or deviancy is a demon meant to be exorcised. As such, we can note, that in much of early twentieth century German and Austrian art, theater, and literature, an interest in humanity's dark side (including criminality) produced motifs of disfigurement and mutilation.[5]

Portraits and Pathologies

In addition to narratives of the dark side, another influential paradigm is the face of "ugliness" in the strange self-portraits of turn-of-the-century Austria and Germany, such as Ernst Ludwig Kirchner's disturbing self-depiction as a one-handed soldier, the terror of war inflected in an imaginary deformity.[6] The Joker is, of course, the ultimate example the Expressionist influence, his face that of a maniacal demon, drawn in bold angular black lines, crisscrossed by feathery sketching and planes, purposefully evoking a sense of irrationality. Perhaps the most iconic Expressionist depictions of a man driven to insanity are Heinrich Davringhausen's 1910 painting *The Madman*.[7] Stylistically, the Madman and the Joker share an expressionist use of color, line, distortion, producing a sense of enclosure and entrapment. At the same time, social degradation, particularly in times of war, is conflated with the "sanity" of culture, and in turn with the mind of the ordinary man. I use the term "man" because Expressionists were primarily concerned with males; the body of artworks depicting the horrors of war and shellshock dealt with the agonies of battle and post-traumatic stress suffered by men sent off to war. To express (and perhaps relish) the suffering and horror of madness, the comic illustrators chose to use Expressionist paradigms to evoke a different sort of agony, that of the hopelessness and brutality of war. In *Batman*, the war is a struggle against wickedness of the mind, and the criminal. This vision strikes an uncanny balance between history, pathology, trauma, and horror.

Interiors and Doctors

As a construct with a strange armature, Arkham is concerned with blood lust and fables of madness, within the dominant image of American insane asylums. Graphic novels such as *Arkham—A Living Hell* and *A Serious House on Serious Earth* employ narratives representing the alleged control, authority, and fallibility of the psychiatric field. Anxieties and mythologies of this nature take the form of horror genre vignettes and storylines. *A Living Hell* begins with a vignette of a switch doctor inflicting a primitive lobotomy on a patient, an exorcism suggesting that the treatment of the mentally ill has a long, cruel history, marked by cruel experimentation. This kind of storyline reflects in

214   Section VII: Literary and Artistic Influences

In *Dr. Jekyll and Mr. Hyde* (1931), Fredric March morphs between good Jekyll and bad Hyde, thanks to ingenious lighting tricks, make-up, costumes, acting skills (and a fictional chemical). The diabolical doctors depicted in *Arkham Asylum* comics, films, TV shows and games show none of the humanitarian traits possessed by Dr. Jekyll prior to his transformation to Hyde. Stevenson's 1886 novella antedated Freud's invention of psychoanalysis, with theories about the *ego, id,* and *superego,* but this filmic rendition of Mr. Hyde, with its Expressionist-style cast shadow, suggests Jungian concepts of the "shadow self" and anticipates film noir's shadows.

contemporary cultural mistrust of institutional psychiatry, leading the viewer to question the authority of place, doctor, diagnosis, and even what is supposedly normative. While the purpose of the polemic remains unclear, we might find Sander L. Gilman's phrase useful: "It is not art which imitates insanity, but the perception of insanity which imitates art."[8]

Nevertheless, it seems we are in an untenable situation. After all, from the highly stylized television series to *Batman Returns* to the horror genre comics, the dominant theme is that the inhabitants of Arkham are the unredeemable. This is where the theme of paranoia is woven into tesserae of psychiatric histories, heroics, and gothic tales. The insane characters represent otherness or the inexplicable. Make no mistake; this is also a carnival for the thrill seeker, who will not mind that historic truths about psychiatry, hospitals, and fiction collide. Rather Arkham proves to be an admixture of the imaginative trajectory of horror, in the tradition of Poe and Lovecraft. Stylized, populated by villains, perverts, seductresses, and hybrids, the world where the protagonists operate is simply chaos. Here there is a confluence of ideas, imaginative trajectories, and visual effects that contribute to a sense of ambivalence and panic. Narrative is important, but one should not expect strict linearity or redemption. Chaos, bloodshed, and hopelessness rule. A fine line divides the sane from the insane. Those not imprisoned in their own wayward minds are captive in a living hell: the cells and hallways of Arkham.

Arkham Asylum: Living Hell *as Assemblage*

In *Arkham: Living Hell*, the asylum is a prison; treatment seems a side issue presented as a half-hearted talk therapy. The psychiatrist herself falls victim to the Cipher, a figure who has no identity herself and wears the skin of her victims, taking on their identities. Pseudo-psychology juxtaposed with horror narratives makes shallow mockery of science. The idea that deviance is a less-than-precise category is manipulated to create a demented sense of pleasure in pain as characters emerge like carnival characters. Does the pathology of madmen reflect a larger social or institutional problem? This is a complex question. The shock-genre motifs of *Batman* move beyond the expressionist idea that the "insane" represented defiance in the role of avant-garde artists and by extension the surrealist interest in mental processes (the unconscious, insanity, automatism, and creativity).[9] The admixture of the naturalism and fantasy weave together to make up a new myth. Strange light, dark and nocturnal, clashes with the artificial brightness, artificiality of institutional lighting, creating a hallucinatory, nightmarish mood. Deformation (a canonical expressionist trope) is central, shadowy crisscrossing lines mean faces are ripped, scored, made grotesque and foreboding. Death is an important theme: self-destruction, the destruction of others, and events leading inexorably to death.[10] As well, all deaths appear to be somehow connected to past deaths.[11] Of course, such idiomatic style is as much about fantasy as actual medical prognosis or experience. Rather, as is typical with horror genres, these morbid conventions lend to the mythic quality of the story. The supernatural merges eerily with the real; a character named Rattle communes with the dead, and a graffiti artist ghoulishly paints in blood like a mythical madhouse inmate. Meanwhile another inmate—a caricature of the 19th-century "imbecilic"— takes apart things and people with no notion of the consequences of his actions or the cannibalistic implications of reassembling human body parts.

Much of this unmediated horror takes place in what appears to be a cavernous, subterranean Arkham. As one of the central characters, Warren White, becomes a victim of the Cipher, he goes further into the underground realm of Arkham. This novel barters in a visual language that menaces the characters and thrills the reader with themes of entrapment, and yet ends in a rather broken way, as a piece of shock genre.[12] The hero or antihero in this and other sagas is Batman, who has survived his own trauma and yet manages to control (albeit messily) the intractable, the damaged, the shell-shocked. Batman is a doppelganger; he has a secret identity, fights criminals, and has his own version of PTSD, for as a child he witnessed the murder of his parents. Rather than senselessly repeating the brutality, Batman uses his resources, especially his considerable wealth, to accumulate gadgets and technologies to help him fight crime. His beacon signifies his dual role rescuer of people in peril, and of himself. He represents reason in a completely unreasonable world. He becomes the wall between the criminally insane and their victims, and of course, society itself. By choosing to fight the criminal world, Batman makes conscious choices without entirely relinquishing his own dark side. The difference between his own trauma and that of the various villains and broken people is nominal at best, suggesting that willpower and masculine rationality may allow one to choose to go to the other side. Conversely, allowing evil, disorder, and madness to consume results in unrelenting chaos, despair, destruction, and never-ending appetite for cruelty. Naturally, without such primal, psychopathic drives (however fictional they may be), there would be no room for heroic tales that so imaginatively blend science, with supernatural events, medicine with eroticism, and violence with redemption.

Somewhere in this anarchy of ideas and visual motifs is a sense of paranoiac panic, an anxious way of seeing the world inside the asylum and outside. The lines between sanity and insanity are blurred as are those between human beings and hybrids, doctors, and patients, cruelty, and treatment, ineptitude and imprisonment. Deviance is embodied in strange creatures, sadistic doctors, in this terrifying prison. Killer Croc, too, embodies the blurring of lines as a demonic doppelganger.

Troublesome characters like Warren White, who land themselves in Arkham, act as the reader's witness. The overall anxiety and ambivalence reflect a cultural mistrust of the restraint and authority of old-fashioned institutions before the anti-psychiatry movement of the 1960s, and of the pharmaceutical industry. These ideas, vaguely understood and genuflected to in graphic novels, narratives, and movies, are related in a diluted way to the anti-institutional (and antipsychiatry) movement that originated in part with Thomas Szasz, The *Myth of Mental Illness* (1960).[13] Clearly the truly criminal, many of whom feature largely in the *Batman* sagas, are not to be reformed by any means. They must be contained. The cause of their intractability may vary, whether past abuse or some sort of demonic connection to the supernatural. This looseness reveals the mercurial nature of the model of Arkham. Equal parts metaphor for mistrust of authority and of psychiatry, the narrative conjoins an abiding interest in metaphysics with a view of madness as a conduit between supernatural and man. Much of this construct is guided by the stories of H.P. Lovecraft, whose tales of horror were founded on the story of his own parents who both died of degenerative syphilis in institutions.[14]

A Serious House on Serious Earth

Grant Morrison and Dave McKean's 2004 *Batman Arkham Asylum: A Serious House on Serious Earth*, DC Comics tells the story of the asylum over fifty years after its founding. Arkham is the repository for Batman's enemies who have taken over the madhouse and "in a harrowing contest of wits with his greatest enemies, the Batman must descend into the heart of darkness, confront his greatest fears and learn the truth of his own experience ... or be broken." Aesthetically, this contemporary book shows the influence of the photography of architectural ruins, the totemic traces of abandoned asylums with their suggestion of lives lost, imprisoned, poetry of suggestive memories, names etched, hieroglyphic images, abandoned suitcases, and prosaic everyday items lined up in disarray or solemn order. Perhaps even a more personal thing or two, drawings, letters, desperate scrawling on a wall— these things we crave for their relic-like romanticism, oscillating between horror and pleasure. The introductory pages show a vignette entitled "The Passion Play," a motif borrowed from Expressionist Christological models to illustrate personal experience and trauma.[15] One of the most distressing passages of *A Serious House*

A monstrous shadow looms large, as unseen beasts emerge from the jungle in Kenton's *Island of Lost Souls* (1931), a cinematic version of H.G. Wells' *Island of Dr. Moreau* (1896). Shipwrecked sailor Edward Parker (Richard Arlen) points to shoot while fiancée Ruth Thomas (Leila Hyams) cowers. The influence of such 19th century literary classics persists in 20th and 21st century film, television, and video games. In TV's *Gotham* (2015–2019), Dr. Hugo Strange resurrects the dead to create a menacing Satanic monster reminiscent of this proto-noir, Expressionist-style scene.

begins, "Spring is a deceitful season and April 1st, 1921 is cold." The scene depicts the grisly murder of the doctor's wife and child by Martin Hawkins ("Mad Dog"), a former patient who the narrator says has been "indescribably violated."

And over this scene lies a veil of smoke and haze, implying a chaos of ghostly memories of a haunted and torturous place. The first memory appears in the journal of

Amadeus Arkham's childhood recollections, interspersed with the hostage situation and Arkham's meeting with Carl Jung and Aleister Crowley.[16] Murder and the descent into madness are the underlying themes, followed by the doctor's torture and murder of his homicidal patient. The book is laid out in long vertical panels, and the vortex-like composition is reminiscent of Otto Dix's *War*.[17] In this picture, Dix uses graphic imagery of death and despair together with atmospheric classicism and shocking realism, an approach we also see in the comic book, which has its own way of combining atmospheric despair with shocking bloodshed, the panels divided and delineated with nocturnal color and chaotic action. I bring up this picture not to make a direct analogy or suggest the Dix picture as a source, but rather to connect the depiction of the sorrows of war—especially the early twentieth century German way of expressing the effects of war, violence and psychological aftershock—with the comic genre's depiction of psychiatric trauma and sexualized murder. However, contemporary expressions of horror and psychiatric deterioration are also informed by a normalization of criminal pathology, and an exoticization of sexual crimes. The mad and the criminal appear often as inseparable categories. These experiences seem informed by the early twentieth century topos of the post–World War I avant-garde, whose experience of the horrors of war are laid out in hundreds of scenes, united by their despairing depiction of death, destruction, loss, abjection, and ensuing madness. We see this from the chaotic ochre and gray masses of people and landscape seen in the work of Ludwig Meidner to the grotesque, marionette-like figures of Beckmann's painting *Nacht*.[18]

Strange Typologies

The categories of inmate and patient are purposefully blurred, and the typology of the subjects is enigmatic. A colorful version of shellshock or post-traumatic stress disorder (or some imagined offshoot of this diagnosis) has changed the landscape of each person or creatures. He is abused, and abuses, she loses and is determined to make everyone she encounters lose something, their dignity, their body parts—whatever it is, perversion rules. Deviance becomes a dance for control. Monsters of mythological power and evil seem to be everywhere. Are they the product of a damaged psyche, or of a broken system? Mental patients include the Joker, Penguin, Poison Ivy, The Riddler, Two-Face, Scarecrow, Bane, Killer Croc, and Harley Quinn. For almost every story told, the dramatic, stylized use of Expressionist gesture and movement evokes a sense of horror, to release inhibitions, and even pleasure in violence. The characters are an enigmatic marriage of mythology, science fiction and archetypes; the reader watches them commit horrific acts or fall victim to torture or death.

And so, we can ask ourselves, what is Arkham? I suppose this is a complex query; after all, every thread threatens to run together with another, creating an entanglement. Arkham seems a locus for anxieties about the other: the mentally ill, the deranged, the criminal, and even the "unnatural." It allows itself a certain imaginative fluidity and allegorical power as a fictional place.[19] This haunting edifice, as well, reflects the gothicizing narrative sensibility of H.P. Lovecraft and, represented with early twentieth century German Expressionist leitmotifs and the stylization of New Objective painting. The uncanny hybridity of fantasy, mythology, and pseudo-psychiatry blend together to form a surreal experience, resembling the ideologies of experimental theater of cruelty.[20]

Arkham, thus, expresses postwar attitudes to authority, particularly the institutional treatment of the mentally ill, mistrust of psychiatrists. Less flatteringly, Arkham reflects the public's voyeuristic appetite for horror as a popular form of entertainment. Even more compellingly, we see a connection to the anti-hero of film noir. If the threat of chaos is part of the allegory, the fable, the visualization of myth, then it is in fact a potent expression of the mayhem of the archetypal myth of the asylum gone wrong. It is not just the characters inhabiting these places that make them strange; the edifices themselves veer between Victorian Kirkbride–style institutions and cold, regimented prisons. The association of the institutionalized asylum with consolidation of authority and a system of cure is a point made by many critics who use both ideological and historic reasoning to explain the problems of imprisonment and definitions of deviance.[21]

However, these concerns are just points of departure for contemporary graphic novels. As tales of horror imagine, curative measures were far from foolproof, often experimental, at times cruel, if not completely inappropriate. The suggestion that authority and knowledge is the sole purview of the medical professional is repudiated over and over, particularly in the stories of doctors whose could themselves be diagnosed as sadists or psychopaths, and who often decline into total insanity and become patients themselves. For example, Dr. Quinn eventually becomes the Joker's lover and a patient herself. Perhaps it is by consuming the other through torture and experimentation she becomes the same as the object of her ministrations. If we add the dark romance of architecture, fiction, and the taste for ghoulish violence, then we have our setting, the fictional Arkham Asylum. This place exemplifies American mythology of the asylum, and the motif of horror and exploitation represents what it might mean to be mad, irreparably so, a vision as embodied in architecture. While forged out of the stylistic distortions of early twentieth century Expressionism, within the graphic work and filmic versions of the great asylum there seems to be as well as conflation of the terror and trauma of war with incumbent madness at the hands of militarized brutality, evident in the mythos of the institutionalized horror chamber. This forms a pastiche of form and theme. The Kirkbride model of the asylum, in its Victorian grandeur and duality, conceals within a majestic exterior a terrible, closeted interior.[22] The characters of the *Batman* saga are elaborately pathologized; thus, Arkham began as a family mansion, devolved into a sanitarium, and was ruled thereafter by various despotic, cruel doctors and other villains who experiment on their prisoners.[23]

Madness has its own narrative, and so this story is a repository of imagination, rebellion and thrilling rebellious acts, often violent, chaotic, and sexualized. These are all well-known themes of fin-de-siècle expressionist art and literature. Add to this that in much of the Arkham series what might turn out to be redemptive climactic drama instead ends in murder. Every element of Arkham's structure is chaotic, unpredictable, and disordered. Disorder is a creative well of ideas, images, and metaphors. This is a dystopia of psychiatry run amuck, a carnivalesque interpretation of the Foucaultian nightmare vision of discipline and punishment, made into a contemporary form of horror interwoven with neo-expressionist sensibility and form.

NOTES

1. Marcel Franciscono, "The Imagery of Max Beckmann's *The Night*." *Art Journal* 33(1) (Autumn 1973): 18–22.

2. Max Beckmann's painting *Die Nacht* (The Night), 1918–19, 52 3/8 in × 60 1/4 inches, oil on canvas, the collection of Kunstsammlung Nordrhein-Westfalen, Dusseldorf, Germany.

220   Section VII: Literary and Artistic Influences

3. Arkham is modeled, at times, on Expressionist aesthetics, such as the vertical geometry of *Dr. Caligari's Cabinet*. See Lotte H. Eisner, *Expressionism in the German Cinema and the Influence of Max Reinhardt. the Haunted Screen* (Berkeley: University of California Press, 1977): 19.

4. See Grant Morrison and Dave McKean's *Batman Arkham Asylum, a Serious House on Serious Earth* (DC Comics, 1998) and Dan Slott's *Arkham—a Living Hell* (DC Comics, 2004). the Rocksteady video game *Batman: Arkham Asylum* takes place in an asylum that has been taken over by the Joker. Insanity becomes a sort of virtual reality, the main player (Batman) is gassed by the Scarecrow and has as well moments of flashbacks, memories, and dreams.

5. This topic is discussed in great depth by Hanis Siebenpfieffer in *Böse Lust: Gewaltverbrechen in Diskursen Der Weimarer Republik* (Böhlau-Verlag, 2005).

6. Ernst Ludwig Kirchner (1880–1938), *Self-Portrait as a Soldier*, 1915, Allen Memorial Art Museum, Oberlin College; Joseph Mashek, "The Horror of Bearing Arms: Kirchner's 'Self-Portrait as Soldier,' the Military Mystique and the Crisis of World War I (with a slip of the Pen by Freud)," *Artforum* 19 (December 1980): 56–61.

7. Works related to the Lustmörder genre include Heinrich Maria Davringhausen, *Madman*, 1910, oil on canvas, 198 × 20 cm, Westfälisches Landesmuseum, Münster and *Der Träumer II* (The Dreamer), 1919, Hessisches Landesmuseum Darmstadt; Otto Dix's *Lustmörder*, 1920. See Maria Tartar, *Lustmord: Sexual Murder in Weimar Germany* (Princeton: Princeton University Press, 1995); and Beth Irwin Lewis, "Lustmord: Inside the Windows of the Metropolis." *Women in the Metropolis: Gender and Modernity in Weimar Culture* (Berkeley: University of California Press, 1997): 202–32.

8. Sander L. Gilman, *Seeing the Insane: A Visual and Cultural History of Our Attitudes Toward the Mentally Ill* (Brattleboro, Vermont: Echo Point Books and Media LLC, 2014: xiii).

9. Gilman, "The German Expressionists Saw in the Image of the Insane the Reification of Their Own Definition of the Artist in Conscious Opposition to the Structures of Society." *Difference and Pathology: Stereotypes of Sexuality, Race, and Madness* (Ithaca: Cornell University Press, 1985), 230.

10. It seems salient to note that Bob Kane's first work (until c.1941) reflected this atmospheric distorted scenic tendency, nocturnal imagery presented in distorted geometry, imbued with a sense of compression and escalating madness and bloodshed.

11. This is of course, related to the work of the architect and film maker Fritz Lang who continually framed his films in the dressings of architecture, the most important to our discussion of Arkham being *The Cabinet of Dr. Caligari* (1919–1920). the demonic doctor's rooms became a canon for the evil doctor, who exists somewhere between alchemist and healer, sadist and fated anti-hero. This doppelganger makes his appearance most notably in the great expressionist classic Dr. Caligari as well as Lang's Mabuse. Even more interesting is film maker Friedrich Wilhelm Murnau's way of making space in pictures like *Nosferatu, a Symphony of Horror.* in his chapter "Experience and Memory: the Visualization of World War I by Artists in Vienna and Berlin" Clemens Klöckner points out the wounded individual is a key theme in post war Expressionist work and that the wartime experience of many of the artists were heterogeneous. *Vienna-Berlin, the Art of Two Cities.* (New York: Prestel, 2013), 175.

12. Alternately, the narrative is set up in a different way in Rocksteady's videogame. It is interesting to see the way the story seems to be told as a subjective experience while it is clear it reflects a larger experience or rather a cultural construct, e.g., that of the insane. Jan-Noël Thon "Subjectivity Across Media: on Transmedial Strategies of Subjective Representation: Contemporary Feature Films, Graphic Novels, and Computer Games." *Storyworlds Across Media. Toward a Media-Conscious Narratology* (Lincoln: University of Nebraska Press, 2014).

13. In addition to Michel Foucault's work such *Madness and Civilization: A History of Insanity in the Age of Reason* (New York: Vintage, 1965), we can refer to the writings of R.D Laing and of course, Dr. Franko Basaglia who is known widely as man who closed the asylums in Italy. Accused at times of abandoning his patients, and alternately of liberating the falsely imprisoned, Basaglia's fallibility and the complexity of his ideas mirror the ambivalence expressed about the mentally ill, the asylum, and the attendant questions about usefulness, control, safety, and the problems of deviance. See also Franko Basaglia's *Die Entscheidung Des Psychiaters* (Psychiatrie-Verlag GmbH, 2000); D. Burston, *The Crucible of Experience: R.D. Laing and the Crisis of Psychotherapy* (Cambridge, MA: Harvard University Press, 2000); R.D Laing, *The Politics of Experience and the Bird of Paradise* (New York: Penguin Books, 1990).

14. Sharon Packer notes: "Lovecraft's Institution Bears Important Parallels to Insane Asylums in Batman While It Recollects Landmark German Expressionist Films About the Charlatan Asylum Superintendent, Caligari, from 1919, and the Self-proclaimed Psychoanalyst, Dr. Mabuse, Who Starred in Dozens of Films, Starting with Fritz Lang's Silent Weimar Cinema of 1923. *Batman* writers and Editors Had Good Reason to Appropriate the Lovecraftian Term—and Not Solely Because of the Content of Lovecraft's Story but Also Because of Lovecraft's Family History. Both Parents Died in Mental Asylums. His Father Went First, When Lovecraft Was Still a Child. His Father's Death Certificate Attributed His Demise to Neurosyphilis. Lovecraft's Mother Became Psychotic Enough to Enter the Same Institution Many Years Later, When H.P. Was Already an Adult." *Mental Illness in Popular Culture* (New York: Praeger, 2017).

15. Among the most trenchant Expressionist examples of this motif is Carl Hauser's 1916 painting *Sol-*

diers, which shows the agonizing moving of a wounded soldier, the composition modeled on the descent from the cross. See Klöckner's discussion of the importance of the motifs of passion of Christ in the work of Hauser and others. Experience and Memory: the Visualization of World War I by Artists in Vienna and Berlin," *Vienna-Berlin, the Art of Two Cities* (New York: Prestel, 2013), 176. German artist Max Beckmann also used passion motifs to depict himself travelling through Berlin in prints such as *Das Martyrium, Die Hölle*, 1919, J.B. Neumann, Berlin, Frankfurt am Main: C. Naumann Druckerei. Kokoschka also integrated passion and Christological motifs in his early visual work, related to the northern interest in paradigm of the man of sorrows.

16. The comic incorporates the style of collected thoughts, fantasies, and nightmares along with various abstractions and symbols like that seen in Jung's T*he Red Book:* Liber Novus. ed. Sonu Shamdasani, tr. M. Kyburz, J. Peck (New York: W.W. Norton, 2009). Both Antony Storr and Paul Stern have asserted the Jung book is representative of the doctor's own period of psychosis, whereas Shamdasani notes that Jung "From December 1913 Onward, He Carried on in the Same Procedure: Deliberately Evoking a Fantasy in a Waking State, and Then Entering Into It as Into a Drama. These Fantasies May Be Understood as a Type of Dramatized Thinking in Pictorial Form...."

17. Otto Dix, *Der Krieg* (War), 1929–1932, tempera on wood, central panel 204 × 204 cm, side panels 204 × 102 cm each, Gemäldegalerie Neue Meister, Dresden.

18. The Expressionist master Beckmann worked as paramedic during the war, and his trauma clearly is relived in the puzzling yet horrifying war time painting. Rose-Carol Washton Long and Maria Makela, ed., "Of 'Truths Impossible to Put in Words,' in *Max Beckmann Contextualized (*Bern, Switzerlan, Peter Lang Publishers, 2009), 85.

19. John Goodwin, "The Horror of Stigma: Psychosis and Mental Health Care Environments in Twenty-First Century Horror Film (Part II)," *Perspectives in Psychiatric Care* 50(4) (2014): 224–34.

20. By experimental theater, I mean the aesthetics and approach of directors like the French Surrealist theorist, actor, and poet Antonin Artaud whose concept of a newly primitive theater of cruelty presented an alternative to rationalism and realism. It is interesting to note that Artaud's major work *Le Théâtre Et Son Double* (1938) is regarded as having been written during a period of "insanity."

21. This field is quite complex; key works include David J. Rothman, *The Discovery of the Asylum: Social Order and Disorder in the New Republic* (Boston and Toronto: Little, Brown and Company, 1971). More recently, Carla Yanni notes in her history of the architecture of asylums that they were expensive public buildings, and as such, legitimized psychiatric knowledge. *The Architecture of Madness. Insane Asylums in the United States* (Minneapolis: University of Minnesota Press, 2007), 8.

22. Yanni also makes note of the issue of control associated with institutionalized asylums pointing to the connection of the development of modern psychiatry and the institutions, as well making the case for the ideological and architectural models of eighteenth and nineteenth century: "In the United States, from About 1830 On, Psychiatry Was Actually Known as "Asylum Medicine," and psychiatrists created a professional organization (the pre-cursor to the American Psychiatric Association) called the Association of Medical Superintendents of American Institutions for the Insane (AMSAII), whose name suggests that they defined themselves as caretakers of large organizations." 2007: p.8.

23. Gilman describes this way of telling stories noting that the multiplicity of the visual motifs which make up the image of the insane; no line can be drawn between the portrait of the madman in the fine arts and that of medical illustration. Painting, sculpture, and photography have been concerned with the madman in their expression of his being in the world. He goes on to point out the intertextuality of these iconographies: these aesthetics structures and their intellectual background have heavily influenced the medial illustration of psychiatric texts. Gilman, 2014: xii.

Surrealism's Influence on Arkham and Psychiatry's Influence on Surrealism

SHARON PACKER, M.D.

German Expressionism, French Surrealism and the Batman Universe

As an admirer of Fritz Lang's *Metropolis* (1927), Batman's creator Bob Kane based the aesthetics of early Batman comics, and of Gotham City in particular, on German expressionism. Decades later, *Metropolis* (1927) held special sway for Tim Burton, director of *Batman* (1989) and *Batman Returns* (1992). The Joker's grin dates to a different German Expressionist film. German expressionism evolved after World War I, as did the French-born Surrealist movement.[1]

Despite this historical link, the Scottish-born creators of the highly influential graphic novel *Arkham Asylum: A Serious House on Serious Earth* (1989) cite Surrealism as their inspiration (along with Jung, Alister Crowley, occultism, Tarot and more generic "Eastern European creepiness," which includes some artists who self-identify as surrealists).[2]

Surrealism's artistic approach was dramatically different from expressionism. Surrealism arose partly in response to World War I trauma and largely in response to psychoanalytic efforts to access the unconscious and interpret dreams. Spiritualist [not spiritual] influences and surrealists' admiration for mediumship also contributed to surrealist credos. Such occult influences parallel the occult interests of *Arkham's* author, Grant Morrison, as he articulated in his interviews.

The creators of *Arkham Asylum: A Serious House on Serious Earth* acknowledge the contemporary Czech surrealist Jan Švankmajer (a prime example of "Eastern European creepiness"), the Brothers Quay, Antonin Artaud and Jean Cocteau. A self-described "poet" who made films, Cocteau's *The Blood of a Poet* (1932) and *Beauty & the Beast* (1946) show striking similarities to surrealist sensibilities but Cocteau himself was rejected by the organized Surrealist society. Antonin Artaud, another surrealist "fellow traveler" who later distanced himself from the group, created his "theater of cruelty." Artaud attained enduring fame for his influential drama theory, yet he spent his last eleven years confined to an asylum, crippled by paranoia and catatonia, with symptoms suggestive of schizophrenia.[3]

The visual imagery of some Dadaist artists, and Dada's penchant for collage, photomontage and text, are evident in some of McKean's drawings. *Arkham* author Grant Morrison's invention of supervillains known as the "Brotherhood of Dada" for *Doom Patrol* comics attests to his first-hand familiarity with Dada. Yet the creators do not mention Dada, a loosely defined, Berlin-based modernist art movement which likewise evolved in response to World War I's devastation. Dada attracted some future surrealists, Breton included, who attended medical school before the war and worked with brain-injured patients during the war. Dada also centered around a medical student, one who would complete his professional studies and become a full-fledged psychiatrist and psychoanalyst (in contrast to Breton, who never returned).[4]

The stupendously successful *Arkham* video games were partly influenced by the graphic novel mentioned above and so those games also appropriate surrealistic imagery. Surrealism's relationship to psychiatry, and to psychoanalysis, is immutable. We can even link surrealism to neuropsychiatry, albeit tangentially, because surrealism's founder, André Breton, had been a medical student before enlisting in the military and working on a ward with head trauma patients, who presumably showed behavioral changes as well as cognitive deficits, sensory loss, movement disorders and probable PTSD (post-traumatic stress disorder). Breton writes about his use of "free association" techniques with his hospitalized head trauma patients.

The text of *Arkham Asylum* screams of surrealist attitudes toward sanity (or lack of it). The morphing graphics show surrealist underpinnings, for they self-consciously evoke the dreamy states admired by surrealists. Even the non-sequential and unpredictable layout of the graphic novel panels recalls the surrealists' "Exquisite Corpse" practice of passing a folded napkin from one person to another, so that all present could add their thoughts without concern for cohesive composition. *Arkham*'s disjointed panels remind readers of the surrealists' game of running from one movie theater to another, never viewing a single film from start to finish.

The Origins of Surrealism

To further appreciate *Arkham*'s relationship to psychiatry, it's worth reviewing the origins of surrealism. Surrealism began in the 20th century, post–World War I. This thoroughly "modern" movement broke with the past, yet still paid tribute to its Symbolist and Romantic—and even medieval—precursors. Surrealism followed in the footsteps of psychoanalysis. It began as a direct response to Freud's fully formulated dream theories and stated as much in its "First Surrealist Manifesto," written by André Breton in 1924 (and revised in 1929). Surrealism also emulated mediumship, which seems a far cry from science, but directly corresponds with Carl Jung's medical school thesis, written before he joined Freud and coined "analytical psychology."

Surrealists' dream themes appear in sharp focus, often depicted in painstaking detail that forces the spectator to identify with the artist, rather than with the artist's subject matter. Their paintings force the spectator's gaze to align with the artist's gaze—in much the same way that cinema does. Spectators see the same scene that the artist sees and can add their own associations or interpret the dreamlike scenes depicted on canvas, as if they were psychoanalysts themselves.

Surrealists probed the unconscious in willful and contrived ways. While they presented random images in irrational ways, to confuse their audiences, they (almost) never confused themselves and remained aware of their intentions. The same could be said of Morrison and McKean, who followed detailed diagrams to create their graphic novel. Morrison annotated his intentions, and McKean was meticulous in his approaches to art and in his use of hand-painted imagery in lieu of hand-drawn comics art, which was standard prior to the ascension of computer-generated comics art. Early Surrealists used "spontaneous writing" and "spontaneous talking" to generate "spontaneous" images but later revised their techniques to avoid untoward and unanticipated after effects.

The Great War and Its Impact on Early Surrealism

The Great War itself, and the profound despair that followed, was an indispensable impetus to the Surrealist sensibility.[5] The war had shattered confidence in the "real world," for the official forces-that-be had destroyed much of the surrounding world. Warfare claimed countless lives in the process. Pre-existing values were devalued. By default, one should look inwards, rather than outward, or toward society, to find viable meanings in individual existence.

Communist and collectivist ideals, which also surfaced in the 20th century, also impacted Surrealist "society." The "Surrealist Manifesto" mimicked the "Communist Manifesto," in name, although not in content. The first "manifesto," authored by André Breton alone, spelled out surrealist goals and methods. It applied the authoritarianism of other totalizing political systems.

The key to understanding the direction Surrealism took lies in the details of Breton's life, and the twists and tangles that the Great War wreaked on his early life aspirations. Breton did not initially intend to be an artist or writer. Rather, he planned to be a doctor. He was a medical student before he enlisted in the French military during World War I.

As a student, Breton studied with Dr. Pierre Janet, the French philosophy professor who became a psychiatrist and a specialist in the study of dissociative disorders and automatic movements. Janet lectured on the relationship between psychiatry and religion, on psychiatry and spiritualism, and on automatisms. Janet gained renown in France, but did not become better known elsewhere, probably because of his retiring—rather than grandstanding—personality.[6]

Having heard Janet's lectures, Breton became familiar French approaches to psychiatry, which differed from approaches in nearby German-speaking countries, where the biologically oriented psychiatrist and future Nobel Laureate Wagner-Jauregg reigned and where the contentious neurologist turned psychoanalyst Sigmund Freud surfaced. Moreover, as a Frenchman, Breton grew up with countrymen who had accepted "mesmerism" as conceived by the Austrian émigré doctor, Franz Mesmer. To the chagrin of official medical societies, Dr. Mesmer became wildly popular with French ladies when he transplanted himself in France, after being banned from practicing his "animal magnetism" (mesmerism) in his native Vienna.

As a medical student, Breton also heard of the innovative research of a still-obscure Viennese neurologist named Sigmund Freud. Armed with information about Janet's "automatic writing," and Freud's "free associations," Breton entered the French army, not a physician, nor even as a medic, but as an ordinary soldier. He was assigned to work on a ward with brain-injured soldiers. Many such persons existed. While casualties of the Great War were astounding, many of those who survived had disabling injuries. Mental breakdowns were commonplace among recruits confined to foxholes for a year or two at a time, cramped alongside the bodies of their dead and decomposing comrades, deafened (metaphorically if not also literally) by the rat-a-tat-tat of constant shelling. The term "shellshock" entered the everyday vocabulary.

Even those who did have complete nervous collapses left the war permanently changed. Their value systems were left in rubbles, shattered like cities destroyed by cannon fire. Lacking new ideals to replace lost faith in the old world, save for a vague hope in "modernism," these men would become members of the "lost generation." Some sensitive souls later became artists.

Breton was one of those "changed men" who did not return to his pre-war life's work. Rather than picking up where he left off, and completing his medical degree, and perhaps pursuing advanced study in psychiatry or neurology, Breton's life took a dramatically different turn. He started an artistic movement, initially intended as a literary venue. It later included art, film, even fashion. Breton did not devalue his earlier medical studies, or his more recent field experience with brain-injured military men, but he reworked his first-hand observations and his intellectual information. He added unique twists of his own, producing the *Surrealist Manifesto*.

In his *Manifesto*, he wrote: "Dear imagination, what I especially like about you is that you do not forgive.... Only imagination makes me aware of the possible, and that is enough to lift a little of the terrible restriction; enough also for me to surrender to imagination without fear of being mistaken.... Hallucinations, illusions, are not a negligible source of pleasure ..."[7] He praised the "the confidences of madmen," affirming that "[he] would spend [his] life provoking them. They are people of a scrupulous honesty, and whose innocence is equaled only by [his own]. Columbus had to sail with madmen to discover America. And see how that folly has taken form and endured."

The *Surrealist Manifesto* elaborated on Breton's ideas about dreams and reality and (surreality) and their relationships to one another. He said, "From the moment that we succeed in realizing the dream in its integrity ... when its contour will develop with unequaled regularity and breadth, we can hope that mysteries—which are not really mysteries—will yield to the great Mystery. I believe the future resolution of these two states, so contradictory in appearance—dream and reality—into a kind of absolute reality, of *surreality*, if one may call it so." Surrealist ideals evolved from this fusion of individualistic nighttime dreams with consensual waking reality.

Surrealism was as much a political statement as a psychological technique, translated into art forms. As New York City's MoMA (Museum of Modern Art) writes, "Surrealists sought to overthrow the oppressive rules of modern society by demolishing its backbone of rational thought" ... and "to tap into the 'superior reality' of the unconscious mind."[8]

Because Breton preferred states of psychological surrender, such as the dream, he devised techniques to enter altered and unencumbered states. Breton specifically spoke of the "prosecution of the real world," and of "breaking free of the tyranny of the unconscious." Unlike many of their Romantic and Symbolist predecessors, most (but not all) Surrealists did not resort to drugs to attain "surreal" states of mind. Still, Surrealism advocated irresponsibility, and recommended escape from the imperatives of a moral order, and from the control of reason.

Dreams were important to Breton for the same reason that they were important to Freud: because dreams permitted closer contact with the unconscious. Breton aped Freud's methods of free association as he excavated dream imagery. Yet his goals differed from the goals of the founder of psychoanalysis—and differed from asylum superintendents in France or just about anywhere else. Breton did not intend to cure patients or to explain the reasons behind their distress. He used art and literature and cinema as vehicles to make the unconscious as accessible as the conscious, and to alter ordinary human experience and to elevate human awareness. Surrealism, as Breton saw it, could reduce the fragmentation of consciousness, and achieve a psychological reconciliation for the total human being. It offered a new outlook on the world, and a different way of experiencing life, without ensuring sanity or conformity as a "cure" might.

The Surrealists celebrated visionary states accessed via automatic writing, automatic speaking, or dreaming. The early Surrealists imitated the spontaneous, unconsciously driven speech of mediums, and combined it with Freudian techniques of "free association." They called their technique "automatic talking." They contrasted automatic talking with the automatic writing of the 19th century spiritualists. Unfortunately, automatic talking proved dangerous when used by the inexperienced or untrained. Breton abandoned automatic speaking to access the unconscious after the technique set off psychotic states, suicide attempts and stabbings at surrealist gatherings.

Perhaps persons who showed such extreme reactions to automatic talking were already in prodromal psychotic states and would have progressed to full psychosis on their own steam. Perhaps the Surrealists' admiration for artists and writers whose lives ended with violence or psychosis—such as such as Lautremont, Rimbaud, Sade or Nerval—encouraged this dark turn or attracted persons who were teetering on the precipice of psychosis. Or perhaps the Surrealists simply lacked the expertise needed for safe journeys into unchartered unconscious terrain. In due time, automatic talking fell out of favor and was officially outlawed in France and condemned by psychoanalytic journals. After Breton introduced more medically oriented techniques, the Surrealists resumed their excursions into the unconscious, this time around, using "automatic writing" in lieu of "automatic talking." They invented a technique they called the *Exquisite Corpse*. They passed around a folded napkin to everyone present, asking each to write his or her thoughts on the visible section of the napkin, without reading the writings of the previous person and without aspiring to cohesion or consistency. A disjointed, dreamlike journal evolved.

Breton's methods and theories were novel enough to convince the esteemed historian of psychiatry, Dr. Henri Ellenberger, that Breton could have started his own school of psychoanalysis, had he returned to medicine, and not defected to art.[9] Yet Breton did not seem to be healer even if he shared some sensibilities with psychiatrists and psychoanalysts and even if he expected surrealism to enhance human awareness and life experience. His dismissive attitudes toward curing psychosis set him apart from asylum superintendents who sought to suppress madness, to isolate the mad from society and to confine these iconoclasts in institutions.[10]

In some ways, Breton's sentiments echoed some "modern" psychoanalysts, such as Jung, who himself had spent seven years in a psychotic "creative crisis" where he communed with spirits. Like Freud, Breton saluted the dream's ability to access the unconscious, and to mimic the psychotic process. Breton also anticipated "anti-psychiatrists" such as the Scottish R.D. Laing, whose London-based Kingsley Hall residential treatment facility used unconventional approaches in a sincere attempt to help persons with schizophrenia. His efforts met with great aplomb but not with great success and eventually proved to be simplistic and overly optimistic.

Kingsley Hall closed within five years of its opening but remained a landmark in the consciousness of the counterculture of the Sixties and Seventies. Laing in turn left a contradictory legacy of erudite writings, thought-provoking theories, appreciation of Chekhov's prescient short stories about psychiatric asylums, and personal proof of the destructive powers of his own alcohol overuse.[11] He appeared to be intoxicated at public appearances in America.[12]

Many generations later, Breton's admiration for madness would be parroted by Dr. Amadeus Arkham in *Batman: Arkham Asylum*. Dr. Arkham not only becomes a patient in his own asylum, but he subsequently extols the virtues of psychosis, and denounces the value of the "Euclidian world." (Compare Arkham's accepting attitude to Dr. Caligari, the icon of German Expressionism and exemplar of the psychotic screen psychiatrist, who never expressed admiration for his deluded state after he was involuntarily admitted to his own asylum.)

Moreau, Sade and Breton: From Symbolism to Sadism to Surrealism

Before linking Breton to Arkham, let us look at Gustave Moreau's influence on Breton. Breton's visit to the Moreau Museum shifted the direction of Breton's artistic efforts and of his life purpose in general. The Moreau Museum is still housed in Moreau's mansion in Paris. Legend says that no one had visited this idiosyncratic space for a span of twenty years prior to Breton's arrival. Moreau's strange Symbolist art, with its many mythological allusions and its luxuriant imagery, had gone underappreciated until Breton recognized the value of this unusual and almost medieval amalgam of collective myth and individual imagination. Symbolism had faded from grace after the world war, dismissed as an irrelevant relic of the past. Breton reignited interest in Moreau, and the Surrealists recycled the introspective spirit of Moreau's work, adding timelier political, scientific, and even medical messages to this otherwise personal approach.

The Surrealist movement also admired the Marquis de Sade, the notorious sadist who spent years confined to prisons and mental asylums. For the Surrealists, Sade epitomized the person who was persecuted by the state because he denounced its moral, sexual, legal, and cognitive control. Moreover, Sade was a prolific writer who recounted his real and imaginary excesses in novels. Sade was as inspiration for emerging Surrealist writers, including Breton.

Sade is not lost on the authors and artist of *Arkham*. Allusions to Sadian characters seep into the text self-consciously. As Morrison explains in his annotations to the 25th anniversary edition, the words, "CHARLOTTE CORDAY! CHARLOTTE CORDAY! CHARLOTTE CORDAY!" [sic] come from the *Marat Sade* play by Peter Weiss. Another expression, "DICTATOR OF THE RATS" –the *Marat Sade*—has the same source. It would be foolish to cite Surrealism as the only possible portal for learning about Sade, for his name is fossilized in psychiatric nosology, and in everyday parlance, but these quotes confirm the author's intentions.

Symbolist Author Gérard de Nerval and Belgian Artist Bosch

Another Symbolist favorite of Breton straddled the nexus between insanity and art, and blended nighttime dream with daytime life: Gérard de Nerval. Nerval produced his best remembered writings while confined to an insane asylum. Despondent over his rejection by singer Jenny Colon, and possibly delusional about the nature of their relationship from the start, Nerval hanged himself just hours before the publication of the second half of his manuscript, *Aurelia* (also titled *Dream and Life*).[13]

Nerval's confusing and disconnected novels, which include fleeting visual imagery, evidence the similarities between dream states and mental disease. His writings also betray the hallucinogenic influence of opium, alcohol, ether, absinthe, and hashish, all of which contributed to his mental decline. Nerval had been influenced by the 18th century German Romantic author and composer, E.T.A. Hoffmann, and by Theophile Gautier, who started the Hashish Club in 1850s France to expose writers and artists to the herb's alleged creativity-enhancing effects.

The 15th century Belgian artist, Hieronymus Bosch, was another Surrealist hero. Bosch's esoteric symbols stand side-by-side with familiar figures, creating incomprehensible combinations that are constantly confusing, but endlessly entertaining. Works such as *The Temptation of St. Anthony* (approximately 1515),[14] *The Garden of Earthly Delight* (1490–1510), and *Ship of Fools* (1490–1500) spoke to the Surrealist aesthetic. The publication of Freud's *Interpretation of Dreams* encouraged admirers to comb the canvas in search of meaningful symbols, just as Freud dissected dreams.

A painting such as *Ship of Fools*[15] was especially relevant, since it depicts madmen who (supposedly) set sail on a hypothetical ship. In *The Temptation of St. Anthony,* Bosch illustrates hallucinations that reportedly appeared when Anthony lived as a solitary desert ascetic, presumably experiencing the psychotomimetic effects of sensory deprivation and possible ergotism. Bosch's *Garden of Earthly Delights* defies explanation, for its candy-colored castles, humongous birds and hybrid beasts inhabit the same landscape as realistically rendered humans.

Unlike Nerval, whose life history was known to the Surrealists, and was much-discussed by psychiatrists of the day, Bosch's life history remains a mystery. Much more is known about the social climate of his times. It is now known that Bosch painted during the heyday of the ergot epidemics, when LSD-like chemicals infiltrated the food supply, and produced bizarre visions, strange sightings, and waking dreams in those afflicted. Perhaps Bosch was exposed to ergot, as were many of his countrymen. This fact may be interesting to us today, as we are more aware of the biological basis of behavior and are reconsidering the medicinal value of once-banned hallucinogenic agents, but this information did not necessarily appeal to psychoanalytically inspired Surrealists, who were more concerned with content than with cause.[16]

Mediums, Spiritualists, Psychoanalysts and Surrealists

Besides valuing these artists and writers of the past, and the dream state itself, Surrealists also admired the altered psychological state of the medium. The Surrealists' fondness for spiritualism differed dramatically from the 19th century Symbolists' attraction to mediums. The Symbolists lived when society was saturated with Spiritualism, séances and even Satanism. They agreed that unseen supernatural sources guided the medium. Surrealists added more modern, psychoanalytically inspired twists to "spiritualist" messages, expressing interest in messages "sent not from the spiritualist hereafter, but from the actual self, hidden by consciousness."

Surrealist experiments with "mediumship" bore striking similarities to Jung's medical school dissertation on the psychological states of mediums, although the Surrealists clearly favored Freud. (The creators of *Arkham* admittedly favor Jung and even devote a page to Dr. Arkham's visit with "Professor Jung," yet their annotations confirm their familiarity with Freud). Before joining forces with his mentor (and father figure and future rival) Freud, Jung researched the mediumistic trances of his cousin Helene, who was a well-known clairvoyant. Jung concluded that mediums "heard" "messages" from their unconscious, which could be retrieved during dissociative "spiritualist" states. Similar altered states occur during the dream state.

By this time, psychoanalytic circles were too skeptical of Surrealism to give much credence to this odd artistic schism. Reports of psychiatric casualties during the surrealists' "automatic writing" escapades had spread beyond the Surrealists and earned them vitriolic condemnation in psychoanalytic journals. Despite Breton's open admiration for Freud and for Freud's newfound "science" of psychoanalysis, Freud himself refused to collaborate with Breton. Freud nevertheless accepted invitations from the Surrealist artist Salvador Dalí many years later. He praised Dalí's artistry and creativity. Most psychoanalysts followed Freud's inclinations and spurned the Surrealists. One exception was the unorthodox French analyst Jacques Lacan.

Ironically, even though Freud disdained the Surrealists generally and Breton in particular, it was the Surrealists who translated and published Freud's dream theories in their official journal in French, and thereby made the French-speaking world aware of Freudian dream theories at a time when Freud's *Interpretation of Dreams* was still marginal to the medical world. It was equally ironic that the Surrealists showed such high regard for Freud, an Austrian import, even though Pierre Janet devoted his career to studying altered states of consciousness in Paris. In yet another note of irony, most Frenchmen and women of the day gravitated to existentialist philosophers such as Jean-Paul Sartre, while iconoclastic Surrealists favored Freud. France preferred the French philosopher Henri Bergson and his book *On Dreams* and resisted the Germanic psychoanalytic ideas. In fact, France was indifferent to psychoanalytic ideas until Jacques Lacan filtered Freud's "voice." Lacanianism in turn became a powerful force in French psychiatry, politics, and culture by the 1950s. By the 1970s, French Lacan–based psychoanalytic theories about cinema stimulated new directions in film criticism. This same contrarian Jacques Lacan had published articles in Surrealist journals at a time when Freud refused to speak with Breton. Lacan also married the ex-wife of well-known Surrealist writer, publisher and pornographer, George Bataille. Lacan later collaborated with Salvador Dalí.[17] It's a small world.

Dalí's Dream Scenes and Surrealist Influences in Cinema and Psychoanalysis

Dalí's influence in art endured and spread to cinema and ultimately to advertising. Dalí's so-called "photographs of dreamscapes" made him one of the most recognized Surrealist artists. He was far more financially successful than other members of this school. He developed a "paranoid-critical" approach to art in collaboration with Lacan and published his theories about the explorations into the unconscious in an often-republished paper by that name. Unfortunately, this paper about his "paranoid-critical"

230   Section VII: Literary and Artistic Influences

approach is too disjointed and incoherent to convey much meaning and sounds more "thought-disordered" (suggestive of psychosis at worst or of limited rhetorical abilities at best). Dalí's skills as a painter and printmaker did not translate into an ability to write. Like his paintings, the exact meanings of Dalí's theories are elusive, and evoke the reader's personal associations more readily than they convey the author's actual intent.

Dalí became more controversial after expressing support for Fascist forces. Unwilling to tolerate his right-wing politics, the Surrealists removed Dalí from their tight-knit, politically sensitive Surrealist circle. Yet Dalí was indirectly instrumental in publicizing psychoanalytic dream theory through his post-war collaboration with Hitchcock in *Spellbound* (1945). In *Spellbound*, a handsome young male psychiatrist (Gregory Peck) loses his memory and is suspected of a murder that he did not commit. He attracts the attention (and affection) of an attractive young female physician/analyst, Dr. Constance Peterson, played by Ingrid Bergman. By dissecting the dreams of the distraught young doctor, the female physician uncovers clues that unmask the identity of the real murderer. The culprit is the departing head of the asylum, who is being replaced by a younger rival. The doctor is played by a withered and whiskered Leo G. Carroll. After Dr. Peterson (Bergman) reveals her theories about the murder, the older doctor pulls a gun from his desk drawer and points it at Dr. Peterson. Unphased, and perhaps overly confident of her psychoan-

Morrison and McKean cite surrealist influences on their graphic novel, *Batman Arkham Asylum: A Serious House on Serious Earth*. Dalí is the best-remembered surrealist and this dream scene of eye-covered curtains in Hitchcock's *Spellbound* (1945) may be the film's most memorable scene. Eye imagery is important to Surrealism, and to *Arkham Asylum* also, for Joker points a pencil at a young female artist's eye, threatening to blind her, unless Batman enters the asylum.

alytic predictions, she turns her back on him and walks away. In one of film's greatest shots, he then holds the same gun to his head, as spectators stare down the barrel.

While Hitchcock's plot twists are compelling, and his actors' performances are laudable, some say that Dalí's Surrealist dream scenes make *Spellbound* so special. Dalí's scenes are enduring, even when other aspects of the film seem dated. Dalí's images of detached eyes are inseparable from the screenplay. This imagery intrigued spectators and sold them on the utility of psychoanalytic dream interpretation. Few viewers remember the details of the convoluted plot, yet virtually every viewer leaves the theater with vivid recollections of Dalí's dream scenes.

Dalí's original dream scene lasted a full thirty minutes but was cut down to two and one-half minutes because it was deemed pornographic. The original was destroyed, and the exact content of Dalí's dream scene is not available, but we can suspect that Dalí's sexual scenarios reflected Freudian emphasis on the sexual symbolism of dream imagery and everything else.

Dalí also collaborated with director Bunuel on a short sadistic, yet influential, Surrealist film entitled *Un Chien Andalou (The Andalusian Dog,* 1929).[18] This film foreshadows the eye imagery in *Spellbound,* but perverts it in a most unpleasant way. Its sadistic mutilation scenes prepare us (if one can ever be prepared) for another influential *Batman* graphic novel, *Batman: The Killing Joke* (1988), by Alan Moore. That 46-page comic won an Eisner Award, and the admiration of many and the condemnation of many more (this author included, as noted in *Superheroes and Superegos: Analyzing the Minds behind the Masks*). The opening scene of *The Andalusian Dog* shows a woman's eyeball being slit open in close-up, as if to symbolize the violent opening of the "mind's eye" and to parallel the violation of the female victim's genital orifice.

Over the years, Dalí's imagery, and the imagery of several other Surrealists, penetrated the American advertising industry. Dalí's painting about *Memory* sold liquor. Belgian Surrealist Rene Magritte's painting of an eye whose pupil opens to the sky outside has become iconic in ads for museums, universities, and other assorted mindscapes. Surrealism's disconnected dream imagery infiltrated the fashion scene by inspiring Elsa Schiaparelli to design a hat from a shoe.

More recently, surrealism entered the emerging world of graphic novels and video games, via *Arkham Asylum: A Serious House on Serious Earth* (1989). *Arkham* will celebrating its 30th anniversary in the year this book is published. It has already been through two anniversary editions (15th and 25th). Its end is nowhere in sight. McKean and Morrison have achieved their goal of "approach[ing] Batman from the point of view of the dreamlike, emotional and irrational hemisphere, as a response to the very literal, 'realistic,' 'left brain' treatment of superheroes which was in vogue at the time, in the wake of *The Dark Knight Returns, Watchmen,* and others."

Not only did the original work eclipse prevailing comics trends of its era, but it persists and reinvents itself, many times over in many media. It makes audiences rethink more metaphysical and artistic ideas about dreams at a time when neurobiology and psychiatric genomics command center stage. Like dreams themselves, its many-layered meanings morph and mutate, communicating with audiences who add their own associations and expand upon the text.

NOTES

1. See Rosa Berland's essay on "Neo-Expressionist Angst" in this book.
2. Dan Franklin, "Portraying Psychological Angst: Dave McKean Interviewed," *Quietus* (April 15, 2015).

http://thequietus.com/articles/17626-dave-mckean-interview Accessed online August 19, 2018; Grant Morrison, *Supergods: What Masked Vigilantes, Miraculous Mutants, and a Sun God from Smallville Can Teach Us About Being Human* (New York: Spiegel & Grau, 2012).

3. For a thoughtful discussion of Artaud and more, see Louis Sass, *Madness and Modernism: Insanity in the Light of Modern Art, Literature and Thought* (Boston: Harvard University Press, 1994).

4. See Sharon Packer, review of *Generation Dada* by Michael White (New Haven and London: Yale University Press, 2013). *metapsychology.com*, December 30, 2014. http://metapsychology.mentalhelp.net. Michael White, *Generation Dada: The Berlin Avant-Garde and the First World War* (New Haven, CT: Yale University Press, 2013). White calls Dada "the Most Indefinable of the 20th Century's Counterculture Movements." Dada once included André Breton, who went on to found the Surrealist movement. Over time, many one-time Dada artists drifted into surrealist circles. the Dadaists wrote the earliest countercultural art manifesto in response to World War I. Hugo Ball and Tristan Tsara were most active, but Richard Huelsenbeck (1892–1974) was also prominent. Like Breton, Huelsenbeck was a medical student when he entered the military and forged his Dadaist ideology. Unlike Breton, Huelsenbeck went on to become a full-fledged physician, psychiatrist and psychoanalyst. A Frick Museum blog at http://www.frick.org/blogs/dadaist_doctor_new_york details Huelsenbeck's post–Dada days, when he worked as a military doctor and later a ship's doctor, before moving to New York, where he worked as an unpaid assistant psychiatrist at NYU Clinic, changed his name to Charles R. Hulbeck, was accepted to Karen Horney's American Institute for Psychoanalysis and subsequently became a lecturer at the Horney Institute. "He credited Horney with sending him many patients and he built up a lucrative practice, enabling him to afford a suite on Central Park West." in his 1969 essay, "On leaving America for Good," he writes, "As a doctor I was a success and as a Dadaist (the thing closest to my heart) I was a failure." [Richard Huelsenbeck, *Memoirs of a Dada Drummer* (Berkeley: University of California Press, 1991).]

5. In the Art Review Section of *The Wall Street Journal* October 22, 2018, Michael Fitzgerald reviews "Our Irrationality Laid Bare." Fitzgerald's 'Monsters & Myths: Surrealism and War in the 1930s and 1940s elaborates on the Wadsworth Atheneum Museum of Art exhibition, which aimed to "capture One of the Most Profound Intellectual Movements of the Century" and "to Capture the Physical and Psychological Violence of the War-torn Decade That Stretched from the Spanish Civil War Through World War II." 31 Henri F. Ellenberger, *Discovery of the Unconscious: The History and Evolution of Dynamic Psychiatry* (New York: Basic, 1970).

6. Henri F. Ellenberger, *Discovery of the Unconscious: The History and Evolution of Dynamic Psychiatry* (New York: Basic, 1970).

7. A Surrealist rival, Yvon Gall, wrote a separate surrealist manifesto in the same year as Breton's better-known publication. André Breton, *First Manifesto of Surrealism* (1924). Accessed online.

8. MOMA.org

9. Henri F. Ellenberger, *Discovery of the Unconscious: The History and Evolution of Dynamic Psychiatry* (New York: Basic, 1970).

10. Patrick Waldberg, *Surrealism* (New York: Thames and Hudson, 1997).

11. Sharon Packer, review of *Portrait of the Psychiatrist as a Young Man: The Early Writings and Work of R.D. Laing, 1927–1960* by Alan Beveridge (Oxford, UK: Oxford University Press, 2011). http://metapsychology.mentalhelp.net (15:50, December 12, 2011).

12. These observations were voiced at the History of Psychiatry section seminar hosted by Cornell-Weill.

13. Joan Kessler, *Demons of the Night* (Chicago: University of Chicago Press, 1992).

14. Bosch paintings are difficult to date precisely, and some wonder if Bosch or a follower painted this triptych.

15. It is doubtful that the proverbial *Ship of Fools* existed in actuality, even though Foucault's much-read anti-psychiatry writings treat it as a concrete entity, analogous to a floating prison.

16. Sharon Packer and Warren Dotz, "Epidemic Ergotism, St. Anthony's Fire and Jewish Mysticism." *Dermatopathology: Practical and Conceptual* 4:3 (July–Sept. 1998): 259–267.

17. Lacan's controversial practices precipitated a split between French and international psychoanalytical circles. He was banned from other psychoanalytic societies because of his unorthodox beliefs and practices. in retrospect, traces of Lacan's early forays into Surrealist studies can be seen in his mature theories. an analyst might say that Lacan's unorthodox embrace of Surrealism foreshadowed his later unorthodox attitudes and practices.

18. Rudolf E. Kuenzli, ed., *Dada & Surrealist Film* (Cambridge, MA: the MIT Press, 1998).

Poe's Place in Arkham Asylum
Precursors and Parallels
Caleb Puckett

Grant Morrison's *Arkham Asylum: A Serious House on Serious Earth* (1989) stands out as one of the most self-consciously "literary" texts in the Batman canon. Unlike the bulk of authors who have presented Batman's adventures, Morrison's approach in *Arkham Asylum* supplants traditional action-oriented plots with a storyline that almost exclusively functions as a psychological examination of the titular character and his alter ego, Bruce Wayne. It is a work focused on the perils and victories played out in Batman's interior world—not the use of criminal detection, gadgetry, and physical force on the streets of Gotham. Morrison's representation of Batman in *Arkham Asylum* goes against the grain of more traditional depictions and the then-prevailing representation of the character as a man driven by great certitude, judgment, and resourcefulness. In fact, as Morrison notes in one of the annotations to the work, he envisioned his version of Batman as a critique of the "violent, driven and borderline psychopathic"[1] representation of the time. By situating Batman as a patient in need of analysis, Morrison unpacks previous portrayals and reassesses the fundamental aspects of the character. Through this approach, Morrison sheds some of the genre-specific limitations to confer a new sense of artistic weight to the Batman story.

In personal interviews and the notes to the 15th anniversary edition of *Arkham Asylum*, Morrison clarifies that he wants readers to take Batman—and indeed his own work as a writer—seriously. To achieve this effect, Morrison shores together and enhances some of the more intriguing psychological, spiritual, and mythic elements which have cropped up over Batman's lifetime, while also forwarding a narrative arc that stands *suis generis* among the titles featuring the character. Morrison's work achieves much of its edge by interjecting those elements of psychology, esoteric thought, and high art into a world still colored by the conventions of the hero pulps. The result is a work that effectively functions as a postmodern patchwork of quotes drawn from both well-known and more arcane source materials.

In interviews and his annotations to the 15th anniversary edition of *Arkham Asylum*, Morrison discloses a range of artistic antecedents and influences he drew upon when creating his version of Batman, including the writers H.P. Lovecraft and Jorge Luis Borges, and the filmmakers Alfred Hitchcock and David Lynch. Interestingly, each of the aforementioned artists also reveals a common influence in their own works: the American writer Edgar Allan Poe. Given Poe's undeniable presence in their respective creations, one can argue that even though Poe's influence on *Arkham Asylum* may appear indirect, it is clearly the most pervasive and deeply embedded influence operating within the graphic novel. In fact, one can claim that Poe's legacy haunts the entire work. Poe is a shade who never brashly confronts readers, but who always remains disquietingly present in every page, for he plays a role in shaping the three most prominent characters in the work—Amadeus Arkham, Joker and Batman—and their intertwining narratives of deep psychological distress. Poe does much to animate the "serious house," for he is among the asylum's most powerful presiding spirits.

As the father of the detective story, early master of psychological storytelling, and seminal practitioner of the American Gothic subgenre, Poe has long informed the Batman universe. This connection is by no means accidental, for the creators of Batman—Bob Kane and Bill Finger—found inspiration in Poe's work. In fact, Kane and Finger even conceived of the idea for Batman while sitting in Edgar Allan Poe Park in New York City. Despite the fact that Poe also exhibited considerable accomplishments in the realm of psychological fiction, Kane and Finger never fully explored that particular strain of Poe's storytelling legacy during their tenures. That strain, in fact, remained largely unexplored by the writers and artists who followed them for the next 50 years. Indeed, while one may find a psychological undercurrent running through many of Batman's tales, stories focusing on the torturous dynamics of Batman's inner life did not truly appear until Morrison took on the character. In pursuing an intensely rendered psychological angle on Batman, Morrison managed to make Batman and his world even more Poe-like than they had been in any of their prior incarnations.

While *Arkham Asylum* shares in that broader spirit of Poe's work, the work also draws on numerous storytelling approaches and story specifics from Poe's short fiction to realize its tone and narrative ambitions. One clear example of this correspondence is the graphic novel's debt to Poe's story "The System of Doctor Tarr and Professor Fether." In Poe's tale, patients at a mental institution have declared their doctors and nurses insane, locked them up, and started subjecting them to a particularly harsh form of treatment. Such a premise is very much at work in Morrison's graphic novel, where the Joker and other rogues have taken over the asylum where they are housed so that they might subject Batman to treatment. Beyond this broad similarity, *Arkham Asylum* also displays a deep and pervasive correspondence with three of Poe's stronger pieces of psychological fiction: "The Masque of the Red Death," "William Wilson," and "The Fall of the House of Usher."

Poe's nightmarish allegory "The Masque of the Red Death" serves as a literary precursor to *Arkham Asylum* primarily through its use of symbolism and structure. Starting with the settings, which function as some of the most significant characters in both stories, we discover a definite parallel between the tales. Morrison's asylum, likes Poe's castle, is "not only a ritual space but a psychological space."[2] It is also a space riddled with inverted values. Rather than serving their traditional symbolic role as protective environments, the asylum and castle represent exposure and sickness. They are traps for those seeking solace. Like Prince Prospero in Poe's tale, the host of Arkham Asylum, the Joker, carefully arranges the space he presides over so that it renders the utmost psychological impression upon those who must journey through it. In Batman's quest through the asylum, he enters a series of rooms where he confronts various villains, including Clayface, Mad Hatter, Scarecrow, Maxie Zeus, Killer Croc, and Two-Face, each of whom represents aspects of his trauma, fear, and crime fighting career. When viewed beside the

A miniaturized Edgar A. Poe puppet casts a harsh shadow in an Expressionist-style alleyway in George Higham's stop-motion animation film, *Annabel Lee* (2001). Poe's influence on the *Arkham* mythos appears in graphic novels, video games, and some comics. The Expressionist influences on Higham's film evoke the Expressionist aesthetics of early *Batman* comics. Like the players in the *Arkham Asylum* video games, puppet Poe meanders through foreboding spaces, where unseen dangers lurk between corners and crevices, ready to appear out of nowhere.

journey the revelers undergo in Prince Prospero's castle, with its seven rooms representing an increasingly disturbing movement through the stages of life, the similarities between the symbolic value of structural properties in Grant Morrison's text and Poe's text become striking.

Like Poe's mask-wearing revelers, the characters in Morrison's work—most conspicuously Batman and the Joker—also wear masks. In both stories, the masks have a multifaceted representable value. They represent the desire for distancing or an attempt to hide or destroy one's experience or identity. The masks also represent the freedom (however terrifying or terrible) to assume a new identity—one either removed from the burdens of past associations or one capable of leveraging those experiences as a source of singular power. The characters in "The Masque of the Red Death" lock themselves away and don their masks in arrogant reverie as the world outside is ravaged by disease. The revelers incorrectly assume the wealth and social privilege which have allowed them to adopt these personas will also exempt them from lethal infection. Unlike those revelers, the Batman of *Arkham Asylum* surrenders any recourse to the shelter afforded by his alter ego's wealth and status, gives over any protections his mask might afford him when confronting malevolence, and willingly enters that realm of disease. Unlike the Batman of old, though, Morrison's Batman is not on a mission to defy the terms of that realm;

rather, he is on a mission to understand his place in it and how he might be transformed by the experience. While Poe's characters die servicing their pride and privilege, Batman sacrifices his pride and privilege, thereby granting himself the opportunity become a healthier man and greater protector of the people of Gotham than he was before entering the asylum.

Along with using masks as means to explore identity, Morrison also utilizes the double or doppelganger throughout *Arkham Asylum* to expose the inner workings of his characters. Morrison's utilization of the double as a central motif and theme in *Arkham Asylum* shares a range of significant similarities with Poe's short story "William Wilson." Of those similarities, two of the most compelling parallels appear within the main characters themselves. Indeed, when one examines the backstories of William Wilson/William Wilson and Bruce Wayne/Batman, and the personality makeup of those same characters, it becomes evident that they conform to a typology Poe utilized throughout his work. In forming Wilson and characters of a similar type, Poe drew on his own life experiences. Poe had experienced the death of his parents as a child and had been adopted into a wealthy family, only to find himself an outsider within that family. Poe was a headstrong and intelligent child who was desirous of admiration, yet he was also a victim of his own Byronic compulsion towards pleasure and subterfuge.

Although Wilson is no orphan, he is an alienated boy who shares numerous biographical correspondences and personal characteristics with Poe. Like Wilson and, by extension, Poe himself, Bruce Wayne is intelligent, headstrong and ostensibly protected by his parent's affluence, yet he is ultimately orphaned, alienated, given to darkness, and in need of discipline lest he slip into destructive self-indulgence and Joker-like anarchy. In *Arkham Asylum*, Morrison utilizes this volatile amalgam of Batman's characteristics and his ever-present potential to slip into an abyss of negative capability to construct his psychodrama and, by extension, deconstruct the influences which have created a host of actual and implied manifestations of the character since its inception.

Readers will note that Wilson and Wayne are emotionally damaged adults seeking rational explanations and even a sense of expiation in their corrupted worlds. This need for guidance—for authority and regulation—manifests itself in the form of a double. This double, which emerges when both characters are children, is born of an acute crisis of identification and consciousness and always manifests itself when the characters are faced with acts of injustice. In each case, that double serves as a mediator of reality and moral regulator for the characters. It maintains an ethereal presence punctuated by a very real and altogether commanding materialization in times of difficulty, which causes the protagonists to both fear and desire the double's power. Whether it be through the parallel narrative involving Amadeus Arkham or Batman's intimate interactions with the Joker, Morrison's Batman is confronted with the horror of acknowledging his shadow self. As Mark P. Williams notes, "The ultimate enemy of Batman is inevitably a dark twin of Batman, a reflection and a double of an already split personality."[3] On a figurative level, Wilson and Batman function as detectives navigating the mysteries of their respective selfhoods. Their choice to run from, or face, the unsettling revelations presented by their double and recognize that double as part of their identity is at the heart of the conflict in both tales.

Just as Poe illustrates Wilson's struggle to acknowledge his doppelganger, Morrison presents Batman's quest throughout Arkham Asylum as a trial of coming to terms with his own double. In both tales, it is by no means coincidental that the protagonists ultimately confront their doubles in spaces populated by other mask-wearing characters. In such spaces, the double's uncanniness and symbolic power increase through the twisted, mirror-like visages surrounding it. They exist in a world of splinters and iterations. Like William Wilson, Batman is tempted to view murder as the ultimate means of escape from his seemingly monstrous shadow self—a crime he might commit for some measure of respite. In his state of confusion and frailty, Batman's impulse for annihilation becomes powerful enough that he even engages in self-harm by stabbing himself with a shard of glass. However, Batman understands that following through with an act of annihilation would ultimately corrupt his core self. By committing such an act, he would forfeit the moral values and potential for wholeness that separate him from the Joker. Batman chooses to uphold his status as a hero and gain future vitality by stifling his that impulse and constructively responding to his shadow. He once again "learns to be Batman" by "negotiat[ing] a relationship with the Joker"[4]—by facing that other, seemingly incomprehensible self. As Timothy Callahan shows, "Batman is not a fully realized 'self' until the end of the graphic novel. At first, and until he achieves victory over the various shadows (as embodied not only by the Joker, but by the other rogues as well), he is a mere *persona*."[5] On the other hand, Wilson has no interest in facing his double. This makes sense, for the William Wilson narrating the tale is much more Joker than Batman in his twisted views and actions. When Wilson kills his double, he eliminates the possibility of making any concessions which might bring about his betterment and solidifies his identity as corruption incarnate. Interestingly, Wilson's solidification of identity also ensures his dissolution, for an identity based on corruption cannot survive. It will continuously degrade itself in a downward spiral until there is nothing left but darkness.

Among Poe's stories, few serve as a clearer literary antecedent and psychological parallel for *Arkham Asylum* than "The Fall of the House of Usher." Like "William Wilson," Poe builds the narrative in "The Fall of the House of Usher" around his protagonist's anguished and ultimately destructive relationship with his double. Correspondingly, the double also serves a symbolic function in the story that suggests a divided identity and moral or spiritual dilemma. Beyond these broader similarities, though, the nature and expression of Poe's psychological crisis in "The Fall of the House of Usher" bears several important distinctions from the one he presents in "William Wilson." In "The Fall of the House of Usher," Poe does not directly trace the protagonist's disturbed state to specific instances of immoral behavior and a pervasive unwillingness or inability to think and behave within the bounds of moral acceptability. Instead, he presents readers with a subtler, more viscerally suggestive tale of psychological distress. Indeed, the atmosphere of the story is infused with decay, menace, and the specter of terrible secrets, but little of the story directly explains what has caused this atmosphere to emerge. The story's protagonist, Roderick Usher, engages in seemingly inexplicable behaviors which suggest—rather than directly identify—a history marred by strange and unspeakable acts and a present rife with intense personal suffering.

The symbolic features of the Gothic setting, along with Usher's grotesque conduct, give rise to several questions regarding the cause and nature of the character's inner turmoil. Readers are left to consider how repressed guilt, psychosexual disorder and inherited illnesses, such as anxiety and depression, can conspire together to create a waking nightmare for an individual despite his or her uncommon intellectual merits. By drawing on the Poe-influenced works of artists such as Lovecraft and Hitchcock, Morrison mirrors many of these same elements, especially when it comes to their symbolic conventions and thematic emphases. In doing so, Morrison subjects *Arkham Asylum*'s readers to a similar series of questions regarding Batman's own internal makeup and ultimate fitness as a heroic figure. Batman, like Poe's famous detective C. Auguste Dupin, is most certainly an Usherian figure attempting to cut through the tumult so that he can piece together a narrative capable of ordering, and thus ending, the horrors he experiences.

A notable story that features a building as a character, "The Fall of the House of Usher" stands out for its symbolic power. Indeed, in many ways readers learn as much or even more about Usher and his malady through the house than they do through the dialogue and actions of the characters in the story. The house of Usher, with its "black and lurid tarn," "vacant and eye-like windows"[6] and former dungeon turned burial vault, functions as a rich metaphor for Usher himself. Indeed, the title itself—"The Fall of the House of Usher"—refers both to the collapse of the structure and the demise of the final member of the Usher family, Roderick Usher. The same may be said about the structure of Arkham Asylum, Amadeus Arkham and the questing hero of the story, Batman. Indeed, Morrison spells out this very connection by having one of villainous inhabitants of the asylum, the Mad Hatter, explain to Batman that "Sometimes I think the asylum is a head. We're inside a huge head that dreams us all into being. Perhaps it's your head, Batman."[7]

Fittingly, Morrison and his critics emphasize the symbolic elements comprising that space. In the notes Morrison includes with the graphic novel, he explains:

> The story is tightly woven around a small number of symbolic elements, which combine and recombine throughout, as if in a dream [...] The construction of the story was influenced by the architecture of a house—the past and the tale of Amadeus Arkham forms the basement levels. Secret passages connect ideas and segments of the book. There are upper stories of unfolding symbol and metaphor [...] The journey through the book is like moving through the floors of the house itself. The house and the head become one.[8]

One could take the previous description of Arkham Asylum's symbolic construction and emphasis on psychology and largely apply it to the house of Usher, for it follows Poe's conception in large measure. In taking this approach, Morrison makes direct use of the literary Gothicism Poe employed in "The Fall of the House of Usher." This element of Morrison's story might be considered a pastiche or homage to Poe—a thoroughly postmodern bit of recycling. However, within the context of a graphic novel featuring Batman, Morrison's approach is transformative, for it takes conceptual cues from an established literary tradition and realizes them in a medium historically reserved for lighter entertainment. The first clue we receive of such intentions lies in the subtitle of the book itself. Morrison has set himself the task of building "a serious house on serious earth." To build his house, Morrison needs Poe.

Alongside the makeup of his asylum, Morrison utilizes Poe-like symbolic conventions as a means to expose the psychological states of his characters. Morrison's connection to Poe in this regard is perhaps most evident in the parallel narratives of Amadeus Arkham and Batman, where he explores repression and psychosis through a series of symbolic female figures (a daughter, mothers and feminized Joker) who serve as expressions of Carl Jung's female archetype, the anima. While Morrison's use of the female figure and anatomical traits (namely abstracted vaginas) point at times to a modern source—namely Hitchcock's *Psycho* and its attendant psycho-sexual readings—it also very much maintains a connection to Poe, a writer for whom dead or dying female figures were "the most poetical topic in the world."[9] Beyond the market considerations of employing such a "poetical" topic, Poe understood the power of the female and feminine principle within male consciousness. Indeed, some of the most memorable male characters in Poe's poems and stories lead tortured inner lives because of their fraught relationships with dead or dying females who simultaneously function as real-world partners and metaphorical signifiers for what is missing in the men. With such characters, Poe uses the female as a cipher to draw out the origins of a psychological or spiritual imbalance within the male characters. In Poe and Morrison, we find also find Jung's anima taking on the aspect of the devouring mother.

Throughout "The Fall of the House of Usher," readers discover that much of Roderick Usher's distress—and his ultimate downfall—may in fact be traced to his bizarre and seemingly unwholesome relationship with his twin sister, Madeline. Madeline represents a crucial part of Roderick that has been buried but not fully relinquished—less an actual sister than an element of his psyche that he has deemed diseased and better removed to the depths of his estate. Relatedly, Morrison's portrayal of Amadeus Arkham's obsessiveness, eventual loss of sanity, and nefarious behavior appears to be rooted in the corrupted or murdered female figures in his life. They are, like Madeline, emblematic of Amadeus Arkham's psychological dissolution. In similar form, Batman's familial trauma and his combative relationship with a twin-like, gender-inverted Joker also suggest that Batman's deeply troubled involvement with the corrupted female figure or feminine principle has driven him to point of psychological crisis.

As many readings of "The Fall of the House of Usher" have asserted, Roderick Usher, Madeline and even the narrator of the tale all constitute a single being who has undergone a fracturing of identity. Viewed in this light, the hints of incest and vampirism Poe writes into the story suggest a self-consuming obsession on the part of Roderick Usher—a spawning of shadow selves capable of warping his sensibilities and draining away his vitality. The whole of the Usher family's history, with its aristocratic remove and indications of inbreeding, occurs within that asphyxiating space of a closed circle. It is a once hermetically sealed existence where the sickness within has started to leach into the visible realm with horrifying results. Roderick Usher, it seems, is the tragic final expression of a genetic and psychic trap that once appeared to protect the unity and ostensible purity of the Usher family.

Amadeus Arkham exists in a state analogous to the one Roderick Usher inhabits. Like Usher, Arkham's past points to incestuous and vampiric behavior—acts born of a deep-seated corruption. In Arkham's words, his sickness is an inevitable result of his heredity: "Madness is born in the blood. It is my birthright." As much as Arkham's incest and familial cannibalism reveal his incontestable monstrousness to readers, these acts also expose his all-consuming obsession with consolidating the pieces of a shattered self and drawing vitality from an ostensibly uncorrupted feminine principle that has long escaped him. Just as Amadeus Arkham preys on his family before creating a closed circle to capture the bat, Batman metaphorically preys on his dead family so that he might acquire the strength to capture his nemesis, the Joker. Batman is caught in a seemingly inescapable circle of trauma and violence. What struck some readers as odd behavior for the fearless, action-oriented Batman of comic books past—Morrison's casting of the hero as a weakened man shrinking from expressions of evil and engaging in self-harm before crying out for his mother—makes sense within this symbolic schema. This is a Batman tangled up in his anima, a Batman battling through the malevolent aspects of himself, lest he become a figure like the Joker, Amadeus Arkham, Norman Bates, or Roderick Usher.

As a result of his malady, or perhaps as a compensatory response to it, Roderick Usher has developed heightened senses and an extreme artistic sensibility. The Joker of *Arkham Asylum* exhibits a comparable condition. A psychotherapist in Arkham Asylum, Ruth Adams, explains to Batman that the Joker's insanity may indeed be a form of "super sanity," which she notes "is a brilliant new modification of human perception."[10] The Joker, it seems, has relinquished his unified sense of self and the ability to filter the myriad influences at play in his environment at a given time. He is a performance artist who has given himself over to an anarchy and perpetual possession; he is a trickster with no center. In discussing Joker's role as a trickster, Hannah Means-Shannon observes that "While the trickster represents a collective social 'dark side,' it relates to an inner 'dark side' known as the shadow."[11] Means-Shannon maintains that Morrison "reinterprets Batman as a response to the Joker, to such an extent that he reimagines Batman's psyche as a direct adaptation of Joker's without the homicidal tendencies."[12] Brilliant or not, the Joker's way of viewing and interacting with the world appears untenable in Batman's eyes, perhaps for no other reason than it is antithetical to the sense of regulation, justice, and peace the hero desperately craves. Batman's will to power is a will to render the world into a rational, rule-bound space.

Curiously, whereas Poe makes it clear that Roderick Usher's powerful perceptual mutations and artistic manifestations cannot help him survive in an outside world constructed of more rational, less volatile stuff, Morrison questions whether that rational outside world—the one Batman most desires—even exists outside of our imagination. Morrison asks readers to consider the Joker's core claim: only the foolish or insane would impose a sense of order and goodness on this undeniably fallen world. In using the Joker to raise such a question, Morrison prompts readers to examine rationality and moral fitness of Batman's raison d'être.

If the Joker, as chief therapist at Arkham Asylum, has exposed Batman's deepest delusion, then what choices does the hero have when it comes to pursuing meaningful truths? Will he leave the Joker unchecked or even join him in his liberating nihilism? By adopting the Joker's perspective, Batman would grant chaos victory over meaning. In the Joker's words, such a choice would allow Batman to join him in claiming his so-called "kingly robes." However, the price of acquiring that sense of awareness and license would prove Faustian, for it would require Batman to admit a traumatic fracturing of identity as a permanent state, to sell himself over to the hell of unmitigated chaos. When the Joker asks Batman to face down his internal chaos or surrender to the ways of that chaos by joining the inhabitants of the asylum, he is presenting Batman with a deeper choice of meaning-making and identification. Should Batman, then, retreat into the reassuring sublimations and inventions of days past? Can those provisions still suffice given his experience in the asylum? Should Batman take the life-affirming existentialist's approach by creating meaning in the face of chaos? That choice would seem a heroic. Or should Batman leave the decision to some power beyond his grasp—perhaps fate?

In a fascinating final parallel with Roderick Usher, whom Poe presents as having no choice but to accept a fate that has been in the making for generations, Batman's release from the asylum comes not with an action-packed showdown where he imposes his will on an opponent, but with the toss of Two-Face's coin. That coin represents Batman relinquishing an illusion of personal control and giving himself over to a cosmic sense of order. Obliquely, it also suggests Batman has gained a sense of solidity and confidence in his path. The irony and ambiguity inherent in such a "choice" and result, coupled with

Hush action figure by DC Direct portrays the bandaged Dr. Tommy Elliott, Bruce Wayne's equally affluent neighbor who orchestrated the death of his father and crippled his mother when he was a child. Although Tommy becomes a surgeon, he envies Bruce and assumes his identity, undergoing plastic surgery to make him resemble Bruce (and hence the facial bandages). Poe's influence reverberates throughout the *Arkham* universe but emerges in full force in *Batman: Hush* (2002–2003), where Jeph Loeb includes Poe's "Purloined Letter" in his story's plot (photograph by George Higham).

the Joker's final reminder that there's always a place for Batman in the asylum, suggests that Batman's triumph is unwilled and temporary. Nonetheless, Morrison informs readers that Batman "has vanquished his shadow. He has merged with his own myth—the Death Bat—and become part man, part numinous legend."[13] Readers, then, leave the text understanding that Batman has gained a profound sense of integrity. Unlike Usher, he has cleansed and stabilized his house.

Fans and critics maintain mixed views regarding Morrison's experiment with Batman in *Arkham Asylum*, particularly when it comes to the work's dense psychological symbolism and literary styling. Viewed favorably or not, it is evident that the work exposes the innerworkings of the hero in manner that still proves illuminating. In looking back at Morrison's tenure with Batman, Mitch Frye sums up his work as "an essentially Lacanian project, with the author offering a psychoanalysis of the Batman's editorial history and identity crisis."[14] That psychoanalytic approach and its attendant connection to Poe continued in Morrison's *Batman: Gothic* (1990) and carried on well after Morrison's time with Batman. Indeed, Poe's influence emerged 12 years later in *Batman: Hush* (2002–2003) when Jeph Loeb chose to include Poe's "Purloined Letter" in his story's plot. During the same period, Len Wein's *Batman: Nevermore* (2003) made liberal use of Poe and his legacy as a writer by actually turning Poe into a character who teams up with Batman in order to solve a series of crimes. Shortly thereafter, in Michael Green's work for the *Batman: Confidential* (2006–2011) series, Batman names one of his most crucial investigative tools—his computer—"Dupin" after Poe's famous detective. Poe, it seems, inhabits the Batcave even as he inhabits Arkham Asylum.

Notes

1. Grant Morrison, *Arkham Asylum: A Serious House on Serious Earth, 15th Anniversary Edition* (New York: DC Comics, 2004).
2. Hannah Means-Shannon, "The Joker Plays King: Archetypes of the Underworld in Grant Morrison and Dave McKean's *Arkham Asylum: A Serious House on Series Earth*," in *The Joker: A Serious Study of the Clown Prince of Crime*, ed. Robert Moses Peaslee and Robert G. Weiner (Jackson, MS: University Press of Mississippi, 2015), 202.
3. Mark P. Williams, "Making Sense Squared: Iteration and Synthesis in Grant Morrison's Joker," in *The Joker: A Serious Study of the Clown Prince of Crime*, ed. Robert Moses Peaslee and Robert G. Weiner (Jackson, MS: University Press of Mississippi, 2015), 221.
4. Williams, "Making Sense Squared," 226.
5. Timothy Callahan, *Grant Morrison: The Early Years* (Edwardsville, IL: Sequart Research & Literacy Organization, 2007), 52.
6. Edgar Allan Poe, *Works of Edgar Allan Poe: Sixty-seven Tales, One Complete Novel and Thirty-one Poems* (New York: Gramercy, 1990), 199.
7. Morrison, *Arkham Asylum*.
8. *Ibid.*
9. Edgar Allan Poe, "The Philosophy of Composition," *Poetry Foundation*, October 13, 2009, www.poetryfoundation.org/resources/learning/essays/detail/69390.
10. Morrison, *Ibid.*
11. Means-Shannon, "The Joker Plays King," 195.
12. *Ibid.*, 212.
13. Morrison, *Ibid.*
14. Mitch Frye, "Seminar on the Purloined Batarang," in *Riddle Me This, Batman! Essays on the Universe of the Dark Knight*, ed. Kevin K. Durand and Mark K. Leigh (Jefferson, NC: McFarland, 2011), 101.

H.P. Lovecraft, Literary Heritage and *Batman: Arkham Asylum*

Eric Sandberg

Many players of *Batman: Arkham Asylum* will be aware of the game's rich comic book heritage. Batman first appeared in *Detective Comics #27* in 1939, and the video game is thus part of a seventy-year long cultural legacy that includes a formidable array of adaptations, appropriations, and revisions. Fewer gamers, however, will be aware of its equally rich, and even older, literary heritage in the works of the early twentieth century master of weird fiction, Howard Philips Lovecraft.

Many of those closely involved in the development of Batman as a character have acknowledged their debt to Lovecraft. Comic book artist Neal Adams, for example, relates how in 1970 he and writer Dennis O'Neil were inspired by both Lovecraft and Edgar Allan Poe. They began to create "Gothic and Spooky" adventures in which Batman, who at that point in his career was a relatively light-hearted character, appeared "like a fish out of water."[1] *Batman: Arkham Asylum*'s eponymous sanatorium entered the Batman universe only four years later, appearing first as the Arkham Hospital in O'Neil's "Threat of the Two Headed Coin" in *Batman #258*. As former DC Comics editor Jack C. Harris writes:

> One summer, I immersed myself in the dark works of H.P. Lovecraft, reading his ghastly and gruesome tales of nether gods and loathsome creatures from the depths of Hell. It was during a conversation with writer Denny O'Neil, before I had even graduated from college, that I suggested that Batman villains such as Two-Face and Joker should never be housed in a common prison; they should be locked away in an insane asylum. And what better asylum could there be for such maniacs than Arkham, the dark dwelling of the tormented souls from Lovecraft's horrific tales?[2]

Thus, the first appearance of the Arkham Asylum in the Batman universe is directly connected to Lovecraft, both as an act of homage to his fiction, and as a way of linking Batman to its disturbing implications. While some readers would contest Harris's characterization of Lovecraft's work (for example, the idea that its monsters arise from "the depths of Hell" is misleading), this acknowledgment of the role of Lovecraft's tales as a source of inspiration in the development of Batman is important.

The asylum has proved a useful addition to the fictional landscape of the Batman comics, as demonstrated by the regularity with which it is has appeared, including—to single out a few highlights—in Grant Morrison's 1989 Dark Age graphic novel *Arkham Asylum: A Serious House on Serious Earth,* and Dan Slott's 2003 six-issue miniseries

Arkham Asylum: Living Hell. Gradually, the dark, morbid, and disturbing atmosphere associated with the asylum—which might well be described as Lovecraftian—has become the default mode for work done in the Batman universe, replacing the earlier playful—even camp—sensibility represented by ABC's 1966-1968 television series *Batman*. Frank Miller's influential 1986 miniseries *The Dark Knight* represents a watershed in the rebranding of Batman as a site of somber, troubled narratives, but it is also possible to attribute this tonal shift, at least in part, to the example and inspiration of Lovecraft. This is, of course, the transformation that has saved Batman from the cultural irrelevance of so many of his crime-fighting peers: without Lovecraft, then, it is likely that Batman would be sharing an ignoble retirement with the likes of Plastic Man instead of appearing in a stream of successful movies and video game adaptations, all of which rely on the darkness of the Dark Knight for their appeal. It is thus well worth considering in more detail the Lovecraftian heritage of Rocksteady Studios' video game.

H.P. Lovecraft: From Obscurity to the Mainstream

During his lifetime, few would have considered Lovecraft to be anything other than a culturally peripheral writer of minimal literary significance. He first published his stories in journals and papers associated with the amateur journalism movement of the late nineteenth and early twentieth centuries. According to S.T. Joshi, these magazines tended to fall in terms of production values, quality, and content somewhere between the relatively high-brow and high-status "little magazines" of the period (often associated with prestigious modernist literary experimentation) and the genre-specific "fanzines" of the later twentieth century.[3] Examples include *The Vagrant*, where early stories like "The Statement of Randolph Carter" and "Dagon" first appeared, and *The United Amateur*, which published "Nyarlathotep" in 1920. Much of his later work appeared in pulp magazines like *Weird Tales* and *Astounding Stories*. Lovecraft's death in 1937 was reported in the March 16 issue of the *New York Times*, but as indicated by the headline "Writer Charts Fatal Malady," this posthumous attention was attributable more to the oddity of the "death diary" he kept chronicling his prolonged and horribly painful illness than to his literary reputation.[4] While his death was certainly noticed and mourned within the limited circles of amateur journalism and weird fiction, if it were not for the dedicated efforts of a number of associates and fans, it is likely that his work would have been forgotten by posterity, at least in the short run. Its survival is largely due to the dedicated efforts of a few individuals, particularly August Derleth, co-founder of the publishing company Arkham House, to collect and publish his work in more durable and accessible forms.

Despite these unpropitious beginnings, there are few American writers of Lovecraft's era who have had a more pronounced and lasting impact on both literary and popular culture. Lovecraft's writing has spawned countless imitations, ranging from the hundreds of fanfiction stories available on the Internet, to the many volumes of Lovecraftian tales published by professional authors. His broader impact on the weird and horror genres is equally significant: no less a figure than Stephen King has described Lovecraft as a "viscerally important" writer.[5] Finally, the gradual introduction of Lovecraftian moods, tropes, and themes into the Batman universe discussed above is but a single example of what has been described as the "gradual percolation of elements of Lovecraftian horror into mainstream popular culture."[6] His characters, settings, and themes have appeared in many comic books since what Mark Jones identifies as the first full-length exploitation of his work in a double-issue 1962 *Justice League of America* story, while the Cthulhu-for-America movement (why vote for the "the middling or lesser evil"?) is an example of Lovecraft's wider cultural influence.[7] The role-playing game *Call of Cthulhu*, first published in 1981, and the 1987 co-operative board game *Arkham Horror*, both of which are still in print, speak to the strong connections between Lovecraft's fiction and gaming communities. There have even been a number of video games based more directly on Lovecraft than *Batman: Arkham Asylum*, although none have been as conspicuously successful in critical and commercial terms. This may change with the release of Focus Home Interactive's *Call of Cthulhu: The Official Video Game* in late 2017, which promises to focus on one of the central themes of Lovecraft's fiction, madness—a theme which is of course central to *Batman: Arkham Asylum*.[8]

Even within the more rarified world of literary and academic culture, Lovecraft's work has steadily gained in both popularity and reputability. The sort of dismissive assessment exemplified by Edmund Wilson's 1945 "Tales of the Marvellous and the Ridiculous," in which he describes Lovecraft's stories as "hack-work" epitomizing "bad taste and bad art" has yielded to the type of institutionalized respectability indicated by the publication of his work in the Library of America in 2005, where it now appears alongside the writings of luminaries ranging from Sherwood Anderson to Edith Wharton, and, in an amusing irony, Edmund Wilson himself.[9] Similarly, academic and critical studies have multiplied, and Lovecraft has even become a central figure in an influential school of contemporary philosophy known as "Speculative Realism."[10]

Lovecraft and Madness: Life and Work

Lovecraft's astounding posthumous success is attributable to many factors—the general increase in the popularity and social acceptability of speculative and fantastic narratives is certainly significant—but his exploration of insanity as a response to the conditions of modernity (albeit conditions filtered through a fantastic imagination) is of central importance, and clearly resonates with the underlying narrative of *Batman: Arkham Asylum*.

It is certainly significant that Lovecraft's life was lived against a background of traumatic mental illness. In April 1893, when Lovecraft was a young child, his father was committed to Butler Hospital in Providence, Rhode Island, where he remained for five years until his death in 1898. This institution originated in the 1841 bequest of one Nicholas Brown, who left $30,000 for the construction of a facility "where the unhappy portion of our fellow beings who are by the visitation of Providence deprived of their reason, may find a safe retreat […]."[11] The hospital is thus the original, if indirect, inspiration for the setting of *Batman: Arkham Asylum*.

Despite its enlightened attitude towards mental health—the institution aimed not just at the protection of the mentally ill, but at the amelioration of their illnesses—there was little Butler Hospital could do for Lovecraft's father. His medical record describes him as being admitted with "obscure symptoms"—terminology which in its ominous ambiguity will resonate with any reader of Lovecraft's work—ranging from "doing and saying strange things" to hallucinations (of his wife's sexual violation) culminating in "extremely noisy and violent behavior."[12] At his death, he was diagnosed as suffering from an anodyne "General Paralysis," but his symptoms (periodic aggressiveness, outbreaks of violent behavior, periodic paranoia, and an exaggerated and delusional sense of self-worth, gradually developing into convulsions, dementia, and a range of painful physical symptoms including ulcers and lesions) are very likely to have arisen from late-stage syphilis.[13] While Lovecraft himself in all likelihood knew little or nothing of the specifics of his father's illness, it is very likely, as his biographer S.T. Joshi argues, that he thought about it a great deal, particularly given his own experiences of mental illness.[14]

These began not long after his father was hospitalized, when Lovecraft began to experience what he described as "nightmares of the most hideous description."[15] In 1898, the same year his father died, he had the first of four nervous breakdowns. While details of these collapses are unavailable, it is clear that Lovecraft's mental condition was poor, ensuring, as Joshi writes, that "he would never lead a 'normal' life."[16] In 1904 a further blow to the family fortunes—his grandfather's death—forced Lovecraft and his mother to leave their beloved home, an event which left Lovecraft disoriented, depressed and, perhaps, suicidal.[17] His lack of mental stability interfered with his studies—he neither graduated from high school nor matriculated at university, despite his clear intellectual aptitude and professed intentions— and spent the years between 1908 and 1913 in isolation, doing little and seeing almost no one. His difficult and probably unhealthy relationship with his mother, with whom he lived alone after his grandfather's death, continued until her death in 1921—a death which came after two years spent in the Butler Hospital, where she was committed for psychological "infirmity & absence," to use Lovecraft's characterization of her condition.[18] Given, then, the fact that both of his parents died in an asylum, and that he himself suffered from mental illness at least intermittently, it is unsurprising that madness appears as central theme in his fiction. While many notable early twentieth century writers were fascinated by insanity and mental aberration, few have articulated more clearly, have evoked more

Cthulhu statue, sculpted by Jason Soles and photographed by George Higham, is based on a relic from Lovecraft's short story, "The Call of Cthulhu." Lovecraft's influence infiltrates the *Arkham* mythos, which borrows the name "Arkham" from a fictional Lovecraft city and which adds "Lovecraftian" character traits to *Arkham's* anti-heroes. Lovecraft's family history of mental illness mirrors major plot points, for both his father and his mother died in psychiatric asylums.

powerfully, and presented more hauntingly dislocated states of consciousness, or have made madness so central to their fiction.[19]

While Lovecraft's writing career was short, lasting roughly fifteen years, he produced a relatively large body of work, and in much of it, insanity plays a significant role. At times, a loss of mental stability occurs as a response to self-alienation. In the macabre tale "The Outsider," for example, the narrator is seen by others—and sees himself—as an "uncanny compound of all that is unclean, uncanny, unwelcome, abnormal, and detestable."[20] Generally, however, this fierce loathing is not directed inwards, but arises from the nature of the world, which is figured in Lovecraft's fiction as a place of dread, terror, and disgust. This occurs through the deployment of what has come to be called the "Cthulhu mythos," an alternate history of the world which radically de-centers humanity, relegating it to the role of a late-coming intruder on a planet vastly older and stranger than conventional history suggests. The creatures of inconceivable power and cruelty whose existence is gradually revealed to Lovecraft's characters through investigation and terrifying first-hand experience are the fictional embodiments of a world-view characterized by what Joshi has described with considerable restraint as a "bleak vision of the world and humanity's place in it."[21] Houellebecq's claim that few authors "have ever been so impregnated, pierced to the core, by the conviction of the absolute futility of human aspiration" makes the same point in considerably stronger terms.[22]

In many of Lovecraft's tales, the response to this existential condition is insanity. "The Call of Cthulhu," for example, opens with a clear assertion of the connection: "We live," the narrator claims, "on a placid island of ignorance in the midst of black seas of infinity": should true knowledge come to us, we will "go mad from the revelation."[23] This possibility—even inevitability—is central to Lovecraftian narrative, in which to understand the true nature of the world is to be condemned, at least metaphorically, to the asylum. It is this fundamental fact that most strongly connects Lovecraft's to *Batman: Arkham Asylum*.

Lovecraftian Elements in Batman: Arkham Asylum

It is certainly true that by the time Arkham and its sanatorium appear in Rocksteady Studios' video game, few of the details of Lovecraft's work remain completely intact. A player need have no familiarity with Lovecraft's work to enjoy and appreciate the dramatic gameplay and multiple narrative strands of *Batman: Arkham Asylum*, yet there are significant parallels between the two that can significantly enrich our understanding of the game as a cultural phenomenon.

The most obvious point of connection is the game's setting. While Butler Hospital may well be in some sense the "original" Lovecraftian asylum, it had already been transposed in Lovecraft's fiction from Providence, Rhode Island, to the fictional town of Arkham, Massachusetts. This town is the center of what is now often called "Lovecraft Country," described in the short story "The Picture in the House" in which Arkhamcenterrst mentioned as "backwoods New England" where the "dark elements of strength, solitude, grotesqueness, and ignorance combine to form the perfection of the hideous."[24] Throughout Lovecraft's work the town is associated with an intangible but persistent sense of horror and decay. Its dreadful past, its "traditions of horror, madness, and witchcraft," have left it open to malign influences in the present day; it is a "crumbling, whisper-haunted" place with "a peculiar vulnerability as regards [...] shadows."[25] This relationship between the town's mysterious past and its terrifying present recurs throughout Lovecraft's oeuvre: Arkham is indeed a "legend-haunted city."[26]

When Arkham (in the shape of the Arkham Asylum) entered the Batman universe, it moved first to the outskirts of Gotham City in comic books and graphic novels, and then to a sprawling complex on an island off the city's coast in the video game, yet as it did so it carried with it many of the characteristics of Lovecraft's most famous setting. Consider, for example, the games' Arkham Chronicle Stones which describe Gotham as a "cursed city" doomed by its past to its present sufferings.[27] Even the appearance of the game's asylum complex bears a physical resemblance to Lovecraft's city with its "clustering gambrel roofs" and "hoary willows."[28] Add to this the eerie, greenish moonlight that illuminates so many of the game's outdoor scenes, which could be compared with, for example, the eponymous colour "not [...] of our earth or heavens" which haunts "the blasted heath" in "The Color Out of Space," and you have a game-world that is at least in part recognizably Lovecraftian.

Of course, the game's setting in the Arkham Asylum is important not just because of physical resemblances, but because of the way it ties in with the theme of madness. There is an important difference here, however, between the video game and Lovecraft's stories. In the latter, mental disturbance generally arises from the encounter between a story's central figure and a terrifying, hidden secret. The protagonist learns too much, or experiences too much, and goes mad as a result: the secrets uncovered, the things seen, are so appalling that this is the only option, and the narrative may well end in the protective environment of the asylum. In "The Festival," for instance, the narrator discovers the truth of "the earth's inner horrors" and, although he survives his encounter with the unspeakable is consigned to "St. Mary's Hospital in Arkham" for treatment for "'psychosis'" and "harassing obsessions."[29] Even more strikingly, in "The Thing on the Doorstep" the narrator kills his best friend, who has been committed to "Arkham Sanatorium" due to his own supernatural experiences, and is likely to end up there himself as his ostensibly rational narrative of the events leading up to the murder (the story itself) will certainly be interpreted as the "wild tales" of a madman.[30] Thus the asylum works in Lovecraft as both a narrative end point, and as a minimal shelter from the terrifying nature of the "real" world. This of course represents a radically different philosophy to that espoused in *Batman: Arkham Asylum* in which the asylum exists less to protect or cure the inmates (despite the unsuccessful attempts in this direction recorded in the game's "interview tapes") than to protect the world outside it from them (with, but for Batman's intervention, a signal lack of success). Another important difference is that while the asylum remains a locus of insanity, Batman himself enters it as an outsider: madness is the problem he confronts, and as epitomized by the Joker and his minions, the enemy he must defeat, rather than the inevitable end result of his own adventures.

Scarecrow: A Lovecraftian Figure

Players of the video game will be quick to point out that there are several prominent exceptions to this generalization surrounding Batman's encounters with Scarecrow. As Benjamin Beil has pointed out, while this character belongs to one of the game's many side-narratives, his three appearances "stand out as especially intense sequences," and they are also particularly interesting in terms of the game's relationship to Lovecraft.[31] Firstly, the three cut-scenes introducing Scarecrow's appearances rely on typically Lovecraftian tropes. In the first, Batman both inhales a "fear toxin" himself, and witnesses its horrifying effects on others. This is directly comparable to Houellebecq's description of Lovecraft's writing as "an open slice of howling fear."[32] It also makes Batman himself, rendered throughout the game as a figure of extreme, if not unstoppable, power vulnerable. As the cut-scene ends and game play resumes the influence of the hallucinogenic drug leads to a number of unsettling—both for the character of Batman and possibly for the player controlling him—elements, such as repeating corridors and rooms, and the apparent death of Commissioner Gordon. The second Scarecrow cut-scene relies on a similar deformation of game-world reality, as Batman enters an endless corridor in which his normal range of actions is unavailable to the player. The hallway gradually transforms into the alley in which his parents were murdered many years ago, while Batman himself becomes a child again. In both cases, the player is left uncertain as the reality-status of what he is observing and participating in, at least until the game's normal status resumes. This is comparable to the profound ontological uncertainty that permeates Lovecraft's narratives, the way in which they constantly challenge their protagonists' sense of what and how the world is. This "narrative unreliability," to use Beil's phrase, is an even more prominent feature of the final Scarecrow cut scene, which uses an apparent technical malfunction to interrupt the game's diegesis, or unfolding narrative. This is followed by an apparent "re-boot" in which the game restarts but with Batman and the Joker's positions exchanged: it is Batman now who is "quite insane" and is being committed to Arkham Asylum by the Joker and his minions.[33] This is, of course, a more Lovecraftian subject position than that which the game normally offers: the equation of the central figure, and thus the player, with stability, order, and rationality is undercut (if only temporarily) by their vulnerability to the mental instability which threatens them and their world.

Of course, this is a video game, so the cut-scenes inevitably give way to the action sequences that constitute the heart of the player experience. But the Scarecrow game sequences that follow these three cut-scenes are also Lovecraftian in an interesting way. Throughout much of the game, players "interact" with their opponents through its much-praised fighting system.[34] While some of Batman's opponents are more difficult to defeat in combat than others, they are all ultimately vulnerable to a particular combat tactic, at least at the hands of a competent player—with the notable exception of Scarecrow. At the conclusion of each of his three cut-scenes, Batman enters a surreal, crumbling obstacle course made up of fragments of the asylum's architecture and landscape surrounding the gigantic, invincible figure of Scarecrow. Rather than kicking, punching, and otherwise manhandling his opponent, the game mechanic here demands that Batman avoid Scarecrow's deadly gaze until he can make his way to a spotlight and project a Bat-signal, which Beil describes as "a manifestation of Batman's willpower," at his enemy.[35] If Scarecrow sees the player, Batman is killed, and the player is offered one of a number of particularly Lovecraftian endgame screens: "And at the end of fear, oblivion."[36] Even if defeated by the Bat-signal, however, Scarecrow reappears to torment Batman (and the player) again.

It is worth comparing these encounters with "The Call of Cthulhu"—the best-known story in Lovecraft's oeuvre—in which the Norwegian seaman Gustaf Johansen encounters the dread Cthulhu in all his terrifying "gelatinous green immensity."[37] This epitome of "shrieking and immemorial lunacy" cannot be fought, only fled.[38] Even when shattered by a collision with Johansen's ship, Cthulhu simply recombines in its "hateful original form."[39] This sort of encounter, between an ordinary man and an inconceivably powerful and utterly undefeatable force of unimaginable malignancy is quintessentially Lovecraftian, and is one of the strongest links between *Batman: Arkham Asylum* and its literary heritage.[40]

Conclusion

If Scarecrow's role in *Batman: Arkham Asylum*, both in terms of the cut-scenes and the unconventional actions sequences in which Batman faces an "undefeatable" enemy represents a powerful connection between the game and the world of Lovecraft's fiction, it also points us in the direction of the single most important distinction between the two. For, while Scarecrow-like Cthulhu is terrifying, powerful, and otherworldly, he is ultimately overcome by Batman: after the third action sequence, the oversized Scarecrow is revealed as a drug-induced hallucination. The "real," human-scale Scarecrow ends up being himself devoured (or at least dragged into the sewers) by another villainous character, Killer Croc, who Batman can then pursue and defeat using his normal equipment and abilities.

This deflation, from mind-numbing horror to routine game play is repeated on a larger scale in the game as a whole. For while in the world of Lovecraftian horror, protagonists face inevitable defeat, death, or madness, no matter how carefully they proceed, how thoroughly they investigate, or how quickly they run (even the sailor Johansen ends up dead, presumably at the hands of cultists, despite his temporary escape from Cthulhu) exactly the opposite is true in *Batman: Arkham Asylum*. In the video game, the player inevitably wins, defeating not just Scarecrow, but all of the villains he faces, including the Joker as a manifestation of madness. They may need to face many taunting game-over screens, may need to replay individual sequences until the particular moves required to defeat a particular opponent or group of opponents are mastered, or even consult online guides and walk-throughs, but with persistence the game has only one ending: Joker defeated, the Asylum brought back under control, and the anarchic energies of madness contained. Nothing could be further from relentless progress of Lovecraft's fiction towards its fundamental realization: that existence terrifyingly exceeds the capacity of humanity to control, or even bear, its horrors.

NOTES

1. Les Daniels, *Batman: The Complete History* (San Francisco: First Chronicle Books 2004), 138.
2. Jack C. Harris, foreword to *The Dark Age: Grim, Great & Gimmicky Post-Modern Comics*, by Mark Voger (Raleigh, NC: TwoMorrows Publishing, 2006), 5.
3. S.T. Joshi, *H.P. Lovecraft: A Life* (West Warwick, RI: Necronomicon Press, 1996), 98.
4. Joshi, *H.P. Lovecraft: A Life*, 630.
5. Stephen King, "Lovecraft's Pillow," introduction to *H.P. Lovecraft: Against the World, Against Life* by Michel Houellebecq (San Francisco: Believer Books, 2005), 14.
6. Mark Jones, "Tentacles and Teeth: the Lovecraftian Being in Popular Culture," in *New Critical Essay on H.P. Lovecraft*, ed. David Simmons (New York: Palgrave, 2013), 226.
7. Ibid., 234. "Meet Cthulhu." *Cthulhu for America*, accessed March 16, 2017, https://cthulhuforamerica.com/about/.
8. Blair Marnell, "New CALL OF CTHULHU Game Trailer Embraces Lovecraftian Madness," last modified January 23, 2017, accessed April 26, 2017, http://nerdist.com/new-call-of-cthulhu-game-trailer-embraces-lovecraftian-madness/.
9. Edmund Wilson, "Tales of the Marvellous and the Ridiculous," in *H.P. Lovecraft: Four Decades of Criticism*, ed. S.T. Joshi (Athens, OH: Ohio State University Press, 1980), 47.

10. See Graham Harman, *Weird Realism: Lovecraft and Philosophy* (Alresford, Hants.: 2012).
11. The Trustees and Superintendent of the Butler Hospital, *The Butler Hospital: Its Story* (n.p. 1926), http://archive.org/details/butlerbook.
12. Quoted in Joshi, *H.P. Lovecraft: A Life*, 13.
13. Joshi, *H.P. Lovecraft: A Life*, 13–14.
14. *Ibid.*, 15.
15. Quoted in Joshi, *H.P. Lovecraft: A Life*, 20.
16. *Ibid.*, 80.
17. Joshi, *H.P. Lovecraft: A Life*, 80.
18. Quoted in Joshi, *H.P. Lovecraft: A Life*, 191.
19. *Ibid.*, 53.
20. H.P. Lovecraft, "The Outsider," in *The Complete Fiction of H.P. Lovecraft* (New York: Chartwell Books, 2016), 180.
21. S.T. Joshi, "Lovecraft and a World in Transition," in Lovecraft and a World in Transition: Collected Essays on H.P. Lovecraft, by S.T. Joshi (New York: Hippocampus Press, 2014), 155.
22. Houellebecq, *H.P. Lovecraft*, 32.
23. H.P. Lovecraft, "The Call of Cthuhlu," in *The Complete Fiction of H.P. Lovecraft* (New York: Chartwell Books, 2016), 381.
24. H.P. Lovecraft, "The Picture in the House," in the Complete Fiction of H.P. Lovecraft (New York: Chartwell Books, 2016), 103. This story was written in late 1920, and first appeared—confusingly enough—in the July 1919 edition of *National Amateur*, which did not appear in print until 1921. See Joshi, *H.P. Lovecraft: A Life*, 242–245.
25. H.P. Lovecraft, "The Shadow Out of Time," in *The Complete Fiction of H.P. Lovecraft* (New York: Chartwell Books, 2016), 1022.
26. H.P. Lovecraft, "The Dreams in the Witch House," in *The Complete Fiction of H.P. Lovecraft* (New York: Chartwell Books, 2016), 924.
27. "Spirit of Arkham," *Batman Arkham Wiki*, http://arkhamcity.wikia.com/wiki/Spirit_of_Arkham
28. H.P. Lovecraft, "The Dreams in the Witch House," 924.; H.P. Lovecraft, "The Silver Key," in *The Complete Fiction of H.P. Lovecraft* (New York: Chartwell Books, 2016), 432.
29. H.P. Lovecraft, "The Festival," in *The Complete Fiction of H.P. Lovecraft* (New York: Chartwell Books, 2016), 287–288.
30. H.P. Lovecraft, "The Thing on the Doorstep," in *The Complete Fiction of H.P. Lovecraft* (New York: Chartwell Books, 2016), 990.
31. Benjamin Beil, "Film Aesthetics and Interactive Representations of Subjectivity in Video Games," in *Subjectivity Across Media: Interdisciplinary and Transmedial Perspectives*, ed. Maike Sarah Reinerth and Jan-Noël Thon (New York: Routledge, 2017), 189.
32. Houellebecq, *H.P. Lovecraft: Against the World, Against Life*, 53.
33. Rocksteady Studios. *Batman: Arkham Asylum*. 2009. PC.
34. See Greg Miller's review of the game at http://www.ign.com/articles/2010/05/27/batman-arkham-asylum-game-of-the-year-review?page = 1 for a discussion of the intricacies of the combat system.
35. Beil, "Film Aesthetics and Interactive Representations of Subjectivity in Video Games," 190.
36. Rocksteady Studios. *Batman: Arkham Asylum*.
37. H.P. Lovecraft, "The Call of Cthulhu," in *The Complete Fiction of H.P. Lovecraft* (New York: Chartwell Books, 2016), 405.
38. *Ibid.*, 405.
39. *Ibid.*, 406.
40. In the Lovecraftian canon it is almost always a man, rather than a woman, who encounters unspeakable horrors: women are peripheral to Lovecraft's fictional imagination.

Section VIII

Mythic and Religious Parallels

Evil Clowns and Acrobats
The Joker and Harley Quinn
Adam W. Darlage

Clowns in the Pale Moonlight

The creators of the Joker for *Batman* #1 from April 25, 1940, could scarcely have imagined the afterlife of Batman's first foe, the "Clown Prince of Crime."[1] For over seventy years, the Joker has dominated Batman storylines, and he routinely appears at or near the top of every ranking of comic book villains.[2] In television and film, the Joker has evolved from the relatively benign Joker portrayed by Caesar Romero in the campy 1960s' *Batman* television series to the loudmouth psychopath portrayed by Jared Leto in *Suicide Squad*.[3] Heath Ledger's murderous Joker in *The Dark Knight* (2008) is perhaps the most notable Joker of recent memory.[4] Fans of the comics and graphic novels are well familiar with his most horrible—and personal—atrocities. The Joker paralyzed Batgirl, Barbara Gordon, in *Batman: The Killing Joke* (1988).[5] In "A Death in the Family" (1988–1989) he blackmailed the mother of the second Robin, Jason Todd, and made her an accessory to the brutal beating and murder of her son.[6]

The Joker represents the madness of a Dionysian orgy, for, as Ledger's Batman put it in *The Dark Knight*, he is an "agent of chaos."[7] Batman, on the other hand, has sublimated his psychological trauma in the name of justice. Despite being a vigilante, he plays by the rules. As Batman's principal arch-nemesis, the Joker relates to Batman as much as Arkham Asylum relates to Gotham City. He represents the psychological chaos that Batman desperately works to overcome. The chaos of the Joker is not simply the disorder of crime and violence, but an emptiness or formlessness that hearkens back to the original meaning of the Greek root χάος (Khaos). The Joker has no moral compass, no ethical frame of reference. He may be a psychopath, or he may have multiple personalities. No one really knows for sure, and that is the point. As his therapist notes in *Arkham Asylum: A Serious House on Serious Earth*, "the Joker seems to have no control over the sensory information he is receiving from the outside world... He has no real personality. He creates himself each day. He sees himself as the Lord of Misrule, and the world as a theatre of the absurd."[8] Above all, the Joker just wants to have fun, and this is what makes him Batman's supreme enemy.

The Joker's allure has much to do with the fact that he is, in fact, a clown. Clowns are questionable, liminal figures somewhere between human and something else. As the famous silent film actor Lon Chaney (1883–1930) once put it, "there's nothing funny about a clown in the moonlight."[9] Jack Nicholson's Joker noted that he asked all his victims the same question: "Have you ever danced with the devil in the pale moonlight?" Perhaps the Joker was implying that he is indeed the devil *qua* clown.[10] Both quotations make it clear that clowns have (or had) their place—in the circus ring or stage, avoiding the dark while painted up and wearing bright baggy clothes and oversized shoes. By the new millennium, the circus clown of yesteryear had largely been displaced by its dark doppelganger, the evil clown. The decision by Ringling Brothers and Barnum & Bailey Circus to hold their final show in May 2017 was not just about elephant cruelty. The entire circus culture hearkens back to a late 19th century entertainment model that cannot compete with easily reproducible digital media in the 21st century; "The Greatest Show on Earth" has been replaced by binge watching on Netflix.

In the history of clowning, the kingly court, the marketplace, the theater, and the circus once bound the clown to familiar venues and artistic forms. However, with the demise of these forms, clowns have been retrofitted to new media contexts, including comic books, movies, TV shows, and video games. Furthermore, the career of the serial killer John Wayne Gacy captured the public's imagination in the late 1970s and accelerated the demise of the trustworthy (or at the very least, innocuous) clown within popular culture.[11] Gacy murdered at least 33 teenage boys during the 1970s while dressed as a clown for charity events. Upon his arrest and imprisonment, Gacy became known as "The Killer Clown" and happily cultivated this image by painting portraits of himself as his alter-ego clown characters, "Patches" and "Pogo." After Gacy, people would never look at clowns the same way again.

The Joker represents an integral part of this pop cultural process. His rictus grin (sometimes a "Glasgow Smile") represents the triumph of the evil clown over circus clowns as well as iconic happy clowns such as Ronald McDonald and Bozo the Clown. His origin stories are legion.[12] According to most accounts, the Joker owes his white skin, green hair, and red rictus grin to an untimely fall into a vat of chemical waste. His earliest origin story, recounted in *Detective Comics* from February 1951 and subsequently adapted in several later storylines, recounts how Batman and a group of college students solve the mystery of "The Man Behind the Red Hood!"[13] In the end, Batman learns that the Red Hood dove into chemical waste to elude the vigilante, and thus became the Joker. In truth, the inspiration for the Joker's smile was Conrad Veidt's tragic hero Gwynplaine in the silent film *The Man Who Laughs* (1928).[14] Directed by the German Expressionist filmmaker Paul Leni, the movie is an adaptation of Victor Hugo's novel *L'Homme qui rit* (1869). The story begins when an agent of the Stuart monarchy disfigures Gwynplaine as a child after murdering his aristocratic father, Lord Clancharlie. Gwynplaine becomes the Laughing Man, the main attraction of a traveling freak show, and along the way finds redemption in his love for his blind friend Dea. He foils the plot of evil jester named Barkilphedro and rejects the moral turpitude of the English nobility.

Other than the rictus grin, the Joker could not be more different than Gwynplaine. He has several visual features that code for the disorderly, evil clown. His hair, his eyes, and other inhuman physical features demonstrate that he is not fully human, but something monstrous.[15] The Joker from *The Long Halloween* is notable for his grotesquely oversized teeth.[16] In *Arkham Asylum: A Serious House on Serious Earth*, Dave McKean draws Joker with bulging red eyes, bright red lips, an oversized chin, and long, claw-like finger nails.[17] The Joker from the video game *Batman: Arkham Asylum* (2009) shares these exaggerated characteristics.[18] Jared Leto's Joker has scars and tattoos in addition to a mouthful of metal teeth. Even the more benign Jokers of *Batman: The Animated Series* (1992–1995) and *Mad Love* (1994), the origin story of Harley Quinn, features a tall, thin Joker with bright red lips and an exaggerated nose and chin.[19] The character Joker from *The Batman* (2004) is known merely as "Joker," and is perhaps the most inhuman of all. He has yellow teeth, a blue tongue, simian hands and feet, and oversized red eyes. His massive head and hulking arms and upper body likewise point to his liminality.[20]

Unlike Batman, whose Batsuit represents efficiency and order (utility belt, etc.), the Joker's ensemble screams physical and psychological disorder. He wears bright, often oversized clothing such as the iconic purple overcoat and green vest or tie that appear in many of his incarnations.[21] The Joker fights with both traditional weapons as well as weapons specific to his clown persona. One of his main weapons is Joker Toxin or Venom, which first appeared in Batman #1 (1940). This weapon recurs often in Joker storylines with more or less the same characteristics. Released in either gas or liquid form, this toxin suffocates its victims by inducing uncontrollable laughter. The toxin ends its deadly work by pulling the mouths of the Joker's victims into a terrible rictus grin in homage to their killer. Jack Nicholson's Joker in *Batman* (1989) uses an Acid Flower, an outlandish long-barreled gun, and an Electric Joy Buzzer. The Joker of *Mad Love* laments that his plan to drop Batman into a tank of piranhas is flawed because piranhas cannot smile at Batman as he is torn to shreds.[22] The Joker is also known to use bombs, grenades, and guns with the iconic Joker face. Sometimes his guns shoot real bullets, while other times a flag bearing the word "BANG!" comes out of the barrel instead.[23]

If the Joker is the "Clown Prince of Crime" in the Batman universe, Harley Quinn is the princess. Paul Dini and Bruce Timm introduced her on September 11, 1992, in an episode from *Batman: The Animated Series* entitled "The Joker's Favor."[24] Harley Quinn's earliest origin story begins at Arkham Asylum in her role as Dr. Harleen Frances Quinzel, counselor for the Joker.[25] *Mad Love* (1994) recounts how the young, single-minded Harleen Quinzel attended Gotham State University on a gymnastics scholarship in the hopes of receiving a degree in Psychology. A poor student, Harley used her sex appeal to make up for her lack of merit among her professors. After her graduation, Quinzel chose to intern at Arkham Asylum. She soon becomes obsessed with the Joker, who professes to be attracted to her name, as it reminds him of the harlequin character. After finally receiving permission from her superiors to have a session with him, the Joker seduces Harley with the lie that his alcoholic father abused him as a child. She became convinced that "the Joker, so often described as a raving homicidal madman, was nothing more than a tortured soul crying out for love and acceptance…. Yes, I admit it, as unprofessional as it sounds…. I had fallen in love with my patient."[26]

Like the Joker, Harley Quinn was inspired by the experience of her real-world creators. Paul Dini based Harley on his friend, actress and comedian Arleen Sorkin, who he called upon to voice Harley Quinn in the popular series. Sorkin played Calliope Jones in *Days of Our Lives* (1984–1990, 1992, 2001, 2006, and 2010). In one episode, she played a jester in a fantasy sequence that Dini points to as his primary inspiration for the character.[27] Hints of Harley Quinn's colorful and domineering personality can be found in Sorkin's portrayal of Geneva, the maid character from the short-lived Fox sitcom *Duet* (1987–1989).[28]

Harley Quinn is not always the Joker's subordinate, especially in more recent incarnations. In *Batman: Harley Quinn* (October 1999), Harley almost breaks away from the

258   Section VIII: Mythic and Religious Parallels

Harley Quinn action figure based on classic animated design is part of the *Batman: Mad Love* Collectors Set by DC Comics. Harley's outstretched arms holds a scepter topped with Joker's head. Harley Quinn had been Dr. Harleen Quinzel, a psychiatry intern and then a staff psychiatrist, before falling in love with Joker and breaking him out of Arkham. Adopting an alternative identity as the acrobatic Harley Quinn, Harley uses her gymnastics training in her new criminal "career." This highly collectible figure skyrocketed in price as Quinn's popularity soared. Paul Dini's one-shot comic book *Mad Love* (1998) recounts Harley and Joker's romance at Arkham Asylum. The final season of TV's *Gotham* (2019) fleshes out Harley's origin story (photograph by George Higham).

Clown Prince. She befriends Poison Ivy and nearly kills the Joker before ultimately reconciling with him.[29] Her "New 52" incarnation is an independent Harley with a new boyfriend, Mason Macabre. In *Harley Quinn #25* (February 2016), she enters the Joker's cell and nearly beats him to death, leaving him with these words: "I'm not yer toy anymore. Unnerstand? You did mean somethin' ta me one time, but that time is over."[30] Finally, in *Suicide Squad*, Margot Robbie's Harley Quinn helps drive the plot as a member of the Suicide Squad.

Like the Joker, Harley Quinn walks the line between human and inhuman, especially after her friend Poison Ivy treats her with an antitoxin that renders Harley immune to most toxins and grants her increased strength and agility.[31] Her face is painted white, and she wears a black mask around her eyes reminiscent of the harlequin character from the stages of 16th and17th street theater known as Commedia dell'Arte.[32] Unlike the Joker, however, Harley is not coded as particularly frightening to the comic book reader. Instead, her looks cater to the libidos of young readers who consume Batman media in the form of comics, video games, and movies. Regardless of whether she is swinging a carnival mallet or a baseball bat, she is invariably portrayed in clothes that highlight her beauty. Her original red and black harlequin outfit with black mask and jester's bells remained relatively unchanged for a long time. The diamonds of her suit signal the patchwork pattern of the early modern harlequin outfit, while the four black and red sections reference a deck of playing cards.

With the release of the video game *Batman: Arkham Asylum* in 2009, Harley's look finally changed. Harley's harlequin costume recedes into the background behind an outfit with the following ensemble: thigh high boots, red and purple corset, white miniskirt, and bloody lab coat. Pigtails and a nurse's hat replace her cap and jester's bells, and her mask has switched from black to purple. The Harley Quinn from the sequel *Batman: Arkham City* (2011) brings back the black and red color theme, retains the new pig-tailed look, but loses the mask in favor of black eyeliner. The Harley Quinn of the fourth installment of the series, *Arkham Knight* (2015), has a similar look.[33] Within print, the fourth volume of the comic *Suicide Squad* came out in the fall of 2011 as part of the major D.C. universe comic reboot known as "The New 52."[34] Within her own comic series that began in 2013, Harley's look remains much the same, with the usual black and red costuming and black and red pigtails.[35] Margot Robbie's incarnation in the film *Suicide Squad* (2016) draws upon these sources, and the Harley Quinn of DC Rebirth in 2016 is true to the new look as well.[36]

"You complete me…"

With these lines, Heath Ledger's Joker sums up his relationship to Batman, which runs far deeper than criminal versus crime fighter?[37] Unlike many of Batman's adversaries, the Joker's appeal is that he represents everything that Batman does not. Batman upholds the traditional values of human society, while the Joker has no agenda other than to incite Batman. As Michael Caine's Alfred from the *Dark Knight* put it in his advice to a bewildered Batman, "some men aren't looking for something logical like money. They can't be bought, bullied, reasoned, or negotiated with. Some men just want to watch the world burn."[38] Most incarnations of the Joker cannot truly love Harley Quinn precisely because he is totally obsessed with Batman, or, perhaps more importantly, being the one who finally beats Batman. Daniel Wallace describes their relationship:

> The Joker needs Batman. The two are a yin-yang swirl of light and dark, though it's the Joker who's always trying to brighten up grim Gotham with his hysterical brand of humor: Batman is the dark element, the shadowy agent of vengeance who rarely speaks and never cracks a smile. If the Joker is the comedian, Batman is his straight man, and his refusal to play by the Joker's rules only reinforces his role. He's the Bud Abbot to the Joker's Lou Costello, even if the Joker is the only one who sees it.[39]

This is why the Joker cannot abide Harley Quinn's successful capture of Batman in *Mad Love*.[40] The Joker would rather kill every other criminal in Gotham City than let anyone else defeat his nemesis. He and Batman are bound together in a cyclical dance of death that Batman cannot end by virtue of his steps within the dance as the protagonist. In Frank Miller's *Batman: The Dark Knight Returns*, it is not Batman who breaks the Joker's neck, but the Joker himself.[41] That is the Joker's power over every Batman narrative: to either end it or renew it. Within most storylines, he is invariably returned to Arkham

260 Section VIII: Mythic and Religious Parallels

Asylum, only to escape yet again and torment Gotham to get Batman's undivided attention.

The art of clowning may help fans of Batman and the Joker better understand their relationship, and perhaps account for why this clown is regarded as Batman's most formidable adversary. Above, Daniel Wallace alludes to the dichotomy between a "straight man" character and the chaotic clown that has long been exploited to comedic effect. A very basic form of this relationship emerges in the form of the fool, who entertained rulers of various cultures, including ancient Egyptian, Greek, Roman and Chinese societies. The medieval and early modern European court jester is perhaps the most well-known. The fools of these eras were usually representative of the lower classes, including peasants, laborers, and servants—or "village idiots"—whose boorish antics entertained higher-class audiences. These clowns represented the cultural traditions of the premodern agricultural underclass, and their performances validated the social superiority of a self-congratulatory elite. If later jesters and clowns could "speak truth" to monarchs, they still only did so at great peril to their own lives.

The early modern street theater known as Commedia dell'Arte is not just the source of the Harlequin character (Arlecchino) after whom Harley Quinn is named. A theatrical tradition that began in Italy in the 16th century, Commedia dell'Arte takes advantage of simple plots based around four character types: the Zanni, the foolish servants; their masters, the Vecchio, or old men; the Captains, proud military men; and the Lovers, the only characters who appear on stage without a mask. Routinely, the Zanni make life difficult for the Vecchio through comic situations, complicating the Vecchio's desire to stop the Lovers from coming together. The Zanni include Zanni, Arlecchino, Columbina, Pulcinella and Brighella. They move the plot and create confusion. As tricksters and clowns, they represent the rustic, lower class in their dress, their masks, and their movement.[42] On the other hand, the Vecchio, like Bruce Wayne, are rich and powerful. These include Pantalone and Il Dottore. John Rudlin notes that "Pantalone is money," a "stabilising figure" who serves to preserve the world, "enabling it to endure while bursting at the seams as the young (the Lovers) and the dispossessed (the zanni) eternally attempt a take-over."[43] Bruce Wayne is Pantalone, but instead of stifling young lovers, he uses his resources to bring justice to the criminals on the streets of Gotham. It is his responsibility to control the passions of criminality.

Later developments within the history of clowning also point to the symbiotic comedic relationship between the "straight man" and the fool. The French *clown blanc*, or Whiteface, is a sad clown akin to the Pedrolino (later, French Pierott) character of Commedia dell'Arte.[44] The bossy Whiteface is paired up with the happy, clumsy, and foolish Auguste. Notably, the Whiteface is dressed neatly despite being a clown, while the Auguste is a disheveled patchwork of color. Abbot and Costello's routine "Who's on

Opposite: In this poster for the *Batman* serial (1943), evil "Japanazi" Dr. Tito Daka grins, and stands to the far right of the seated Batman (Lewis Wilson), whom he turns into a zombie via his brain machine. Dr. Daka represents the racist "Yellow Menace" meme that invaded American culture, and that predated disclosure of Japanese wartime medical experiments on mostly Chinese and other Asian prisoners. We wonder if casting the versatile Asian American actor B.D. Wong as Dr. Strange in the *Gotham* TV series intentionally recollects the equally evil Dr. Daka- or if this casting choice plays on Wong's role as a sinister scientist in the *Jurassic* franchise or his dramatically different persona as a pensive and soft-spoken FBI psychiatrist in TV's *SVU* series.

262   Section VIII: Mythic and Religious Parallels

First?" is a classic example of the comedic power of this relationship.[45] The usually well-dressed Bud Abbot calmly tries to explain the creation of a baseball team to Lou Costello, who is dressed in ill-fitting clothes and usually bears the props of a baseball hat, bat, and a glove. Costello simply cannot follow the names of the ball players, including "Who," "What," and "I Don't Know," among others. The bit works because the semantic word play confuses Costello to the point that he begins yelling and gesticulating in frustration. It ends with no resolution, with Abbot introducing the name of a final player, the shortstop, "I Don't Give A Darn," whose name reflects Costello's angry resignation. Like Abbot and Costello's famous "Who's on First?" routine, Batman comics, movies, TV shows, graphic novels, and video games may be forever serialized and improvised as long as Batman and the Joker play their roles in this archetypal comedic relationship.

The Joker's popularity within the DC Universe is not surprising given his deep archetypal connections to the world of ancient, medieval, and modern tricksters, clowns, and comedic duos. Further, the setting of Batman and the Joker's myriad battles only encourages continued serialization. Batman has Wayne Manor and the Batcave on the outskirts of Gotham City. These represent wealth, stability, and suburban distance from the criminal dregs of Gotham. The Joker invariably has a hideout (often called a "Ha-Hacienda" in the comics) that is full of booby-traps. As for Arkham Asylum, Daniel Wallace notes it "felt as if it had belonged there all along" after it was introduced in 1974.[46] This is because Arkham Asylum is a dark, Gothic house of horrors that deftly inverts almost everything about Wayne Manor and the Batcave. It is run down, poorly run, and notoriously easy to break out of. As such, it provides the Joker with exactly what he needs: a place to recover from his defeats and a place from which to escape with relative ease. As long as the Joker gets away, Batman will be compelled to hunt him down.

NOTES

1. Bob Kane and Bill Finger, *Batman #1*(DC Comics, 1940). on the controversy over Jerry Robinson's role in the creation of the Joker, see *The Joker: A Serious Study of the Clown Prince of Crime*, ed. Robert Moses Peaslee and Robert G. Weiner (Jackson, MI.: University Press of Mississippi, 2015), XVI.
2. For example, Comic Vine lists the Joker as #1, "Top 100 DC Villains," comicvine.gamespot.com/profile/idea/lists/top-100-dc-villains/49775/ (Accessed 17 April 2017) as does IGN Entertainment, "The Top 25 Villains of DC Comics," www.ign.com/articles/the-top-25-villains-of-dc-comics (Accessed 17 April 2017).
3. *Batman*, created and produced by William Dozier (Los Angeles, CA: Greenway Productions, 1966–1968); *Suicide Squad*, directed by David Ayer (Burbank, CA: DC Entertainment, RatPac-Dune Entertainment, Atlas Entertainment, 2016).
4. *The Dark Knight*, directed by Christopher Nolan (New York: Warner Bros. Pictures, 2008).
5. Alan Moore et al., *Batman: The Killing Joke* (New York: DC Comics, 1988).
6. Jim Starlin et. al., *Batman #426–429*, "A Death in the Family" (New York: DC Comics, December 1998 to January 1999).
7. *The Dark Knight*.
8. Grant Morrison and Dave McKean, *Arkham Asylum: A Serious House on Serious Earth* (New York: DC Comics, 1997), 29.
9. Quoted in Marc Dery, *The Pyrotechnic Insanitarium: American Culture on the Brink* (New York: Grove Press, 1999), 65.
10. *Batman*, directed by Tim Burton (Guber-Peters Company, PolyGram Pictures, 1989).
11. Adam Darlage, "From Pogo to Pennywise: the Rise of the Evil Clown in American Pop Culture Since 1978," in *A History of Evil in Pop Culture: What Hannibal Lecter, Stephen King, and Vampires Reveal About America*, Vol. 2, ed. Sharon Packer and Jody Pennington (Santa Barbara, CA: ABC-CLIO, 2014), 137–148.
12. Peaslee, Introduction to *The Joker: A Serious Study of the Clown Prince of Crime*, XVIII.
13. For example, *The Killing Joke* is loosely based on *Detective Comics #168*, "The Man in the Red Hood," by Bill Finger, Lewis Sayre Schwartz, George Roussos, and Win Mortimer (New York: DC Comics, 1951).
14. *The Man Who Laughs*, directed by Paul Leni (Los Angeles: Universal Pictures, 1928).
15. Noël Carroll has argued that clowns have an "alternate Biology" much like monsters in horror movies, "Horror and Humor," *The Journal of Aesthetics and Art Criticism*, Vol. 57, No. 2, Aesthetics and Popular Culture (Spring, 1999): 145–160, 155.

16. Jeph Loeb and Tim Sale, *The Long Halloween* (New York: DC Comics, 2011).
17. Morrison, *Arkham Asylum: A Serious House on Serious Earth*.
18. *Batman: Arkham Asylum* (2009), directed by Sefton Hill (New York: Warner Bros. Interactive Entertainment).
19. *Batman: The Animated Series*, developed by Bruce Timm and Eric Radomski (New York: Warner Bros. Animation, 1992–1995); Paul Dini and Bruce Timm, *The Batman Adventures: Mad Love* (New York: DC Comics, 1994). Notably, Mark Hamill began his iconic role as the Joker in *Batman: The Animated Series*.
20. *The Batman*, produced by Alan Burnett and Sander Schwartz (Burbank, CA.: Warner Bros. Animation and DC Entertainment, 2004–2008).
21. The Joker from *Batman Beyond: Return of the Joker*, directed by Curt Geda and screenplay by Paul Dini (New York: Warner Bros. Family Entertainment, Warner Bros. Animation, 2000) is a notable exception. This older Joker has trimmed his green hair and wears an efficient all-black ensemble.
22. *Mad Love*.
23. For example, in *Batman Beyond: Return of the Joker*, one of the Jokerz (the Joker's henchmen) named Bonk challenges the Joker, who promptly terrifies him with a gun to his face. Bonk says, "Take It Easy, I Was Just Kidding," to which the Joker shoots the "BANG" flag and says, "So Was I," and laughing maniacally afterward. of course, as Bonk turns around to walk away, the Joker shoots him with the "BANG" flag harpoon in the heart, saying, "Oops! No I Wasn't…"
24. "The Joker's Favor," *Batman: The Animated Series*, Episode 7; first aired September 11, 1992.
25. Like the Joker, Harley Quinn has alternate origin stories, including her fall into the vat of chemicals in her New 52 continuity. Comic Vine presents a good summary of these narratives at comicvine.gamespot.com/harley-quinn/4005–1696/ (Accessed 17 July 2017).
26. *Mad Love*.
27. Johnny Chu, "Confirmed: Harley Quinn Based on Arleen Sorkin's Role on Days of Our Lives," www.geekynews.com/confirmed-harley-quinn-based-on-arleen-sorkins-role-on-days-of-our-lives-14220/ (Accessed 17 April 2017).
28. *Duet*, created by Ruth Bennet and Susan Seeger (Hollywood, CA.: Paramount Television, 1987–1989).
29. Paul Dini et al., *Batman: Harley Quinn* (New York: DC Comics, 1999).
30. Amanda Conner and Jimmy Palmiotti, *Harley Quinn #25* (New York: DC Comics, 2016).
31. Dini et al., *Batman: Harley Quinn*.
32. John Rudlin, *Comedia Dell'Arte: An Actor's Handbook* (New York: Routledge, 1994), 34–37.
33. *Batman: Arkham Asylum*, 2009; *Batman: Arkham City*, 2011; and *Batman: Arkham Knight*, 2015; directed by Sefton Hill (New York: Warner Bros. Interactive Entertainment).
34. Adam Glass et al., *Suicide Squad, Volume 4* (New York: DC Comics, 2011).
35. Amanda Conner et al., *Harley Quinn* (New York: DC Comics, 2013).
36. Amanda Conner et al., *Harley Quinn* (New York: DC Comics, 2016).
37. *The Dark Knight*.
38. *Ibid*.
39. Daniel Wallace, with an introduction by Mark Hamill, *the Joker: A Visual History of the Clown Prince of Crime* (New York: DC Comics, 2011), 37.
40. *Mad Love*.
41. Frank Miller, *Batman: The Dark Knight Returns* (New York: DC Comics, 1986), 151.
42. John Rudlin gives detailed information about the appearance, posture, gait, and speech patterns of the stock characters. for example, Arlecchino and the other Zanni should stoop when they walk, evidence of their lower status, *Comedia Dell'Arte*, 69–70.
43. Rudlin, *Comedia Dell'Arte*, 92.
44. *Ibid.*, 134.
45. Bud Abbot and Lou Costello, "Who's on First?"
46. Wallace, *The Joker: A Visual History*, 55.

Matricide and Myth

Daniel R. Fredrick

Ancient Greek myths have never shunned the topic of *oikos,* or familial slayings whether parents are committing prolicide, siblings committing fratricide or sororicide, or children committing patricide or matricide. Matricide in ancient Greek myth rises most prominently in Sophocles' well-known play the *Libation Bearers* which tells the story of Orestes killing his mother Clytemnestra. Orestes' reason? Clytemnestra has murdered the king, his father Agamemnon. There is also a similar, albeit shorter, lesser-known tale, in Apollodorus' *Bibliotheca*, which tells of Alcmaeon killing his mother Eriphyle for urging the father to partake in a futile attack on Thebes. Ever since the writing of these dramatic ancient Greek myths, tales of matricide have resurfaced throughout Western culture, and we can find them even in the world of modern comics. In the long-running series *Batman*, for example, the theme of matricide (which is so prevalent in the *Libation Bearers*) is central particularly as it relates to the tale of Arkham Asylum. Because Greek myths still influence our culture, it is both intriguing and revealing to investigate comparisons between the two fictional worlds. This essay will examine matricide in *Arkham Asylum*, specifically how Amadeus Arkham's murder of his mother compares in terms of mental illness and motive to mythological precedents such as Orestes and the lesser hailed Alcmaeon.

The Guilt of the Mothers: Elizabeth Arkham, Eriphyle and Clytemnestra

Because matricide is one of the most heinous and unnatural crimes, any mother, even fictional, who is murdered at the hands of her child should undergo some interrogation so that there is a fuller understanding of her role in the crime. Was there something crooked about the mother? Did she torment her son to the point of murderous rage? Or was the mother simply an innocent victim of her bad seed, a victim of morally defective genetics, of an extremely diabolic and vicious offspring? In other words, to what extent are these mothers—Elizabeth Arkham, Eriphyle, and Clytemnestra—guilty of provoking their sons to commit matricide? A brief look at some pertinent details regarding the relationships of Elizabeth Arkham, Eriphyle, and Clytemnestra with their sons will be useful to gain psychological insights of both victim and assailant.

Elizabeth Arkham appears to be innocent of any wrong doing against Amadeus. Elizabeth is troubled psychologically yet induces neither harm nor torment on her son. Unlike Eriphyle and Clytemnestra, Elizabeth is not conniving. She does not plot against her husband nor her children. Elizabeth's troubles are personal. She battles with her own psychotic afflictions, which are assuaged by her doting son who tenderly cares for her. The dark secret of course is that Amadeus cared for his mother up until the moment he actually killed her, fabricating the cause of his innocent mother's death, claiming that she committed suicide. Because of Amadeus' betrayal, we have great empathy for Elizabeth. Indeed, among the three mothers discussed here, Elizabeth seems to be the only one who is completely innocent.

Alcmaeon's mother Eriphyle, surely, is guilty of a great sin, for she sells (indirectly) her husband's life to acquire a piece of jewelry, the infamous and cursed *Necklace of Harmonia,* which was reputed to restore to and retain youth in its possessor. However, this necklace, forged by Hephaestus, was designed to entrap any who possessed it. It was worn, for example, by the fated Jocasta, Oedipus' mother, who committed suicide after learning that she had married her own son. This damned necklace was kept in the Oedipus family heirloom, and after his death, Oedipus' son Polynices kept it, not for himself but to entice the vain and gullible, to entice someone like Eriphyle. And so, when Polynices' brother Eteocles gained control over Thebes, their shared inheritance, Polynices gifted the necklace to Eriphyle with the agreement that she would encourage her husband Amphiaraus, a seer, to join in the battle famously known as the *Seven Against Thebes.* But Amphiaraus originally protested the war, warning the military that it would surely perish in the battle. But the military charged ahead anyway. (The words of seers always fall on deaf ears in ancient tales). Amphiaraus reluctantly had to participate, dying in battle with most of his comrades just as he foresaw. Eriphyle is guilty because she knew that the price of the necklace was her husband's life. To retaliate, Amphiaraus, while dying, whispered to his son the story of his mother's horrible trade, his life for the necklace, a dark secret which burdened Alcmaeon, like Orestes, to avenge his father's death. Obliged, Alcmaeon was forced to kill his own mother. Indeed, Alcmaeon faced the same philosophical conundrum as Orestes. The key difference to note is that Eriphyle did not directly kill Amphiaraus, meaning she did not grasp and drive a blade into a vital organ (as does Clytemnestra). Eriphyle's crime is betrayal, selling her husband for the promise of eternal youth. In short, Eriphyle is guilty for her choice, not her action.

As for Clytemnestra, she is incontrovertibly guilty. At a key point in the play, she enters the stage, covered in Agamemnon's blood that he vomited all over her as a result of getting struck three times with an axe. This gross blood splatter does not cause any revulsion in Clytemnestra. In fact, the blood spray causes a paroxysm of pleasure: Hear her delight: "And I rejoiced [after being sprayed with his blood]—just as the fecund earth rejoices when the heavens send spring rains, and new-born buds burst into bloom."[1] That Clytemnestra revels in her husband's blood contrasts her greatly with the other mothers, showing her to be the guiltiest of the three. Unlike Eriphyle who merely succumbed to a moment of greed, Clytemnestra "brooded on this struggle [the murder] many years."[2] Hers was not a crime of sudden passion but a premeditated crime, the spilling of blood and the taking of life with her own hands. Whereas Clytemnestra is on the dark side of the guilt spectrum, Eriphyle is in the gray zone, and Elizabeth, the light.

The Visions

From the brief description above, one can see that Elizabeth Arkham is different from Eriphyle and Clytemnestra in that she is innocent of committing a crime against her husband or son. If we examine the mothers from another perspective—from their tendency to be affected by psychotic visions—Arkham and Clytemnestra are more easily paired, with Eriphyle having no psychotic vision. If we were to force some analyses on Eriphyle and what might be called her "visions," we could conclude that she is obsessed by the fantasy of regaining her youth. But fantasies are generated by one's own desires, so they are not visions per se. Eriphyle has control over her "vision" whereas Arkham and Clytemnestra do not.

Both Arkham and Clytemnestra, indeed, are haunted by visions. Arkham, for example, is haunted by a gigantic vampire bat (a vampire bat is presumed here, for other bats, e.g., fruit bats, would cause little anxiety beyond a brief spell of horripilation). Clytemnes-

Close-up of Batman action figure designed by Hot Toys and based on *Batman: Arkham City* (2011) game. Expressionist-style cast shadow was added by photographer George Higham, in homage to cast shadows of Gotham City skyscrapers in comics. Batman's image is ubiquitous in American culture. Batman himself is one of only three surviving superheroes since the start of the superhero genre. Batman remains the most popular superhero, rivaled only by Spider-man (photograph by George Higham).

tra too is haunted by visions. Instead of a bloodthirsty bat, Clytemnestra envisions she has birthed a snake, which, when offered one of her teats, fangs out life-draining blood rather than nutrient-rich colostrum. It is interesting that Clytemnestra's vision is about breastfeeding particularly because she did not breastfeed Orestes. Breastfeeding was the responsibility of the nurse-servant.[3]

Although both Elizabeth and Clytemnestra are haunted by visions, Elizabeth's visions, according to Sharon Packer, are a result of a "destructive neurodegenerative and psychotogenic gene."[4] Both Elizabeth's defective gene and her haunting bat visions will be passed on to her murderous son Amadeus, and likewise to the other inmates in the asylum.[5] In contrast to Arkham's vision which becomes communal in a sense, Clytemnestra's vision of the snake is exclusively her own. Furthermore, Clytemnestra has a strong hunch what the vision of the snake means. The snake that Clytemnestra births is certainly none other than Orestes who will fatally pierce her—not with fangs—but with a blade. That Orestes is the snake of Clytemnestra's vision is underscored in Orestes' own analysis of it:

> I think it matches me in every point. That snake came from the same womb as did I—it was wrapped up in my swaddling clothes and sucked the milk that nourished me, mixing it with blood so that she screamed. It portends that she will die by violence, from nursing such a violent beast. Me. I am that snake. And I will kill her. That is the meaning of this dream.[6]

Orestes' erroneous belief that he was breastfed deserves a few words, for it shows he is unaware of the roots of his mother's deception. Clytemnestra uses the idea of breastfeeding to plead for mercy, crying "Hold! My son, my child, take pity on these breasts. Here you often lay asleep and sucked milk that made you strong."[7] Yet, if we scroll back a few lines in the play, we learn that Orestes suckled not from his mother's but from the Nurse's breast. Orestes of course would have had no memory of his nursing. However, the trope of breastfeeding is powerfully intimate, and Clytemnestra is able to "milk" pity from him. The emotional appeal works for a moment, for when Clytemnestra reveals her breasts, Orestes halts his urge to kill, turning to his cohort and asking, "Pylades, what do I do? I cannot [at the sight of my mother's breast] kill my own mother."[8] Pylades, neither daunted by the family platitudes nor the breast, reminds Orestes of his duty to avenge his father. Orestes follows his companion's sobering advice, his misgivings fleeting. In the final decision, Orestes is not the breastfed infant, but the deadly snake.

What we can conclude is that Clytemnestra's vision of the nursing snake is not a result of a neurodegenerative and psychotogenic gene as is the case with Arkham, but is rather a result of a guilty conscious, of perhaps dealing with the stress of being marked for murder by her own son. In short, each mother—Eriphyle, Arkham, and Clytemnestra—experiences visions in varying degrees and for varying reasons. Eriphyle's is a desire, fueled by nothing more than fantasy and greed. Clytemnestra's is a guilt-driven vision which reveals her fear of her vengeful son. Finally, Arkham's vision is a product of psychotic delusions.

Motives and Murders: Amadeus Arkham, Alcmaeon and Orestes

As reviewed above, the mothers have varying degrees of guilt and varying mental problems. The motives of the murderers must also be reviewed so that a supple comparison between ancient culture and popular culture can be appreciated. Recall Orestes' second thought to kill his mother when he beholds his mother's breast, a maternal symbol which neutralizes momentarily his passion for revenge. Affected by the symbolism of the breast, Orestes questions his cultural obligation to avenge his murdered father based on the perplexity of the situation, for to take the life of the life-giver defies the logic inherent in natural law. However, Orestes may also intuit that the female breast is not only a symbol of infancy but also one of adult sexuality. Although Clytemnestra took a principled risk to defuse the situation by presenting her breast to her adult son, her gamble failed. The reason is that Orestes was not the sole viewer of the breast; Pylades was there as well, and thus Clytemnestra's breast became embarrassingly public. Other than a cultural obligation, what further excites Orestes to murder his mother is his role as leader of the undertaking. His sister Elektra played a role, and Pylades, an even greater asset, was a close partner, tense and primed to assist in a murder that they all condoned and corroborated upon.

But Orestes needs to do more than murder Clytemnestra. He desires to shame and torture her. Unlike Amadeus Arkham who euthanizes his mother out of compassion, Orestes is vindictive. To elaborate, Orestes drags his mother to the bloodied corpse of Aegisthus, her adulterous lover and accomplice in the murder of Agamemnon. Pushing Clytemnestra down on Aegisthus' fresh corpse, Orestes lashes out that his mother, now lying on top of the dead body, can continue in her adulterous union even in (and throughout) death. This perverse act allows Orestes both to punish Clytemnestra as well as to help himself cope with his murderous obligation by envisioning their adulterous affair, a disgusting image which will further ignite his rage. But even as Orestes drags his mother, there is something unique during this stage of the murder that differs from the Arkham murder: dialogue between mother and son.

As the murder is drawn out, Clytemnestra has a voice, at times of pity, at others protest, unlike Arkham who, while being unknowingly euthanized, is silent. To Orestes, Clytemnestra pitifully begs for a different outcome. "Can't we grow old together?"[9] But Orestes refuses. When this plea does not work, does Clytemnestra continue to beg? No, like so many characters in Greek drama, Clytemnestra turns to *eristic* rhetoric, or put simply, a wrangling style of argument and debate, a hallmark of the ancient Greek world. Clytemnestra, even while facing immediate and inevitable death, continues to argue: *Destiny*, not her, she asserts, is to blame for Agamemnon's death. But Orestes too is a product of his rhetorical culture, delaying the murder to refute her with a classic strategy (using her own argument against her): if *destiny*, not Clytemnestra, is to blame for Agamemnon's death, then it is also destiny—not Orestes—who is to blame for her death. Orestes feels the need to win both the verbal as well as the physical fight. After a few more desperate and failed attempts to scare and shame Orestes, Clytemnestra realizes her tears are "useless," an admission suggesting that those tears were disingenuous, for tears of utility are more suspicious than tears of sorrow.[10] It is easy to see that not only are the tears useless, but so are the words. And yet the final words—the message—from Orestes at the end of this scene is useful in that it reveals the interplay between his pride and his mental torment. After committing matricide, Orestes strides out into the spotlight, mocking the illicit lovers who are now "clinging" in death. But we should interject, "How did these dead bodies end up in such an erotic embrace?" Orestes, engaging in pseudo-necrophilia, manipulated the arms and the legs to make the corpses appear as if lovemaking, no easy task with rigor mortis setting in. After showcasing their morbid consummation, Orestes presents forensic evidence (Agamemnon's robe etc.), to establish his innocence, asserting the reasons why he is justified for matricide as highlighted in the passage below. Notice that mental anguish will be the price for his vengeance.

> I feel like some chariot racer lashing on my team, but we have strayed way off the course.... My mind is racing ... it has lost control. Something overpowers me ... carries me off.... Deep in my heart, fear prepares a furious song and dance. So while I still have my wits about me, to all my friends I publicly proclaim I killed my mother justly.[11]

The hounds of hell—the Furies—symbols of haunting guilt and regret will come for him. Orestes will be hunted by a guilty conscious for the rest of his life.

Like Orestes, both Amadeus and Alcmaeon will suffer mental distress after murdering their mothers. The opportunity to elaborate on this point, however, is difficult because the literature regarding the murder of Elizabeth Arkham (by Amadeus) and the murder of Eriphyle (by Alcmaeon) is not as detailed as it is for the murder of Clytemnestra. Still, a few observations can be made. The Arkham family's "sordid history" takes "center stage" in Grant Morrison's graphic novel *Arkham Asylum: A Serious House on Serious Earth*.[12] From it, we learn that Amadeus' mother was mentally ill (recall her tormented visions of the bat). Amadeus provided home care for Elizabeth, which puts him in a category far different than Orestes or Alcmaeon who played no nurturing role nor offered any palliative care. However, there is a sinister side to Amadeus' story. One night, while Amadeus was "caring" for his mother, he saw his mother's bat, a vision that horrified him. Fear and mental stress taking hold, Amadeus ran a razor across his mother's throat, killing her instantly. However, Amadeus represses the memory of the matricide and constructed a believable narrative (even to himself) that his mother committed suicide. Whereas Orestes and Alcmaeon publically admit the murders, Amadeus covers it up, making him in a way more deceitful and therefore more sinister than the duty-bound Greeks. Amadeus avoided being discovered as the murderer, but his crime came to light when he beheld the murdered bodies of his own wife and daughter (discussed below). And so, unlike Orestes, Amadeus, after slicing his mother's throat, feels no guilt nor need to justify the murder, for in Amadeus's mind, there was no murder, only a tragic suicide. Thus, Amadeus offers not a public defense of the murder, but a public dedication for her suicide, specifically converting the Arkham family mansion into Arkham Asylum, a hospital dedicated to the care of those who also suffer from mental illness. But the Arkham hospital was a cursed place just as the house of Atreus (e.g., Agamemnon, Orestes) was a cursed place.

The information regarding Alcmaeon's murder of Eriphyle is almost as sparse as the murder of Elizabeth Arkham. We can find the story in Apollodorus' chapter on the *Seven Against Thebes*. From Apollodorus we learn that, like Orestes, Alcmaeon, after consulting the oracle, receives a divine order to avenge his father's death. In another account, in Euripides' fragment from *Alcmaeon in Corinth*, we learn about the mental consequences Alcmaeon suffers after killing his mother: Alcmaeon goes insane (like Amadeus) and is motivated to kill his mother because of his rage. In brief, all three sons suffer mental illness to some degree, with Amadeus suffering prior to the killing while Orestes and Alcmaeon suffer after. These mental illnesses that occur after the murder deserve further discussion.

Mental Consequences of Matricide

Though Orestes and Alcmaeon justify their acts of matricide, choosing to define it not as matricide but as an obligation to avenge their fathers' deaths, they are still unable to walk away with a clear conscious, an idea symbolized in their flight from the Furies. The Furies were the "embodiment of the act of self-cursing."[13] Or, put simply, they were a representation of one's guilty conscious, following him wherever he went, inescapable and maddening. The Furies remind us (and Orestes and Alcmaeon) that though they may have been justified in the eyes of an ancient Greek jury, they cannot shrug off the fact that they still killed their mothers and will be consequently haunted—or should we say hunted—by that guilt.

Orestes' situation is especially tragic, perhaps more so than Alcmaeon's, for Orestes, according to Clytemnestra, was supposed to be the one to break the curse of the Furies that haunted the members of the house of Atreus.[14] In other words, mental illness was supposed to cease with Orestes and his descendants. But ironically, it is Orestes himself who incites and inflames the Furies. The last male heir of Agamemnon thus continues rather than cuts down that curse. As for Alcmaeon, he too shares the same consequence of mental illness that results from committing matricide. Alcmaeon's crime awakens the chthonic Furies who spew out from the belly of the earth (the deep recesses of the mind) to possess if not devour the entire conscience of the guilty.

If the Furies are a type of madness that stems from a guilty conscience, where are Amadeus' Furies? Put another way, how does Amadeus' madness as well as guilt from the murder manifest itself? First, Amadeus' madness is clearly genetic, for he is haunted by the same bat that haunted his mother. On this point, he is different from Orestes and Alcmaeon who were haunted by the Furies *after* the murders. Amadeus may have subconsciously believed that his mother was causing the bat to appear and thus may have reasoned that, to destroy the specter, all he had to do was destroy where it came from. Second, that Amadeus suppresses the murder also shows the extent of his mental illness. Amadeus falls into severe madness when he saw his wife Constance and daughter Harriet slaughtered and defiled by Martin "Mad Dog" Hawkins who hunted them down after Amadeus analyzed Mad Dog's psyche for the police. To get revenge, Mad Dog rapes, kills, and mutilates them both. And to truly earn the nickname, he severs the little girl's head, so he can prop it up like a toy inside her dollhouse. A macabre artist proud of his work, Mad Dog even signs his name on the young girl's severed torso.

Walking in on this horror, Amadeus suddenly remembers the murder scene of his mother and that he himself was to blame. The resulting mental breakdown he suffers sends him—ironically—to his own asylum.[15] To Amadeus, Mad Dog thus functions as a kind of male Erinys whose murderous pursuit forces Amadeus into a life of mental illness. After Amadeus collapses in sorrow among the pieces of his butchered wife and daughter, he puts on Elizabeth's wedding dress, symbolizing his union with horror and psychotic illness, and proceeds to feast on their corpses (as the graphic novel insinuates), a ghoulish wedding banquet so to speak.

Amadeus' mental breakdown is different from Orestes' and Alcmaeon's, first, because it is more severe, and second, because the end result of the illness turns Amadeus from a hunted one to a hunter. Said differently, Amadeus is hunted by his "fury" Mad Dog. Later, the roles are reversed, and Amadeus becomes an Erinys himself, pursuing and ultimately murdering Mad Dog through electroconvulsive therapy while serving as his therapist. Eventually, the mental illness conquers Amadeus, and he dies in Arkham Asylum.

Tales this tragic should force us to wonder if any healing could ever come to the house of Atreus or the house/asylum of Arkham? This question is indeed a part of Sophocles' drama. For example, the chorus in the *Libation Bearers* believes that the house of

Atreus can break its curse, but the answer as to how it can break that curse, stated in the final scene, is predictably ambiguous. The chorus chants:

> The third storm [Orestes] has broken savagely over the palace and run its course. First, came the torments of those children slaughtered for Thyestes' food. Next came the suffering of a man, our warrior lord, Achaea's king. And now the third—do I call him rescuer or destroyer? When will all this end?[16]

This question—"When will it all end?"—asked in a play written 2500 years ago is still relevant if applied to the characters at Arkham Asylum, continually filled with villains of the worst kind.[17] When will all these insane criminals stop filling up Arkham Asylum? The answer in the *Batman* comic series is just as ambiguous. We are certain of only one thing: The two homes of Orestes and Amadeus are places of perpetual darkness. Give thanks they are fictional.

NOTES

1. Aeschylus, The Oresteia, trans. Ian C. Johnston (Arlington, VA: Richer Resources, 2007), 19.
2. Aeschylus, The Oresteia, 19.
3. Aeschylus, The Oresteia, 15.
4. Sharon Packer, "Arkham Asylum's Criminally Insane Inmates and Psychotic Psychiatrists," in Mental Illness in Popular Culture, ed. Sharon Packer (Santa Barbara, CA: Praeger, 2017), 260.
5. Of course, we cannot help but wonder to what extent this bat is related to Batman who haunts so to speak all of the criminals of Gotham.
6. Aeschylus, The Oresteia,11.
7. Aeschylus, The Oresteia, 10.
8. Aeschylus, The Oresteia, 19.
9. Aeschylus, The Oresteia,19.
10. Aeschylus, The Oresteia, 20.
11. Aeschylus, The Oresteia, 23.
12. Bradley J. Daniels, "Arkham Asylum: Forensic Psychology and Gotham's (Not So) 'Serious House,'" in The Psychology of Superheroes: An Unauthorized Exploration, ed. Robin S. Rosenberg and Jennifer Canzoneri (Dallas, TX: BenBella, 2008), 205.
13. Walter Burkert, Greek Religion (Boston: Harvard University Press, 1977), 198.
14. Aeschylus, The Oresteia, 14.
15. Daniels, "Arkham Asylum," 206.
16. Aeschylus, The Oresteia, 24.
17. One noteworthy example is in the TV series *Gotham* when Jerome Valeska is sent to Arkham after murdering his mother.

Appendix
Unethical Experiments in Modern Genetics Research

Dr. Linda Friitawa, the disgraced doctor who lost her medical license because of unauthorized genetics experiments, is a fictional character in the Arkham mythos, as is Dr. Hugo Strange, the psychiatrist who creates bizarre mutations in his Indian Hill hideaway beneath Arkham Asylum for the Criminally Insane. But fact and fantasy can collide in science fiction, and today's fiction may become tomorrow's fact.

CRISPR technology that allows gene manipulation and substitution arrived decades after these curious characters came into being, but the availability and affordability of this easy-to-use innovation makes Dr. Strange's unethical experiments more relevant than ever before. The November 26, 2018, edition of the *New York Times* describes a Chinese scientist named He Jianku. Dr. Jianku claims that he edited the genes of twin embryos before re-implanting the genetically modified twins into the mother's uterus.

In contrast to the fictional Dr. Friitawa or Dr. Strange, Dr. Jianku's expressed intentions were benevolent: he strived to make the babies resistant to H.I.V. infection. Yet he faced worldwide condemnation, and the opprobrium of fellow Chinese scientists, who feared that this unsanctioned step could start a slippery slope, whereby prospective parents pick and choice specific traits in their offspring as casually as people order a sandwich with or without mustard—or on whole wheat or rye—at the corner deli.

At the time of this writing, it is unclear how many other scientists will attempt similar procedures in the near future—and it is unclear if the scientist's still unpublished claims conform to his reports. Yet other inheritable conditions beg for intervention. Sickle cell anemia, an autosomal recessive blood disorder that mostly affects persons of African ancestry as well as some Middle Eastern or Mediterranean people, results from single genetic mutation. This disease may be prevented by gene manipulation, provided that the ethical sanctions against such manipulation are lifted. Sickle cell anemia shortens lifespans and results in painful crises and swollen joints. Blood clots in the spleen interfere with the spleen's ability to ward off infection. Sickle cell can leave some young persons cognitively impaired or crippled when sickle-shaped cells obstruct blood flow in the brain. Even persons who carry only one sickle cell gene (and hence are "heterozygous") can suffer untoward effects under severe atmospheric stress. Flying in unpressurized plans or engaging in rigorous boot camp activities at high altitude have harmed heterozygous military recruits who previously appeared healthy. There is every reason to hope for help.

Sadly, horrific precedents set by Josef Mengele and his ilk continue to ignite fear and dampen enthusiasm about genetics advances. The public outcry against genetic modification often focuses on the production of "perfect" children via CRISPR, like the blond-haired, blue eyed children featured in Franklin Schaffner's triple Academy Award nominee, *The Boys from Brazil* (1978), which was based on Ira Levin's novel by the same name. It is no accident that the births of Aryan-appearing children in *The Boys from Brazil* were linked to Nazi escapees.

The role of the Reich still hangs over society. Representations of geneticists in comics reflected the fear generated by Nazi geneticists. Even before the Nazi killing machine sprang into motion, first-generation comic book readers encountered villainous geneticists early on. Dr. Hugo Strange was one of the earliest *Batman* villains. Strange began as a geneticist before he morphed into a sinister psychiatrist and asylum superintendent in response to the anti-comics crusade led by psychiatrist Dr. Wertham.

Batman debuted as a character in 1939, a few months before World War II began in September 1939, when Germany invaded Poland and France and Britain declared war on Germany in response. *Batman* comics came into being the following year, in 1940.

The geneticists in the Arkham mythos remind us of the double-edged sword that hangs over scientists as they tip-toe into unchartered territory. The intrepid are willing to tolerate uncertainty and to run the risk of worsening a bad situation, instead of standing still and accepting the certainty of a devastating disease. The cautious will wait for ethics committees, as well as scientific reviews, to green light such novel experiments. Only time will tell which way the pendulum will swing—but I predict that the trepidations expressed at recent CRISPR experiments may fade to grey within a decade, if the current controversial experiments succeed. Alternatively, unforeseen adverse outcomes—which are equally possible—could stymie future attempts for the foreseeable future.

About the Contributors

Aaron **Barlow** teaches English at the New York City College of Technology (CUNY). A specialist in American popular culture, he earned his doctorate from the University of Iowa with a dissertation on the science-fiction writer Philip K. Dick.

Rosa JH **Berland** holds an MA in fine art history from University of Toronto. She is an art historian and curator of modern and contemporary art. As a specialist in Expressionist art, she served as a curator at the Museum of Modern Art and worked for the Solomon R. Guggenheim Museum and The Frick Collection, New York.

Matthew **Brown**, D.O., is a physician and psychiatrist who is board certified in child and adult psychiatry and holds an MBA in healthcare leadership. He has published in peer-reviewed journals and book chapters and presented at conferences on trauma, attachment, and psychedelics as medicine. His private psychiatry practice uses holistic approaches.

Jeffrey **Bullins** is an assistant professor of communications at Plattsburgh State University of New York. His research interests include sound design for film and television as well as genre studies, particularly horror. He is also a freelance sound designer and audio engineer.

Adam W. **Darlage** is a lecturer in the Department of Humanities and Philosophy at Oakton Community College in Des Plaines, Illinois, where he teaches courses in world religions and world mythologies. His research interests include the historical and religious roots of contemporary pop cultural archetypes and symbols.

Shawn **Edrei** completed his Ph.D. at Tel-Aviv University, where he teaches a course on gaming. He continues to pursue the field of digital narratology, exploring the ways in which new technologies have changed our perspectives on storytelling and authorship. He has published on interactive storytelling, video games, and virtual narrative.

Jason W. **Ellis** is an assistant professor of English at the New York City College of Technology, CUNY, and formerly, a Marion L. Brittain Fellow at the Georgia Institute of Technology. He holds a Ph.D. in English from Kent State University, M.A. in science fiction studies from the University of Liverpool, and B.S. in science, technology, and culture from Georgia Tech.

Fernando Espí **Forcén**, M.D., was born and educated in Spain. He earned his M.D. from the Medical School at the University of Murcia and a Ph.D. on the history of psychiatry. His interests include philosophy, art history, rock music, gastronomy and cinema.

Daniel R. **Fredrick** is an assistant professor of writing at the American University of Sharjah, United Arab Emirates. He has written and presented on Chaucer, Cicero, and rhetoric-related topics.

Susan Hatters **Friedman**, M.D., is a forensic psychiatrist and a maternal mental health specialist. She is also an associate professor at the University of Auckland. Her research has focused on violence within the family and her clinical work entails evaluation and treatment of women in prison who have mental health issues.

About the Contributors

Brenda S. **Gardenour Walter** holds a Ph.D. in medieval history from Boston University and is a professor of history at the Saint Louis College of Pharmacy. Her research examines the role of Aristotelian discourse, learned medicine, and scholastic theology in the construction of alterity and the continued influence of medieval otherness on dark culture.

Jaq **Greenspon** is a professional writer who spent his formative years in Hollywood, where he wrote movies and TV shows as well as numerous books and articles about the entertainment industry. He is now an associate professor at Vytautas Magnus University in Kaunas, Lithuania.

Rasa **Greenspon** is a Ph.D. candidate in comics studies. She is a native of Lithuania and lives in Kaunas, Lithuania, with her husband Jaq Greenspon, which whom she collaborates on comics studies projects.

Ryan C.W. **Hall**, M.D., practices psychiatry and forensic psychiatry. He is also an associate professor of the Department of Psychiatry at the University of Central Florida College of Medicine; an affiliate associate professor at the University of South Florida (Tampa); and an adjunct faculty member at Barry University Dwayne O. Andreas School of Law (Orlando).

Darren **Harris-Fain** received his Ph.D. in English from Kent State University and is a professor of English at Auburn University at Montgomery, where he teaches British and American literature as well as fantastic fiction and graphic novels. He has published essays on literary fiction, science fiction, fantasy, and comics in more than thirty books.

Kristi Rowan **Humphreys** is a full-time faculty member in the Department of English at Baylor University and author of the monograph *Housework and Gender in American Television*. She holds a Ph.D. and is also a professional actor and an author.

Timothy W. **Kneeland** is a professor and Chair of the History and Political Science Department at Nazareth College in Rochester, New York. He has authored numerous chapters and encyclopedia articles on the history of psychiatry, American politics and natural disasters. He also provides political analysis for local media in Upstate New York.

Michael **Markus** is an associate professor of history at Alabama State University. He holds a Ph.D. in history from Washington University in St. Louis. His research focuses on 19th-century British political history, and on the history of British imperialism, as well as the depiction of mental illness in popular culture, particularly in the horror genre.

Sharon **Packer**, M.D., is a physician and psychiatrist, as well as a clinical assistant professor at Icahn School of Medicine at Mount Sinai and Albert Einstein College of Medicine. She has presented at medical school Grand Rounds, American Psychiatric Association conferences, science fiction forums and Comic-Con. She is the author and editor of numerous books and articles.

Caleb **Puckett** works at Park University in Parkville, Missouri. He is active in a range of pursuits, including writing, editing, and instructional design. His creative and academic work has appeared in a host of publications, both in the U.S. and abroad.

Eric **Sandberg** completed his Ph.D. at the University of Edinburgh and is an assistant professor at City University of Hong Kong and a docent at the University of Oulu. His research interests range from modernism to the contemporary novel. He is the lead researcher on a project exploring nostalgia in contemporary culture.

Eric J. **Sterling** earned his Ph.D. in English, with a minor in drama and theater, at Indiana University. He is the Ida Belle Young Endowed Professor of English at Auburn University at Montgomery, where he has taught since 1994. He has published four books and more than six dozen refereed articles.

Elyse D. **Weiner**, M.D., is board-certified in adult psychiatry and psychosomatic medicine. She is a fellow of the Academy of Consultation-Liaison Psychiatry and is also a clinical assistant professor of psychiatry at SUNY Downstate Medical Center and the New York University School of Medicine.

Filmography

Annabel Lee (2001): George Higham.

Batman (1966–1968): William Dozier.
Batman (1989): Tim Burton.
Batman (2004–2008): Vietti, Brandon, dir.
Batman Arkham Asylum (2009): Rocksteady Studios.
Batman: Arkham City (2011): Sefton Hill.
Batman: Arkham Knight (2015): Sefton Hill.
Batman Begins (2005): Christopher Nolan.
Batman Beyond (1999–2000): Butch Lukic, dir.
Batman Beyond: Return of the Joker (2003): Curt Geda.
Batman: Mask of the Phantasm (1993): Eric Radomski and Bruce Timm.
Batman: The Animated Series (1992–1995): Bruce Timm and Eric Radomski, dir.
Beauty and the Beast (1946): Jean Cocteau.
Bedlam (1946): Mark Robson.
Beetlejuice (1988): Tim Burton.

The Cabinet of Dr. Caligari (1919): Robert Weine.
Charlie and the Chocolate Factory (2005): Tim Burton.
A Clockwork Orange (1971): Stanley Kubrick.
Convicted by Hypnotism (1912): Eclair (production company).
The Criminal Hypnotist (1909): D. W. Griffith.

The Dark Knight (2008): Christopher Nolan.
Die Hard (1988): John McTiernan.
Die Hard 2: Die Harder (1990): Renny Harlin.
Die Hard with a Vengeance (1995): John McTiernan.
Dr. Dippy's Sanitarium (1906): American Mutascope (production company).
Dr. Jekyll and Mr. Hyde (1912): Lucius Henderson.
Dr. Jekyll & Mr. Hyde (1920): John S. Robertson.
Dr. Jekyll and Mr. Hyde (1931): Rouben Mamoulian.
Dr. Jekyll and Sister Hyde (1970): Roy Ward Baker.
Dr. Mabuse, der Spieler [*Dr. Mabuse, the Gambler*] (1922): Fritz Lang.
The Doctor's Secret (*Hydrothérapie Fantastique*) (1910): Georges Méliès.
"Dreams in Darkness." *Batman: The Animated Series*. Dick Sebast, dir. Season 3, episode 28. Aired November 3, 1992.
Dressed to Kill (1980): Brian De Palma.
Drugstore Cowboy (1989): Gus Van Zant.
Duet (1987–1989): Iris Dugow, dir.
The Dybbuk (1937): Michal Waszynski.

eXistenZ (1996): David Cronenberg.
The Exorcist (1973): William Friedkin.
The Exorcist II: The Heretic (1977): John Boorman.
The Fifth Floor (1978): Howard Avedis

Frankenstein (1931): James Whale.
The French Connection (1971): William Friedkin.
The Game (1997): David Fincher.
Gaslight (1944): George Cukor.
Gothika (2003): Mathieu Kassovitz

Hannibal (2001): Ridley Scott.
House on Haunted Hill (1959): William Castle.
House on Haunted Hill (1999): William Malone.
The Hypnotic Eye (1960): George Blair.
The Hypnotic Violinist (1914): Warner Brothers (production company).
The Hypnotic Wife (1909): Pathé (production company)
Hypnotism (1910): Lux (production company).
The Hypnotist at Work [*Le Magnétiseur*] (1897): Georges Méliès.

In Dreams (1999): Neil Jordan.
The Island of Dr. Moreau (1977): Don Taylor.
The Island of Dr. Moreau (1996): John Frankenheimer.
The Island of Lost Souls (1933): Erle C. Kenton.

The Jacket (2005): John Maybury.
Jacob's Ladder (1990): Adrian Lyne.
Judgment at Nuremberg (1961): Stanley Kramer.

King of Hearts (1966): Philippe de Broca.

M (1931): Fritz Lang.
The Man Who Laughs (1928): Paul Leni.
The Manchurian Candidate (1962): John Frankenheimer.
The Manchurian Candidate (2004): Jonathan Demme.
Metropolis (1927): Fritz Lang.
A Nightmare on Elm Street (1984): Wes Craven.

One Flew Over the Cuckoo's Nest (1975): Miloš Forman.

Psycho (1960): Alfred Hitchcock.
Psycho (1998): Gus Van Sant.

Quills (2000): Philip Kaufman.

Rosemary's Baby (1968): Roman Polanski.

Scarface (1993): Brian De Palma.
Session 9 (2001): Brad Anderson.
Shock Corridor (1963): Samuel Fuller.
The Silence of the Lambs (1991): Jonathan Demme.
Silent Hill (2006): Christophe Gans.
The Snake Pit (1948): Anatole Litvak.
Spellbound (1945): Alfred Hitchcock.
Spider (2002): David Cronenberg.
Star Wars (1977): George Lucas.
Suicide Squad (2016): David Ayer.
The System of Dr. Tarr and Professor Fether (1912): Maurice Tourneur.

The Testament of Dr. Mabuse (1933): Fritz Lang.
"**This Ball of Mud and Meanness.**" John Behring, dir. *Gotham*. Season 2, episode 14. Aired March 14, 2016
The Tingler (1959): William Castle.

A Vilna Legend (1924): Zygmund Turkow.
The Vow (1937): Henryk Szaro.

When Clouds Roll By (1919): Victor Fleming.
"**Whom Gods Destroy.**" *Star Trek*. Season 3, episode 14. Herb Wallerstein, dir. Aired January 3, 1969.

Young Frankenstein (1974): Mel Brooks.

Bibliography

Aarseth, Espen. *Cybertext: Perspectives on Ergodic Literature.* Baltimore: John Hopkins University Press, 1997.

Aeschylus. *The Oresteia.* Translated by Ian C. Johnson. Arlington, VA: Richer Resources, 2007.

Allahverdipour, Hamid, Mohsen Bazargan, Abdollah Farhadinasab, and Babak Moeini. "Correlates of Video Games Playing Among Adolescents in an Islamic Country." *BioMed Central PublicHealth* 10 (2010): 286, doi: 10.1186/1471-2458-10-286.

Alper, Thelma. "An Electric Shock Patient Tells His Story." *Journal of Abnormal and Social Psychology* 43 (1948): 201–210.

American Psychiatric Association. *Diagnostic and Statistical Manual of Mental Disorders,* 5th ed. Washington, D.C.: American Psychiatric Association, 2013.

American Psychological Association. "Today's Superheroes Send Wrong Image to Boys, Say Researchers: Masculine Stereotype Not Healthy for Relationships." *American Psychological Association,* August 15, 2010. http://www.apa.org/news/press/releases/2010/08/macho-stereotype-unhealthy.aspx.

Anderson, Craig A. "Media Violence Effects on Children, Adolescents and Young Adults." *Health Progress* 97 (2016): 59–62.

Anderson, Craig A., Akiko Shibuya, Nobuko Ihori, Edward L. Swing, Brad J. Bushman et al. "Violent Video Game Effects on Aggression, Empathy, and Prosocial Behavior in Eastern and Western Countries: A Meta-Analytic Review." *Psychological Bulletin* 136 (2010): 151–73.

Arieti, Silvano. *Interpretation of Schizophrenia.* New York: Basic, 1974.

Arnheim, Rudolf. *Film as Art.* Berkeley: University of California Press, 1957.

atomicpoet. "Is Catcher in the Rye [sic] an Assassination Trigger?" *Wordpress,* January 31, 2012. http://atomicpoet.wordpress.com/2012/01/31/is-catcher-in-the-rye-an-assassination-trigger/.

Bailey, Dale. *American Nightmares: The Haunted House Formula in American Popular Fiction.* Bowling Green, OH: Bowling Green State University Popular Press, 1999.

Bakhtin, Mikhail. *Rabelais and His World.* Translated by Hélène Iswolsky. Cambridge, MA: MIT Press, 1968.

Ballinger, Alexander, and Danny Graydon. *The Rough Guide to Film Noir.* New York: Rough Guide, 2007.

Basaglia, Franco. *L'instituzione Negata.* Torino, Italy: Einaudi, 1973.

Beatty, Bart. *Fredric Wertham and the Critique of Mass Culture.* Jackson: University of Mississippi, 2005.

Beil, Benjamin. "Film Aesthetics and Interactive Representations of Subjectivity in Video Games." In *Subjectivity Across Media: Interdisciplinary and Transmedial Perspectives,* edited by Maike Sarah Reinerth and Jan-Noël Thon. New York: Routledge, 2017.

Bender, H. Erik, Praveen R. Kamban and Vasilis Pozios. "Putting the Caped Crusader on the Couch." *New York Times,* September 20, 2011.

Benton, Mike. *The Illustrated History of Horror Comics.* Dallas, TX: Taylor Publishing, 1991.

Berger, Arthur Asa. *The Comic-Stripped American: What Dick Tracy, Blondie, Daddy Warbucks, and Charlie Brown Tell Us About Ourselves.* New York: Walker, 1973.

Bergfelder, Tim, Erica Carter and Deniz Gokturk. *The German Cinema Book.* London: BFI, 2002.

Bergstrom, Janet, ed. *Endless Night.* Berkeley: University of California Press, 1999.

Bernstein, Matthew, and Gaylyn Studlar, ed. *Visions of the East.* New Brunswick, NJ: Rutgers University Press, 1997.

Biesen, Sheri Chinen. *Blackout: World War II and the Origins of Film Noir.* Baltimore: Johns Hopkins University Press, 2005.

Bould, Mark: *Film Noir: From Berlin to Sin City.* London: Wallflower, 2005.

Bourde, Raymond, and Étienne Chaumeton. *A Panorama of American Film Noir: 1941–1953.* Translated by Paul Hammond. San Francisco: City Lights, 2002.

Bourget, Dominique, Pierre Gagné, and Mary-Eve Labelle. "Parricide: A Comparative Study of Matricide Versus Patricide." *Journal of the American Academy of Psychiatry and the Law* 35 (2007): 306–12.

Bradbury, Ray. "Usher II." *The Martian Chronicles.* Garden City, NJ: Doubleday, 1958.

Braslow, Joel T. *Mental Ills and Bodily Cures: Psychiatric Treatment in the First Half of the Twentieth*

Century. Berkeley: University of California Press, 1997.

Breggin, Peter. *Electroshock: Its Brain-Disabling Effects.* New York: Springer, 1979.

Bridwell, E. Nelson. Introduction to *Superman from the Thirties to the Seventies,* edited by National Periodical Comics. New York: Crown Publishers, 1971.

Brooker, Will. *Batman Unmasked: Analysing a Cultural Icon.* London: Continuum, 2001.

Brown, Jeffrey. "Comic Book Masculinity and the New Black Superhero." *African American Review* Spring 1999.

Budd, Mike, ed. *The Cabinet of Dr. Caligari.* New Brunswick, NJ: Rutgers University Press, 1990.

Buhle, Paul, ed. *Jews and American Comics: An Illustrated History of an American Art Form.* New York: New Press, 2008.

Burns, Sarah. "Better for Haunts: Victorian Houses and the Modern Imagination." *American Art* 26, no. 3 (Fall 2012): 2–25.

Bushman, Brad J., and Craig A. Anderson. "Comfortably Numb: Desensitizing Effects of Violent Media on Helping Others." *Psychological Science* 20 (2009): 273–277.

Callahan, Timothy. *Grant Morrison: The Early Years.* Edwardsville, IL: Sequart Research & Literacy Organization, 2007.

Campbell, Joseph. *The Hero with a Thousand Faces.* Princeton: Princeton University Press, 2004.

Campbell, Joseph. Introduction to *The Portable Jung.* By C.G. Jung. New York: Penguin, 1971.

Campbell, Joseph. *The Masks of God: Creative Mythology.* New York: Penguin, 1968.

Campbell, Joseph, Bill Moyers and Betty Flowers. *The Power of Myth.* New York: Knopf Doubleday Publishing Group, 1988.

Campion, John, James M. Cravens, Alec Rotholc, Henry C. Weinstein, Fred Covan and Murray Alpert. "A Study of 15 Matricidal Men." *American Journal of Psychiatry* 142 (1985): 312–7.

Cardno, Alistair, E. Jane Marshall, Bina Coid, Alison Macdonald, Tracy Ribchester, Nadia Davies, Piero Venturi, Lisa Jones, Shon Lewis et al. "Heritability Estimates for Psychotic Disorders: the Maudsley Twin Psychosis Series." *Archives of General Psychiatry* (February 1999): 56: 162–168.

Carroll, Noël. "Horror and Humor." *The Journal of Aesthetics and Art Criticism* 57, no. 2 (Spring 1999): 145–160.

Chabon, Michael. *The Amazing Adventures of Kavalier and Clay.* New York: Picador, 2000.

Chabon, Michael. "Introduction to Metropolitan Museum of Art." *Superheroes: Fashion and Fantasy.* New Haven: Yale University Press, 2008.

Chandler, Raymond. *Farewell, My Lovely.* New York: Knopf Doubleday, 1940.

Charney, Dennis. "Psychobiological Mechanism of Resilience and Vulnerability: Implications for Successful Adaption to Extreme Stress." *American Journal of Psychiatry* 2 (2004): 368–391.

Charney, Leo, and V.R. Schwartz. *Cinema and the Invention of Modern Life.* Berkeley: University of California Press, 1995.

Chu, Johnny. "Confirmed: Harley Quinn Based on Arleen Sorkin's Role on *Days of Our Lives.*" *Geeky News.* www.geekynews.com/confirmed-harley-quinn-based-on-arleen-sorkins-role-on-days-of-our-lives-14220/.

Clark, S.A. "Matricide: The Schizophrenic Crime?" *Medicine, Science and the Law* 33 (1993): 325–8.

Cocks, Geoffrey. *Psychotherapy in the Third Reich.* 2d ed. New Brunswick, NJ: Transaction Publishers, 1997.

Coles, Robert, ed. *The Erik Erikson Reader.* New York: Norton, 2000.

Conner, Amanda, Jimmy Palmiotti and Chad Hardin. *Harley Quinn.* New York: DC Comics, 2013.

Conner, Amanda, Jimmy Palmiotti, John Timms and Chad Hardin. *Harley Quinn.* Burbank, CA: DC Comics, 2016.

Coogan, Peter. *Superhero: The Secret Origin of a Genre.* Austin, TX: Monkey Brain Books, 2006.

Cooper, D.G. *Psychiatry and Anti-Psychiatry.* Oxon, UK: Routledge, 2007.

Cooper, David. *The Death of the Family.* Harmondsworth, UK: Penguin, 1980.

Cox, Brian. Review of *Shyness: How Normal Behavior Became a Sickness* by Christopher Lane. *New England Journal of Medicine* 358 (2008): 539–540.

Craddock, Jim, ed. *Videohound's Golden Movie Retriever 2007.* Detroit: Thomson Gale, 2007.

Daniels, Bradley J. "Arkham Asylum: Forensic Psychology and Gotham's (Not So) Serious House." In *The Psychology of Superheroes,* edited by Robin Rosenberg and Jennifer Canzoneri. Dallas, TX: SmartPop Books, 2008.

Daniels, Les. *Batman: The Complete History.* San Francisco: First Chronicle Books, 2004.

Daniels, Les. *DC Comics: A Celebration of the World's Favorite Comic Book Heroes.* New York: Watson-Guptill, 2003.

Daniels, Les. *Wonder Woman: The Life and Times of the Amazon Princess: The Complete History.* San Francisco: Chronicle Books, 2000.

Darlage, Adam. "From Pogo to Pennywise: the Rise of the Evil Clown in American Pop Culture Since 1978." In *A History of Evil in Popular Culture: What Hannibal Lecter, Stephen King, and Vampires Reveal About America.* Vol. 2, edited by Sharon Packer and Jody Pennington. Santa Barbara, CA: ABC-CLIO, 2014.

Day, Terri, and Ryan C.W. Hall. "Déjà Vu: From Comic Books to Video Games: Legislative Reliance on 'Soft Science' to Protect Against Uncertain Societal Harm Linked to Violence V. the First Amendment." *Oregon Law Review* 89 (2010): 415–452.

DeCamp, Whitney, and Christopher Ferguson J. "The Impact of Degree of Exposure to Violent Video Games, Family Background, and Other Factors on Youth Violence." *Journal of Youth Adolescence* 46, (2017): 388–400.

Depra, Dianne. "5,000,000: Number of 'Batman: Arkham Knight' Copies Sold Since Launch." *Tech Times.* http://www.techtimes.com/articles/95196/20151015/5-000-000-number-of-batman-arkham-knight-copies-sold-since-launch.htm.

Dery, Marc. *The Pyrotechnic Insanitarium: American Culture on the Brink.* New York: Grove, 1999.

Dini, Paul, and Bruce Timm. *The Batman Adventures: Mad Love.* New York: DC Comics, 1994.

Dini, Paul, and Bruce Timm. *Mad Love.* New York: DC Comics, 2009.

Dini, Paul, Yvel Guichet, Aaron Sowd, Don Kramer, Wayne Faucher, Joe Quinones, Neil Googe and Alex Ross. *Batman: Harley Quinn.* New York: DC Comics, 1999.

DiPaolo, Marc. *War, Politics, and Superheroes: Ethics and Propaganda in Comics and Film.* Jefferson, NC: McFarland, 2011.

Donn, Linda. *Freud and Jung. Years of Friendship, Years of Loss.* New York: Collier, 1988.

Donovan, Sarah K. "Under the Mask." In *Batman and Philosophy: The Dark Knight of the Soul,* edited by William Irwin, Mark White, and Robert Arp. Hoboken, NJ: Wiley, 2008.

Dostoyevsky, Fyodor. *The Idiot.* Columbia, SC: Digreads, 2018.

Doyle, Kathryn. "Violent Video Games May Be Tied to Aggressive Thoughts." *Reuters Health News.* http://www.reuters.com/article/us-violent-videogames-idUSBREA2N1MC20140324.

Duncan, Randy, and Matthew J. Smith, ed. *Icons of the American Comic Book: From Captain America to Wonder Woman.* Santa Barbara, CA: ABC-CLIO, 2013.

Durand, Kevin K., and Mark K. Leigh, ed. *Riddle Me This, Batman! Essays on the Universe of the Dark Knight.* Jefferson, NC: McFarland, 2011.

Ebaugh, Franklin G., Clarke H. Barnacle and Karl T. Neuberger. "Fatalities Following Electric Convulsive Therapy." *Archives of Neurology and Psychiatry* 49, no. 1 (1943), 107–117.

Eisner, Lotte H. *Fritz Lang.* New York: Da Capo, 1976.

Eisner, Lotte H. *The Haunted Screen.* Berkeley: University of California Press, 1952.

Eisner, Lotte H. *The Haunted Screen: Expressionism in the German Cinema and the Influence of Max Reinhardt.* Translated by Roger Greaves. Berkeley: University of California, Press, 1977.

Elferen, Isabella. "Sonic Descents: Musical Dark Play in Survival and Psychological Horror." In *The Dark Side of Game Play: Controversial Issues in Playful Environments,* edited by Torill Elvira Mortensen, Jonas Linderoth, and Ashley ML Brown. London: Routledge, 2015.

Eliade, Mircea. *Shamanism.* Princeton, NJ: Bollingen,1972.

Eliot, Alexander, Joseph Campbell and Mircea Eliade. *The Universal Myths.* Markham, Ontario: New American Library, 1990.

Ellenberger, Henri. *Discovery of the History of the Unconscious: The History and Evolution of Dynamic Psychiatry.* New York: Basic Books, 1970.

Elsaesser, Thomas. *Fassbinder's Germany.* Amsterdam: Amsterdam University Press, 1981.

Elsaesser, Thomas: *Weimar Cinema and After.* London: Routledge, 2001.

Erikson, Erik. *Childhood and Society.* 2d ed. New York: Norton, 1950.

Estes, Clarissa Pinkola. *Women Who Run with the Wolves: Myths and Stories of the Wild Woman Archetype.* New York, Random House, 1992.

Eury, Michael, and Michael Kronenberg. *The Batman Companion.* Raleigh, NC: TwoMorrows Publishing, 2009.

Feiffer, Jules. *The Great Comic Book Heroes.* New York: Bonanza Books, 1965.

Fenichel, Otto. *The Psychoanalytic Theory of Neurosis.* New York: Norton, 1945.

Ferguson, Christopher J., and John Kilburn. "Much Ado About Nothing: The Misestimation and Overinterpretation of Violent Video Game Effects in Eastern and Western Nations: Comment on Anderson et al. (2010)." *Psychological Bulletin* 136 (2010): 174–178.

Finger, Bill, Lewis Sayre Schwartz, George Roussos and Win Mortimer. "The Man in the Red Hood." In *Detective Comics* #168. New York: DC Comics, 1951.

Fingeroth, Danny. *Disguised as Clark Kent: Jews, Comics, and the Creation of the Superhero.* New York: Continuum, 2007.

Fingeroth, Danny. *Superman on the Couch: What Superheroes Really Tell Us About Ourselves and Our Society.* New York: Continuum, 2004.

Fisher, William A., Taylor Kohut, Lisha A. Di Gioacchino, and Paul Fedoroff. "Pornography, Sex Crime, and Paraphilia." *Current Psychiatry Reports* 15(6) (2013): 1–8, https://doi.org/10.1007/s11920-013-0362-7.

Fitrakas, Bob. "The Columbus Sniper, Video Games and the New Manchurian Candidates." *The Free Press,* August 29, 2004. http://freepress.org/article/columbus-sniper-video-games-and-new-manchurian-candidates

Fleischhacker, H.H. "Some Neurological and Neurovegetative Phenomena Occurring During and After Electroshock." *Journal of Nervous and Mental Disease* 102, no. 4 (1945): 185–190.

Forcén, Carlos Espí, and Fernando Espí Forcén. "Demonic Possessions and Mental Illness: Discussion of Selected Cases in Late Medieval Hagiographical Literature." *Early Science and Medicine* 19, no. 3 (2014): 258–79.

Forcén, Fernando Espí. "A Hospital for the Mentally Ill in the Middle Ages—Psychiatry in History." *The British Journal of Psychiatry* 208, no. 2 (2016): 103.

Forcén, Fernando Espí. *Monsters, Demons and Psychopaths: Psychiatry and Horror Film.* Boca Raton: CRC, 2017.

Foster, William. *Looking for a Face Like Mine.* Waterbury, CT: Fine Tooth Press, 2005.

Foucault, Michel. *Discipline and Punish: The Birth of the Prison.* New York: Vintage, 1995.

Foucault, Michel. *Madness and Civilization: A History of Insanity in the Age of Reason.* New York: Vintage, 1988.

Fox News. "Controversial Video Game Gun Study Gets Retracted." *Fox News,* January 25, 2017. http://www.foxnews.com/tech/2017/01/25/controversial-video-game-gun-study-gets-retracted.html

Franciscono, Marcel. "The Imagery of Max Beck-

mann's *The Night*." *Art Journal* 33, no. 1 (1973): 18–22.
Franz, Alexander, and Sheldon Selesnick. *The History of Psychiatry*. Northvale, NJ: Jason Aronson, 1966.
Frazer, James. *Folklore in the Old Testament* (abridged edn.). New York: Avenel, 1988.
Frazer, James. *The Golden Bough: A Study in Magic and Religion* (abridged edn.). New York: Penguin. 1996.
Friedberg, John. *Shock Treatment Is Not Good for Your Brain*. San Francisco: Glide Publications, 1975.
Friedman, Lawrence: *Menninger: The Family and the Clinic*. New York: Knopf. 1990.
Friedman, Susan Hatters, Fernando Espí Forcén, and John Preston Shand. "Horror Films and Psychiatry." *Australasian Psychiatry* 22, no. 5 (2014): 447–49.
Friedman, Susan Hatters, Fernando Espí Forcén, John Preston Shand, and Praveen R. Kambam. "Horror Films and Forensic Psychiatry." *Newsletter of the American Academy of Psychiatry and the Law* 42 (2017): 11.
Friedman, Susan Hatters, and Phillip J. Resnick. "Child Murder by Mothers: Patterns and Prevention." *World Psychiatry* 6 (2007): 137–141.
Friedman, Susan Hatters, and Ryan C.W. Hall. "Star Wars: the Force Awakens Forensic Teaching About Patricide." *Journal of the American Academy of Psychiatry and the Law* 45 (2017): 726–32
Fromm, Erich. *Escape from Freedom*. New York: Henry Holt, 1969.
Gabbard, Glen, and K. Gabbard. *Psychiatry and the Cinema*, 2d ed. Washington, D.C.: American Psychiatric Press, 1999.
Gabler, Neal. *An Empire of Their Own*. New York: Anchor Books, 1988.
Gabler, Neal. *Life: The Movie: How Entertainment Conquered Reality*. New York: Vintage, 2000.
Gay, Peter. *A Godless Jew: Freud, Atheism, and the Making of Psychoanalysis*. New Haven: Yale University Press and Hebrew Union College Press, 1987.
Genrile, Douglas A., Dongdong Li, Angeline Khoo, Sara Prot, and Craig A. Anderson. "Mediators and Moderators of Long-term Effects of Violent Video Games on Aggressive Behavior: Practice, Thinking, and Action." *Journal of American Medical Association Pediatric* 168 (2014): 450–7.
Gertz, Stephen. *Dope Menace: The Sensational World of Drug Paperbacks 1900–1975*. Portsend, WA: Feral House, 2008.
Giannetti, Louis, and S. Eyman. *Flashback*, 4th ed. Upper Saddle River, NJ: Prentice Hall, 2001.
Gilman, Charlotte Perkins. "The Yellow Wallpaper." *The New England Magazine*, January 1892.
Gilman, Sander L. *The Case of Sigmund Freud. Medicine and Identity at the Fin De Siècle*. Baltimore: Johns Hopkins University Press, 1993.
Gilman, Sander L. *Difference and Pathology: Stereotypes of Sexuality, Race and Madness*. Ithaca, NY: Cornell University Press, 1985.
Gilman, Sander L. *Disease and Representation: Images of Illness from Madness to AIDS*. Ithaca, NY: Cornell University Press, 1988.
Gilman, Sander L. *Seeing the Insane. a Visual and Cultural History of Our Attitudes Toward the Mentally Ill*. Brattleboro, VT: Echo Point Books and Media LLC, 2014.
Girard, Rene. *Violence and the Sacred*. Baltimore: Johns Hopkins University Press, 1977.
Glass, Adam, Federico Dallocchio, and Ransom Getty. *Suicide Squad, Vol. 4*. New York: DC Comics, 2011.
Goffman, Erving. *Asylums: Essays on the Social Situation of Mental Patients and Other Inmates*. Chicago: Aldine Publishing, 1961.
Goldsmith, Gary. Review of "Freudian Fraud: The Malignant Effect of Freud's Theory on American Thought and Culture" by E. Fuller Torrey. *New England Journal of Medicine* 328, no. 15 (1993): 1131–1132.
Gomel, Elana. *Narrative Time and Space: Representing Impossible Topologies in Literature*. New York: Routledge, 2014.
Goode, Erica, Serge Kovaleski, Jack Healy, and Dan Frosch. "Before Gunfire, Hints of 'Bad News.'" *New York Times*, August 26, 2012. http://www.nytimes.com/2012/08/27/us/before-gunfire-in-colorado-theater-hints-of-bad-news-about-james-holmes.html
Goodwin, John. "The Horror of Stigma: Psychosis and Mental Health Care Environments in Twenty-First Century Horror Film (Part II)." *Perspectives in Psychiatric Care* 50, no. 4 (2014): 224–242.
Gordon, Ian, Mar Jancovich, and Matthew McAllister. *Film and Comic Books*. Jackson: University Press of Mississippi, 2007.
Gould, Michael: *Surrealism and the Cinema*. London: Tantivy Press, 1976.
Gralnick, Alexander. "A Fatality Incident to Electroshock: A Review of the Subject and Autopsy Report." *Journal of Nervous and Mental Disease* 102, no. 5 (1945): 483–495.
Grant, Alan. *Batman: Shadow of the Bat: The Last Arkham #1*. New York: DC Comics, June 1992.
Grant, Alan. *Batman: The Last Arkham*. New York: DC Comics, 1992.
Grant, Alan, and Alcatena (artist). *The Batman of Arkham*. New York: DC Comics, 2000.
Gravett, Paul, and Peter Stanbury. *Holy Sh*t! The World's Weirdest Comic Books*. New York: St. Martin's Press, 2008.
Green, Christopher M. "Matricide by Sons." *Medicine, Science and the Law* 21 (1981): 207–14.
Greenberg, Harvey Roy. *Screen Memories*. New York: Columbia University Press, 1993.
Greitemeyer, Tobias, and Silvia Osswald. "Effects of Prosocial Video Games on Prosocial Behavior." *Journal of Personality and Social Psychology* 98 (2010): 211–221.
Gunning, Tom. *The Films of Fritz Lang*. London: BFI, 2000.
Gunter, Barrie, and Jill McAleer. *Children and Television*. 2d ed. London: Routledge, 2005.
Hajdu, David. *The Ten-Cent Plague: The Great*

Comic-Book Scare and How It Changed America. New York: Picador, 2008.
Hale, Nathan G. "American Psychoanalysis Since World War II." In *American Psychiatry After World War II, 1944–1994*, edited by Roy W. Menninger and John C. Nemiah. Washington, D.C.: American Psychiatric Press, 2000.
Hall, Ryan, Terri Day, and Richard Hall. "A Plea for Caution: Violent Video Games, the Supreme Court, and the Role of Science." *Mayo Clinical Proceedings* 86 (2011): 315–321.
Hammond, Paul, ed. and trans. *The Shadow and Its Shadow*, 3rd ed. San Francisco: City Lights, 2000.
Harman, Graham. *Weird Realism: Lovecraft and Philosophy.* Alresford: Zero Books, 2012.
Harris, Jack C. Foreword to *The Dark Age: Grim, Great & Gimmicky Post-Modern Comics.* By Mark Voger. Raleigh, NC: TwoMorrows Publishing, 2006.
Hayman, Ronald. *A Life of Jung.* New York: Norton, 1999.
Heide, Kathleen M. "Matricide and Step-matricide Victims and Offenders: an Empirical Analysis of U.S. Arrest Data." *Behavioral Sciences and the Law* 31 (2013): 203–14.
Heide, Kathleen M., and Autumn Frei. "Matricide: a Critique of the Literature." *Trauma, Violence, & Abuse* 11 (2010): 3–17.
Heide, Kathleen M., and Denise Paquette Boots. "A Comparative Analysis of Media Reports of U.S. Parricide Cases with Officially Reported National Crime Data and the Psychiatric and Psychological Literature." *International Journal of Offender Therapy and Comparative Criminology* 51 (2007): 646–75.
Hewetson, Alan. *The Complete Illustrated History of the Skywald Horror-Mood.* Manchester, UK: Critical Vision, 2004.
Hill, Geoffrey. *Illuminating Shadows: The Mythic Power of Film.* Boston: Shambala, 1992.
Hine, David, and Jeremy Haun. *Batman: Arkham Asylum #1.* New York: DC Comics, 2009.
Hine, David, and Jeremy Haun. *Batman: Arkham Reborn #1.* New York: DC Comics, 2009.
Hine, David, and Jeremy Haun. *Batman: Arkham Reborn #2.* New York: DC Comics, 2010.
Hine, David, and Jeremy Haun. *Batman: Arkham Reborn #3.* New York: DC Comics, 2010.
Hoberman, J., and Jeffrey Shandler. *Entertaining America.* Princeton, NJ: the Jewish Museum with Princeton University Press, 2003.
Houellebecq, Michel. *H.P. Lovecraft: Against the World, Against Life.* Translated by Dorna Khazeni. France: iUniverse, 1991.
Hubben, William. *Dostoevsky, Kierkegaard, Nietzsche and Kafka.* New York: Touchstone, 1952.
Huesmann, Rowell L. "Nailing the Coffin Shut on Doubts That Violent Video Games Stimulate Aggression: Comment on Anderson et al. (2010)." *Psychological Bulletin* 136 (2010): 179–81.
Huskey, Darry. "A Complete History of Batman Video Games." *IGN.* October 8, 2014. http://www.ign.com/articles/2014/10/08/a-complete-history-of-batman-video-games.
Huston, Aletha C., et al. "From Attention to Comprehension: How Children Watch and Learn from Television." In *Children and Television: Fifty Years of Research*, edited by Norma Pecora, John P. Murray, and Ellen Ann Wartella. Mahwah, NJ: Lawrence Erlbaum, 2007.
IGN Entertainment. "The Top 25 Villains of DC Comics," www.ign.com/articles/the-top-25-villains-of-dc-comics.
Itzkoff, Dave. "Scholar Finds Flaws in Work by Archenemy of Comics." *New York Times.* February 19, 2013. http://www.nytimes.com/2013/02/20/books/flaws-found-in-fredric-werthams-comic-book-studies.html
Jackson, Shirley. *The Haunting of Hill House* (1959). New York: Penguin, 1984, reprint.
Jones, Gerard. *Men of Tomorrow.* New York: Basic Books, 2004.
Jones, Mark. "Tentacles and Teeth: The Lovecraftian Being in Popular Culture." In *New Critical Essays on H.P Lovecraft*, edited by David Simmons. New York: Palgrave Macmillan, 2013, 227–247.
Joshi, S.T. *H.P. Lovecraft: A Life.* West Warwick, RI: Necronomicon Press, 1996.
Joshi, S.T. "Lovecraft and a World in Transition." In *Lovecraft and a World in Transition: Collected Essays on H.P. Lovecraft*, edited by S.T. Joshi. New York: Hippocampus Press, 2014.
Jung, C.G. *Man and His Symbols.* New York: Anchor, 1964.
Jung, C.G. *Memories, Dreams, Reflections*, revised ed., edited by Aniela Jaffe. Translated by Richard and Clara Winston. New York, Vintage: 1989.
Jung, C.G. *The Portable Jung*, edited by Joseph Campbell. New York: Penguin, 1971.
Jung, C.G. *The Red Book: Liber Novus*, edited by S. Shamdasani. Translated by M. Kyburz, J. Peck. New York: W.W. Norton, 2009.
Kalat, David. *The Strange Case of Dr. Mabuse.* Jefferson, NC: McFarland, 2001.
Kalinowski, Lothar, and Paul Hoch. *Somatic Treatments in Psychiatry: Pharmacotherapy; Convulsive, Insulin, Surgical Other Methods*, 2d ed. New York: Grune & Stratton, 1952.
Kalman, Thomas. "FRONTLINE—Clinical Encounters with Internet Pornography." *Journal of the American Academy of Psychoanalysis and Dynamic Psychiatry* 36, no. 4 (2008): 593–618.
Kane, Bob, and Bill Finger. *Batman #1*, New York: DC Comics, 1940.
Kane, Joseph. "Batman and Psychiatry." *British Journal of Psychiatry* 199 (2011): 359
Kaplan, Arie. *From Krakow to Krypton: Jews and Comic Books.* Philadelphia: JPS, 2008.
Kaplan, E. Ann, ed. *Psychoanalysis & Cinema.* New York: Routledge, 1990.
Kaplan, Harold I., and Benjamin J. Sadock. *Kaplan & Sadock's Comprehensive Textbook of Psychiatry.* Philadelphia: Lippincott Williams & Wilkins, 2009.
Kater, Michael H. *Doctors Under Hitler.* Chapel Hill: University of North Carolina, 1989.
Kellogg, Carolyn. "Fire Department Links '50 Shades' to Handcuff Help Calls." *Los Angeles Times*, July

29, 2013. http://www.latimes.com/books/jacketcopy/la-et-jc-fire-department-50-shades-handcuff-help-calls-20130729-story.html.

Kenrick, Douglas, and Virgil Sheets. "Homicidal Fantasies." *Evolution and Human Behavior* 14 (1993): 231–246.

Kerkhoff, Jack. *How Thin the Veil: A Newspaper Man's Story of His Own Mental Crackup and Recovery.* New York: Greenberg, 1952.

Kesey, Ken. *One Flew Over the Cuckoo's Nest.* New York: Signet, 1962.

Kieth, Sam, Michelle Madsen, Dave Stewart, Steve Wands and Bob Kane. *Arkham Asylum: Madness.* London: Titan, 2011.

King, Stephen. *Danse Macabre.* New York: Everest House, 1981.

King, Stephen. "Lovecraft's Pillow." Introduction to *H.P. Lovecraft: Against the World, Against Life.* By Michel Houellebecq. San Francisco: Believer Books, 2005.

King, Stephen. *The Shining* (1977). New York: Anchor Books, 2012, reprint.

Kinnard, Roy. *Horror in Silent Films.* Jefferson, NC: McFarland, 1995.

Kirsch, Thomas B. *The Jungians.* London: Routledge, 2000.

Klock, Geoff. *How to Read Superhero Comics and Why.* New York: Continuum, 2002.

Klöckner, Clemens. "Experience and Memory: The Visualization of World War I by Artists in Vienna and Berlin." In *Vienna-Berlin, the Art of Two Cities,* edited by Berlinische Galerie and Belvedere Vienna. Munich, London: Prestel, 2013.

Kneeland, Timothy W. Review of *Hurry Tomorrow,* directed by Richard Cohen. *Educational Media Reviews Online,* December 2, 2010. http://emro.lib.buffalo.edu/emro/emroDetail.asp?Number=4253.

Kneeland, Timothy W. "ECT as Miracle Maker, Crucifier & Resurrector: Christian Imagery and ECT 1940–Present." Popular Culture Conference, 1999.

Kneeland, Timothy W., and Carol Warren. *Pushbutton Psychiatry: A History of Electroshock in America.* Westport, CT: Praeger, 2002.

Knight, J. "Comic Books and Psychiatry: An Innovative Way to Teach Mental Health Issues." *British Medical Journal* 340 (2010): 1388.

Knoll, James L., IV. "In Memoriam—Thomas Stephen Szasz, MD." *Psychiatric Times,* September 13, 2012.

Knowles, Christopher. *Our Gods Wear Spandex: The Secret History of Comic Book Heroes.* San Francisco: Weiser, 2007.

Kolker, Robert. *A Cinema of Loneliness,* 3rd ed. New York: Oxford University Press, 2000.

Kolocotrnis, Cyril. "The Truth About Electro-Shock Treatments." *Madness Network News Reader.* San Francisco: Glide Publications, May 1973.

Kracauer, Siegfried. *From Caligari to Hitler: A Psychological History of the German Film,* edited by Leonardo Quaresima. Princeton, NJ: Princeton University Press, 2004.

Kracauer, Siegfried. *From Caligari to Hitler.* Princeton, NJ: Princeton University Press, 1947.

Kranzler, Henry, and Domenic A. Ciraulo. *Clinical Manual of Addiction Psychopharmacology.* Washington, D.C.: APPI Press, 2005.

Laing, R.D. *The Divided Self, Etc.* Harmondsworth, UK: Penguin, 1965.

Lane, Christopher: *Shyness: How Normal Behavior Became a Sickness.* New Haven, CT: Yale University Press, 2007.

Lang, Derrik. "Colorado Massacre Casts Ugly Scar on Batman Mythology." *Associated Press,* July 26, 2012. https://www.usnews.com/news/entertainment/articles/2012/07/26/colo-massacre-casts-ugly-scar-on-batman-mythology.

Langford, Barry. *Film Genre: Hollywood and Beyond.* Edinburgh, UK: Edinburgh University Press, 2005.

Lebeau, Vicky. *Lost Angels.* London: Routledge, 1995.

Lebeau, Vicky. *Psychoanalysis and Cinema.* London: Wallflower, 2001.

Lewis, Beth Irwin. "Lustmord: Inside the Windows of the Metropolis." In *Women in the Metropolis: Gender and Modernity in Weimar Culture,* edited by Katharina Von Ankum. Berkeley: University of California Press, 1997.

Lichtenfeld, Eric. *Action Speaks Louder.* Westport, CT: Praeger, 2004.

Lifton, Robert Jay. *The Nazi Doctors: Medical Killing and the Psychology of Genocide.* New York: Basic Books, 1986.

LoCicero, Don. *Superheroes and Gods: A Comparative Study from Babylonia to Batman.* Jefferson, NC: McFarland, 2008.

Lodge, David. *Consciousness and the Novel.* Harvard University Press, 2002

Loeb, Jeph, and Tim Sale. *The Long Halloween.* New York: DC Comics, 2011.

Loeb, Jeph. *Emperor Joker.* London: Titan, 2007.

Long, Rose-Carol Washton, and Maria Makela, ed. *Of 'Truths Impossible to Put in Words': Max Beckmann Contextualized.* Bern, Switzerland: Peter Lang Publishers, 2009.

Longfellow, Henry Wadsworth. "The Masque of Pandora." In *The Masque of Pandora and Other Poems.* Boston: Osgood, 1876.

Longhurst, Robin. *Bodies: Exploring Fluid Boundaries.* London: Routledge, 2001.

Lovecraft, H.P. "The Call of Cthuhlu." In *The Complete Fiction of H.P. Lovecraft.* New York: Chartwell Books, 2016.

Lovecraft, H.P. "The Dreams in the Witch House." In *The Complete Fiction of H.P. Lovecraft.* New York: Chartwell Books, 2016.

Lovecraft, H.P. "The Festival." In *The Complete Fiction of H.P. Lovecraft.* New York: Chartwell Books, 2016.

Lovecraft, H.P. "The Outsider." In *The Complete Fiction of H.P. Lovecraft.* New York: Chartwell Books, 2016.

Lovecraft, H.P. "The Picture in the House." In *The Complete Fiction of H.P. Lovecraft.* New York: Chartwell Books, 2016.

Lovecraft, H.P. "The Shadow Out of Time." In *The Complete Fiction of H.P. Lovecraft.* New York: Chartwell Books, 2016.

Lovecraft, H.P. "The Silver Key." In *The Complete*

Fiction of H.P. Lovecraft. New York: Chartwell Books, 2016.
Lovecraft, H.P. "The Thing on the Doorstep." In *The Complete Fiction of H.P. Lovecraft.* New York: Chartwell Books, 2016.
Macfie, Alexander Lyon. *Orientalism: A Reader.* New York: New York University Press, 2000.
Maidenbaum, Aryeh, ed. *Jung and the Shadow of Anti-Semitism.* Berwick, ME: Nicolas-Hays, 2003.
Makari, George. *Revolution in Mind: The Creation of Psychoanalysis.* New York: Harper Perennial, 2008.
Marleau, Jacques D., Frédéric Millaud and Nathalie Auclair. "A Comparison of Parricide and Attempted Parricide: a Study of 39 Psychotic Adults." *International Journal of Law and Psychiatry* 26 (2003): 269–79.
Marnell, Blair. "New CALL OF CTHULHU Game Trailer Embraces Lovecraftian Madness," modified January 23, 2017. http://nerdist.com/new-call-of-cthulhu-game-trailer-embraces-lovecraftian-madness/.
McGinn, Colin. *The Power of Movies.* New York: Pantheon, 2005.
Means-Shannon, Hannah. "The Joker Plays King: Archetypes of the Underworld in Grant Morrison and Dave McKean's *Arkham Asylum: A Serious House on Series Earth.*" In *The Joker: A Serious Study of the Clown Prince of Crime*, edited by Robert Moses Peaslee and Robert G. Weiner. Jackson: University Press of Mississippi, 2015, 194–208.
Means-Shannon, Hannah. "On the Scene: Sparks Fly at 'Surely You're Joking, Dr. Wertham' Event." www.comicsbeat.com.
Medawar, Jean, and David Pyke. *Hitler's Gift: The True Story of the Scientists Expelled by the Nazi Regime.* New York, Arcade, 2000.
Metropolitan Museum of Art. *Superheroes: Fashion and Fantasy.* New Haven, CT: Yale University Press, 2008.
Middleton, Robin. "Sickness, Madness and Crime as the Grounds of Reform." *AA Files: Architectural Association School of Architecture*, no. 25 (1993): 14–29.
Miller, Dinah, and Annette Hanson. *Committed.* Baltimore: Johns Hopkins University Press, 2016.
Miller, Frank, Klaus Janson and Lynn Varley. *Batman: The Dark Knight Returns.* New York: DC Comics, 1986.
Miller, Greg. Review of *Batman: Arkham Asylum*, developed by Rocksteady Studios, Feral Interactive, and Virtuos. *IGN*, May 26, 2010. http://www.ign.com/articles/2010/05/27/batman-arkham-asylum-game-of-the-year-review?page=1.
Miller, Gregory M., and Justin P. Wade. "Physician and Hospital *Amici CURIAE Volk V. Demeerleer.*" Signatory organizations: Washington State Medical Association, Washington State Hospital Association, American Medical Association, Washington Chapter—American College of Emergency Physicians, Washington State Council of Child & Adolescent Psychiatry, Washington Academy of Family Physicians, and American Psychiatric Association. Submitted to court October 21, 2015.
Millet, John A.P., and Eric P. Mosses. "On Certain Psychological Aspects of Electroshock Therapy." *Pyschosomatic Medicine* (1944): 341.
Moon, Graham, Robin Kearns and Alun Joseph. *The Afterlives of the Psychiatric Asylum: Recycling Concepts, Sites and Memories.* Burlington VT: Ashgate, 2015.
Moore, Alan, Brian Bolland and John Higgins. *Batman: The Killing Joke.* New York: DC Comics, 1988.
Morris, Tom, and Matt Morris, ed. *Superheroes and Philosophy: Truth, Justice and the Socratic Way.* Chicago: Open Court, 2005.
Morrison, Grant. *Arkham Asylum: A Serious House on Serious Earth.* Burbank, CA: DC Comics, 1989.
Morrison, Grant, and Dave McKean. *Arkham Asylum: A Serious House on Serious Earth.* New York: DC Comics, 1997.
Morrison, Grant, and Dave McKean. *Arkham Asylum: A Serious Place on Serious Earth, 15th Anniversary Edition.* New York: DC Comics, 2004.
Morrison, Grant, and Dave McKean. *Arkham Asylum: A Serious House on Serious Earth, 25th Anniversary Deluxe Edition.* New York: D.C. Comics, 2014.
Morrison, Grant. *Supergods: What Masked Vigilantes, Miraculous Mutants, and a Sun God from Smallville Can Teach Us About Being Human.* New York: Spiegel & Grau, 2011.
Moskowitz, Andrew. "Dissociation and Violence: A Review of the Literature." *Trauma, Violence, & Abuse* 5 (2004): 21–46.
Murphy, Timothy. *Case Studies in Biomedical Research Ethics.* Cambridge, MA: MIT Press, 2004.
Murray, Murray. *Hamlet on the Holodeck: The Future of Narrative in Cyberspace.* Cambridge, MA: MIT Press, 1998.
Murry, David J. *A History of Western Psychology,* 2d ed. Englewood Cliffs, NJ: Prentiss Hall, 1988.
Naremore, James. *More Than Night: Film Noir in Its Contexts.* Berkeley: University of California Press, 1998.
National Periodical Comics. *Superman from the Thirties to the Seventies.* New York: Crown Publishers, 1971.
Neiva, Eduardo, and Carlo Romano. "The Semiotic Immersion of Video Games, Gaming Technology and Interactive Strategies." *The Public Journal of Semiotics* 1, no. 2 (2007) 31–49.
Noll, Richard. *The Jung Cult: The Origins of a Charismatic Movement.* Princeton, NJ: Princeton University Press. 1994.
O'Brien, Geoffrey. *The Phantom Empire.* New York: Norton, 1993.
Oliver, Kelly, and Benigno Trigo. *Noir Anxiety.* Minneapolis: University of Minnesota Press, 2002.
O'Neil, Denny. "The Threat of the Two-Headed Coin." In *Batman #258.* New York: DC Comics, 1974.

Osborne, Jennifer. *Monsters*. New York: Del Ray Books, 2006.
Packer, Sharon. "Ancient Myth and Modern Pharmacology." *Hellenic Medical Society Bulletin*. Spring, 2000.
Packer, Sharon. *Cinema's Sinister Psychiatrists: From Caligari to Hannibal*. London: McFarland, 2012.
Packer, Sharon. *Dreams in Myth, Medicine, and Movies*. Westfield, CT: Praeger, 2002.
Packer, Sharon: "Jewish Mystical Movements and the European Ergot Epidemics." *Israel Journal of Psychiatry* 35, no. 3 (1998): 227–239.
Packer, Sharon. *Mental Illness in Popular Culture*. Santa Barbara, CA: Praeger, 2017.
Packer, Sharon. *Movies and the Modern Psyche*. Westfield, CT: Praeger, 2007.
Packer, Sharon. *Neuroscience in Science Fiction Film*. Jefferson, NC: McFarland, 2015.
Packer, Sharon. "Stress & Religion." In *Encyclopedia of Stress*, vol. III. edited by M. Fink. Cambridge, MA: Academic Press, 1998.
Packer, Sharon. "Stress & Religion." In *Encyclopedia of Stress*, 2d ed., edited by M. Fink. Cambridge, MA: Academic Press, 2007.
Packer, Sharon. "Stress and Religion After 9/11." In *Encyclopedia of Stress*, 2nd ed, edited by M Fink. Cambridge, MA: Academic Press, 2007.
Packer, Sharon. "Stress, Religion & Superheroes." In *Stress: Concepts, Cognition, Emotion, and Behavior. Handbook of Stress*, vol. I, edited by M. Fink. Cambridge, MA: Academic Press, 2016.
Packer, Sharon. *Superheroes and Superegos: Analyzing the Minds Behind the Mask*. Santa Barbara, CA: Praeger, 2010.
Packer, Sharon, and Jody Pennington, ed. *Evil in American Popular Culture: What Hannibal Lecter, Stephen King, and Vampires Reveal About America*. Santa Barbara, CA: ABC-CLIO, 2014.
Packer, Sharon, and Warren Dotz. "Epidemic Ergotism, St. Anthony's Fire, and Jewish Mysticism." *Dermatopathology Practical and Conceptual* 4 (1998): 259–267.
Parkinson, David. *History of Film*. New York: Thames & Hudson, 1995.
Parks, Alison, Helen Sweeting, Daniel Wight and Marion Henderson. "Do Television and Electronic Games Predict Children's Psychosocial Adjustment? Longitudinal Research Using the UK Millennium Cohort Study." *Archives of Disease in Children* 98 (2013): 341–348.
Parteger, William. *Observations on Maniacal Disorders* (Reading: for the Author, 1792) cited in Andrew Scull, *Madhouse: A Tragic Tale of Megalomania and Modern Medicine*. New Haven, CT: Yale University Press, 2005.
Patrick, Christopher. "Psychophysiological Correlates of Aggression and Violence: An Integrative Review." *Philosophical Transactions of the Royal Society B Biological Sciences* 363 (2008): 2543–2555.
Peaslee, Robert Moses, and Robert G. Weiner, ed. *The Joker: A Serious Study of the Clown Prince of Crime*. Jackson, MI.: University Press of Mississippi, 2015.
Pelak, Victoria, and Grant Liu. "Visual Hallucinations." *Current Treatment Options in Neurology*, no. 6 (2004): 75–83. doi:10.1007/s11940-004-0041-4
Pidd, Helen. "Anders Breivik 'Trained' for Shooting Attacks by Playing Call of Duty." *The Guardian*, April 19, 2012. https://www.theguardian.com/world/2012/apr/19/anders-breivik-call-of-duty.
Poe, Edgar Allan. "The System of Dr. Tarr and Prof. Feather." *Graham's Magazine* XXVIII, no. 5 (1845).
Poe, Edgar Allan. *Works of Edgar Allan Poe: Sixty-seven Tales, One Complete Novel and Thirty-one Poems*. New York: Gramercy, 1990.
Poetry Foundation. "The Philosophy of Composition." *Poetry Foundation*. October 13, 2009. www.poetryfoundation.org/resources/learning/essays/detail/69390.
Polan, Dana. *Power and Paranoia*. New York: Columbia University Press, 1986.
Prawer, S.S. *Caligari's Children*. Oxford, UK: Oxford University Press, 1980.
Proctor, Robert N. *Racial Hygiene: Medicine Under the Nazis*. Boston: Harvard University Press, 1988.
Rahman, Tahir, Resnick Phillip and Harry Bruce. "Anders Breivik: Extreme Beliefs Mistaken for Psychosis." *Journal of American Academia of Psychiatry and the Law* 44 (2016): 28–35.
Ramsland, John. "Mettray: A Corrective Institution for Delinquent Youth in France, 1840–1937." *Journal of Educational Administration and History* 22, no. 1 (1990): 30–46.
Rank, Otto. *Art and Artist*. New York: Norton, 1989.
Rank, Otto. *The Myth of the Birth of the Hero*. 1909.
Rehak, Bob. *The Video Game Theory Reader*. London: Routledge, 2003.
Reynolds, Richard. *Super Heroes: A Modern Mythology*. Jackson, MI: University Press of Mississippi, 1992.
Roach, David. *The Superhero Book*, edited by Gina Misiroglu. Detroit: Visible Ink, 2004.
Robinson, Daniel N. *An Intellectual History of Psychology*, 3rd ed. Madison: University of Wisconsin Press, 1995.
Robinson, David. *Das Cabinet Des Dr. Caligari*. London: BFI, 1997.
Rosenberg, Robin, and Jennifer Canzoneri, ed. *The Psychology of Superheroes: An Unauthorized Exploration*. Dallas: Benbella Books, 2008.
Ross, Alex. *Mythology: The DC Comics Art of Alex Ross*. New York: Pantheon. 2005.
Roth, Michael. *Freud: Conflict and Culture*. New York: Vintage, 1998.
Rothman, David J. *The Discovery of the Asylum: Social Order and Disorder in the New Republic*. Boston: Little, Brown, 1971.
Rubin, Lawrence, ed. *Using Superheroes in Counseling and Play Therapy*. New York: Springer-Verlag, 2006.
Rudlin, John. *Comedia Dell'Arte: An Actor's Handbook*. New York: Routledge, 1994.
Sadawski, Greg. *Supermen: The First Wave of Comic Book Heroes 1936–41*. Seattle: Fantagraphics Books, 2009.

Sadowsky, Jonathan. *Electroconvulsive Therapy in America: The Anatomy of a Medical Controversy*. New York: Routledge, 2017.
Said, Edward. *Orientalism*. New York: Vintage, 1979.
Salisbury, Mark. *Burton on Burton*. London: Faber & Faber, 1995.
Santos, Marlisa. *The Dark Mirror: Psychiatry and Film Noir*. Lanham, M.D.: Rowman and Littlefield, 2010.
Sarwer, David, Gregory Brown, and Dwight Evans. "Cosmetic Breast Augmentation and Suicide." *American Journal of Psychiatry* 164 (2007): 1006–1013.
Schelde, Per. *Androids, Humanoids, and Other Science Fiction Monsters*. New York: New York University Press, 1993.
Schlozman, Steven. "What Happened to Mental Illness by the 23rd Century?" In *Star Trek Psychology: The New Frontier*, edited by Travis Langley. New York: Sterling, 2017.
Schwab, Gerald. *The Day the Holocaust Began*. Westport, CT: Praeger, 1990.
Scott Snyder, *Batman Zero Year Savage City*. New York: DC Comics, September 2014.
Scull, Andrew. *Madness in Civilization: A Cultural History of Insanity from the Bible to Freud, from the Madhouse to Modern Medicine*. Princeton, NJ: Princeton University Press, 2015.
Segal, Robert A. *The Gnostic Jung*. London: Routledge, 1992.
Senate Subcommittee Hearings into Juvenile Delinquency, with the special focus on Comic Books. April 21, 1954, testimony by Dr. Fredric Wertham. http://www.thecomicbooks.com/wertham.html.
Sergi, Joe. "Tales from the Code: Spidey Fights Drugs and the Comics Code Authority." *Cbdlf.org*. http://cbldf.org/2012/07/tales-from-the-code-spidey-fights-drugs-and-the-comics-code-authority/.
Shamdasani, Sonu. *Cult Fictions: C.G. Jung and the Foundations of Analytical Psychology*. London: Routledge, 1998.
Shamdasani, Sonu. *Jung and the Making of Modern Psychology: The Dream of a Science*. Cambridge, UK: Cambridge University Press, 2003.
Shand, John Preston, Susan Hatters Friedman and Fernando Espí Forcén. "The Horror, the Horror: Stigma on Screen." *The Lancet Psychiatry* 1, no. 6 (2014): 423–425.
Shand, John Preston, Susan Hatters Friedman, Renee M. Sorrentino, and George W. Schmedlen. "And Then I Woke Up in Jail: Amnesia Claims in Evaluations." Research poster presentation at American Academy of Psychiatry and the Law annual meeting, October 2013, Coronado, CA.
Shorter, Edward. *A History of Psychiatry: From the Era of the Asylum to the Age of Prozac*. New York: Wiley, 1998.
Shorter, Edward, and David Healy, *Shock Therapy: A History of Electroconvulsive Treatment in Mental Illness*. New Brunswick, NJ: Rutgers University Press, 2007.
Siebenpfieffer, Hanis. *Böse Lust: Gewaltverbrechen in Diskursen Der Weimarer Republik*. Böhlau-Verlag, 2005.
Siever, Larry. "Neurobiology of Aggression and Violence." *American Journal of Psychiatry* 165 (2008): 429–442.
Sievers, Melissa. "Brains, Brawn, Breasts: How Women Are Depicted in Today's Action/Adventure Comic Books." MA thesis, University of North Carolina–Chapel Hill, 2003.
Sievers, W. David. *Freud on Broadway*. New York: Hermitage House, 1955.
Silver, Alain, and Elizabeth Ward. *Film Noir*, 3rd ed. Woodstock, NY: Overlook Press, 1992.
Silver, Alain, and Paul Ursini. *Film Noir Reader 4*. New York: Limelight Editions, 2004.
Silver, Alain, and Paul Ursini. *Film Noir*, edited by Paul Duncan. Los Angeles: Taschen, 2004.
Simmons, David, ed. *Essays on H.P. Lovecraft*. New York: Palgrave, 2013.
Sims, David. "Gotham's Arkham Asylum Is Too Bland to Be Scary." *The Atlantic*, January 6, 2015. https://www.theatlantic.com/entertainment/archive/2015/01/gothams-arkham-asylum-is-too-bland-to-be-scary/384244/.
Singer, Marc. *Grant Morrison: Combining the Worlds of Contemporary Comics*. Jackson: University Press of Mississippi, 2012.
Skolnick, Evan. *Video Game Storytelling: What Every Developer Needs to Know About Narrative Techniques*. Berkeley, CA: Watson-Guptill Publications, 2014.
Slocum, J. David. *Violence and American Cinema*. New York: Routledge, 2001.
Slott, Dan, and Ryan Sook. *Arkham Asylum Living Hell*, Chapter 2. New York: DC Comics, August 2003.
Slusser, George, and Gary Westfahl, ed. *No Cure for the Future: Disease and Medicine in Science Fiction and Fantasy*. Westport, CT: Praeger, 2002.
Smith, Daniel. "Shock and Disbelief." *The Atlantic Monthly* 287, no. 2 (2001): 79–90.
Soren, David. *The Rise and Fall of the Horror Film*, revised ed. Baltimore: Midnight Marquee, 1997.
Starlin, Jim, Jim Aparo, Mike DeCarlo, Adrienne Roy, John Costanza and Mike Mignola. "A Death in the Family." *Batman* #426–429. New York: DC Comics, Dec. 1998¬–Jan. 1999.
Staub, Michael E. *Madness Is Civilization: When the Diagnosis Was Social, 1948–1980*. Chicago: University of Chicago Press, 2011.
Stern, Fritz. *Einstein's German World*. Princeton, NJ: Princeton University Press, 1999.
Stokes, Melvyn, and R. Maltby, ed. *Hollywood Spectatorship*. London: BFI, 2001.
Storr, Anthony, and Anthony Stevens. *Freud and Jung: A Dual Introduction*. New York: Barnes & Noble, 1998.
Szasz, Thomas. *The Myth of Mental Illness*. New York: J. Norton, 1974.
Szasz, Thomas, ed. *The Age of Madness: The History of Involuntary Mental Hospitalization*. New York: Jason Aronson, 1974.
Tartar, Maria. *Lustmord: Sexual Murder in Weimar Germany*. Princeton, NJ: Princeton University Press, 1995.
Tear, Morgan J., and Mark Nielsen. "Failure to Demonstrate That Playing Violent Video Games

Diminishes Prosocial Behavior." *Plos One* 8 (2013): doi: 10.1371/journal.pone.0068382.
Thompson, Don, and Maggie, ed. *Comic-Book Superstars*. Iola, WI: Krause, 1993.
Thon, Jan-Noël. "Subjectivity Across Media: On Transmedial Strategies of Subjective Representation: Contemporary Feature Films, Graphic Novels, and Computer Games." In *Storyworlds Across Media: Toward a Media-Conscious Narratology*, edited by Jan-Nol Thon and Marie-Laurie Ryan. Lincoln: University of Nebraska Press: 2014.
Thurber, James. "The Secret Life of Walter Mitty" reprinted in *Thematic Guide to Popular Short Stories*. Edited by Patrick A. Smith. Westport, CT: Greenwood, 2002.
"Top 100 DC Villains." *Comic Vine—Gamespot*. http://www.comicvine.gamespot.com/profile/idea/lists/top-100-dc-villains/49775/.
Torrey, E. Fuller. *Freudian Fraud*. New York: HarperCollins, 1992
Tyler, Parker. *The Hollywood Hallucination*. New York: Creative Age Press, 1944.
Tyrone, Cannon, Jaakko Kaprio, Jouko Lönnqvist, Matti Huttunen and Markku Koskenvuo. "The Genetic Epidemiology of Schizophrenia in a Finnish Twin Cohort: A Population-Based Modeling Study." *Arch Gen Psychiatry* 55 (January 1998): 67–74.
Uricchio, William. "The Batman's Gotham City™: Story, Ideology, Performance." *Comics and the City: Urban Space in Print, Picture and Sequence*. New York: Continuum, 2010.
van der Kolk, Bessel A., and Rita Fisler. "Dissociation and the Fragmentary Nature of Traumatic Memories: Overview and Exploratory Study." *Journal of Traumatic Stress* 8 (1995): 505–25.
Voger, Mark. *The Dark Age: Grim, Great & Gimmicky Post-Modern Comics*. Raleigh, NC: TwoMorrows Publishing, 2006.
Wagner, Matt. *Batman & the Monster Men*. New York: DC Comics, 2006.
Wallace, Daniel, with an introduction by Mark Hamill. *The Joker: A Visual History of the Clown Prince of Crime*. New York: DC Comics, 2011.
Walsh, Doug. *Batman: Arkham Asylum Signature Series Guide*. Indianapolis: Bradygames, 2009.
Weinstein, Rabbi Simcha. *Up, Up and Oy Vey*. Baltimore: Leviathan Press, 2006.
Werthem, Fredric. *Seduction of the Innocent*. New York: Rinehart, 1954.
Werthem, Fredric. *A Sign for Cain: An Exploration of Human Violence*. New York: Macmillan, 1966.
West, Sara G., and Mendel Feldsher. "Parricide: Characteristics of Sons and Daughters Who Kill Their Parents." *Current Psychiatry* 9 (2010): 20–38.
Williams, Mark P. "Making Sense Squared: Iteration and Synthesis in Grant Morrison's Joker." in *The Joker: A Serious Study of the Clown Prince of Crime*, edited by Robert Moses Peaslee and Robert G. Weiner, 209–228. Jackson: University Press of Mississippi, 2015.
Wilson, Claire. "How Mental Illness Is Portrayed in Children's Television: A Prospective Study." *British Journal of Psychiatry* (2000): 176.
Wilson, Edmund. "Tales of the Marvelous and the Ridiculous." In *H.P. Lovecraft: Four Decades of Criticism*, edited by S.T. Joshi. Athens, OH: Ohio State University Press, 1980.
Wolf, Mark J.P. *The Video Game Theory Reader*. London: Routledge, 2003.
Wright, Bradford W. *Comic Book Nation: The Transformation of Youth Culture in America*. Baltimore: Johns Hopkins University Press, 2003.
Wright, Nicky. *The Classic Era of American Comics*. London: Prion, 2000.
Wurtz, James F. "'Out of the Asylum': Physical, Mental, and Structural Space in Grant Morrison and Dave McKean's 'Arkham Asylum: A Serious House on Serious Earth.'" *Amerikastudien / American Studies* 56, no. 4 (2011): 555–71.
Yanni, Carla. *The Architecture of Madness: Insane Asylums in the United States*. Minneapolis, MI: University of Minnesota Press, 2007.
Yanni, Carla. "The Linear Plan for Insane Asylums in the United States Before 1866." *Journal for the Society of Architectural Historians* 62, no. 1 (2003): 24–49.
Yoe, Craig. *Secret Identity: The Fetish Art of Superman's Co-Creator Joe Shuster*. Introduction by Stan Lee. New York: Abrams ComicArts, 2009.
Young-Eisendrath, Polly, and Terence Dawson. *The Cambridge Companion to Jung*. Cambridge, UK: Cambridge University Press, 1997.
Yudofsky, Stuart C. "Commentary: Contracting Schizophrenia: Lessons from the Influenza Epidemic of 1918-1919." *Journal of the American Medical Association* (2009) 324–326: 301(3).
Yudofsky, Stuart C., and Robert E. Hales. "Neuropsychiatry and the Future of Psychiatry and Neurology." *American Journal of Psychiatry* 159, no. 8 (2002): 1261–1264.
Zaretsky, Eli. *Secrets of the Soul: A Social and Cultural History of Psychoanalysis*. New York: Vintage, 2004.

Websites

www.atkinsononfilm.com.
www.boxofficemojo.com
www.geektyrant.com
www.imdb.com
www.seductionoftheinnocent.com
www.superdickery.com
www.wikipedia.com

Index

Numbers in **bold italics** indicate pages with illustrations

AA *see* Alcoholics Anonymous (AA)
Abbot, Bud 259–262, 263*n*45
Abel-Blouet, Guillaume 191
abuse 39, 70, 105, 118, 129–130, 135, 140, 165, 185, 211, 216; child 130; drug 34; physical 91, 118; sexual 91, 118, 127; verbal 127; *see also* alcoholism (alcohol use disorder); substance use
Academy Award 97, 103, 128, 130, 274
acid 46, 153, ***174***, 257; *see also* LSD
acrobat 20, 105–106, ***157***, 255, ***258***
action-adventure 3–4, ***79***, 118
Action Comics 5, 203
action figure ***44***, ***66***, ***71***, ***84***, ***156***, ***241***, ***258***, ***266***
Adams, Neal 243
Adams, Dr. Ruth 38, 40, 141, ***152***, 175–176, 178, 240; treatment of Two-Face 178–179
addiction *see* substance use
Aeschylus 271*n*1, 271*n*2, 271*n*3, 271*n*6, 271*n*7, 271*n*8, 271*n*9, 271*n*10, 271*n*11, 271*n*14, 271*n*16
affair 103, 137, 268
The Affair 73
After Mein Kampf 116
aggression 47, 58–64, 166–167, 172*n*6, 246; *see also* intimate partner violence (IPV)
AIDS 15, 29, 31, 143*n*6
Alabama 116–118; *see also* experimentation, Tuskegee
albino ***71***, 110, 125
Alcmaeon 12, 264–265, 267, 269–270
alcohol 27, 44, 72, 227–228
Alcoholics Anonymous (AA) 44, 51*n*3
alcoholism (alcohol use disorder) 27, 44–45, 51, 66, 68, 74, 83, 198, 227, 257
Alfred 9, 49, 52, 65, 82, 151, 259
Alice 9, 80, 85, 119; *see also* Sinner, Alyse; Synner, Alice; Tetch, Alice

Alice and the Looking Glass 20
Alice's Adventures in Wonderland 84, 141, 203
Alice's Restaurant 10
Allahverdipour, Hamid 59, 62*n*14
Alper, Thelma 40, 42*n*36
alter ego 8, 47, 106, 115, 233, 235
altruism 67–69, 72–74, 79, 83; altruistic infanticide 68; altruistic matricide 68–69, 73
Alzheimer's disease 10, 11, 12, 30, 31; *see also* dementia; frontotemporal dementia (FTD); Huntington's disease (HD); Lewy body dementia (LBD)
Amanita muscaria 15
Amazing Spider-Man 62
Amazing Stories 83
Ambiguously Gay Duo 85
American Gothic 234
American Horror Story: Asylum 97
American Psychiatric Association (APA) 3, 14, 21*n*1, 22*n*18, 32, 32*n*4, 180*n*12, 221*n*22
American Psychological Association (APA) 62, 64*n*30
amnesia 4, 16, 69, 71–72, 74, 75*n*40, 76
amniocentesis 31
amniotic fluid 48
amphetamine 27
Amphiaraus 265
amygdala 45
analytical psychology 15, 223; *see also* Jung, Carl Gustav
Anderson, Craig A. 58–59, 63*n*10, 63*n*12, 63*n*13
anesthesia 38, 49, 116
anima 238–239
animal ***18***, 30, 111, 114, 126, 149, 152; instincts 113–114
animal magnetism 224
animation 1, 9, 19, 38, 105, 107, 110, 145, 151, 165–167, ***166***, 171, 211, 234, ***235***, 257, ***258***; *Animated Series* 49, 104–105, 107–108, 151, 165, 167; computer 110;

Disney animation 110; stop-motion animation ***235***
Annabel Lee ***235***; *see also* stop-motion animation
Annilia see Distress'd Orphan; or Love in a Mad-house
anorexia 45
Ansberry, Clare 12
antibiotics 29
antidepressants 78, 51*n*8, 133, 133*n*7
anti-hero ***50***, 150, 161, 219, 220*n*11, ***246***
anti-psychiatry 17, 20, 38, 41*n*15, 45, 49, 78, 91–94, 97–99, ***98***, 137, 143*n*8, ***189***, 216, 226, 232*n*15
anti-psychotics ***32***, 34; *see also* chlorpromazine; Thorazine (phenothiazine)
anti-Semitism 5, 15
anti-social personality disorder (ASPD) 106, 177; antisocial behavior 55, 60, 70, 75, 104, 110, 145; *see also* sociopath
Antos 117, 177
APOE gene 11, 31
Apollodorus 264, 269
April Fools' Day 142, 153, 175
Aqualad 159
archetype 141, 156, 219, 238, 242*n*2, 256, 262
architecture 1, 19, 93, 98, 101, 184, 191, 198, 216, 219, 221*n*21, 221*n*22, 238, 249; Fritz Lang 220*n*11; Kirkbride 93, 98; Victorian 195, 198, 198*n*6
Archives of General Psychiatry 44
Arieti, Dr. Silvano 95, 99*n*3
aripiprazole (Abilify) 37; *see also* anti-psychotics
aristocracy 223
Arkham 109
Arkham, Dr. Amadeus 5, 16, 9, 20, 25–26, 30, 38, 66, 72–73, 137, 140–142, 150, 176, 184, 193, 198, 218, 239, 270–271; Joker 234, 236; journal 184–185, 188, 218; Jung 238; murder of Mad Dog

292   Index

Hawkins 25–26, 72, 141–142, 150; murder of mother 12, 25, 67, 264–265, 269–270; murder of wife and daughter 26, 66, 193–194, 217; patient in his asylum 227; spirit 185, 187–188; trauma 198; zebra fish 194
Arkham, Elizabeth 10, 12, 16, 21, 25–26, 28–29, 31, 34, 36, 70, 80, 87, 98, 124, 134, 145, 193–194, 264–265; and madness 266–267; as mother 264; murder of 12, 25, 67, 98, 264–265, 269–270; wedding dress 72, 125, 177, 194, 270; *see also* Elizabeth Arkham Asylum for the Criminally Insane
Arkham, Harriet 72, 142, 270
Arkham, Dr. Jeremiah 9, 10, 30–31, 40, **66**, 74, 80, 98, 125, 129, 152; *see also* Black Mask
Arkham Asylum 55, 57; official guide 185–186
Arkham Asylum: A Living Hell 40, 124, 211, 213, 215, 244
Arkham Chronicle Stones 248
Arkham City **77**, 107, 149–150, 186, 190, **192**, 259, **266**
Arkham Horror 245
Arkham Hospital 8–9, 25, 86, 145–146, **147**, **152**, 243
Arkham House 244
Arkham Island 8, 184–185, 189
Arkham Knight **47**, **56**, 57, 149, 151, 259
Arkham: Living Hell 44
Arkham Manor 149
Arkham mythos 3, 6–9, 11, 16, 80–81, **84**, 124, 184, **235**, **246**, 273–274
Arkham Origins 149
Arkham Sanitarium 145, 248; *see also* Arkham Hospital; sanitarium
Arkowitz, Hal 145
Arlecchino 20, 260; *see also* harlequin
Armageddon 58
Arrhenothelus, Zeus 194
Arrow *see* Green Arrow
Arrowverse 156
arsenic 29
Artaud, Antonin 221n20, 222, 232n1
Asperger's Syndrome 131; *see also* autism; autism spectrum disorder (ASD)
Association of Medical Officers of Asylums and Hospitals for the Insane 137
Astounding Stories 244
Asylums 96, 137, 143n9, 148; *see also* Goffman, Erving
Athena 173
Aurelia (Dream and Life) 228
Aurora, Colorado 56, 76–80; *see also* *The Dark Knight Rises*, movie massacre in Aurora, Colorado; Holmes, James; mass murders

Austin Powers 58, 62, 93, 127,
Austria 83, 93, 127, 133n3, 137, 213, 224
autism *see* autism spectrum disorder (ASD)
autism spectrum disorder (ASD) 34, 39, 44, 131; *see also* Asperger's Syndrome
automatic talking 226
automatic writing 224, 226, 229
autopsy *see* post-mortem exam
autosomal dominant disorder 10, 26, 30–31
avant-garde 205, 209n6, 215, 219–220, 232n4
Avedis, Howard 138

"Bad Place" 141
BAFTA 128
Bagley, Dr. 170
Bailey, Dale 141
Bakhtin, Mikhail 175–176, 180n5
Bale, Christian **4**
Bane 48, 151–153, 162, 218
Barkilphedro 256
Barnes, Nathaniel 9
Barthes, Roland 11
Bartholomew, Dr. 49, 165, 167–169
Basaglia, Franco 96, 100n7, 220n13
Basaglia Law 96, 104
"The Bat in the Belfry" 145, 171
Bataille, George 229
batarang **56**, **60**, 153n13, 242n14
Batcave 49, 242, 262,
Bates, Norman 15, 98, 125, 132–133, 145, 176, 194, 239; *see also* Perkins, Anthony; *Psycho*
Batgirl 107, 257
The Batman 145, 151, 156, 165, 170–171, 257
Batman: Arkham Asylum 7, 9, 19, **112**, 148–149, **157**, 184, 191, 193, 195, 243, 245, 247, 246, 256; official guide 185–187; Spirit of Arkham subplot 188
Batman: Arkham City **77**, 86, 190, 149, **192**, 259, **266**
Batman: Arkham Knight **51**, **61**
Batman Begins 3–4, **4**, **44**, 126, 148, 195
Batman Beyond: Return of the Joker 151, 263n21, 263n23
Batman: Confidential 242
Batman: Gothic 242
Batman: Harley Quinn 257–258
Batman: Hush 242, 260
Batman: Nevermore 242
Batman Returns 214, 222
Batman: Savage City 40
Batman: Shadow of a Bat **112**
Batman: The Animated Series 47, 49, 51, 104–105, 107, 145, 151, 165, 167, 171n1, 172n8; 257, 263n19, 263n24; "Dreams in Darkness" 49, 51n12, 165, 167, 171n1; "Lock-up" 168, 172n7
Batman: The Dark Knight Returns 63n41, 231, 259

Batman: The Killing Joke 65, 107, 231, 255
Batman Unmasked 146
Batmobile 9, 48–49, 82, 148
battle fatigue *see* shell shock
Baudelaire, Charles 29
Beacon Asylum 197–198
The Beatles 46, 55, 57, 61
Beatty, Scott 106–107, 109n16
Beauty and the Beast 222
Beckmann, Max 211, 218, 219n1, 221n15, 221n18
Beecher, Dr. Henry 117, 120n7
behavior modification 118; *see also* behavioral conditioning
behavioral conditioning 104, 110
Beil, Benjamin 248
Bell Tower shooting *see* Texas Bell Tower
Belle Reve Penitentiary 155, 166
Bellevue 69, 103
berdache 15
Berger, Arthur Asa 177
Bergholzi 102; *see also* Jung, Carl Gustav
Bergman, Ingrid 230
Bergson, Henri 229
The Bible 39, 57, 143n3, 187
Bibliotheca 264
biopsychosocial model 99
bipolar disorder 21n7, 32, 68
Birds of Prey 105, 107, 109n13
Birth Perinatal Matrices (BPM) 48
Bizarro 203–209
Black Canary 105, 114
black mask 258–259
Black Mask 30–31, 33, **66**; *see also* Arkham, Dr. Jeremiah
Black Mask II 80
Blackgate Prison 133, 148–149
blindness 27, 29, **77**, 117, **130**, **248**, 256
Blood, Jason 124
The Blood of a Poet 222
The Blue Angel 108
Bolland, Brian 179
Bolton, Lyle 168–170
Bonnet, Dr. Charles 26
Bono, Chelsea "Chastity" 15
boomerang **56**
Boomerang, Captain 156–158, 161, 162n7
Boondocks 203
Booth, John Wilkes 30
Borges, Jorge Luis 233
Bosch, Hieronymus 111, 228, 232n14
Boundaries and Boundary Violations in Psychoanalysis 103, 108n5
"Boundaries in clinical Practice" 103, 108n7
boundary breaking 17, 101–102, 103–104, 106–108
bovine spongiform encephalopathy 29–30; *see also* mad cow disease
Bozo the Clown 257
Bradbury, Ray 20, 207

Brady, James 128
brain injury 4, 20; *see also* traumatic brain injury (TBI)
Breivik, Anders Behring 56, 60, 63*n*2
Breton, André 20, 46, 50, 223–224, 227, 229; Freud; 20, 224–225; medical student 20, 46, 223; *Surrealist Manifesto* 224, 232*n*7; World War I 224–225
Brody, Adrien 4
Bronze Tiger 156
Brooker, Will 179
Brooklyn 117, 119
Brooklyn Bridge 119
"Brotherhood of Dada" 222–223, 232*n*4; *see also* Dada
Brothers Quay 222
Brown v. Board of Education 85
Brown v. Entertainment Merchants Assoc. 58, 63*n*9
Buffy the Vampire Slayer 150
bulimia 45; *see also* anorexia
Bullock 105; *see also* Bullock, Det.
Bullock, Det. 105
Burrell, James 150, 154*n*22
Burton, Tim 7, 83, 222
Bushman, Brad J. 58–59
butler *see* Alfred
Butler Hospital 245–247, 251*n*11
Byrne, John 158

The Cabinet of Dr. Caligari 111, 118, 123, **124**, 127, 145, 220*n*11, 220*n*14
Caine, Michael 259
Caligari, Dr. 18, 87, 88*n*2, 123, **124**, 127, 132, 150, 220*n*3, 227
"Call of Cthulhu" (short story) 245, 247, 249, 251*n*37, 264, **264**
Call of Cthulhu: The Official Video Game 245, **246**, 250*n*8, 263
Call of Duty 57, 60
Call of Duty: Black OPS 60, 63*n*2
Cameron, Dr. Donald Ewan 118
Canada 70, 96, 118, 150
Canadian Psychiatric Assocation 118
cancer 27, 45, 112, 117
Cannon, Danny 107, 124
Captain Boomerang *see* Boomerang, Captain
carnival 127, 148, 175–176, 214–215, 219, 259
Carpenter, John 18, 81
Carroll, Leo G. 4, 230
Carroll, Lewis 20, 84, 141, 203–204
cartoons 7, 19, 58, 79, 82, 119, 126, 146, 169; Batman 165–167; 82; Joker 105–106, 188; Quinzel, Dr. (Harley Quinn) 104–106; Strange, Dr. Hugo; *see also* animation
Carvey, Dana 85
Castellanos, Sebastian 198
Castle, William 88*n*2, 114–115
catatonia 32, 94, 99, 138, 222
The Catcher in the Rye 56–57
Catwoman 107
Caucasian **87**

Cavendish, Dr. Charles 15, 39, 43, 125, 141–142, 152, 175–177, 243
CCA (Comics Code Authority) 8, 62, 64*n*26
Center of the Cyclone 44, 51*n*2; *see also* Lilly, Dr. John
Cerletti, Dr. Ugo 35, 38, 40, 94; *see also* electroconvulsive therapy (ECT); shock therapy
Cesare **124**, 127, 137, 150; *see also* Caligari, Dr.
Chandler, Raymond 206
Chaney, Lon 256
The Changling 129, 139
Chapman, David Mark 56–57
Charcot, Dr Pierre 127
Charenton 191
Charles Bonnet syndrome 26
Chicago Psychoanalytic Institute 96
Un Chien Andalou (*The Andalusian Dog*) 231
Chinese 84, 118, 137, 260, **260**, 273; Chinese-American 110
chlorpromazine 81, 94, 99; *see also* anti-psychotics; Thorazine
chorionic villus sampling 31
Christianity 20, 91, 98, 104, 116
christological models or motifs 216, 221*n*15
chromosome 30–31; *see also* genetics
CIA 43, 45, 47, **92**, 97, 118
Cinema's Sinister Psychiatrists 3, 5, 10, 18, 123, 143*n*19
circus 82, 105, 108, **157**, 256
Clayface 153, 170, 234
Clockwork Orange **50**, 110, 150
clown 20, 105–106, 108, 115, 255, 260, 262; clown fish 142; *258*; Garth 175; *see also* Clown Prince of Crime
Clown Prince of Crime 34*n*1, 175, 242*n*2, 242*n*3, 255, 257–258, 262*n*12, 263*n*39
Clytemnestra 20, 264–270
Cobblepot, Oswald **50**, 148; *see also* Penguin
cocaine 27
Cocteau, Jean 222
cognitive deficit or decline 11, 35, 65, 80, 83, 185, 223, 273; symptoms 19, 30
collage 222
Colon, Jenny 228
"Color Out of Space" 248
Colorado 16, 56, 76, 78–79, 196; *see also* Aurora, Colorado; *The Dark Knight Rises*, movie massacre in Aurora, Colorado
Columbine High School 13
Columbus, Christopher 29, 225
comic book 5, 6*n*3, 8, 16, 26–27, 55, 61, 80, 103–105, 107, 151, 157, 218, 243, **258**, 274; comic book industry 62, 203; *Luke Cage* comic book 116, 118
Comics Code 8, 62; *see also* CCA (Comics Code Authority)

Commedia dell'Arte 20, 260
commitment 73, 113, 129, 131
Committed (Miller and Hanson) 14
congenital tabes 29; *see also* syphilis
Conroy, Kevin 55
Conspiracy Theory **92**, 118–119
contagion 56, 137–138, 150–151, **166**, 194
convulsion 35, 40, 246; *see also* seizures
Cooper, Dr. David 95–96, 99
corpse 193, 195, 209, 223, 226, 268, 270; *see also* Exquisite Corpse; surrealism
Cory, Donald 173–174, 176–178
Costello, Lou 259–260, 262
couch 35, 38, 40, 50, 102, 105–106
counseling, Christian 104, 113
counterculture 15, 45–46, 49, 97, 227, 232*n*4
countertransference 102, 125
Craig, Yvonne 173
Crane, Dr. Gerald 47, **47**, 51, **51**, 126
Crane, Dr. Jonathan 3, **4**, 17, 36, **44**, 47–48, **48**, 86, **92**, 125–127, 148, 150, 187, 218, 248–250; Arkham psychiatrist 17–18; psychology professor 86, 167–168; *see also* Scarecrow
Cranford, Peter 39
Cream 46
Creutzfeldt-Jakob disease 29–30
crime 9, **50**, 57, 61, 65, 67–68, 80, 82, 86, 103, 108, 115, 130, 215, 218, 234, 237; classical literature 264–266, 269; Crime Alley 65, 126; crime boss 9, **44**, **50**, 140, 153; crime fighter 82, 107, 177, 179, 234, 259; war crime 115; *see also* Clown Prince of Crime
criminal justice 3, 129, 138
CRISPR 273–274
critical psychiatry 91; *see also* anti-psychiatry
Cronenberg, David 4, 102, 150
crossdresser 15, 125; *see also* transvestite
Crowley, Alister 218, 222
Cruising 103
Cthulhu **246**, 246–247, 249–250; **264**; *Call of Cthulhu* 245, **246**, 249; Cthulhu-for-America movement 245

Dada 222–223, 232*n*4, 239
"Dagon" 244
Daka, Dr. 82, 84, **87**, **260**
Dalí, Salvador 229–230, **230**, 231
A Dangerous Method 102
Dark Castle Entertainment 115
Dark Knight **56**, 150, 153, 244
The Dark Knight 203, 244, 255, 259
The Dark Knight Returns 231, 259
The Dark Knight Rises 16, **60**, 153; movie massacre in Aurora, Colorado 16–17, 56, 77–80

A Dark Night in Aurora (Reid) 78
Darkseid 158
Darlage, Adam 118n15
Davis, Viola 161
Davringhausen, Heinrich 213, 220n7
The Days of Our Lives 257
DC Comics 1, 5, 80–81, 106–108, 124, 134, 155, 184, 204, 216, 243, **258**
DC Comics Encyclopedia 106
DC Universe 66, 155, 205–207, 262; *see also DC Comics Encyclopedia*
DC Universe: Assault in Arkham 38
Deadshot 156, 161
Death, Dr. 80
death camps 83; *see also* Third Reich; Treblinka; Nazis
"A Death in the Family" 65, 70, 99, 105, 149, 255
The Death of the Family 99, 160
Declaration of Helsinki 111, 116, 120, 125
deinstitutionalization 81, 93, 96, 132, 139–140
déjà vu 142
delirium 16, 26–27, 99
delirium tremens (DTs) 27
dementia 5, 9–11, 25–26, 29–30, 69, 105, 117, 125, 215, 246; *see also* Alzheimer's; frontotemporal dementia (FTD); Huntington's disease (HD); Lewy body dementia (LBD)
demons 98, 134, 140, 213
Dent, Harvey **152**, 153, ***174***; *see also* Two-Face
De Palma, Brian 15, 125
dependent 68–70, 75
depersonalization 71–72
depression **4**, 32, 45, 49, 59, 68–69, 78, 98, 133, 237, 246
depth psychology 83; *see also* Jung, Carl Gustav
derealization 71–72
Derleth, August 244
de Sade, Marquis 226–227; *see also* sadism
detective 8, 9, 107, 198, 234, 236, 238, 256
Detective Comics 8, 126, 136, 243, 256
deviance 36, 39, 150, 152, 179, 192, 211, 213, 215–216, 218–219
Diagnostic and Statistical Manual of Mental Disorders 5 (DSM-5) 32
DiCaprio, Leonardo **130**
Dietrich, Marlene 108
differential diagnosis 16, 21n7, 25–26
Digital Arkham 195, 198
diminished capacity 76, 78, 128
Dini, Paul 104, 257
The Dirty Dozen (film) 155
The Dirty Dozen (novel) 155
The Discovery of the Unconscious 114

Disney 110, 193
displacement 138, 140
dissociation 16, 67, 70–74, 125, 190, 196, 224, 229
Distress'd Orphan; or Love in a Mad-house 135
The Divided Self 95
Dix, Dorothea 125
Dix, Otto 218, 220n7, 221n17
doctor *see* physician
Dr. Bagley *see* Bagley, Dr.
Dr. Bartholomew *see* Bartholomew, Dr.
Dr. Caligari *see* Caligari, Dr.
Dr. Daka *see* Daka, Dr.
Dr. Death *see* Death, Dr.
Dr. Frankenstein *see* Frankenstein, Dr.
Dr. Jekyll *see* Jekyll, Dr.
Dr. Jekyll and Mr. Hyde **2**, **17**, 113–114, **214**
Dr. Loomis *see* Loomis, Dr.
Dr. Mabuse *see* Mabuse, Dr.
Doctor Mabuse 127
Dr. Meredith *see* Meredith, Dr.
Dr. Strange (Stephen Vincent) **84**, 85
Doctor Tarr 20, 234; *see also* "The System of Dr. Tarr and Prof. Fether"
domestic violence *see* intimate partner violence (IPV)
Donner, Richard 118
Don't Look at the Basement 97
Doom Patrol 223
doppelganger 215–216, 220n11, 236, 256
Dostoyevsky, Fyodor 208
Drake, Tim 151
"Dreams in Darkness" 49, 165, 167
Dressed to Kill 15, 125
DSM *see Diagnostic and Statistical Manual of Mental Disorders 5 (DSM-5)*
Duell, William **97**
Duke Nukem 58
Dupin, C. Auguste 238, 242
dybbuk 124

Early History of Boundary Violations in Psychoanalysis 103
Eastern State Penitentiary 191–192
Eastwood, Clint 129
Easy Rider 46
ECT (electroconvulsive therapy) *see* electroconvulsive therapy (ECT)
EEG (electroencephalogram) *see* electroencephalogram (EEG)
ego dissolution 45
Eichmann trial 115
Eidos Interactive 184–185
Eisner, Lotte 213, 220n5
Eisner Award 231
Elba 173, 175, 177–178
electroconvulsive therapy (ECT) 16, 22, 35, **36**, **37**, 37–41, 81, 94–99, 128, 270
electroencephalogram (EEG) 82

electroshock therapy *see* electroconvulsive therapy (ECT)
electrotherapy 38; *see also* electroconvulsive therapy (ECT)
Elizabeth Arkham Asylum for the Criminally Insane 9, 25, 36, 80, 87, 134, 145, 155
Ellenberger, Dr. Henri 114, 226
Elliott, Dr. Thomas (Tommy) 92, **241**; *see also* Hush
emotionally disturbed persons (EDP) 105
Emperor Joker 204, 206, 208–209
The Emperor Jones 206
Enchantress 156
England 68, 134–135; *see also* London
USS *Enterprise* 174, 177–178, 186
epidemiology 10
Epimetheus 173, 185
Eriphyle 21, 264–266, 269
Erwin, Lee 173
Esquirol 93
Eteocles 265
euthanasia 12–13, 29, 31, 34, 82, 86, 125, 268
Evil in American Popular Culture 17
The Evil Within 19, 191, 193, 198
existentialism 45, 95, 99, 103, 229, 240, 247
exorcism 91, 98, 124, 213
The Exorcist 113
experimentation 17; ethical experimentation 111–113; hallucinogens 44, 94, 119; human experimentation 114, 116; Nazis 18, 115, 120; Strange, Dr. **44**, 118;Tuskegee 117; unethical 18, 114–115, 117, 119–120, 150, 196, 213, 244, 273–274
Expressionism 87, 111, **214**, **217**, 218, **235**, **266**; German Expressionism 18, 20, **37**, 80, 87, 98, 106, 108, 111, 123, 145, 211–213, **212**, 218–219, 220n3, 220n8, 220n11, 220n14, 220n15, 220n17, 222, 227, 256
Exquisite Corpse 223, 226
extreme risk protective orders (ERPO) 14

Falcone, Carmine 148
"The Fall of the House of Usher" 234, 237–239, 252
Farewell, My Lovely 206
fascist 85, **186**, 230
Fat Lady 159; *see also* Waller, Amanda
FBI 106, 110, 126, **197**, **260**
FDA (Federal Drug Administration) 12, 112
fear toxin 47, **47**, 50–51, **51**, 66, 150, 167, 249
feature film 19, **79**, 156
femme fatale 18, 19
Fenichel, Otto 40
Fenton, Dr. Lynn 78
Ferenzi, Sandor 103

"The Festival" 248
fetish 39, 106
Fiennes, Ralph 4
The Fifth Floor 138
film noir 36, 80, 108, **214, 217**, 219
Final Solution *see* death camp
Finger, Bill 126, 234, 252
fingernail 11, **47**, 256
Fingeroth, Danny 188, 204n20
"The First Surrealist Manifesto" 223–225, 232n7
Flag, Rick 156–161
The Flash 156
flashbacks *see* memory
Flashpoint 65, 67
Fleming, Dr. 29
Fleming, Victor 111
Fletcher, Louise 128–129
Folie à deux 73
Folie et Déraison 96
Fonda, Peter 46
forensic psychiatry 4–5, 8, 14, 16, 25, 30, **47**, 68–69, 72, 86, 103, 106, 128, 268
Forman, Miloš 97, **97**, 128
Foucault, Michel 96, 104, 109n18, 192, 219, 220n13, 232n15
Fox Kids 165
Frankenheimer, John 114
Frankenstein, Dr. **40**, 113, 122, 127, 145, 150
Frankenstein (novella) **37**
Freddy (Kruger) 128
free association 12, 127, 223–226
Freeman, Dr. Walter 94
Freeze, Mr. 148, 153
The French Connection 103
Freud, Sigmund 4, 20, 83, 102–103, 114; dreams 223; free association 225–226; Freudian 46, 82, 98, 114, 193–194, 226, 229, 231; hypnosis 127, 179, 193–194; surrealism 223–226, 229; Wagner-Jauregg 133n3
Friedkin, Thomas 103
Fright **66, 71**, 80, 125; *see also* Friitawa, Dr. Linda
Friitawa, Dr. Linda **66, 71**, 80, 110–111, 125, 273
From Caligari to Hitler 88n2, 123, 127
frontal lobes 94
frontotemporal dementia (FTD) 30, 32
FTD *see* frontotemporal dementia (FTD)
Fuller, Samuel 138
funny farm 5, 129, **130**
The Furies 269–270
Future Cop 58

Gabbard, Dr. Glen 103
Gacy, John Wayne 256
The Garden of Earthly Delights 228; *see also* Bosch, Hieronymus
Garrett 207
Garth 173–179
gas chamber 83, 116
Gautier, Theophile 228

GCPD (Gotham City Police Department) *see* Gotham City Police Department (GCPD)
gender 30, 70, 101, 106, 211; gender-affirming surgery 15; gender boundaries 176; gender equality 91; gender fluidity 39, 41n8; gender inverted 239; gender transitions 14
General Hospital 101
general paralysis 29, 31, 246; *see also* neurosyphilis
general paresis of the insane 31; *see also* general paralysis
geneticist 11, 38, 31, **66**, 80, 83, 85, 110, 185, 274
genetics 5, 21, 30–31, 125, 273–274
genocide 83, 177
German Expressionism 18, 20, **37**, 80, 87, 98, 106, 108, 111, 123, **212**, 213, 218, 220n14, 222, 227, 256
Gernsback, Hugo 83
Ghost Adventures 191
ghosts 18, 115–116, **137**, 140–141, 143, 145–146, 150, 191, 193, 217
Gibson, Mel **92**, 118–119
Gilman, Sander L. 214
Ginsberg v. New York 57–58
"Glasgow Smile" 256
Glider Pro 58
Goffman, Erving 20, 96, 98, 104, 137–138, 141
Golden Globe 128
Goldstein, Andrew 131, 133n5
Gordon, Barbara 95, 107, 195–196, 255
Gordon, Comm. *see* Gordon, Jim (James)
Gordon, Det. Jim (James) 9, 47, 139, **139**, 151
Gotham 2, **9**, 9, 40, 47, 82–83, 107, 110, 123–124, 126–127, **139**, 151, 157, **192, 197, 217, 258, 266**
Gotham City 1, 98, 133, 146, 148, 151, 169, 170–171, 175, 179, 184–186, 190, 194–197, 205, 222, 233, 248, 255, 259–260, 262; monsters 186–187
Gotham City Police Department (GCPD) **139**
Gotham City Sirens 107
Gotham Examiner **147**
Gotham Gazette 177
Gotham House of Madness and Ill Humors 174
Gotham State Prison 146
Gothika 140, 150
grand mal seizures 28, 35, 38; *see also* convulsion; seizures
Grand Theft Auto IV 60
grapnel gun **56**
Great Recession 5
Great War (WWI) 137; surrealism 222, 224–227; *see also* World War I
Greek 5, 20, 173, 255, 260, 264, 268–270; ancient 264, 268, 270; classical 20; language 255; mythology 173, 264

Green Arrow 9
Greenberg, Clement 204–205
Greenwich Village 107
Grob, Dr. Charles S. 45
Grof, Stanislav 48
Guatemala 117–117
guns 13–14, **56**, 58, 62, 66, 86, 128, 130–131, 165, 167–168, 230–231, 257; gun control 13, 141
Guthiel, Dr. Thomas 103
Guthrie, Arlo 10
Guthrie, Woody 10
Gwynplaine 256
gynecologist 101, 197
Gypsies 116

Ha-Hacienda 262
Haight-Ashbury 46
Halloween 19, 81, 87, 145, 153; *The Long Halloween* 256
Halloween 40, 79, 107, 115
hallucinations: auditory hallucinations 4, 32, 47–48; Batman 168, 170, 194; Bosch 55; drug-induced 250; hypnogogic hallucinations 28; Lilliputian hallucinations persecutory 4, 34n1; surrealism 225; visual hallucinations 26–28, 31–33, 34n1, 49, 73, 177
hallucinogen 3, **4**, 15–16, 17, 43, **44**, 47, 49, 50, 86, **92**, 126, 228, 249; *see also* psychedelics
haloperidol (Haldol) 34; *see also* anti-psychotics
Hamill, Mark 55
Hanson, Dr. Annette 14
Harkness, "Digger" 156; *see also* Boomerang, Captain
Harlem 85
harlequin 20, 105–106, 108, **157**, 258–260
Harley Quinn *see* Quinn, Harley
Harvard 104
Hashish Club 228
The Haunting of Hill House 141; *see also House on Haunted Hill*
Hawkins, Martin ("Mad Dog") 25–26, 38–39, 66–67, 72–73, 125, 140, 142; *see also* "Mad Dog"
Heavenly Creatures 73
Helena (Huntress) 107
Hell 240, 243–244, 269; *A Living Hell* 40–42, 124, 211, 213, 215, 244
Heller, Bruno 107, 124
Hell's Crucible 126
Helms, Richard 119; *see also* CIA
hepatitis 29, 116–117
hepatolenticular degeneration (Wilson's disease) 28
Hephaestus 173, 265
Herod 85
Hinckley, John, Jr. 128
Hippocrates 91
Hitchcock, Alfred 15, 46, 73, 81, 125, 132, 145, 176, **230**, 230, 233, 237–238; *see also Psycho*
Hitler, Adolf 5, 29, 114–115, 127
HIV 29; *see also* AIDS

Hobart, Rose *17*
Hoffmann, Dr. Albert 119, 128
Hoffmann, E.T.A. 228
Hofmann, Dustin 119
Holmes, James 56, 76, 78–80, 84, 87, 131; *see also* The Dark Knight Rises, movie massacre in Aurora, Colorado
The Holy Mountain 46
homicide 26, 67–69, 70–72, 106, 169, 198, 218, 240, 257
L'Homme qui rit (The Man Who Laughs) 256
homosexuality 8, 39, 62, 85, 103, 128
Hopkins, Miriam *17*
Hopper, Dennis 46
hospice 12
Hostess Twinkle Defense 78, 128
House of Pain *18*, *36*, 114
House of Wax 115
House on Haunted Hill 114–115, 129, *137*, 140, 150
HUAC (House Un-American Activities Committee) 8; *see also* McCarthy, Sen. Joseph "Joe"
Hugo, Victor 21
Huntington's chorea 10
Huntington's disease (HD) 10–11, 21n10, 30–31; *see also* dementia
Huntress (Helena) 107; *see also* Helena (Huntress)
Hush 86, *241*, 242, 260; *see also* Elliott, Dr. Thomas (Tommy)
Hyde, Mr. *2*, *17*, 113–114, 150, *214*; *see also* Jekyll
Hydrothérapie Fantastique 88n9
hydrotherapy 81, 88n9
hypnosis 44, 118, *124*, 127

The Idiot 208
The Immortal Life of Henrietta Lacks 111–112
In Dreams 140
incarceration 1, 5, 9, 13, 17, 69, *77*, 98–99, 113, 129–131, *139*, 150, 155, 158, *189*
Indian Hill *18*, *84*, 85, *90*, 110, 126, *192*, *197*, 273
Injustice Squad 159
insane asylum 192, *197*, 198n1, 213, 220n14, 221n21, 227, *246*, 247; *see also* mental asylum; sanitarium; state hospital
insanity defense 17, 76–77, 87, 97, 128; *see also* not guilty by reason of insanity (NGRI)
Insanity Defense Reform Act 128
Institute of Psychiatric Services 3
institutionalization 1, 13, 81, 93, 96, 129, 132, 138–140, 159, 219, 245
insulin coma therapy (ICT) 34, 35, 93
intermittent irregular reinforcement 104
Interpretation of Dreams 20, 228–229

Interpretation of Schizophrenia 95
intimate partner violence (IPV) 104, 108
in-vitro fertilization (IVF) 31
The Island of Dr. Moreau 114, *217*
Island of Lost Souls 18, 114, *217*
isolation 1, 13, 46, 118, 127, 192, 196, 246; isolation cells or rooms 43, 96, 191; isolation tank 43, 46
Italian Mental Health Act (1978) 96

The Jacket 4, 150
Jackson, Peter 73
Jackson, Shirley 141
Jade 103
JAMA (Journal of American Medical Association) *see* Journal of American Medical Association (JAMA)
Janet, Dr. Pierre 127, 224, 229
Jannings, Emil 19
Japan 19, 82, 84, 142, 193, *197*, 198, 160, *260*
Japanazi 82, 84, *87*, *260*
Jason (Voorhees) 152
Jaspers, Dr. Karl 95–96
Jefferson Airplane 46
Jekyll, Dr. *2*, *17*, *17*, 112–114, 127, 150, *214*
Jenner, Caityn [Bruce] 15
Jerusalem 115
jester 20, 106, 175, 256–257, 259–260
Job 111
Jocasta 265
Jodorowsky, Alejandro 46
"Johnny Panic and the Bible of Dreams" 39–40
Jones, Ernst 103
Jones, Jackson 159
Jones, Mark 245
Jones, Waylon *see* "Killer Croc"
Joshi, S.T. 244, 246–247
Judgment at Nuremberg 115–117
Journal of American Medical Association (JAMA) 113
Jung, Carl Gustav 15–16, 20, 46, 67, 83, 98, 102, *174*, *214*, 218, 222–223, 226, 229, 238–239
Jurassic 110, 126, *197*, *260*; *Jurassic Park* 126; *Jurassic World: Fallen Kingdom* 126
Justice League *44*, 80, 159, 161–162, 245
juvenile delinquency 8, 61

Kane, Bob 20, *37*, 80, 123, 126, *212*, 222, 234
Karloff, Boris *37*
Katz, David 131
Kefauver, Sen. Estes 8
Kendra's Law 131
Kennedy, Sen. Robert 118
Kennedy, Sen. Ted 119
Kenton, Erle C. 114, *217*
Kesey, Ken 39, 45, *97*, 97, 138, 206
ketamine 45, 49

Killer Croc 36, 153, 186, 216, 218, 250
The Killing Joke 65, 107, 231, 255
Kilmer, Val 114
King, Stephen 141, 151, 244
King Lear 3–4
King of Hearts 150, 161
Kingsley, Ben *130*
Kingsley Hall 95, 226–227
Kirchner, Ernst Ludwig 213
Kirk, Captain 173–177, 179, 180n2
Kirk, James T. 173–177, 179–180
Kirkbride 93, 98, 195, 198, 219
kitsch 204–206, 209
Klein, Alan 46
Klein-Rogge, Rudolf *79*
Knightfall 151–152
Koran 57
Kracauer, Siegfried 127
Kramer, Stanley 115
Krauss, Werner *124*
Krimson City 198
Kristallnacht (Night of Broken Glass) 5
Kubrick, Stanley *50*, 110
Kyle, Selina 82; *see also* Cat-woman

laboratory *2*, 45, 48, 52, 59–60, *84*, *186*, *192*
Lacan, Jacques 229, 232n17, 241, 246
LaGrieve, Simon 156, 158–159
Laing, Ronald David (R.D.) 95, 103, 220n13, 226–227
Lammers 60
Lang, Fritz *79*, 80, 127–128, *212*, 220n11, 220n14, 222
Lanza, Adam 67, 131
Lassick, Sydney *97*
"The Laughing Fish" 105
Laughing Man 156
Laughton, Charles *18*
Lautremont 226
Lawton, Floyd 156, 159–161, 166; *see also* Deadshot
Leatherface 152
Lecter, Hannibal 106, 128, 130, 148, 151, 198; *From Caligari to Hannibal* 123
Ledger, Heath 79, 83, 203, 255, 259
Leland, Joan 169
Lemmings 60
Leni, Paul 20, 106, 256
Lenin, Vladimir 29
Lennon, John 46, 56, 116–117
lesbianism 39
Leto, Jared 255, 257
leucotomy 94, 102; *see also* lobotomy; psychosurgery
Lewy body dementia (LBD) 30
Libation Bearers 264, 270–271
Lifton, Robert J. 116
Lilliputian hallucinations 34n3
Lilly, Eli 119
Lilly, Dr. John 43–44, 47
Lima, Dr. Pedro 94
Lincoln, Abraham 29

linear media 183
Lloyd, Christopher **97**
lobotomy 94, 97, 128–129, 137–138, 213; see also psychosurgery
"Lock-up" on Batman: The Animated Series 168–169
Loeb, Jeph **241**, 242
London 98, 113, 191, 226; see also England
The Long Halloween 256
Longfellow, Henry Wadsworth 173
Looking Glass 19, 203, 209; see also Alice
Loomis, Dr. 145, 153; see also Halloween
Loony Tunes 203
lost generation 225
Love in a Mad-house 135
Lovecraft, H.P. 20, 178, 185, 206, 216, 220n14, 233, 238, 243–250
Lovecraft Country 247
LSD 27, 43–46, 97, 118–119, 228; see also acid; psychedelics
Ludovico Technique **50**, 110
Luke, Keye 173–174
Luke Cage 116, 118
lunatic 50, 169, 171, 175, 196, 208
lurasidone (Latuda) 34
Luthor, Lex 209
Lynch, David 233

M. Butterfly 110
Mabuse, Dr. 18, 127–128, 212, 220n11, 220n14
Macabre, Mason 258
mad cow disease 29–30; see also bovine spongiform encephalopathy; prion disease
"Mad Dog" 25–26, **36**, **37**, 38, 72–73, 98, 125, 128, 140, 142, 150, 270; "pack o'mad dogs" 152; see also Hawkins, Martin
Mad Hatter 9, 17, 80, 82, 84–85, 142, 150, 204, 234, 238
"Mad Love" (cartoon) 169, 151
Mad Love (graphic novel) 104, 113, 257, **258**, 259
Mad magazine 203
mad scientist see scientist
Maddon, Joe 204
The Madman 213
Madness and Civilization 96; see also Foucault, Michel
Mafia 125
magic 73, 85, 133, 184
Magritte, Rene 231
Maillard, Monsieur 137
Mal de San Vito (Sickness of Saint Vitus) 10, 11; see also Huntington's disease (HD)
Malone, William 114
malpractice 26, 78, 102, 132
Mamoulian, Robert **2**, **17**, 114
Man and His Symbols 15–16
"The Man Behind the Red Hood" 256
"The Man Who Laughs" 20–21, 78, 106, 256
managed care 129, 132

Manchuria 84
Manchurian Candidate 114, **186**
Maniac 112
maniac 81, 105, 169, 171; megalo-maniac 207
Manning, Chelsea 15
Manson, Charles 56–57
Marathon Man 119
March, Fredric **2**, **17**, 114, **214**
Marco, Major **186**
Maria **79**
Marine 9
Marlowe, Philip 206
Marta 173–174, 176–177, 179–180
Marvel 18, 65, **84**, 116
Marx, Karl 95, 104
masculinity 69, 64n30, 216
mask 20–21, 40–41, **44**, 49, 77, 83, 126, 146, 149, 152, 184, **186**, 230–232, 235–237, 258–260; see also Black Mask; Black Mask II
"The Masque of Pandora" 173
"The Masque of the Red Death" 234–235, 252
mass murders 61, 76–79, 83, 87, 129
massacre of the innocents 85
matricide 5–6, 12, 16, 21, 67–70, 73–74, 264, 268–270
Maupassant, Guy de 29
Maxie Zeus see Zeus, Maxie
mayor 110, 148–149
Mayor Moscone see Moscone, Mayor
Mazas Prison 191
McCarthy, Sen. Joseph "Joe" 8, 85
McCoy, Charles 58
McCoy, Dr. Leonard "Bones" 179
McDowell, Malcolm **50**
McGuffin 16
McKean, Dave 7, 10, 19, 149, 178–179, 184–185, 188, 216, 223–224, **230**, 231–232, 256
McKenzie, Ben **139**
McMurphy, Randle 39, 128, 149, 206–208
MDMA 27, 49
Medea 5
medical license **66**, 80, 110, 125
medieval 20, 98, 175, 233, 237, 260, 262
meditation 95
mediumship 222–223, 226, 228–229, 238
medsploitation 113
Medula, Dr. Ladislas 94
Méliès, George 81–82
"The Meltdown" 170
memory 10, 12, 25, 35, 40, 49, 67, 71–73, **87**, 105, 111, 125, 141, 150, 192–193, 216–217, 230, 255, 267, 269; Joker 105–106, **157**; screen memories 82; *Spellbound* and memory 230–231; see also dementia; repression
Memory 231
"men in white coats" 129
Mengele, Josef 110, 116, 126, 274
mental asylum 134–135, 140,

220n14, 227; see also psychiatric hospital; sanitarium; state hospital
mental breakdown 20, 151, 270, 224–225
Mental Illness in Popular Culture 5
mental patients 13, 19, 81, 83, 96, 116, 131–133, 137–138, 145–146, 150–153, **166**, 218
mentalist 193
Meredith, Dr. 87
mescaline 27
Mesmer, Dr. Franz 224
mesmerism 224
metaphysics 208, 231
metrazol 35
Metropolis 70, 73, 124
Metropolis **79**, 80, **85**, **212**, 222
Mettray 191
Metzel, Dr. Jonathan 14
Middle Ages 91
migraine 28, 119
Mikama, Shinji 198
Milk, Harvey 78, 128
millennials 12, 115
millennium 60, 256
Miller, Dr. Dinah 14
Miller, Frank 65, 244
Milo, Professor 150
Ministry of Fear 80
Ministry of Science 80–81, 125
Mr. Freeze see Freeze, Mr.
Mr. Hyde see Hyde, Mr.
Mr. Science 81
Mr. Zsasz see Zsasz
MKUltra 43, 45, 50, 118–119
mobster **44**, 86, **174**
MoMA (Museum of Modern Art) see Museum of Modern Art (MoMA)
Moniz, Dr. Antonia Egaz 94; see also lobotomy; psychosurgery
monster **37**, 85, 110, 126, 145, 150, 186–187, 207, **217**, 243
Moore, Alan 65, 107, 231; see also Batman: The Killing Joke
Moral Treatment 93
Moreau, Gustave 227
Moreau Museum 227, 244
morgue 47
Mortal Kombat 58
Moscone, Mayor 128
Moscoso, Victor 46
Mount Massive Asylum 196–198
MRI 28, 45
Much Ado About Nothing 59
multiple sclerosis (MS) 73
murder see homicide
Murphy, Cillian 3–4, **4**, **44**, 86, 126
Murray, Janet 3, 183–184
Museum of Modern Art (MoMA) 20, 225
music 5, 21, 46, 49, 56, 61, 98, 110, 127, 195, 198, 205
mutilation **36**, 213, 231; self-mutilation **112**
Mxyzptlk 209
Myers, Michael 19, 145, 153, 156

The Myth of Mental Illness 38, 96–97, **112**, **189**, 216
mythos 124, 184, 187, 219, **235**, **246**; Arkham mythos 3, 6–9, 11, 16, 80–81, **84**, 124, 184, **235**, **246**, 273–274; Batman mythos 2; Cthulhu 247

Nacht 211, 218–219
Naish, J. Carrol **87**
narcissistic personality 85, 177
narcolepsy 28, 30
narrative unreliability (unreliable narrator) 249
Nathanson, E.M. 155
National Institute of Health (NIH) 119
National Institute of Mental Health (NIMH) 43, 45, 119
The Nazi Doctors 116; see also Lifton, Robert J.
Nazis 5, 16, **79**, 83–84, 113–116, 119–120, **137**, 274; extermination of mentally and physically handicapped persons 83–84; see also Hitler, Adolf; Operation T-4; Third Reich
Necklace of Harmonia 265
Negrette, Dr. Americo 10–11, 21n10
Nerval, Gérard de 226–228
neurodegenerative disease/disorder 10–12, 30, 86, 125, 267
neurologist 20, 25, 35, 94, 127, 224–225
neuropathology 93–94
neuropsychiatry 5, 117, 223
neuroscience 16, 76, 79, 82, 86, 99, 131
neuroscientist 17, 79–80, 83–85; sinister scientist **66**, 111, 126, **197**, **260**; see also Ministry of Science
neurosurgeon 18, **84**, 85, 94
neurosyphilis 29, 93, 117, 220n14; see also congenital tabes; general paresis of the insane
New Age 14–15
New Batman Adventures The 104, 165, 169
New England 8, 247
New England Journal of Medicine 113, 116–117, 122
"New 52" 66, 74, 149, 258–259
Nicholson, Jack 38, 46, 83, **97**, 128, 256–257
nightmare 72, 194, 206, 219, 237, 246
A Nightmare on Elm Street 128
NIMH see National Institute of Mental Health
Nimoy, Leonard 173
9/11 4–5, 160, 6n1
No Good Deed 12–13
Nolan, Christopher 3, 83
North Korea 57, **186**
Norway Shooter 56; see also Breivik, Anders Behring
not guilty by reason of insanity (NGRI) 70, 76, 78, 128, 155

Novartis 119; see also Sandoz Laboratories
Novick, Irv 8
Nuremberg Code (Race Laws) 5, 116–117, 120, 125; Nuremberg Trials 115–116; see also *Judgment at Nuremberg*; Nazis
nurses 12, 36, 79, 97, 99, 107, **157**, 167, 207, 234, 259, 267
"Nyarlathotop" 244
Nygma, Ed 9 110; see also Riddler
NYPD 126

Obama, Pres. Barak 161
obscenity 57
Observations on Maniacal Disorders 134–135, 145
obsessive-compulsive disorder 3, 45, 65, 78, 99, 190, 239
occipital cortex 28, 45
occultism 15–16, 124, 213, 222
Oedipus 82, 89, 265
oikos 264
olanzapine (Zyprexa) 34; see also anti-psychotics
Olson, Dr. Frank 119
On Dreams 229
One Flew Over the Cuckoo's Nest (film) 38–39, **97**, 128, 138, 149–150
One Flew Over the Cuckoo's Nest (novel) 39, 45, 97, 138, 206
O'Neil, Dennis 8, 9, 243
Operation Paperclip 115
Operation T-4 83
Oracle see Gordon, Barbara
Orange Is the New Black 13
The Oresteia 291
Orestes 12, 265, 267–271
orphan 82, 86, 88, 126, 135, 208, 236
Oscar 114
Ostrander, John 155–156, 158–162
Oswald, Lee Harvey 57
OTC medications (over-the-counter) see over-the-counter medications (OTC)
Outlast 19, 191, 193
Outlast: Whistle Blower 196–197
"The Outsider" 247
over-the-counter medications (OTC) 27

palliative care 12–13, 269
Pandora 173
Pantalone 260
parahippocampus 45
paranoia 26, 30, 34, 68, 70, 85, 112, 214, 216, 222
paranoid-critical approach 229–230
Park, Waylon 197–198
parole 78, 116, 133n5
parricide 16, 70–71, 73–75, 80n24; see also matricide; patricide
Parteger, William 134–135
Partisan Review 204
"Passion Play" 216
Patches 256

patricide 73–75, 264; see also parricide
Pauline Parker-Juliet Hulme case 73
PCP (phencyclidine) 20, 27
Pearson, Ivy **17**
Peck, Gregory 230
pedophile 8, 85
Penguin 9, 36, 40, 49, **50**, 98, 110, 148, 150, 152–153, 218; see also Cobblepot, Oswald
penicillin 29, 117; see also Fleming, Dr.; syphilis
Pennyworth, Alfred 65; see also Alfred
Pentonville Prison 191
period piece 129
peritraumatic dissociation 71, 76
Perkins, Anthony 132; see also Bates, Norman; *Psycho*
Persona 3
persona 40, **174**, 176, **197**, 237, 257, **260**
personality disorder 68, 70, 82, 106, 177
PGD (prenatal genetic diagnostic testing) see prenatal genetic diagnostic testing (PGD)
phantom limb 27
phobia 47, **47**, 86, 150
physician-assisted suicide (PAS) 12–13, 26; see also euthanasia
physicians 3, 9–10, 12, 14, 26, 30, 37, 39, 66, 83, 93, 96, 101–105, 115–116, 125, 127, 134, 137, 208, 224 230, 232n4
"The Picture in the House" 247
Pinel, Dr. Philippe 93, 125
Pink Floyd 46
plastic surgery 86, **241**
Plastique 156
Plath, Sylvia 39
pneumonia 31
Poe, Edgar Allan 20, 214, 233–234, **235**, 235–242, 243; influence on Arkham 20
Pogo 256
Poison Ivy 36, 49, 187, 218, 258
poisoning, mercury 29
police 9, 37, 76, 78, 107, 124, 145, 148, 168–169, 171, 185–186, 270
police procedural 9, 124
Pollack, Andrew 14
Polynices 265
Pong 55
possession 18, 91, 187, 240
post-mortem exam 30
Post-Traumatic Stress Disorder (PTSD) 4, 49, 71, 116, 198, 215, 218, 223
postnatal biography 48
pregnancy 29, 31, 36, 39, 77, 119; termination of pregnancy 31
prenatal genetic diagnostic testing (PGD) 31, 34
Price, Vincent 114–115, **137**
prion disease 29–30
prison 5, 8, 13, 16, 19, 25, 36, 73, 94, 106, 113, 125, 128–129, 130–

131, 137, 139, 153, 156, 160, 197, 211, 215–219, 227, 243, 256, *260*; Blackgate Prison 133, 148–149; and *Cuckoo's Nest* 149; and Foucault 191–193; and Gotham State Prison 146; and Goffman 141; and Nuremberg Code 116–119; and *Star Trek* 173, 175–178, 184
prognosis 1–3, 5, 10, 215
Prometheus 173
Prospero, Prince 234–235
Protestant 102
Providence, RI 243, 245, 247
pseudo-necrophilia 268
pseudo-psychology 215, 218
pseudo-science 116
psilocybin 45, 49, 55*n*7
Psych Out 46
psychedelics 17; 43–51, 73, 86, 94, 118; psychedelic art 50; *see also* hallucinogens
psychiatric hospital *see* insane asylum
Psychiatric News 14, 118
Psychiatry and Anti-Psychiatry 95
Psychiatry and the Cinema 103
psychic phenomena 140
Psycho 15, 19, 73, 81, 98, 111, 125, 132, 145–146, 176, 238
psychoanalysis 38, 40, 43, 44, 93, 102–103, 114, 127, *214*, 223–224, 226, 228–229, 241–242
psychologist 11, 40, 58–59, 62, 85, 91, 104, 132, 148, 151, *186*
psycholytic therapy 44
psychometric testing 69
psychopathological proximity stress disorder 196
psychosis *see* mental breakdown
psychosurgery 94, 99; *see also* leucotomy; lobotomy
psychotherapy 38, 44, 49, 97–99, 133, 140, 240; *see also* psychoanalysis
psychotic identification 79–80, 125
PTSD (Post-Traumatic Stress Disorder) *see* Post-Traumatic Stress Disorder (PTSD)
pulps 8, 205, 233, 244, 251
Puma 159–160
Purloined Letter" *241*, 242
Pylades 267–268

quetiapine (Seroquel) 34
Quinn, Harley 16, 35–36, 38, 125–126, 156, *157*, 160, 168–169, 218–219, 257–259, *258*; and Joker 101–109, 126, 187; *see also* cartoons, Quinzel, Dr. (Harley Quinn)

Rabelais and His World 173, 175, 187
racism 118, 157, *260*
Ra's al Ghul 146
Ratched, Nurse 128
Reagan, President Ronald 56, 128
The Reaper *66*, 80–81

"Recommendation to Physicians Practicing Psycho-analysis" 108*n*4
Redfield, William *97*
Reid, Dr. William H. 78
Ren, Kylo 74
Renaissance 96
repression 67, 71–72, 114, 237–239
"Research with Vulnerable Populations" 119
Resident Evil 198
residential treatment facility (RTF) 99, 226
restraints, chemical 132
"revolving door" policy 131, *147*, 169
Richmond, Fred 73
Richmond, Linda M. 14
Riddler 9, 38, 82, 110, 148, 189, 218
right-to-die 12–13
Rimbaud 226
Ringling Brothers and Barnum & Bailey Circus 256
risperidone (Risperdal) 34
Rivera, Geraldo 116–117
Robbie, Margot 258
Roberts, Julia *92*, 118–119
Robin 8, 49, 62, 82, 85, 151, 255
Rock, Sgt. 159
The Rocky and Bullwinkle Show 203
Rogues' Gallery 40, *84*, 156
Rogues Gallery *84*, 156
Romero, Cesar 83, 255
Ronald McDonald 256
Rorschach test 5–6, 10
Rotwang *79*
Rudlin, John 260
Russia 95, 102, 113, 208
Ruvik 198

sadism 38, 62, 66, 103, 162, 207, 216, 219, 227, 231
safety valve theory 59
Saint Mary of the Innocents Hospital 93
St. Mary's Hospital in Arkham 248
Saint Vitus 10
St. Vitus' Dance 21*n*9
Sakel, Dr. Manfred (Menachim) 93; *see also* insulin coma therapy (ICT)
Salk, Dr. Jonas 81, 87
San Francisco 46, 78, 128
Sandoz Laboratories 44–45, 119
Sandy Hook School 67
sanitarium 129, *130*, 145, 191, 193, 219
Sara, Mia 107
Sartre, Jean Paul 95–96, 229
Satan 76, *217*, 228
Saturday Night Live (SNL) 85
Scarecrow 3, *44*, 47, 47–51, *66*, 86, 125–126, 148, 150, 167–169, 187, 195, 218, 234, 248–250; *see also* Crane, Dr. Jonathan; Murphy, Cillian
Schaffner, Franklin 274

Schiavelli, Vincent *97*
schizoaffective disorder 32
schizophrenia 28, 32, *32*, 34, 35, 38, 67–70, 81, 94–95, 131–132, 138, 145, 222, 226
Schlozman, Steven 178
Schopenhauer, Arthur 99
Schubert, Franz 29
Schwartz, Alvin 204
science 1–2, *37*, 81, 93, 96, 116, 178, 180, 215–216, 223, 229; Ministry of Science 80–81, 125; Mr. Science 81; Nazi science 116; *Scientific American* 153*n*2
science fiction 19, 81, 83, 110–111, 211, 213, 218, 273
scientists 10–11, 17, 19, 45, 66, 81, 83, *84*, 95, 110–111, 119, *124*, 125–126, 132, *197*, 273–274; Chinese scientist 273; mad scientist *2*, 17, 19, *79*, 81, 83, 111, 126, 150
Scotland 19, 68, 95, 118, 178, 222, 226
Scott, Sir Walter 204, 219
Second Sino-Japanese War 84
Seconds 114
seduction 105, 115, 174, 187
Seduction of the Innocent 62, 85; *see also* Wertham, Dr. Fredrick
Sefton Hill *47*, *112*, *186*, *189*, *192*
seizures 26–28, 35, 38, 94; partial seizures 28; tonic-clonic seizures 28; *see also* convulsion; grand mal seizures
sensory deprivation 43, 118, 228
Sgt. Pepper's Lonely Hearts Club Band 46, 50
Sermo.com 104
sertraline (Zoloft) 78
Session 9 140, 191
Seven Against Thebes 265, 269
sex-link 26, 30; *see also* genetics
sexuality 8, 73, 101, 104, 114, 118, 227, 231, 237–238; sexual aggression 59, 118, 245; sexual exploitation or harassment 102–103; sexual minorities 14; sexual misconduct 102–103; sexual orientation or preference 39, 101; sexual relations 29; sex worker (prostitute) 86; transsexual 14–15; *see also* homosexuality
shadow 17, *166*, *217*, *235*, 186, 196, *214*, 240–241, 248, *266*
shadow self *17*, 20, *174*, *214*, 236–237, 239, 240–241
Shakespeare, William 3–4, 29
shamanism 14–15, 95
shapeshifting 173–174, 176–179
Sharp, Mayor 149
Sharp, Warden Quincy 148, 187–190
Shatner, William 173
shell shock 127, 213, 215, 218, 225, 137; *see also* Post-Traumatic Stress Disorder (PTSD)
The Shining 142
The Ship of Fools 228, 232*n*15; *see also* Bosch, Hieronymus

Shoah 5
Shock Corridor 1389
Shuster, Joe 5
Shutter Island 129, **130**, 139
sickle cell anemia 273
side effects 16, 34–35, 94
Side Effects 103–104
Siegel, Jerry 5; and Shuster 5
The Silence of the Lambs 106, 130
Silent Hill (film) 140, **197**
Silent Hill (game) 19
The Simpsons 203
Sinatra, Frank **186**
Sinister Psychiatrists in Cinema 3; *see also* Cinema's Sinister Psychiatrists
Sinner, Alyse [Alice] 80, 125
Skulldugger 82
sleep 28, 67, 72, 93, 101, 267
Smith's Grove Sanitarium 145
soap opera 17, 101
sociopath **54**, 106, 126, 130; *see also* anti-social personality disorder (ASPD)
Sohl, Erwin and Jerry 173
Soles, Jason **246**
somnambulist **124**, 127, 150
Sophocles 264, 270
Sorkin, Arleen 55, 104, 257
South America 11, 21*n*10
speculative realism 245
Spellbound 4, 46, **230**, 230–231
Spider 4
Spider-Man 262, **266**
Spielrein, Dr. Sabina 102
Spirit of Arkham 185, 187–189; *see also* Sharp, Warden Quincy
spiritualism 91, 141, 222, 224, 226, 228–229
SPMI (serious and persistent mental illness) 130
Spock, First Officer 173–176, 177–179, 185
spongiform encephalopathy (bovine spongiform encephalopathy) 29–30; *see also* mad cow disease
Sputnik 81
Star Trek 19, 173–174, 179–180
Star Wars: The Force Awakens 73–74
Starling, Agent 106; *see also The Silence of the Lambs*
state asylum *see* insane asylum
state hospital 13, 81, 113, 117, 129, 131–132
"The Statement of Randolph Carter" 244
Staten Island 117
Stekel, Wilhelm 103
STEM 198
Sternberg, Josef von 108
steroids 27
Stewart, Patrick **92**, 119
stigma 2, 62, 171
stockbroker 10, 73
stop-motion animation **235**
Strange, Dr. Hugo 18, **18**, 36, 39–40, 50, **66**, 80, 82, **84**, 85–86, **87**, 110, 125–126, 149–150, **186**, **192**, **197**, **217**, **260**, 273–274; experiments of 50, 80, 85–86, 110, 125–126, **186**, **192**
Strange, Dr. Stephen Vincent 18, **84**, 85
The Strange Case of Dr. Jekyll and Mr. Hyde 2, 114
A Streetcar Named Desire 155
sub-narratives 183
substance use 13–14, 57, 60, 72; substance use disorders 21, 72; *see also* alcoholism (alcohol use disorder)
suicide 4, 8, 12, 25–26, 30, 36, 45, 72, 99, 103–104, 111, 125, 128, 151, 226, 246, 265, 269; and matricide 67, 69; and Olson, Dr. 45, 119; and Szasz 99
Suicide Squad 19, 107, 151, 155–156, 158, 159–162
Suicide Squad (comics) 19, 107, 155–161, **255**, 258–259
Suicide Squad (film) 107, 117, 151, 255, 259
Suicide Squad: Rebirth 160–161
suicide tourism 12
Supergods 174–175
Superheroes and Superegos 231
Superman 5, 20, **56**, 85, 203–205, 208–209
Superman (video game) 5, 55
Superman Complex 62–62
supernatural 18–19, 115, 129, 134, **137**, 138, 140–143, 151, 211, 215–216, 228, 248
surrealism 12, 20, 46, 111, 215, 222–230, **230**, 231–232; and Great War 224–227
"Surrealist Manifesto" 223–225
Švankmajer, Jan 222
Svengali 127
Svengali 127
SVU: Law & Order 19*n*22, 110, 126, **197**, **260**
Sydenham's chorea *see* St. Vitus' Dance
symbolism 15, 46, 67, 72–73, 227–229, 231, 234, 241, 268
Symbolist 223, 225, 227–228
Synner, Alice *see* Sinner, Alyse
syphilis 29, 93, 117, 216, 246; *see also* congenital tabes; general paresis; neurosyphilis
"The System of Dr. Tarr and Prof. Fether" 137, 208, 234
Szasz, Dr. Thomas 38, 42, 96–97, **97**, 98, **112**, **189**, 216

taboo 101
Tango Gameworks 198
Tarasoff Act 13, 78
Tarot 15, **152**, 178, 222
taxi driver 118–119
Taxi Driver 56
Taylor, Don 114
TCMS *see* transcutaneous magnetic stimulation
temporal lobe epilepsy *see* seizures
The Temptation of St. Anthony 228
tertiary syphilis *see* general paralysis
Tetch, Alice 9, 85
Tetch, Jervish 84–85, 204
Tetch virus 9, 21*n*4
Texas Bell Tower 67
theater of cruelty 218, 221*n*20, 222
Third Reich 15, 114, 123; *see also* Hitler, Adolf; Nazis
Thompkins, Dr. Leslie 9
Thorazine (phenothiazine) **32**, 34, 81; *see also* anti-psychotics
The Thousand Eyes of Dr. Mabuse **212**
"The Threat of the Two Headed Coin" 243
3D Pinball 58
Tibet 85
Timm, Bruce 104, 257
Todd, Jason 65, 99, 255
Tolstoy, Leo 29
Tompkins, Dr. Leslie 9
tonic-clonic seizures 28; *see also* convulsion; grand mal seizures
El Topo 46
Topsy-Turvy 20, 123, 170, 208
Torah 57
torture 36–39, 48, 86, 115, 119, 125, 151, 169, 174, 179, 211, 218–219, 239, 257, 268
"total institution" 96, 98, 137
toys **44**, **174**, 258
Tracy, Dick 83
"trans-institutionalization 13–14
transcutaneous magnetic stimulation (TCMS) 82
transference 102, 106, 125
transsexual 14–15
transvestite 15; *see also* crossdresser
trauma 48–49, 66–67, 70–72, 74, 82–83, 86, 151, 159, 179, 196, 198, 213, 215–216, 218–219, 224, 239–240, 245, 255; birth trauma 48–49; traumatic amnesia 71–72; war trauma 20, 222–223; *see also* Post-Traumatic Stress Disorder (PTSD); traumatic brain injury (TBI)
traumatic brain injury (TBI) 4
treatment-resistant depression (TRD) 49
Treblinka 83; *see also* Nazis; Shoah; Third Reich
treponema pallidum 29; *see also* congenital tabes; syphilis
trickster 20, 106, 240, 260, 262
The Trip 46
tuberculosis sanitorium **166**
Tuke, William 125
tumors 28, 111, 149
Tuskegee syphilis study 116–118
12 Monkeys 150
twins 34, 116, 236–237, 239, 273
Two-Face 36, 83, 140, **147**, 152–153, **174**, 218, 234, 240, 243; and coin 8, 146, **152**, 178, 240

Uncle Ben 65
unconsciousness 11, 44, 49, 108, 114, 119, 215, 222–223, 225–226, 229 243
UK Millennium Cohort Study 60
The United Amateur 244
U.S. Holocaust Memorial Museum 116
U.S. Public Health Service 18, 116
United States Senate Subcommittee on Juvenile Delinquency 61
U.S. Supreme Court 58, 60
Upshur, Miles 196
uranium 8
Usher, Madeline 239
Usher, Roderick 20, 237–241
"Usher II" 20, 207
USSR *see* Russia

vaccine 29, 81, 117
The Vagrant 244
Vale, Viki 149
Van Gogh, Vincent 29
Vannacutt Psychiatric Institute for the Criminally Insane **137**
variable-obscenity standard 57
Veidt, Conrad 20–21, 78, **124**, 256
vengeance 38, 66–67, 85–86, 98, 142, 145, **147**, 177, 185–186, 259, 265, 267–270
Venom 50, 257
Victorian 85, 93, 98, 113, 124, 192, 195–196, 198, 219
video games **192**, **217**, **235**
Virchow 95

Wagner-Jauregg, Julius 224; Wagner-Jauregg Trial 127, 133n3, 138
Wallace, David Foster 128
Waller, Amanda 19–20, 156–162
War 218
Watchmen 231
Watts, Dr. James 94
Wayne, Bruce 8–9, 40, 48, 50, 65–66, 82, 168, 233, 236, **241**, 260; and Wertham 85–86
Wayne, Martha 65–67
Wayne, Dr. Thomas 66–67
Wayne Manor 9, 262
wedding dresses 72, 125, 177, 194, 270
Wein, Len 86
Weine, Robert 111
Weird Tales 244
Weiss, Peter 227
Wells, H.G. **18**, **217**
Wertham, Dr. Fredrick 8, 55, 61–62, 85, 274; *see also* Comics Code; *Seduction of the Innocent*
West, Adam 146
Wexler, Dr. Nancy 11
Whales, James **37**
When the Clouds Roll By 111
Whitaker, Robert 14
White, Warren 215–216
"White Angel" 119
Whiteface 260
Whitman, Charles *see* Texas Bell Tower
Whom Gods Destroy see Antos

"William Wilson" 20, 234, 236–237
Williams, Rob 160
Williams, Tennessee 155
Willowbrook School 116–117
Wilson, Bill *see* Alcoholics Anonymous (AA)
Wilson, Edmund 245
Wilson, Wes 46
Wilson, William 20
Wilson's disease (hepatolenticular degeneration) 29
Wizard of Oz 111
Wolf, J.P. 185
the womb 48, 192–194, 198, 267
Wong, B.D. **87**, 110, 126, **197**, **260**
World of Zoo 60
World War I 20, 111, 123, 127, 218, 221–224, 232n4
World War II 5, 82–84, 94–95, 115, 132, 137, 203–205, 218, 222, 274

Year One 65
Yellow Menace 82, **260**
"The Yellow Wallpaper" 20, 207

Zauzmer, Julie 115
Zeus 173, 194
Zeus, Maxie 39–40, 234
Zeus Arrhenothelus *see* Arrhenothelus, Zeus
Zsasz, Mr. Victor 36, 38, **97**, 98–99, **112**, 153, **183**, **189**
Zwingli 102

www.ingramcontent.com/pod-product-compliance
Ingram Content Group UK Ltd.
Pitfield, Milton Keynes, MK11 3LW, UK
UKHW051850210426
5322IPUK00025B/647